Huhh?
Toyotarou's Art
Huh?
Toriyama Sensei's Correction

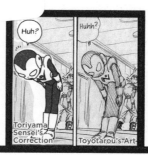

Toriyama Sensei gave me some pointers
on how to bow correctly.

I'm talking about how to draw someone bowing!!
(LOL)

—Toyotarou, 2019

Toyotarou

Toyotarou created the manga adaptation for the *Dragon Ball Z* anime's 2015 film, *Dragon Ball Z: Resurrection F*. He is also the author of the spin-off series *Dragon Ball Heroes: Victory Mission*, which debuted in *V-Jump* in Japan in November 2012.

Akira Toriyama

Renowned worldwide for his playful, innovative storytelling and humorous, distinctive art style, Akira Toriyama burst onto the manga scene in 1980 with the wildly popular *Dr. Slump*. His hit series *Dragon Ball* (published in the U.S. as *Dragon Ball* and *Dragon Ball Z*) ran from 1984 to 1995 in Shueisha's *Weekly Shonen Jump* magazine. He is also known for his design work on video games such as *Dragon Quest*, *Chrono Trigger*, *Tobal No. 1* and *Blue Dragon*. His recent manga works include *COWA!*, *Kajika*, *Sand Land*, *Neko Majin*, *Jaco the Galactic Patrolman* and a children's book, *Toccio the Angel*. He lives with his family in Japan.

SHONEN JUMP Manga Edition

STORY BY **Akira Toriyama**
ART BY **Toyotarou**

TRANSLATION **Caleb Cook**
LETTERING **Brandon Bovia**
DESIGN **Joy Zhang**
EDITOR **Rae First**

DRAGON BALL SUPER © 2015 BY BIRD STUDIO, Toyotarou
All rights reserved. First published in Japan in 2015 by SHUEISHA Inc., Tokyo.
English translation rights arranged by SHUEISHA Inc.

The stories, characters and incidents mentioned
in this publication are entirely fictional.

Printed in Italy

Published by VIZ Media, LLC
P.O. Box 77010
San Francisco, CA 94107

10 9 8 7 6 5
First printing, December 2020
Fifth printing, November 2023

PARENTAL ADVISORY
DRAGON BALL SUPER is rated T for
Teen and is recommended for ages 13
and up. This volume contains realistic
and fantasy violence.

DRAGON BALL

SUPER

GREAT ESCAPE

11

STORY BY
Akira Toriyama

ART BY
Toyotarou

CAST OF CHARACTERS

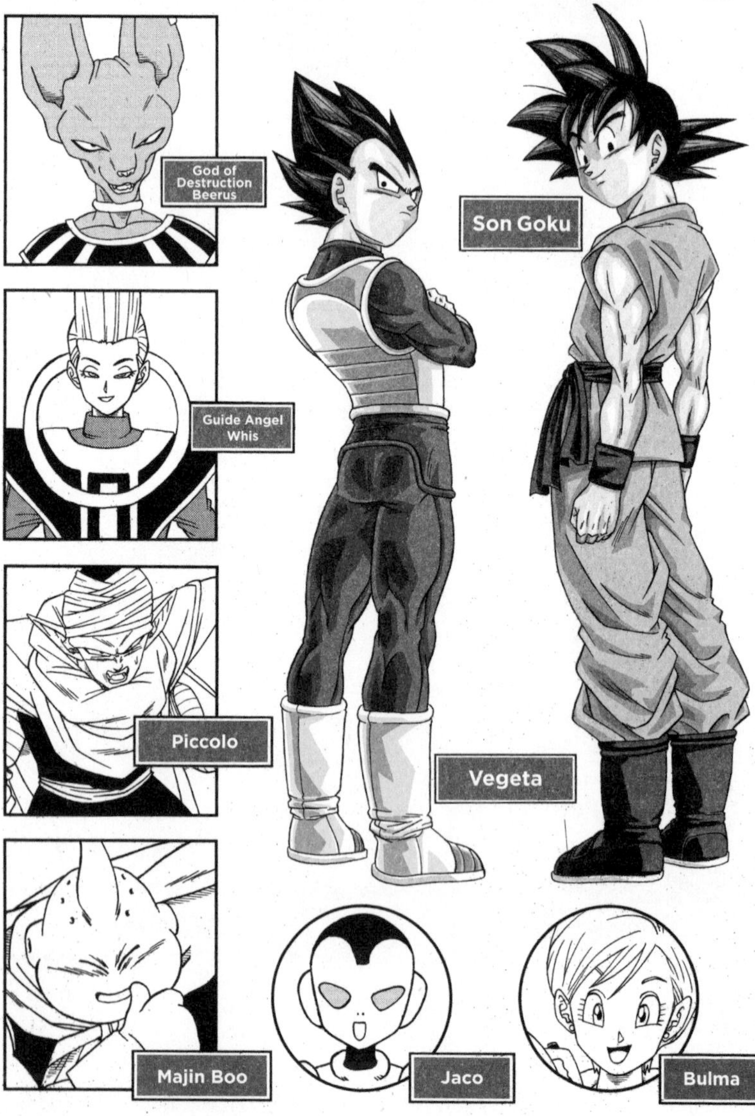
Son Goku
Vegeta
God of Destruction Beerus
Guide Angel Whis
Piccolo
Bulma
Jaco
Majin Boo

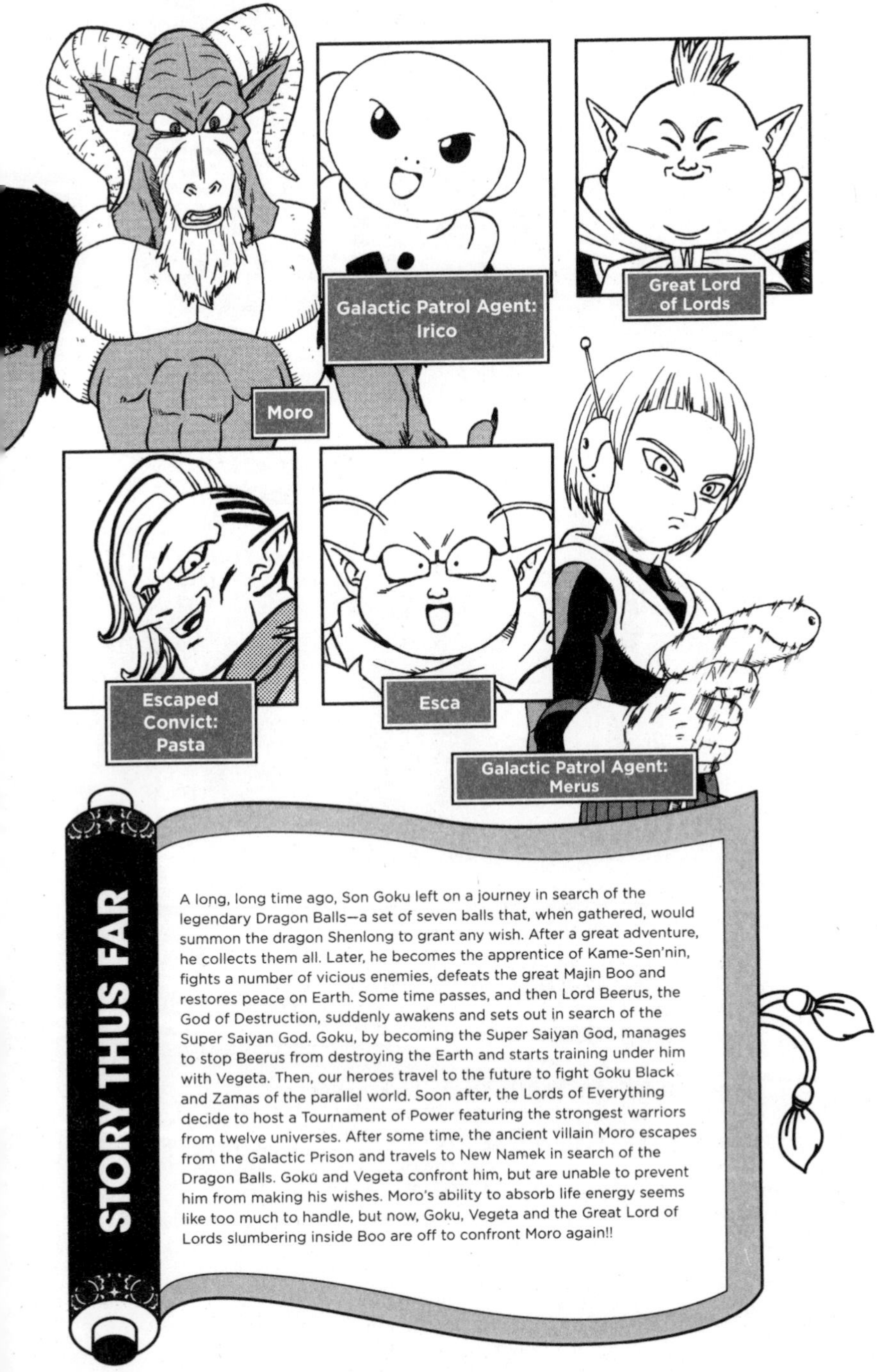
Great Lord of Lords
Galactic Patrol Agent: Irico
Moro
Galactic Patrol Agent: Merus
Esca
Escaped Convict: Pasta

STORY THUS FAR

A long, long time ago, Son Goku left on a journey in search of the legendary Dragon Balls—a set of seven balls that, when gathered, would summon the dragon Shenlong to grant any wish. After a great adventure, he collects them all. Later, he becomes the apprentice of Kame-Sen'nin, fights a number of vicious enemies, defeats the great Majin Boo and restores peace on Earth. Some time passes, and then Lord Beerus, the God of Destruction, suddenly awakens and sets out in search of the Super Saiyan God. Goku, by becoming the Super Saiyan God, manages to stop Beerus from destroying the Earth and starts training under him with Vegeta. Then, our heroes travel to the future to fight Goku Black and Zamas of the parallel world. Soon after, the Lords of Everything decide to host a Tournament of Power featuring the strongest warriors from twelve universes. After some time, the ancient villain Moro escapes from the Galactic Prison and travels to New Namek in search of the Dragon Balls. Goku and Vegeta confront him, but are unable to prevent him from making his wishes. Moro's ability to absorb life energy seems like too much to handle, but now, Goku, Vegeta and the Great Lord of Lords slumbering inside Boo are off to confront Moro again!!

11

DRAGON BALL SUPER

TABLE OF CON-TENTS

DRAGON BALL SUPER

CHAPTER 49: OUTER SPACE BATTLE

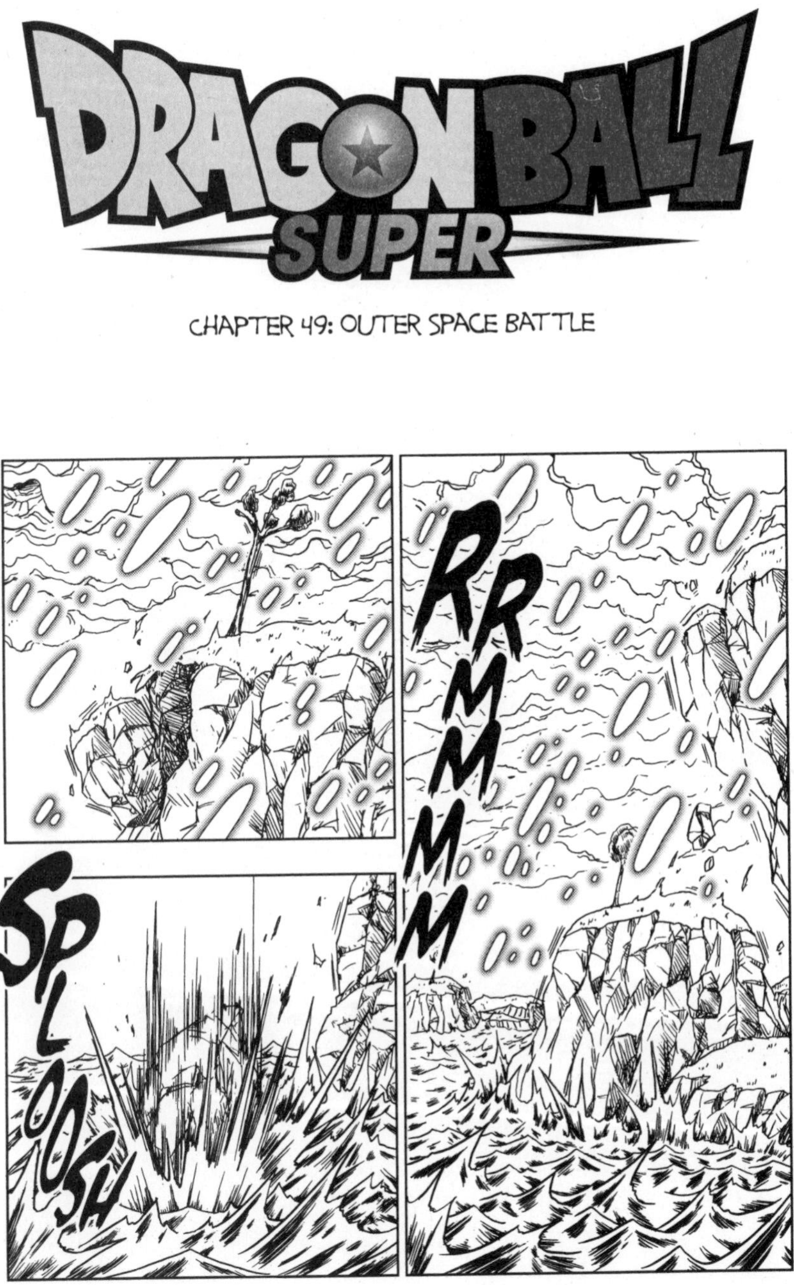
RRMMMM
SPLOOSH

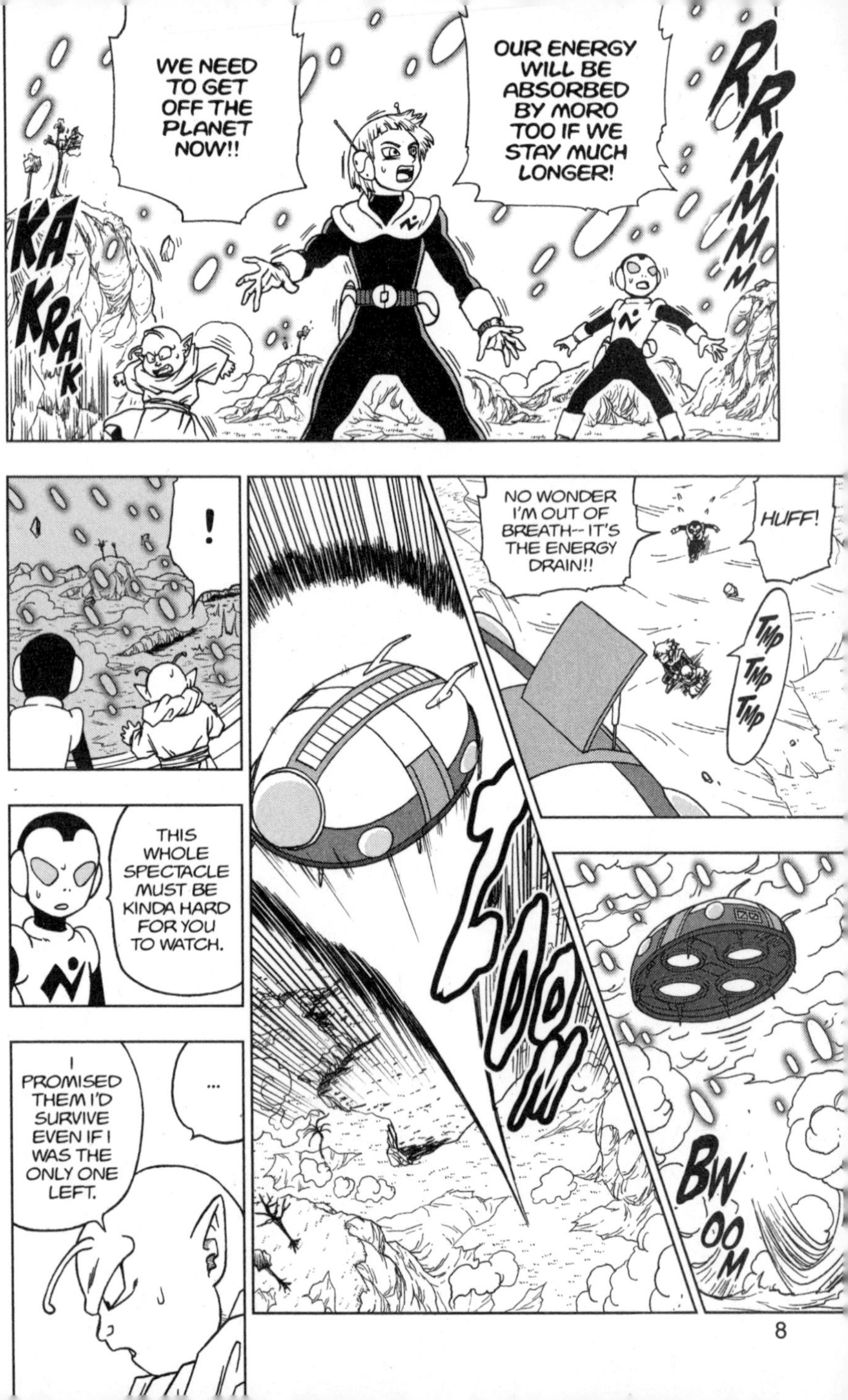
RRMMMMMM
OUR ENERGY WILL BE ABSORBED BY MORO TOO IF WE STAY MUCH LONGER!
WE NEED TO GET OFF THE PLANET NOW!!
KA KRAK
HUFF!
NO WONDER I'M OUT OF BREATH-- IT'S THE ENERGY DRAIN!!
TMP TMP TMP
BWOOM
ZOOOM
!
THIS WHOLE SPECTACLE MUST BE KINDA HARD FOR YOU TO WATCH.
...
I PROMISED THEM I'D SURVIVE EVEN IF I WAS THE ONLY ONE LEFT.

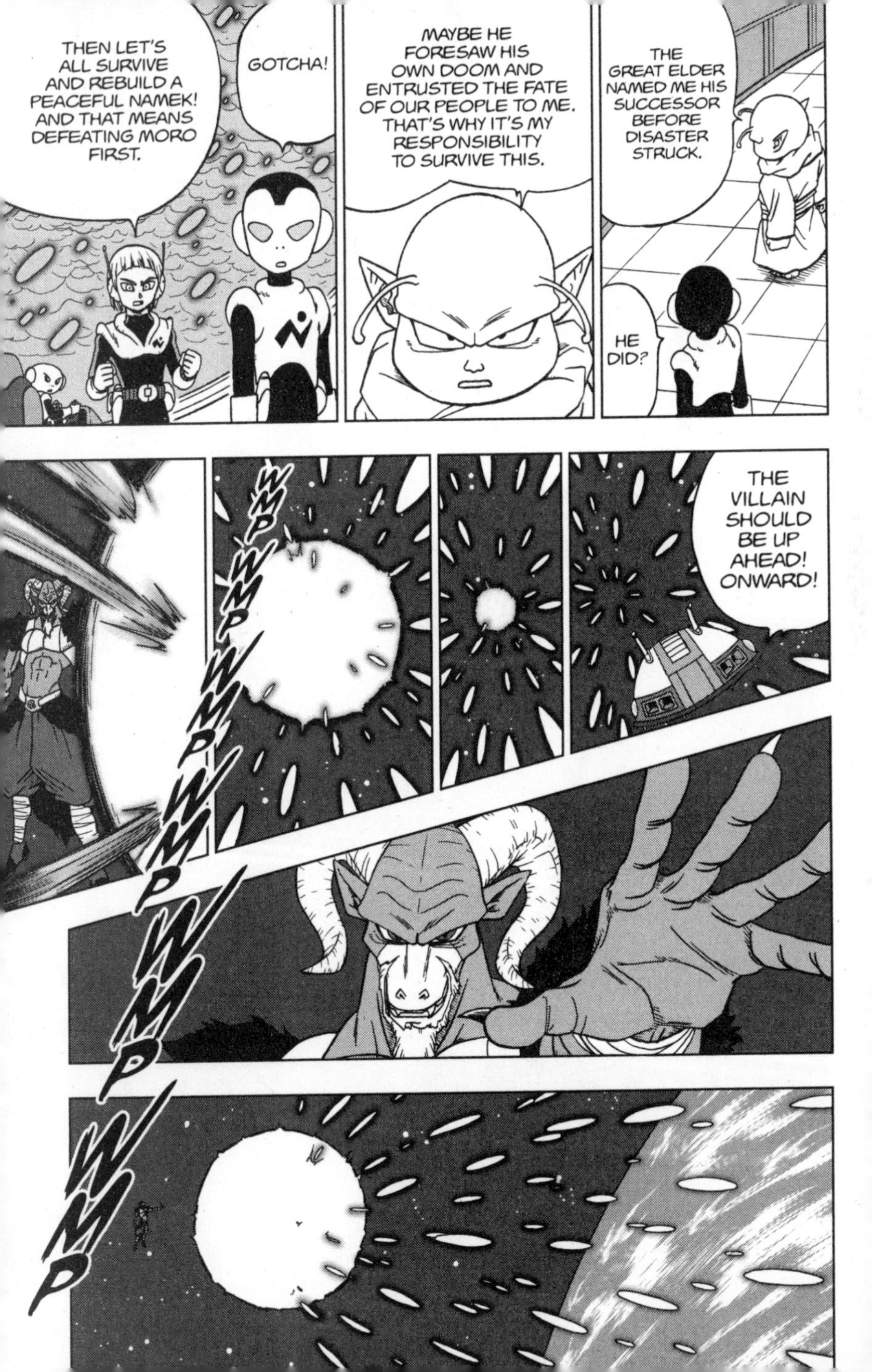
THE GREAT ELDER NAMED ME HIS SUCCESSOR BEFORE DISASTER STRUCK.
HE DID?
MAYBE HE FORESAW HIS OWN DOOM AND ENTRUSTED THE FATE OF OUR PEOPLE TO ME. THAT'S WHY IT'S MY RESPONSIBILITY TO SURVIVE THIS.
THEN LET'S ALL SURVIVE AND REBUILD A PEACEFUL NAMEK! AND THAT MEANS DEFEATING MORO FIRST.
GOTCHA!
THE VILLAIN SHOULD BE UP AHEAD! ONWARD!
WMP WMP WMP WMP WMP WMP

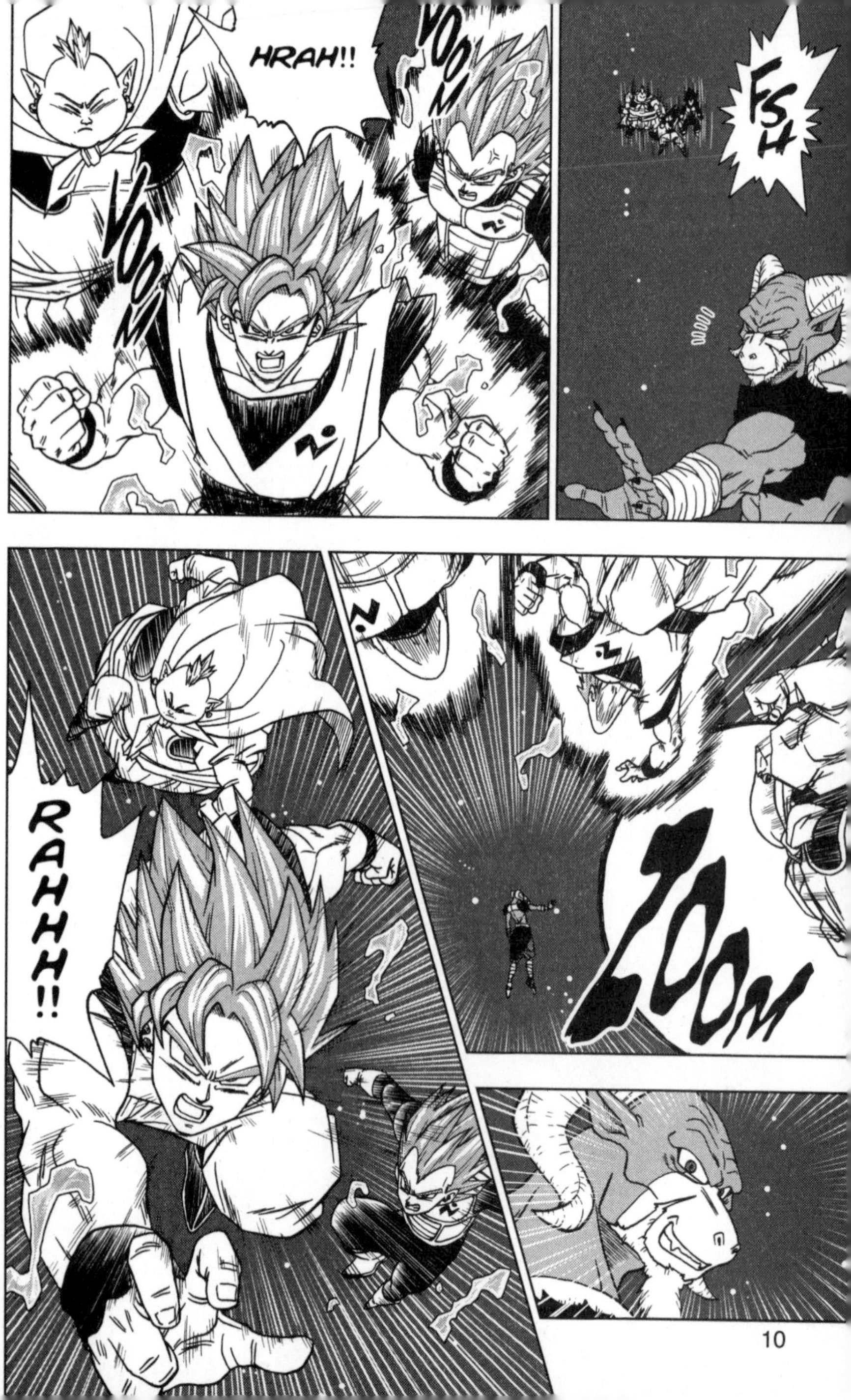
FSH
HRAH!!
VOOM
VOOM
ZOOM
RAHHHH!!

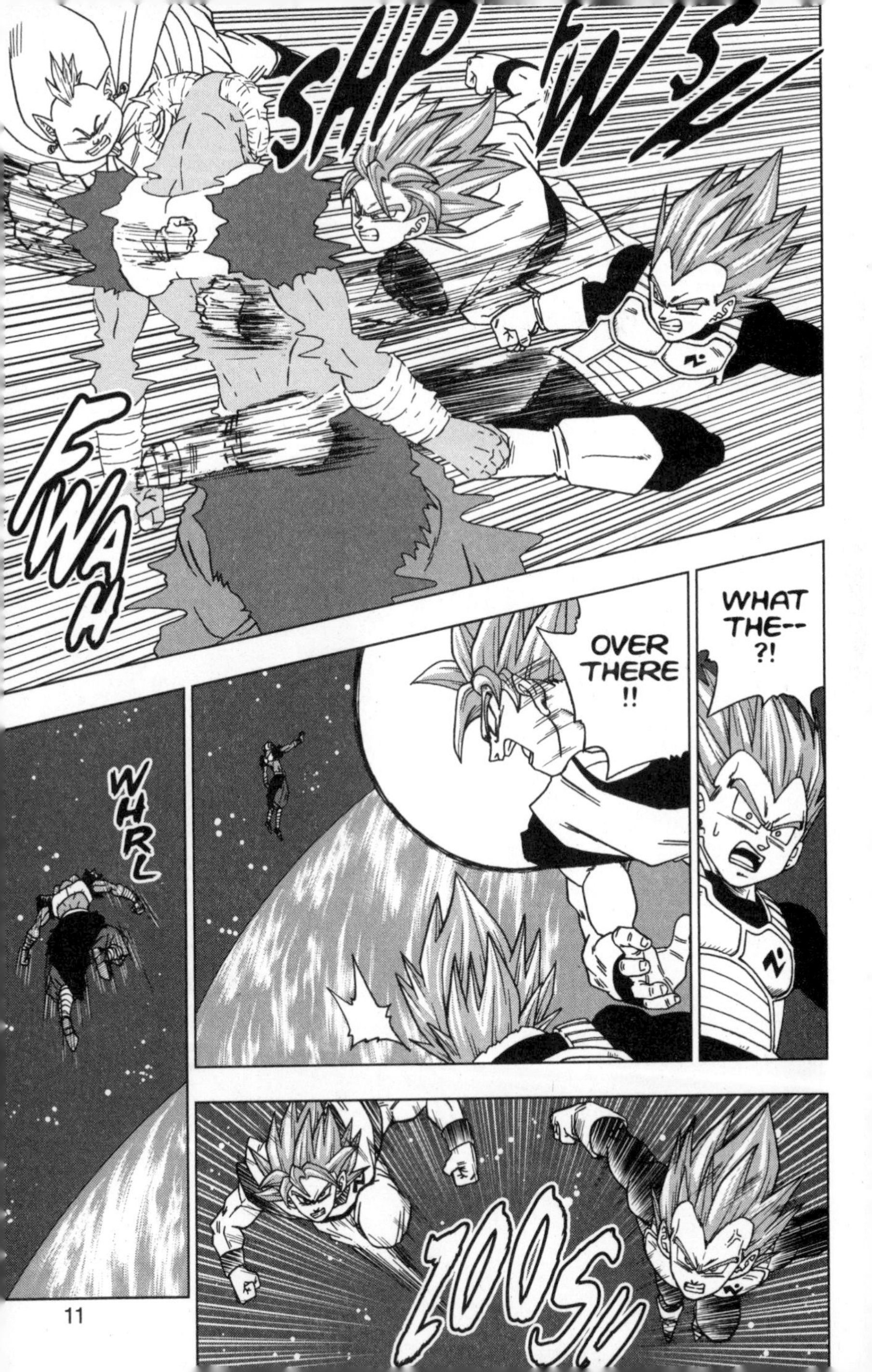
SHP
WISH
FWAH
WHAT THE-- ?!
OVER THERE !!
WHRL
ZOOSH

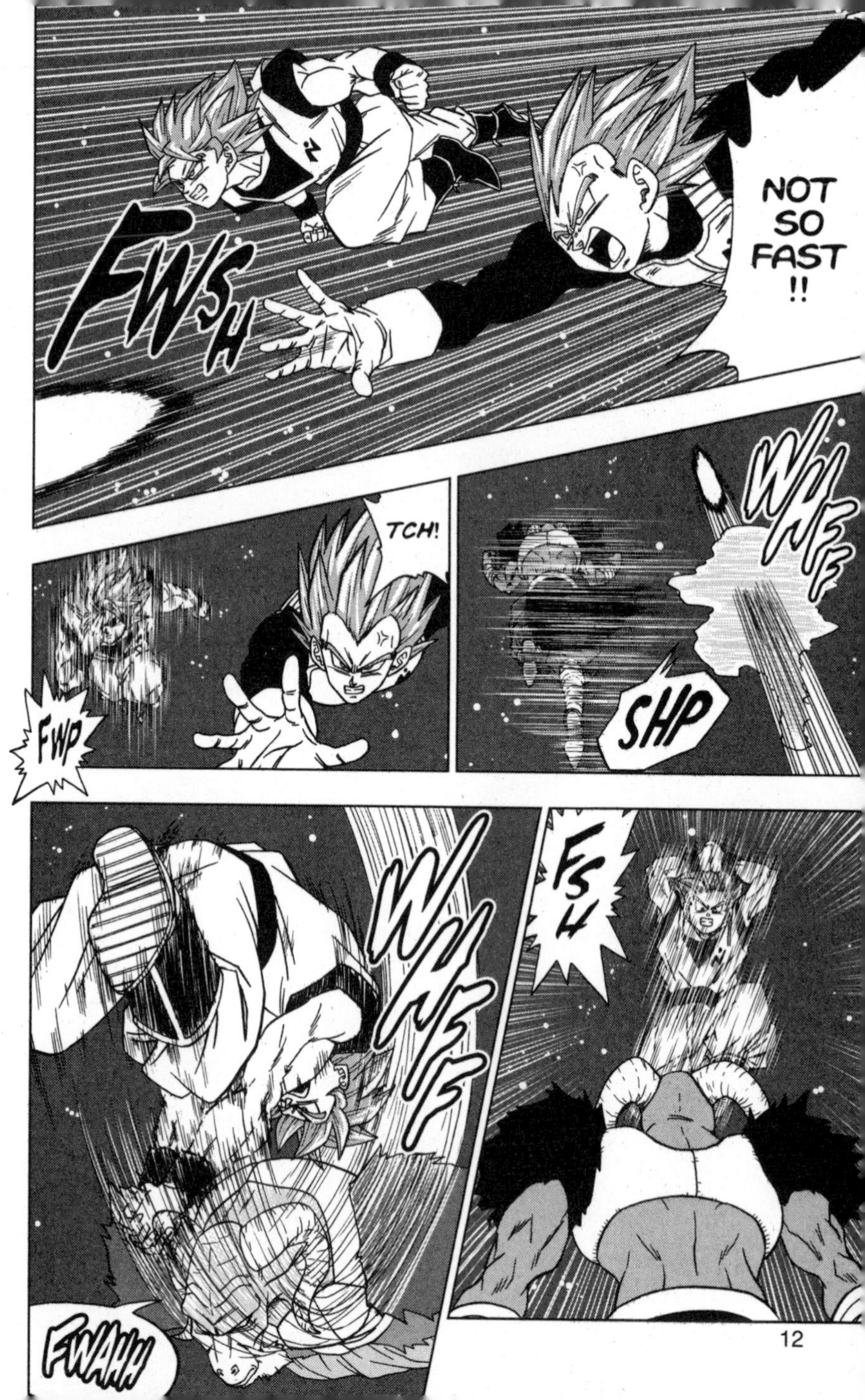
NOT SO FAST!!
FWSH
WHFF
SHP
TCH!
FWP
FSH
WHFF
FWAHH

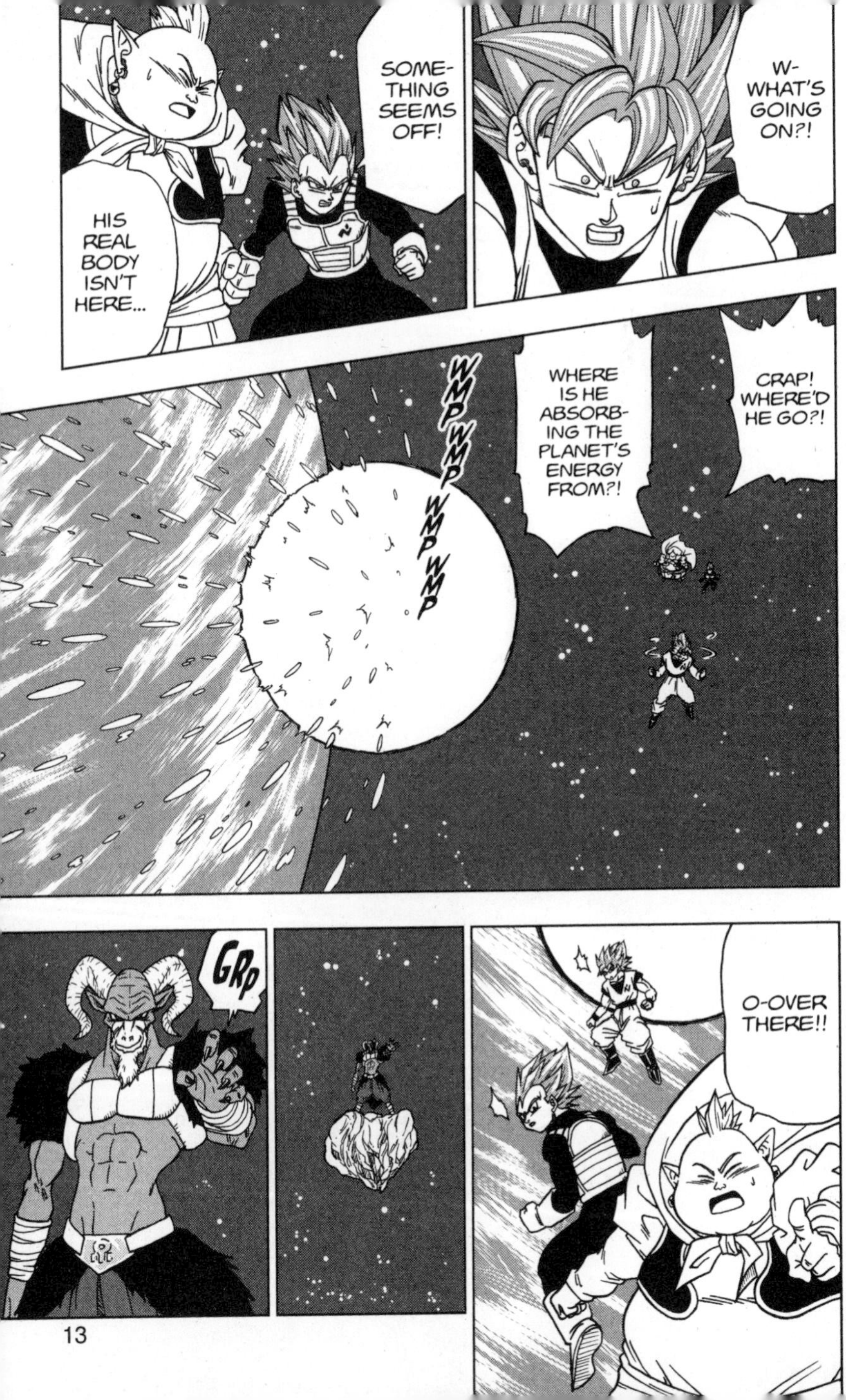
W-WHAT'S GOING ON?!
SOME-THING SEEMS OFF!
HIS REAL BODY ISN'T HERE...
CRAP! WHERE'D HE GO?!
WHERE IS HE ABSORB-ING THE PLANET'S ENERGY FROM?!
WMP WMP WMP WMP
O-OVER THERE!!
GRP

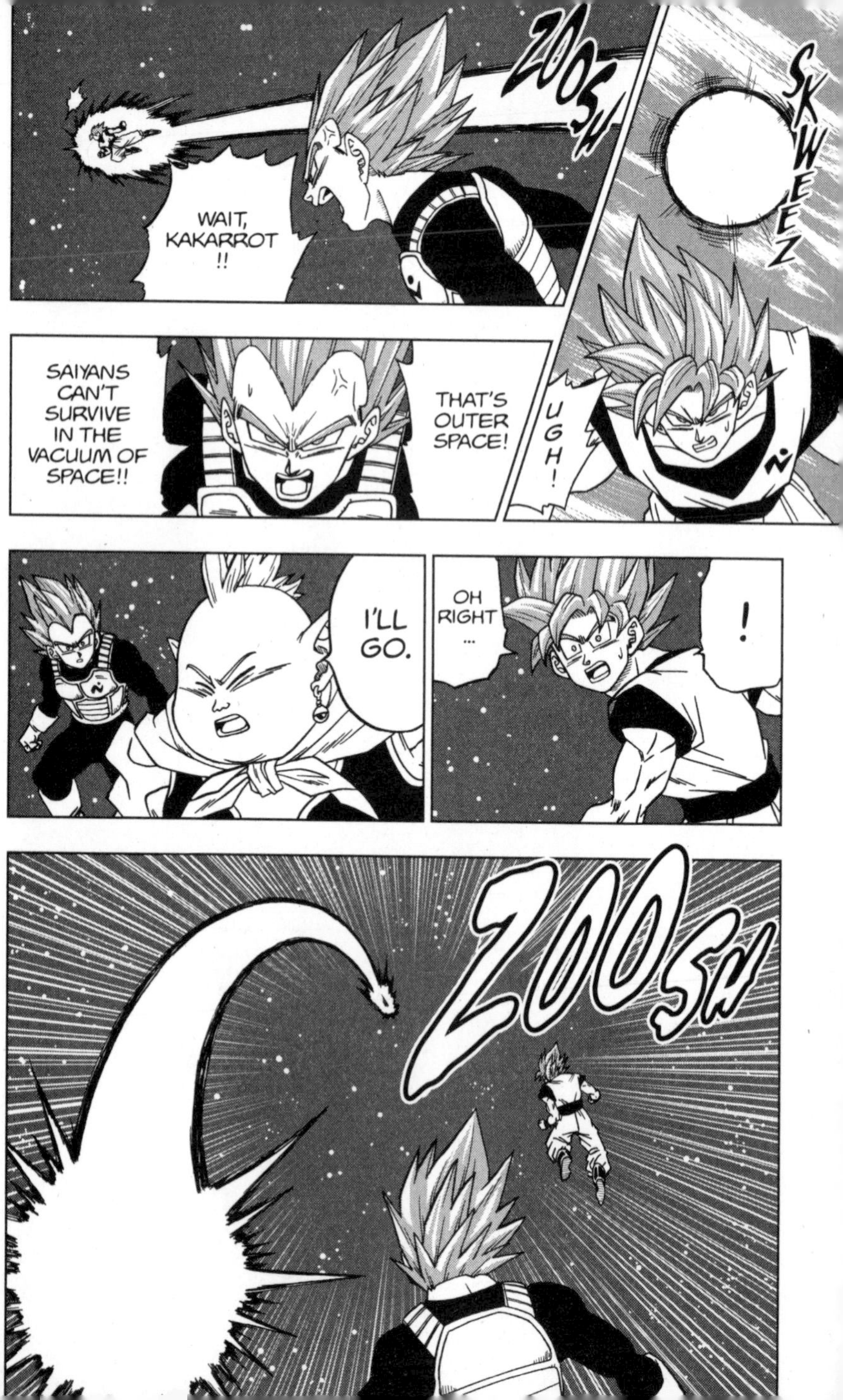
SKWEEZ
UGH!
ZOOSH
WAIT, KAKARROT !!
THAT'S OUTER SPACE!
SAIYANS CAN'T SURVIVE IN THE VACUUM OF SPACE!!
!
OH RIGHT ...
I'LL GO.
ZOOSH

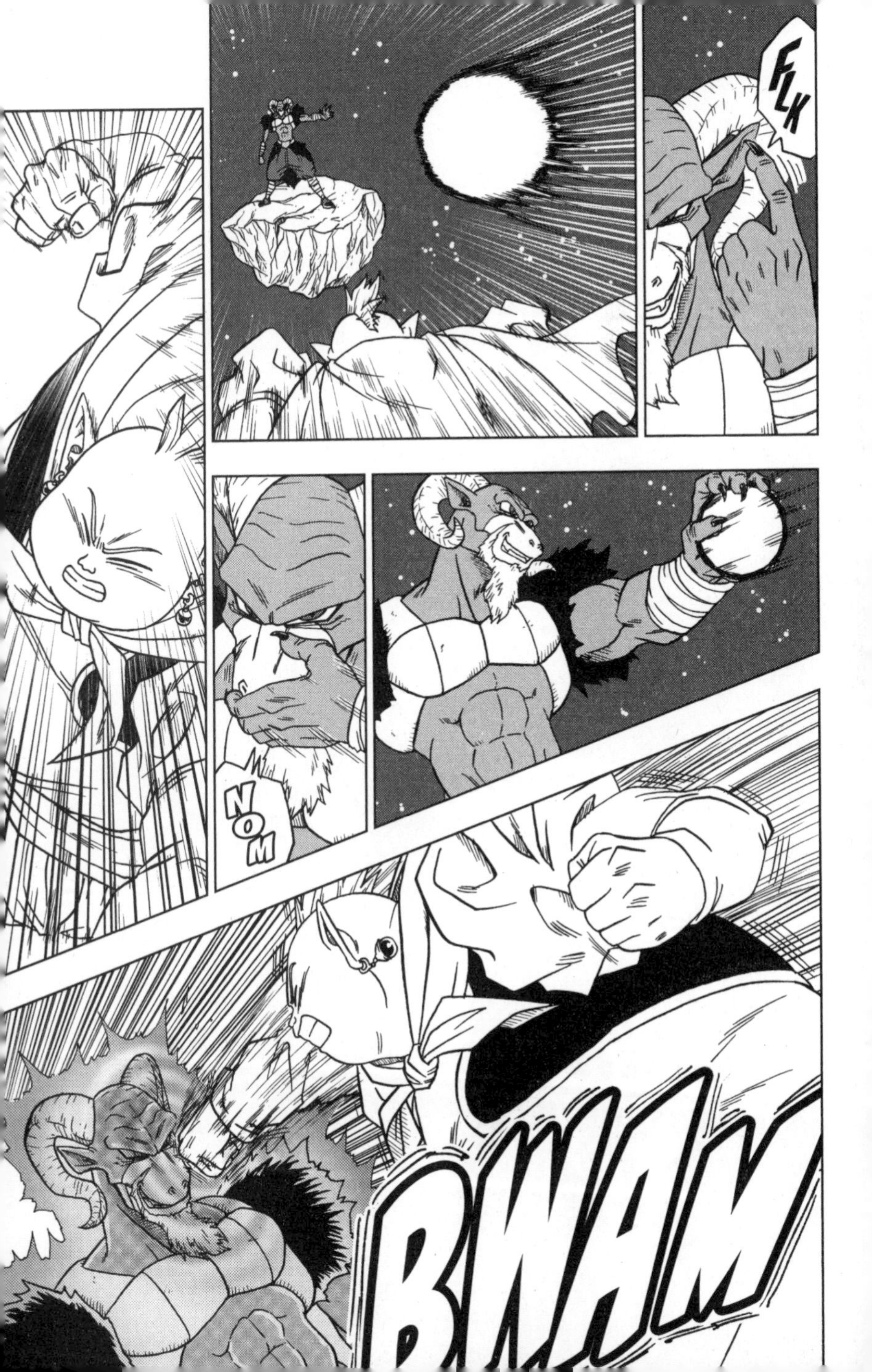
FLK
NOM
BNHAM

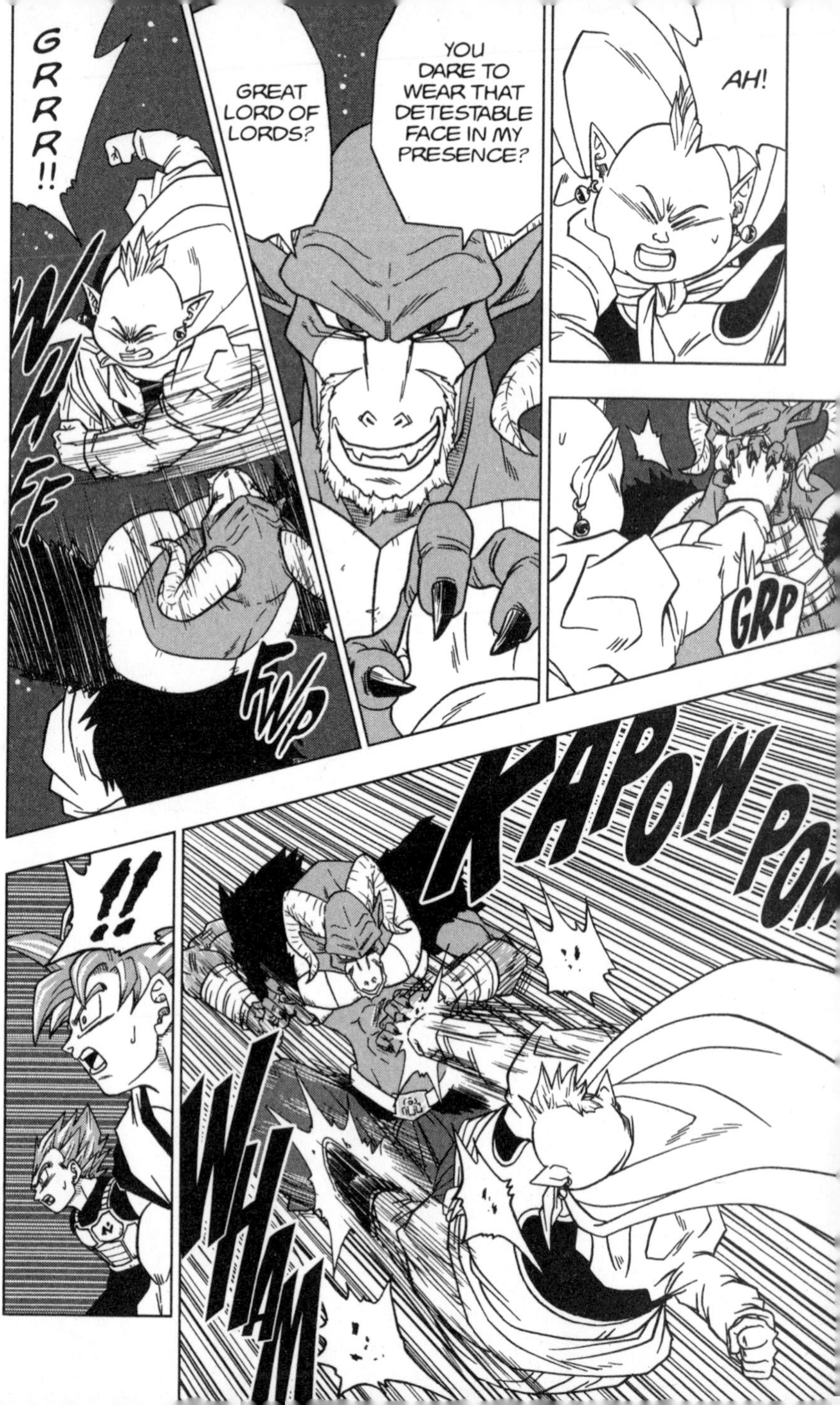
AH!
GRP
YOU DARE TO WEAR THAT DETESTABLE FACE IN MY PRESENCE?
GREAT LORD OF LORDS?
FWP
GRRRR!!
WHIFF
KAPOW
POW
WHAM
!!

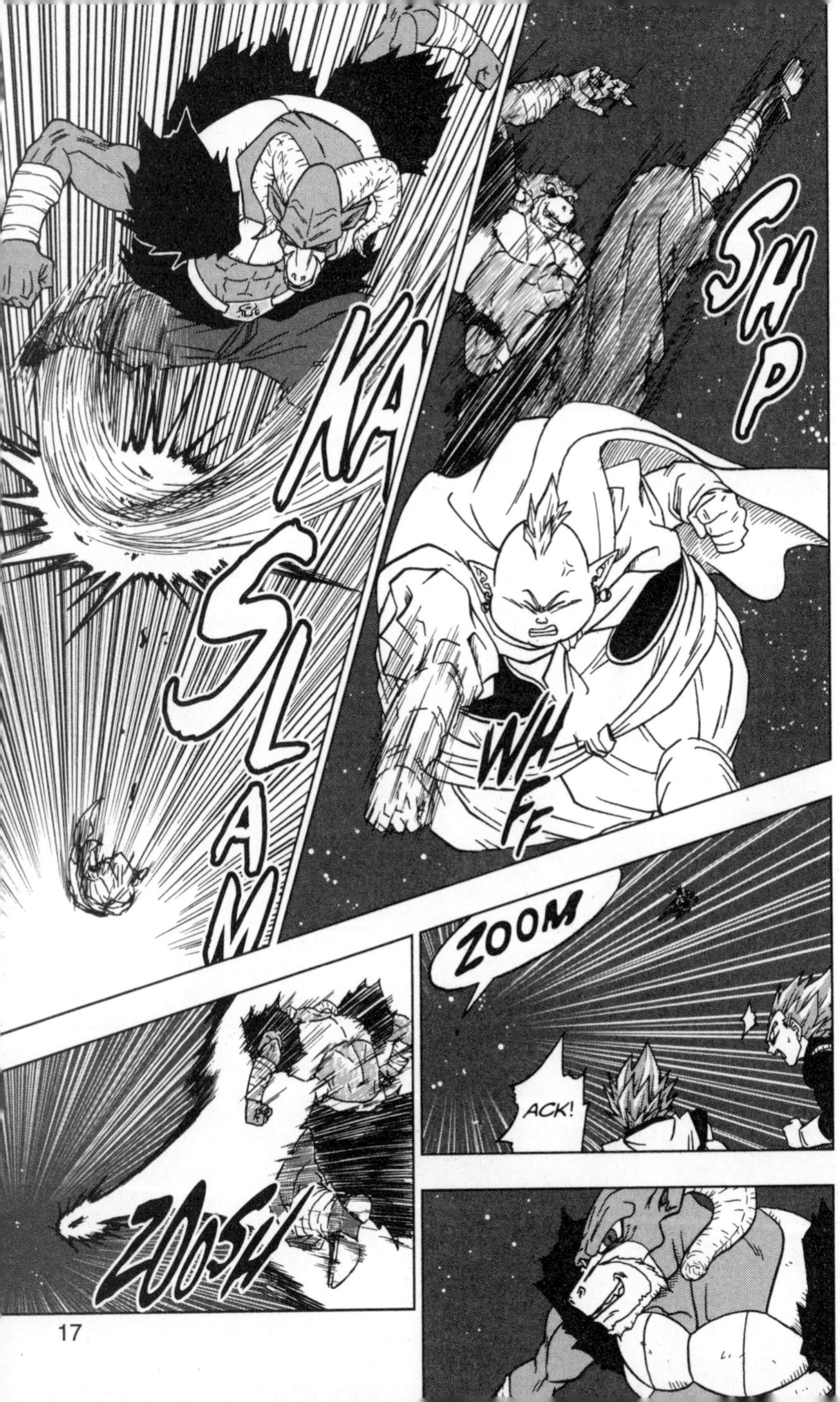
SHP
WHIFF
KA
SLAM
ZOOM
ACK!
ZOOSH

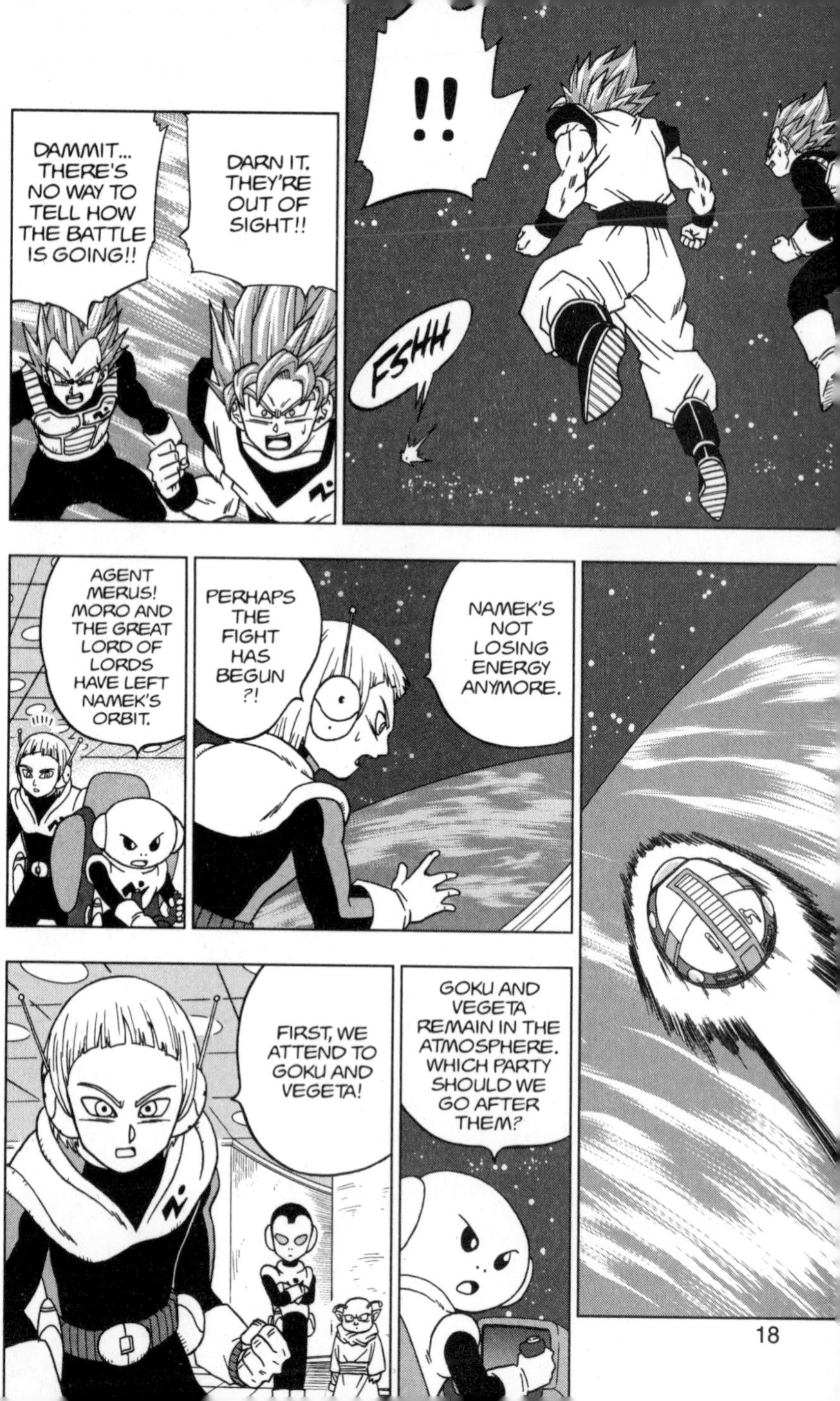
!!
FSHH
DARN IT. THEY'RE OUT OF SIGHT!!
DAMMIT... THERE'S NO WAY TO TELL HOW THE BATTLE IS GOING!!
NAMEK'S NOT LOSING ENERGY ANYMORE.
PERHAPS THE FIGHT HAS BEGUN?!
AGENT MERUS! MORO AND THE GREAT LORD OF LORDS HAVE LEFT NAMEK'S ORBIT.
GOKU AND VEGETA REMAIN IN THE ATMOSPHERE. WHICH PARTY SHOULD WE GO AFTER THEM?
FIRST, WE ATTEND TO GOKU AND VEGETA!

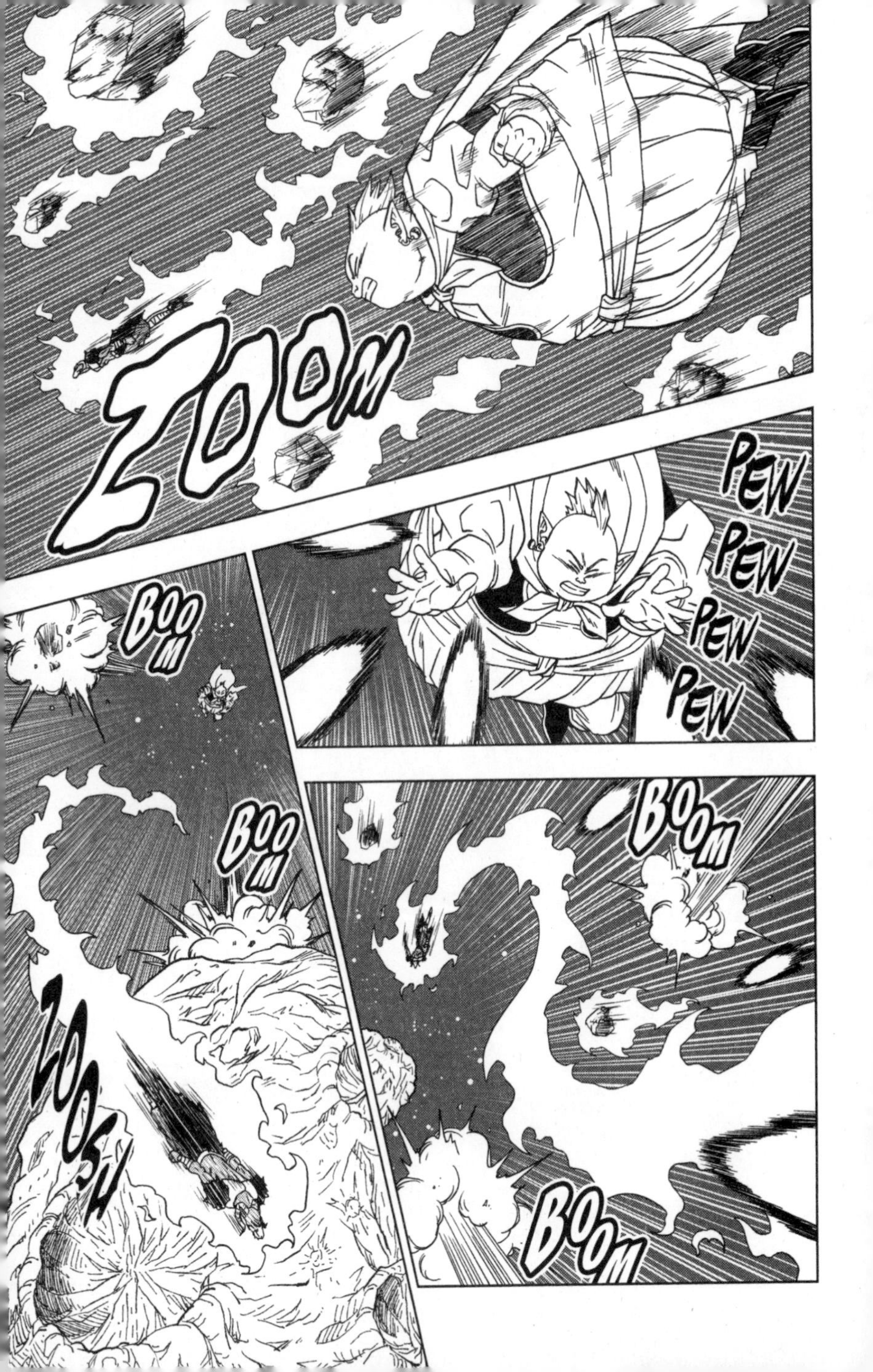
ZOOM
PEW PEW PEW PEW
BOOM
BOOM
BOOM
ZOOSH
BOOM

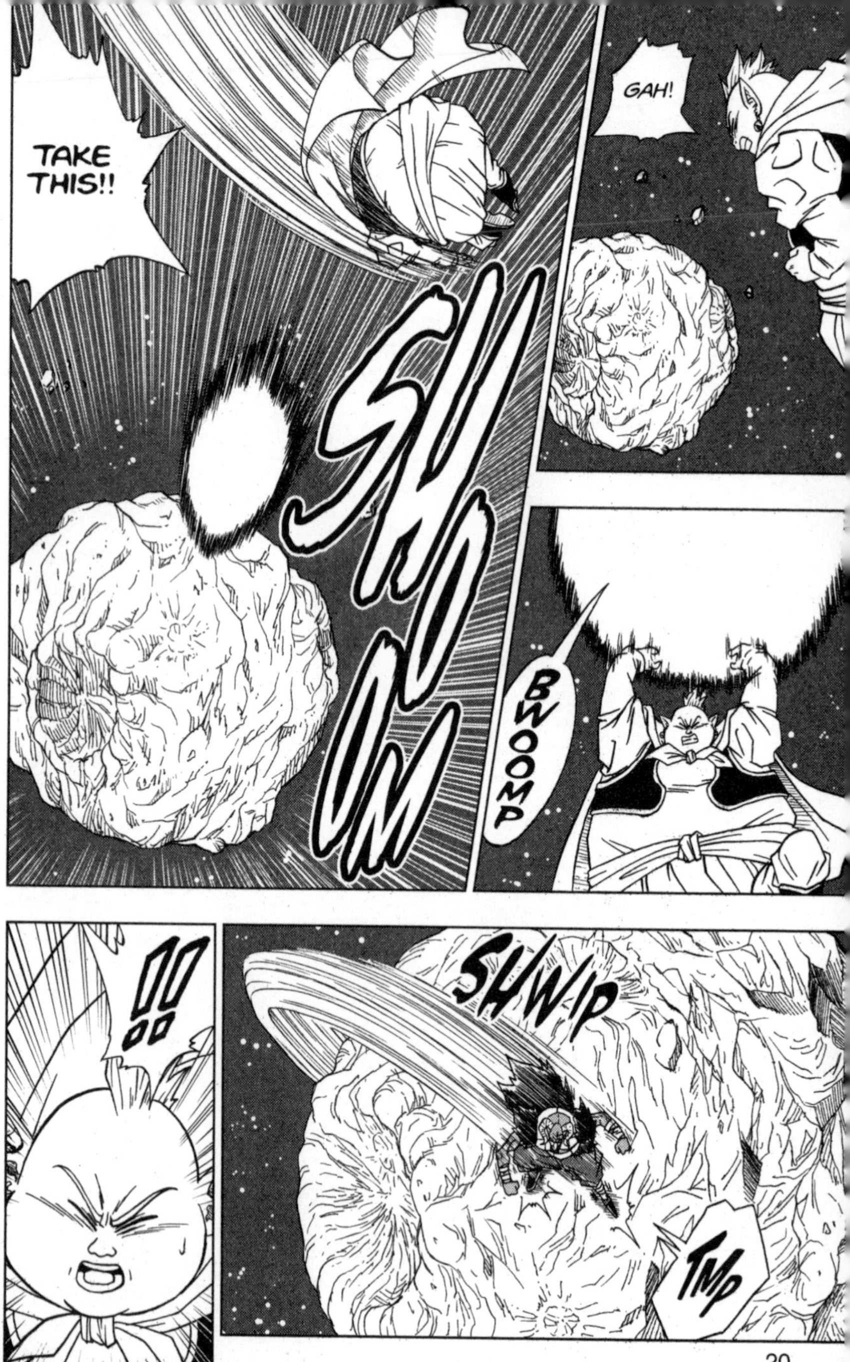
GAH!
BWOOMP
TAKE THIS!!
SHOOM
SHWIP
TMP
!!

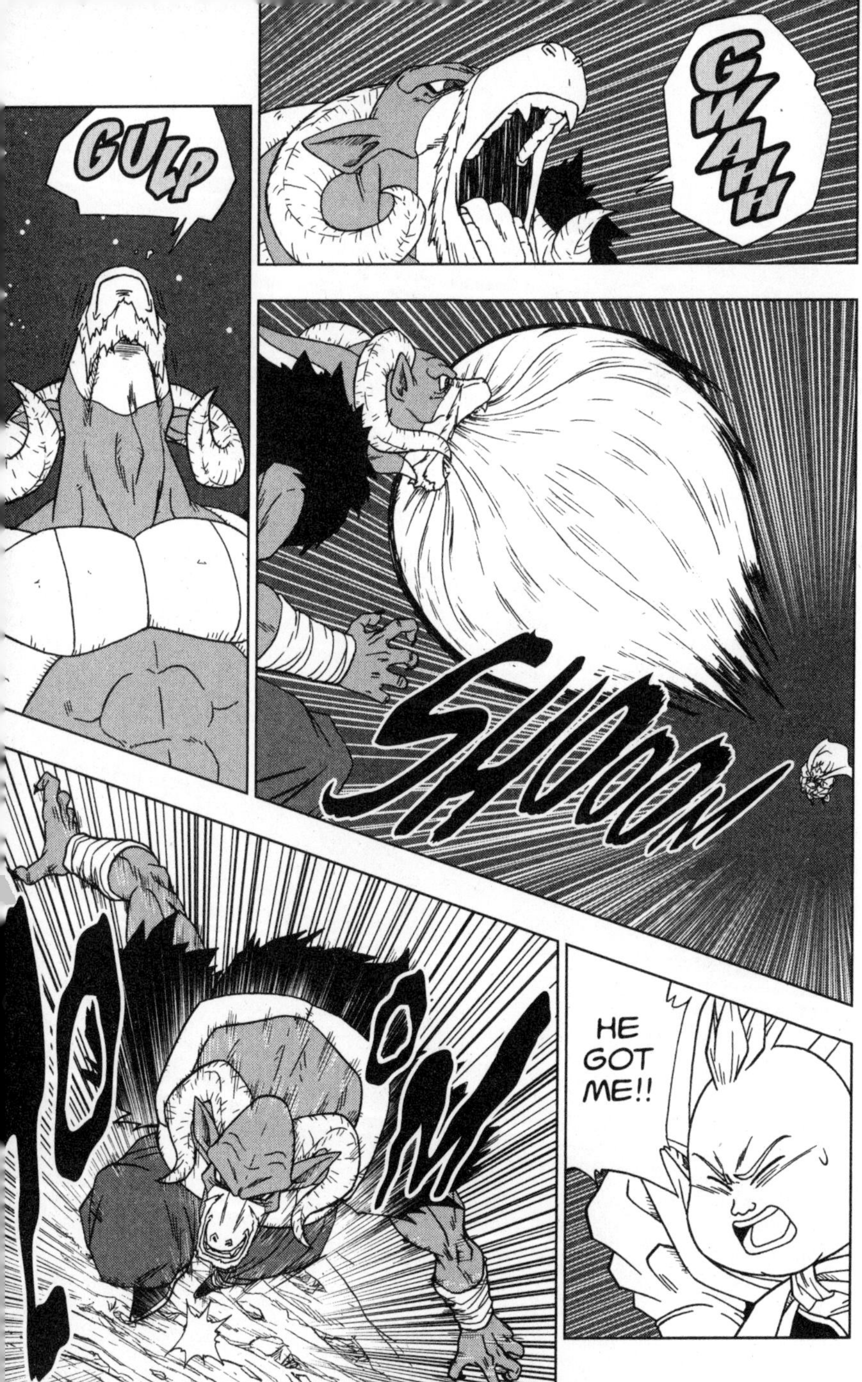
GWAHH
SHOOOM
GULP
HE GOT ME!!

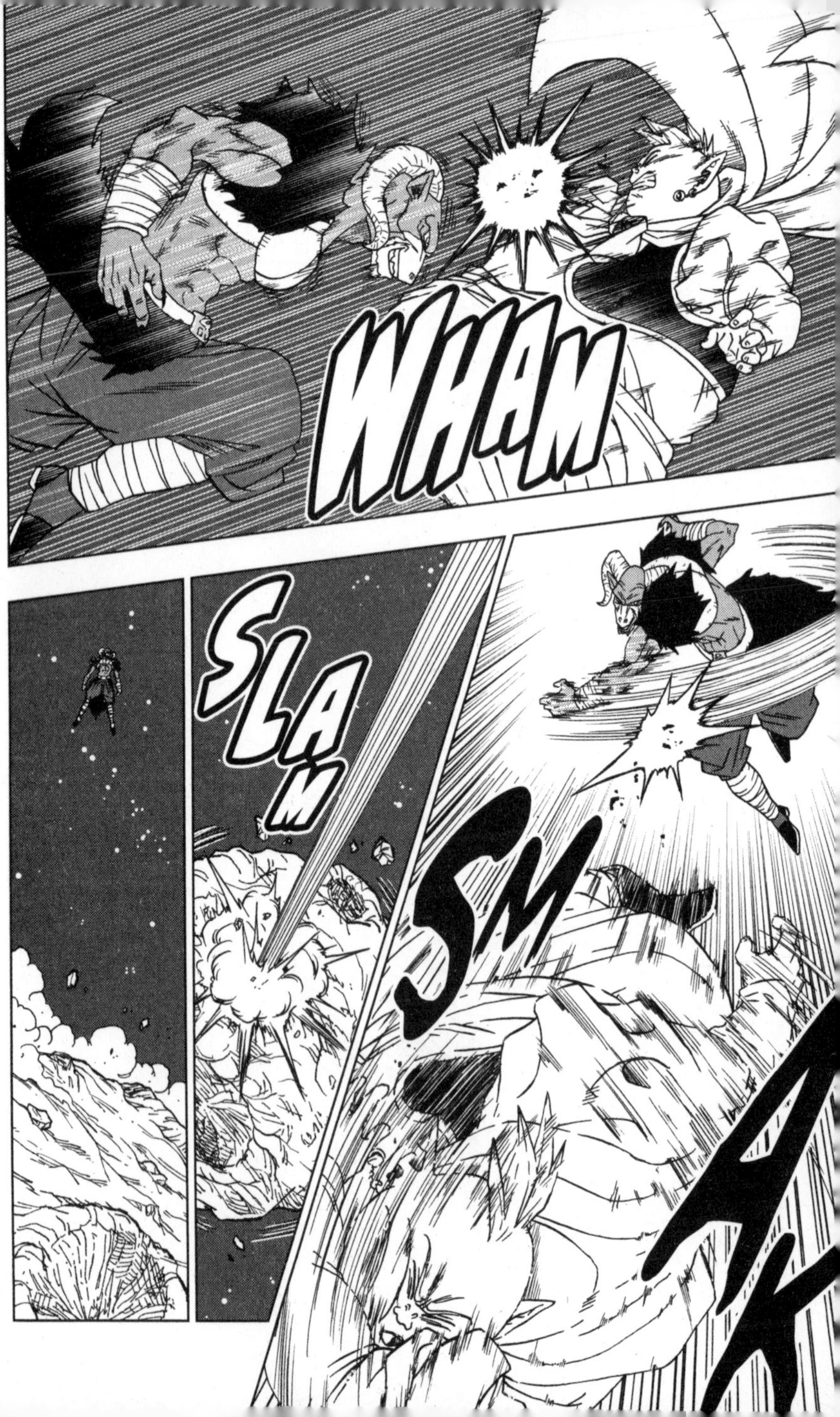
WHAM
SLAM

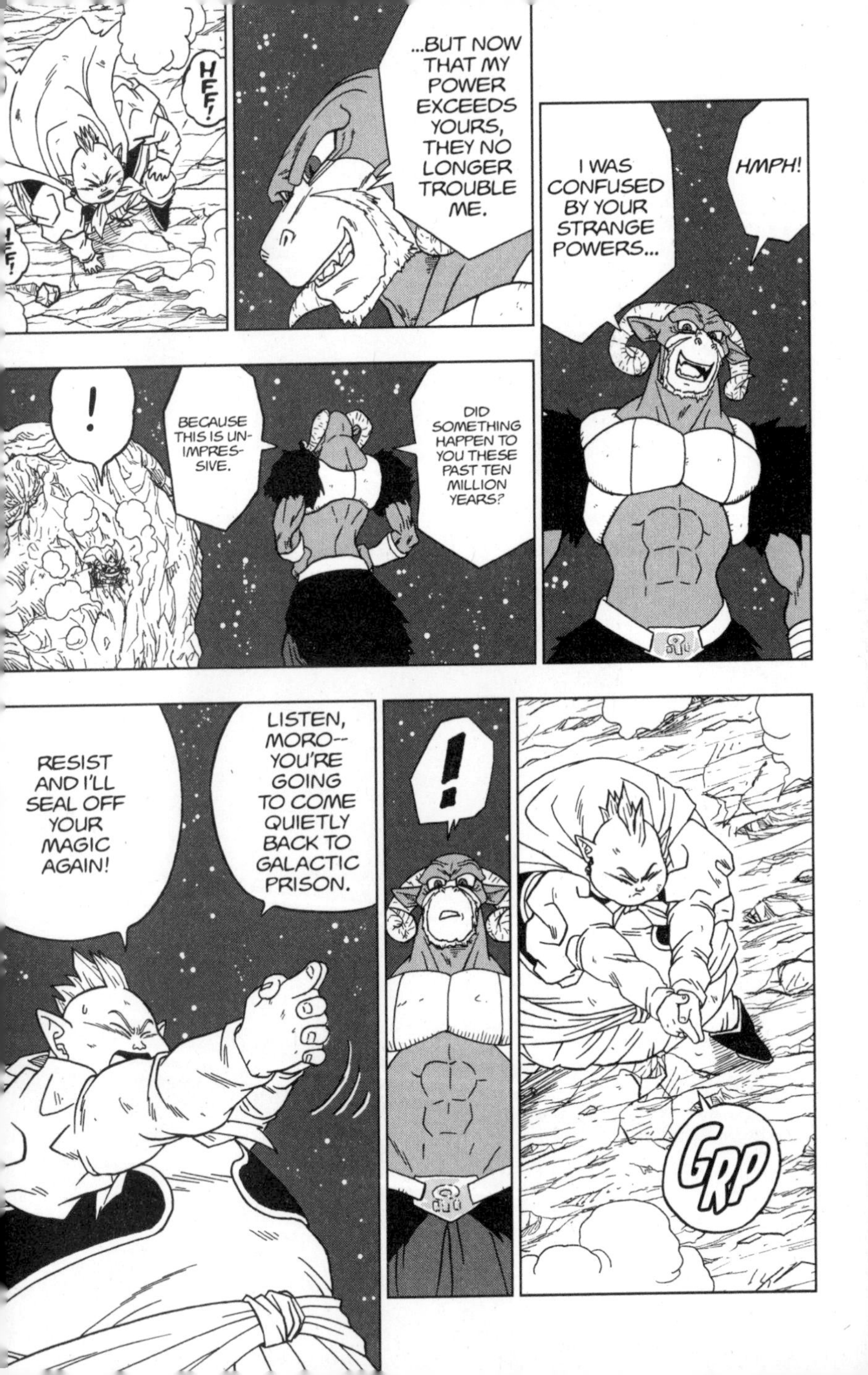
HMPH!
I WAS CONFUSED BY YOUR STRANGE POWERS...
...BUT NOW THAT MY POWER EXCEEDS YOURS, THEY NO LONGER TROUBLE ME.
HFF!
HFF!
DID SOMETHING HAPPEN TO YOU THESE PAST TEN MILLION YEARS?
BECAUSE THIS IS UN-IMPRES-SIVE.
!
GRP
!
LISTEN, MORO-- YOU'RE GOING TO COME QUIETLY BACK TO GALACTIC PRISON.
RESIST AND I'LL SEAL OFF YOUR MAGIC AGAIN!

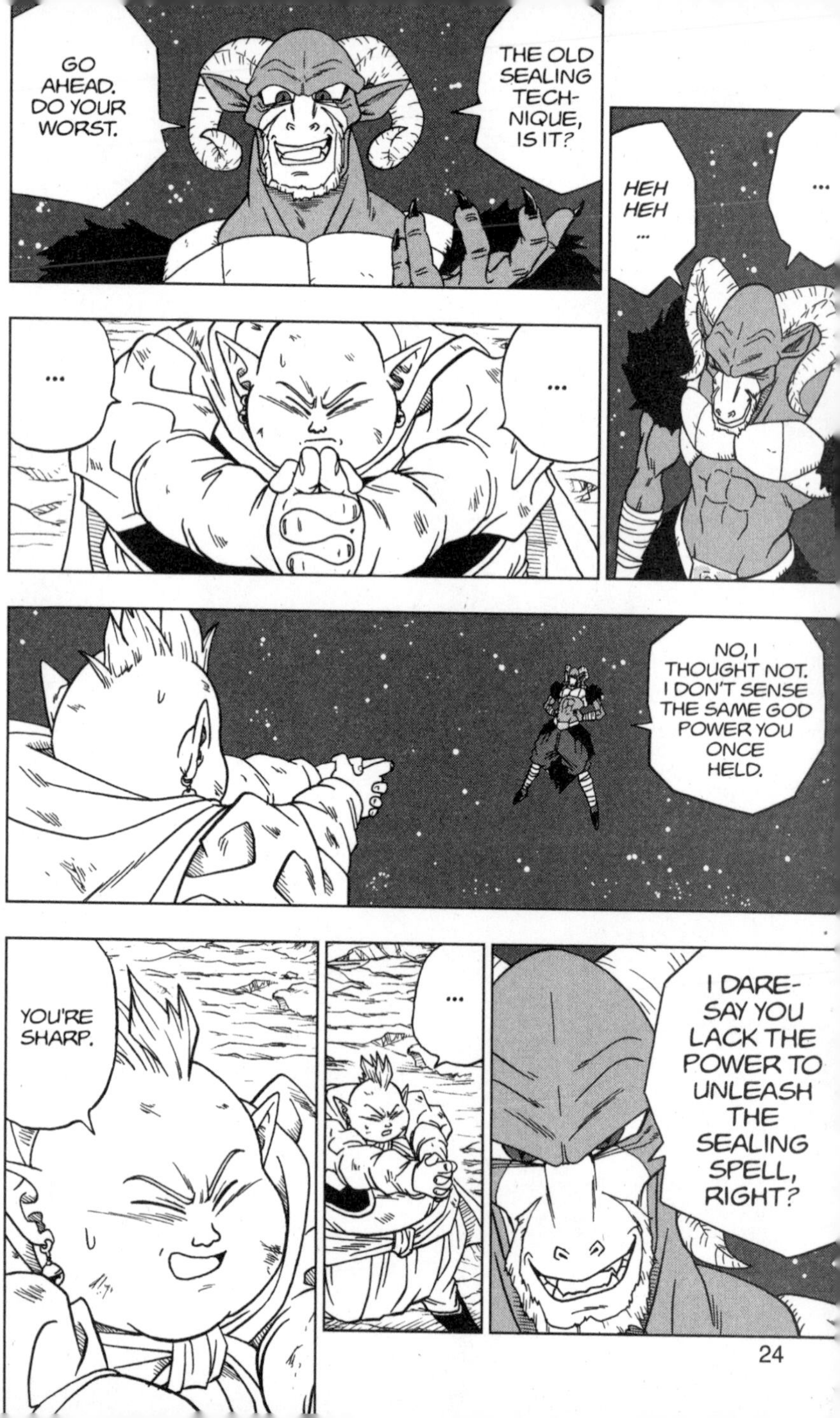
...
HEH HEH ...
THE OLD SEALING TECH-NIQUE, IS IT?
GO AHEAD. DO YOUR WORST.
...
...
NO, I THOUGHT NOT. I DON'T SENSE THE SAME GOD POWER YOU ONCE HELD.
I DARE-SAY YOU LACK THE POWER TO UNLEASH THE SEALING SPELL, RIGHT?
...
YOU'RE SHARP.

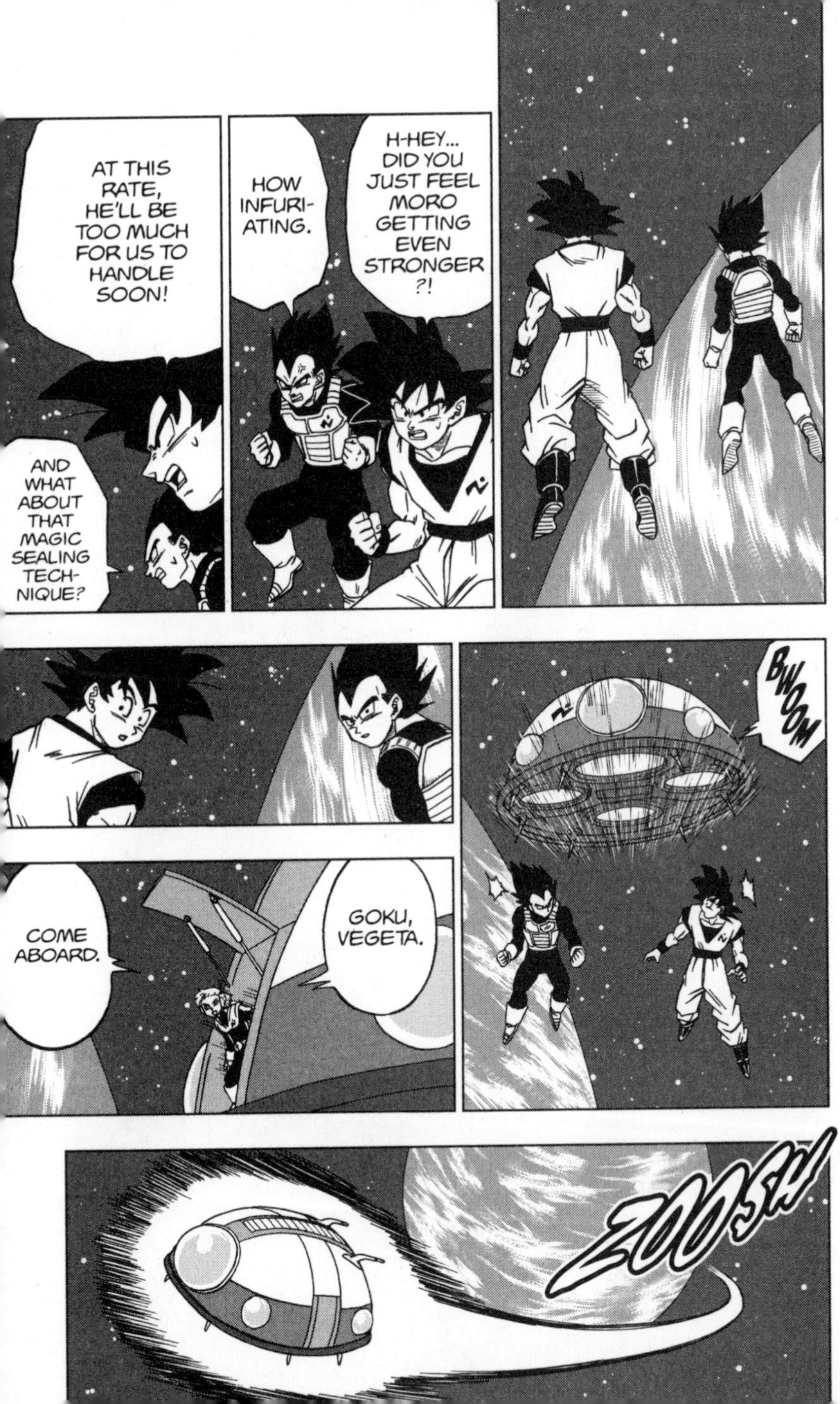
H-HEY... DID YOU JUST FEEL MORO GETTING EVEN STRONGER?!
HOW INFURIATING.
AT THIS RATE, HE'LL BE TOO MUCH FOR US TO HANDLE SOON!
AND WHAT ABOUT THAT MAGIC SEALING TECHNIQUE?
BWOOM
GOKU, VEGETA.
COME ABOARD.
ZOOSH

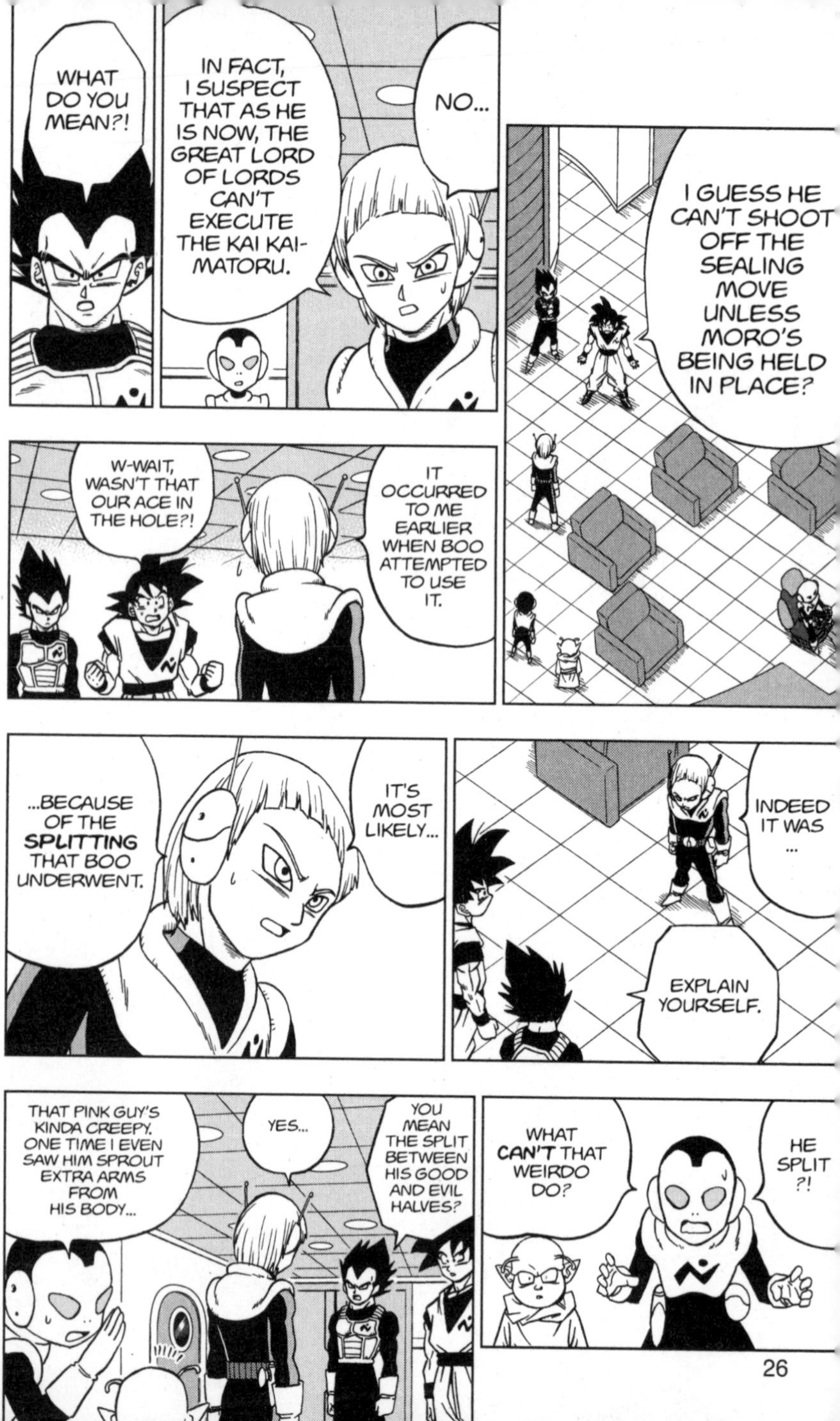
I GUESS HE CAN'T SHOOT OFF THE SEALING MOVE UNLESS MORO'S BEING HELD IN PLACE?
NO...
IN FACT, I SUSPECT THAT AS HE IS NOW, THE GREAT LORD OF LORDS CAN'T EXECUTE THE KAI KAI-MATORU.
WHAT DO YOU MEAN?!
IT OCCURRED TO ME EARLIER WHEN BOO ATTEMPTED TO USE IT.
W-WAIT, WASN'T THAT OUR ACE IN THE HOLE?!
INDEED IT WAS ...
EXPLAIN YOURSELF.
IT'S MOST LIKELY...
...BECAUSE OF THE **SPLITTING** THAT BOO UNDERWENT.
HE SPLIT ?!
WHAT **CAN'T** THAT WEIRDO DO?
YOU MEAN THE SPLIT BETWEEN HIS GOOD AND EVIL HALVES?
YES...
THAT PINK GUY'S KINDA CREEPY. ONE TIME I EVEN SAW HIM SPROUT EXTRA ARMS FROM HIS BODY...

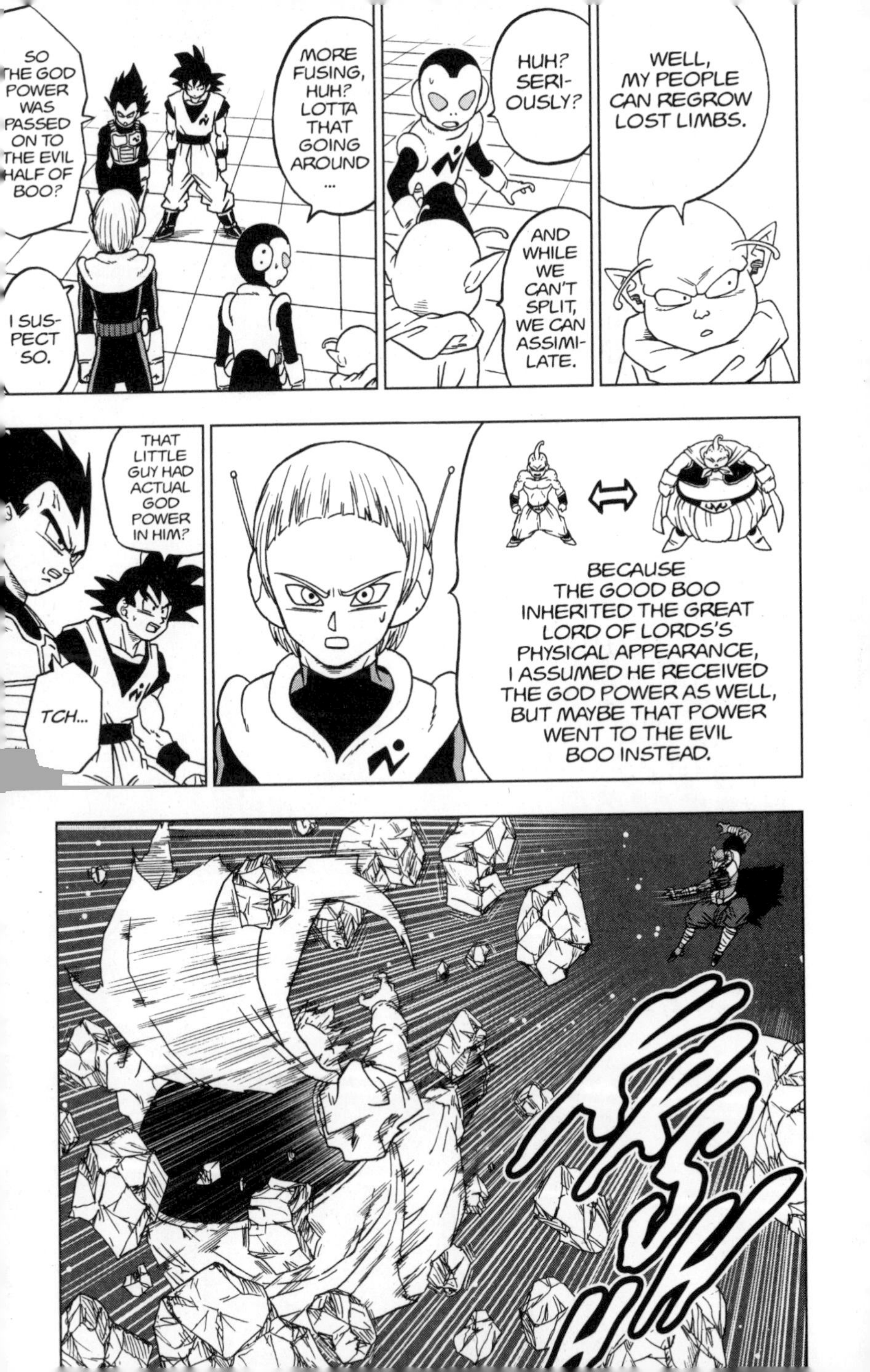
WELL, MY PEOPLE CAN REGROW LOST LIMBS.
HUH? SERIOUSLY?
AND WHILE WE CAN'T SPLIT, WE CAN ASSIMILATE.
MORE FUSING, HUH? LOTTA THAT GOING AROUND ...
SO THE GOD POWER WAS PASSED ON TO THE EVIL HALF OF BOO?
I SUSPECT SO.
BECAUSE THE GOOD BOO INHERITED THE GREAT LORD OF LORDS'S PHYSICAL APPEARANCE, I ASSUMED HE RECEIVED THE GOD POWER AS WELL, BUT MAYBE THAT POWER WENT TO THE EVIL BOO INSTEAD.
THAT LITTLE GUY HAD ACTUAL GOD POWER IN HIM?
TCH...

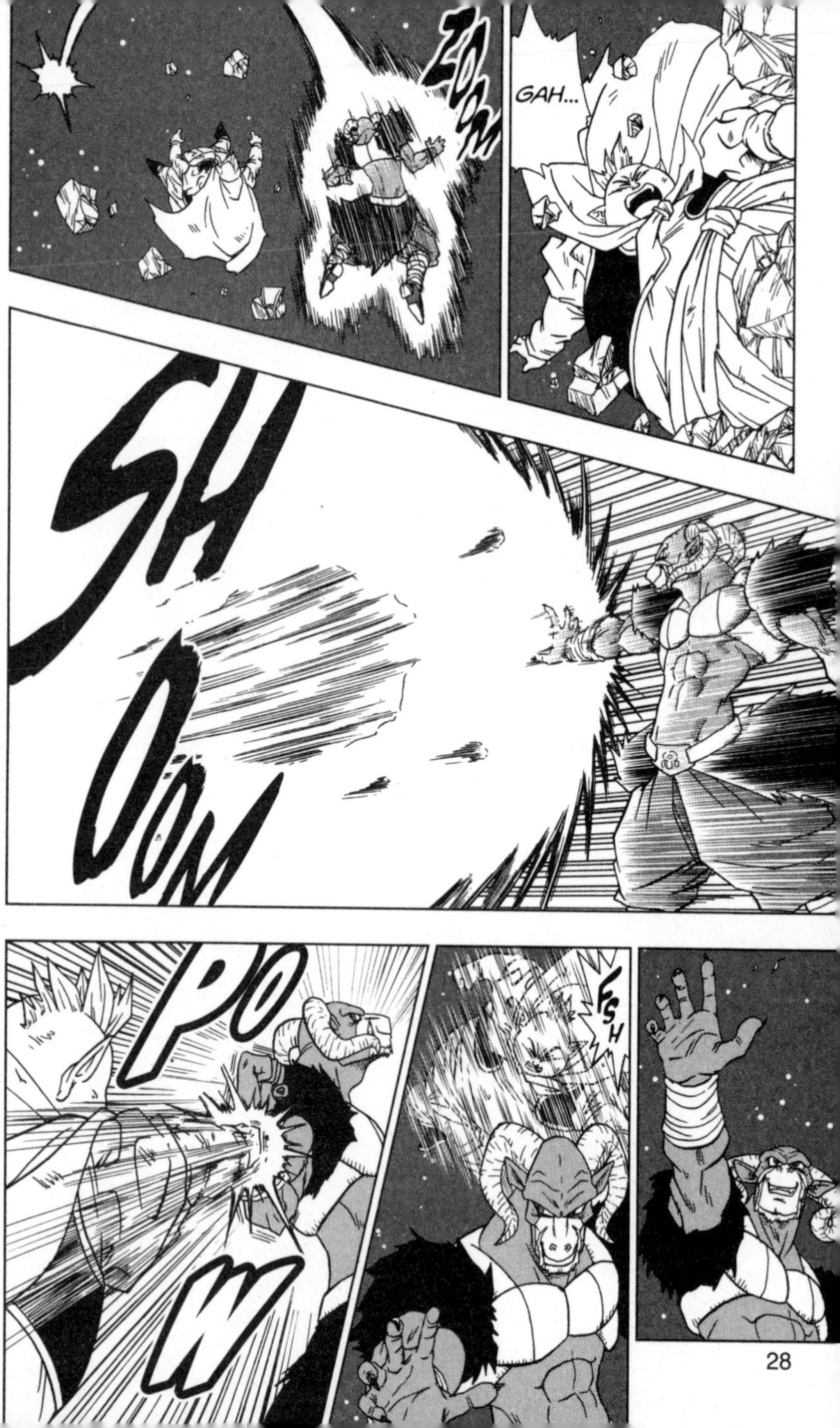
GAH...
ZOOM
SHOOM
FSH
POW

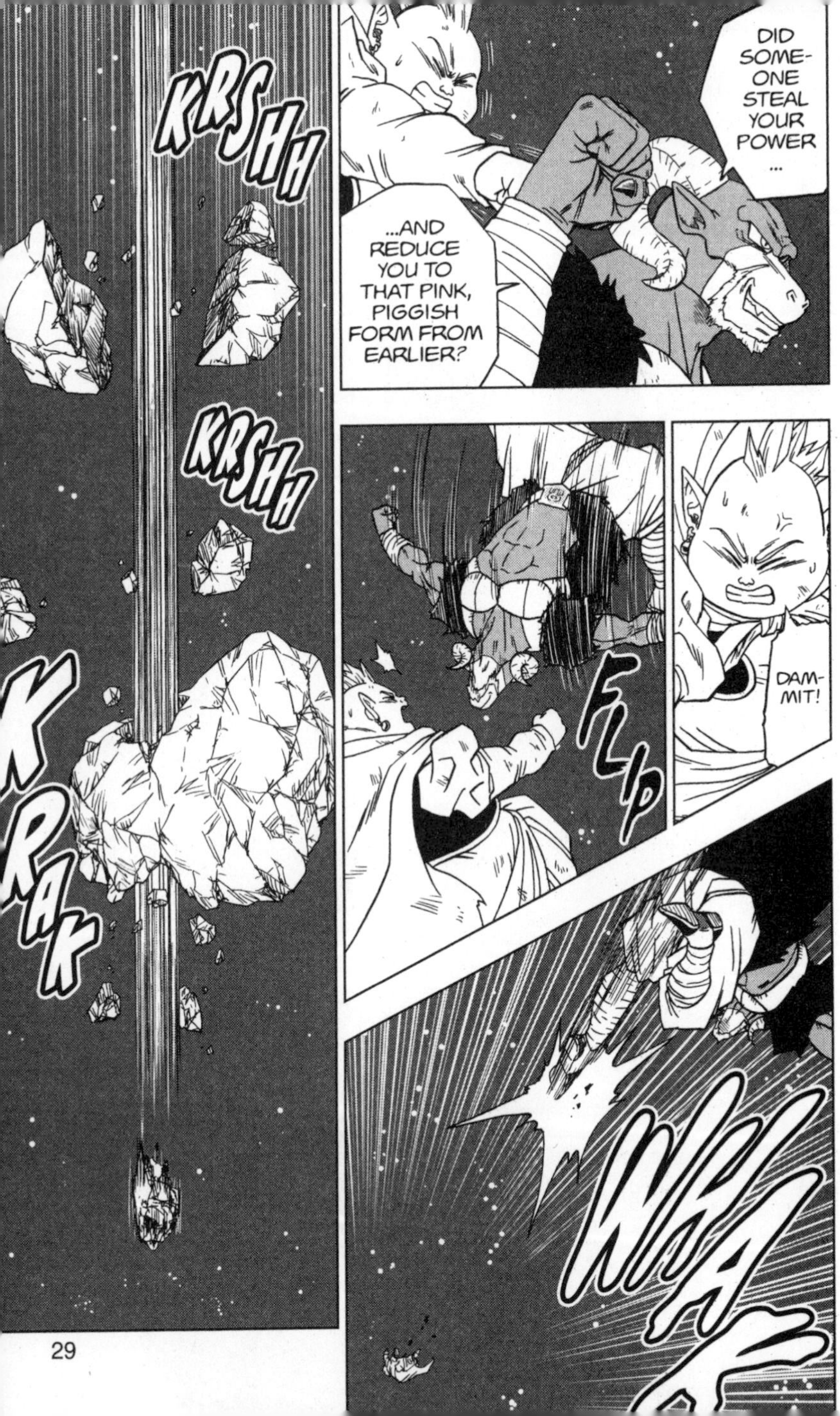
DID SOME-ONE STEAL YOUR POWER ...
...AND REDUCE YOU TO THAT PINK, PIGGISH FORM FROM EARLIER?
DAM-MIT!
FLIP
WHA
KRSHH
KRSHH
KRAK

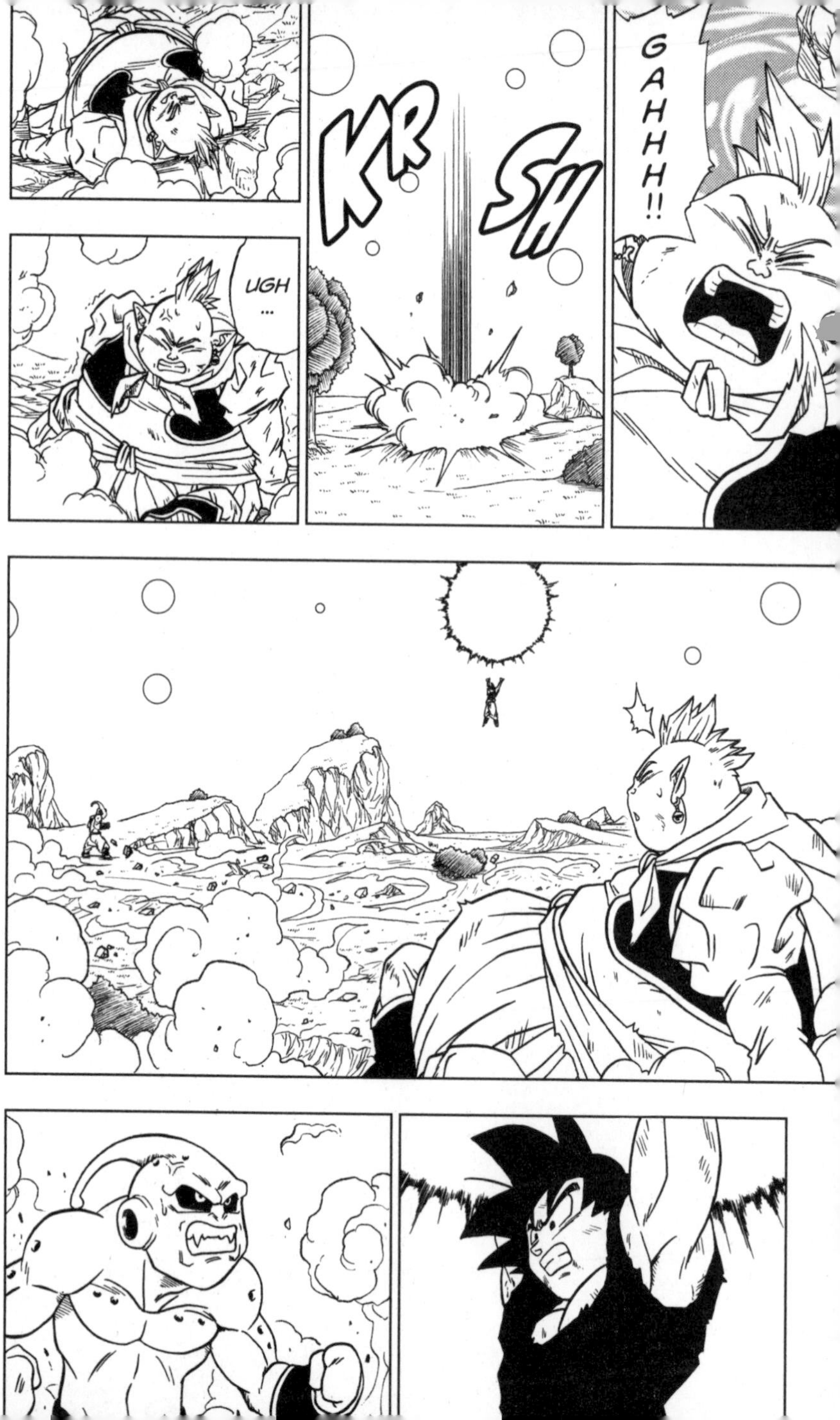
GAHHHH!!
KR SH
UGH ...

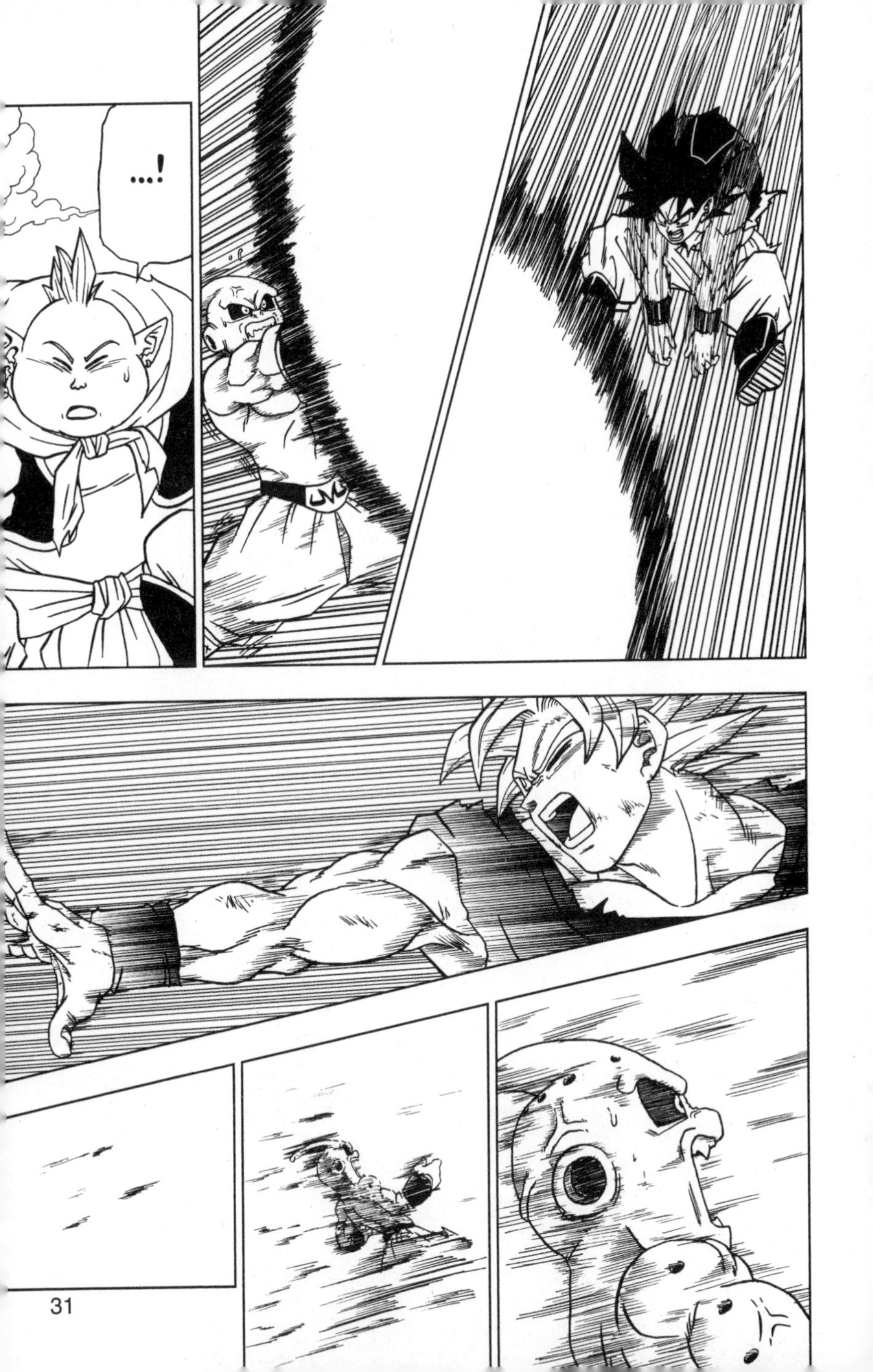
...!

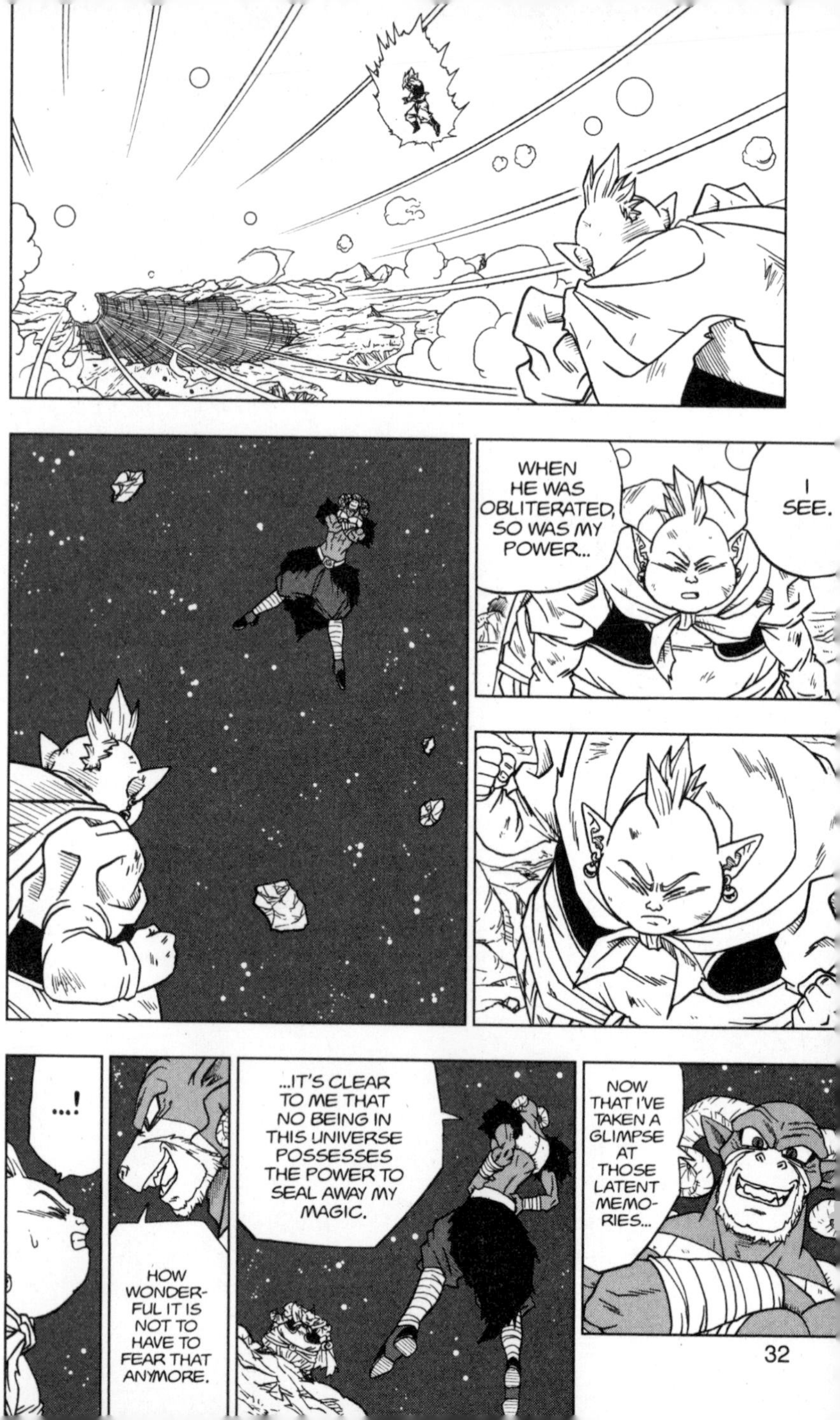
I SEE.
WHEN HE WAS OBLITERATED, SO WAS MY POWER...
NOW THAT I'VE TAKEN A GLIMPSE AT THOSE LATENT MEMO-RIES...
...IT'S CLEAR TO ME THAT NO BEING IN THIS UNIVERSE POSSESSES THE POWER TO SEAL AWAY MY MAGIC.
HOW WONDER-FUL IT IS NOT TO HAVE TO FEAR THAT ANYMORE.
...!

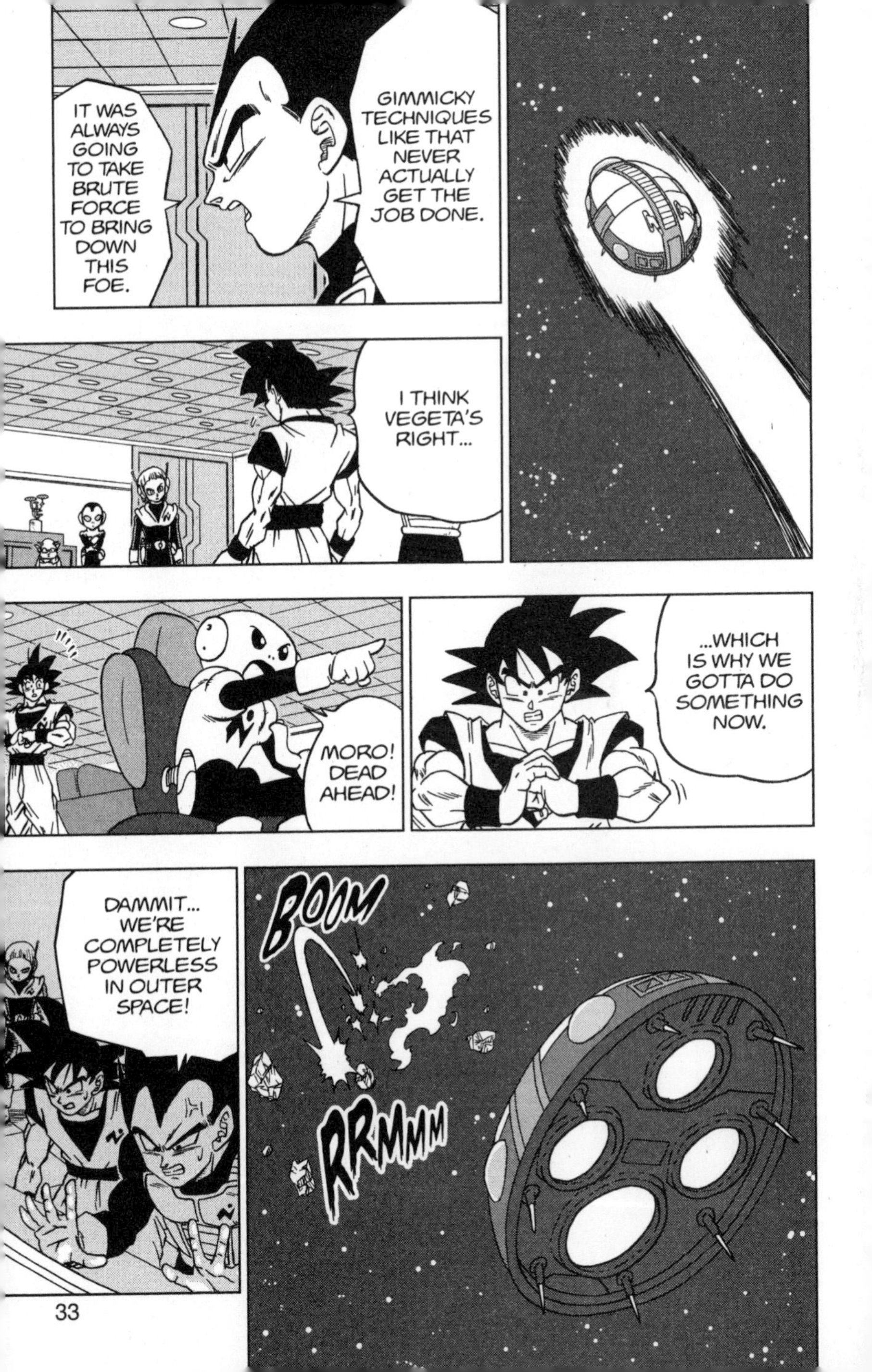
GIMMICKY TECHNIQUES LIKE THAT NEVER ACTUALLY GET THE JOB DONE.
IT WAS ALWAYS GOING TO TAKE BRUTE FORCE TO BRING DOWN THIS FOE.
I THINK VEGETA'S RIGHT...
...WHICH IS WHY WE GOTTA DO SOMETHING NOW.
MORO! DEAD AHEAD!
BOOM
RRMMM
DAMMIT... WE'RE COMPLETELY POWERLESS IN OUTER SPACE!

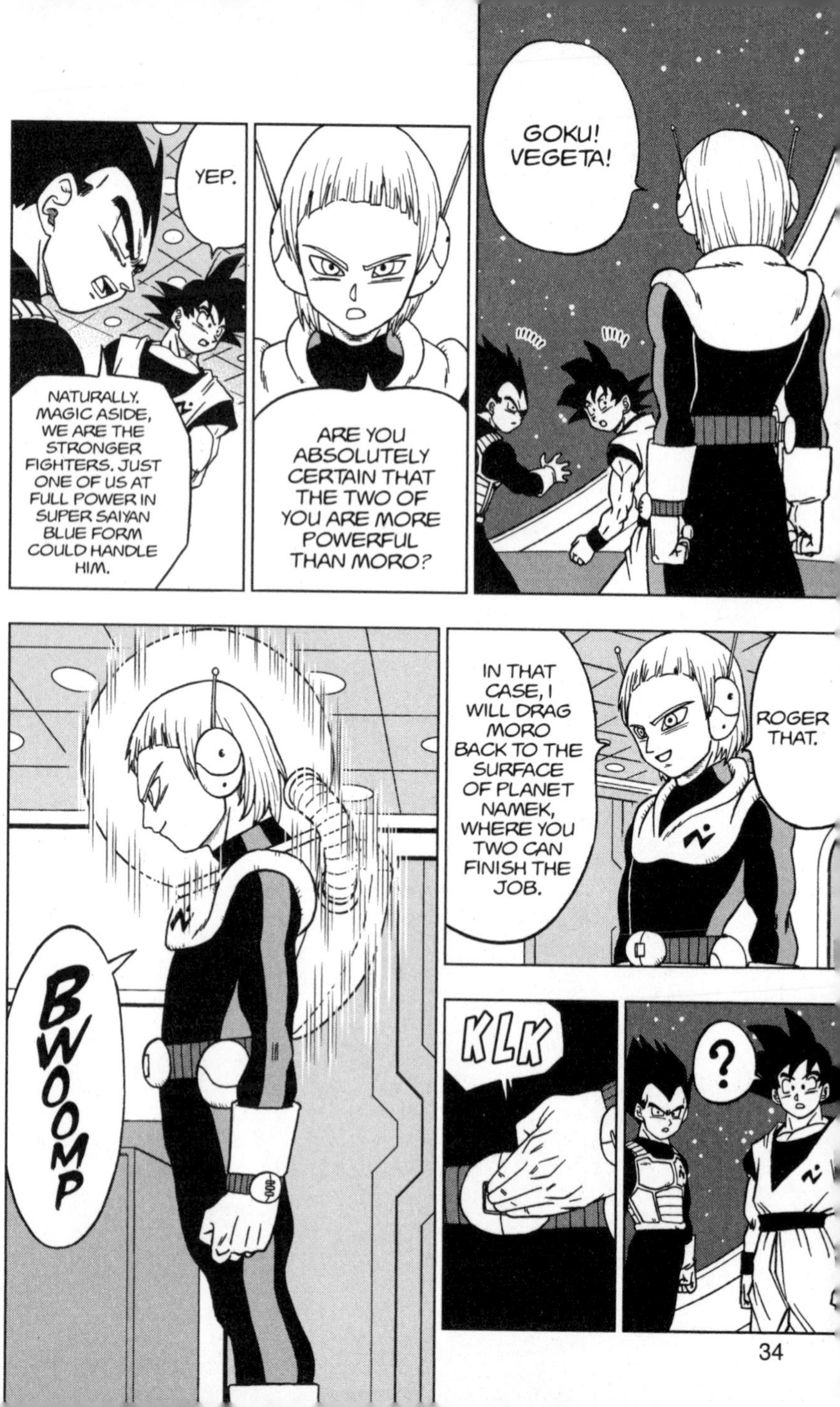
GOKU! VEGETA!
ARE YOU ABSOLUTELY CERTAIN THAT THE TWO OF YOU ARE MORE POWERFUL THAN MORO?
YEP.
NATURALLY. MAGIC ASIDE, WE ARE THE STRONGER FIGHTERS. JUST ONE OF US AT FULL POWER IN SUPER SAIYAN BLUE FORM COULD HANDLE HIM.
IN THAT CASE, I WILL DRAG MORO BACK TO THE SURFACE OF PLANET NAMEK, WHERE YOU TWO CAN FINISH THE JOB.
ROGER THAT.
?
KLK
BWOOMP

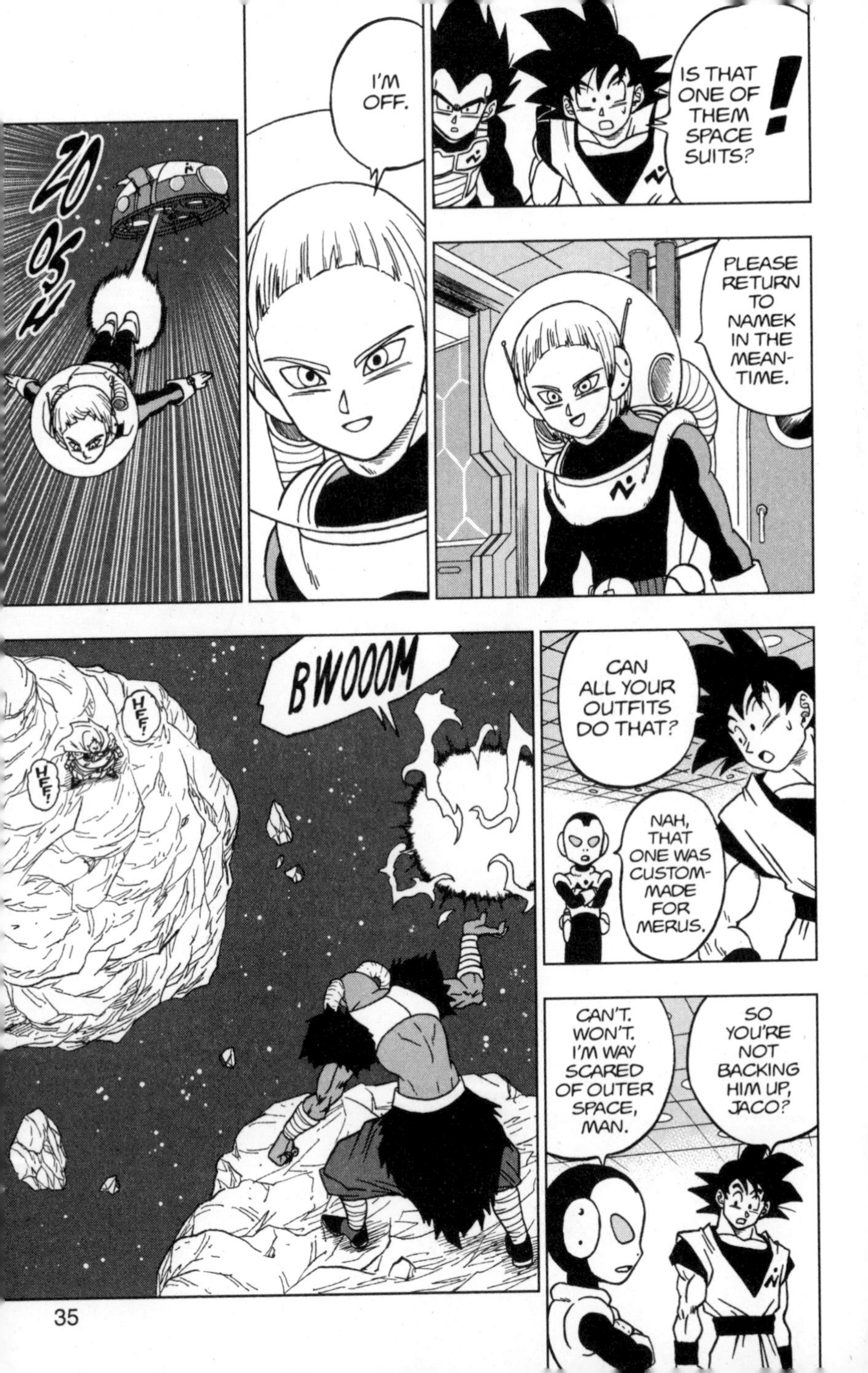
IS THAT ONE OF THEM SPACE SUITS?
!
PLEASE RETURN TO NAMEK IN THE MEAN-TIME.
I'M OFF.
ZOOSH
CAN ALL YOUR OUTFITS DO THAT?
NAH, THAT ONE WAS CUSTOM-MADE FOR MERUS.
SO YOU'RE NOT BACKING HIM UP, JACO?
CAN'T. WON'T. I'M WAY SCARED OF OUTER SPACE, MAN.
BWOOOM
HEF!
HEF!

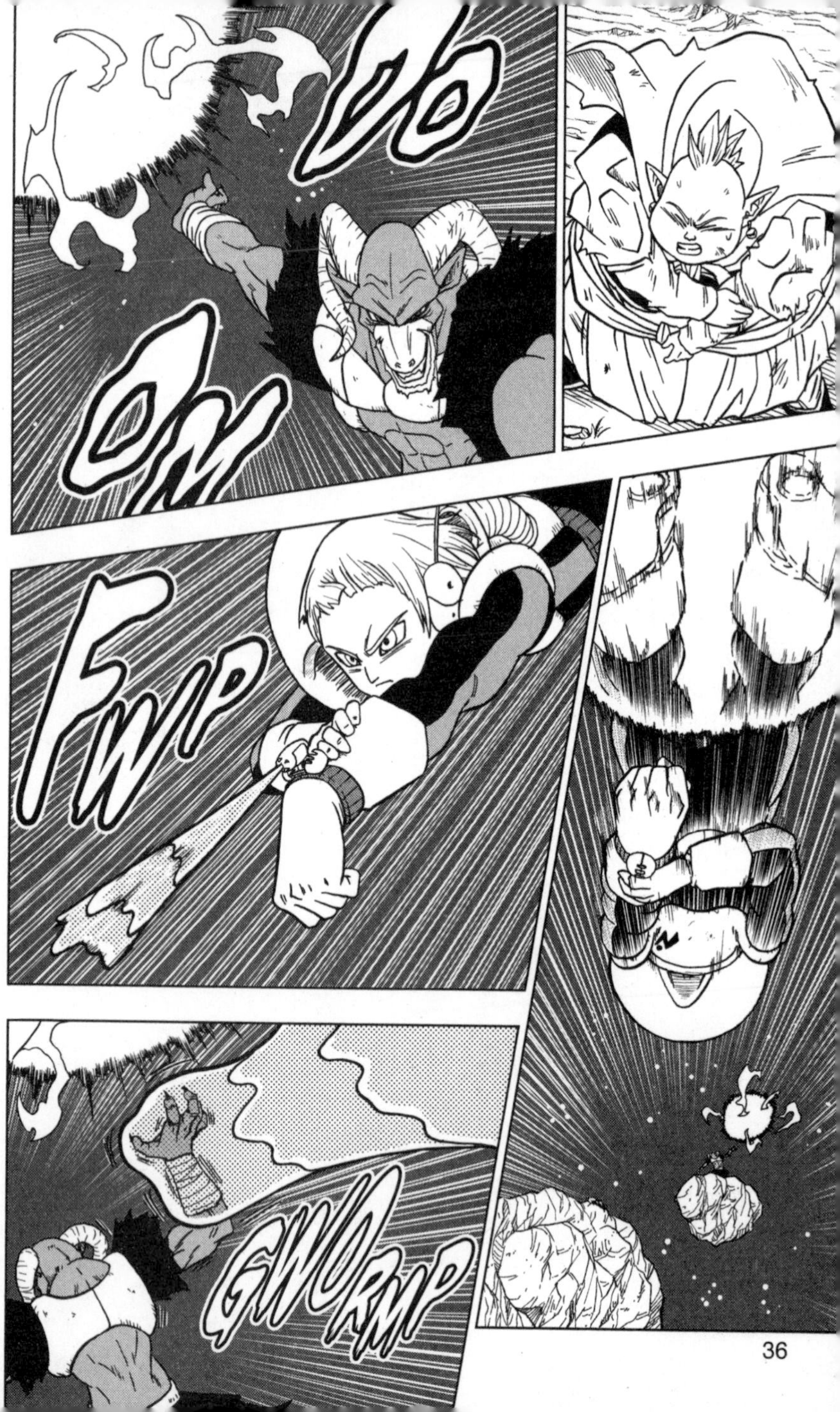
FWIP
GWORMP

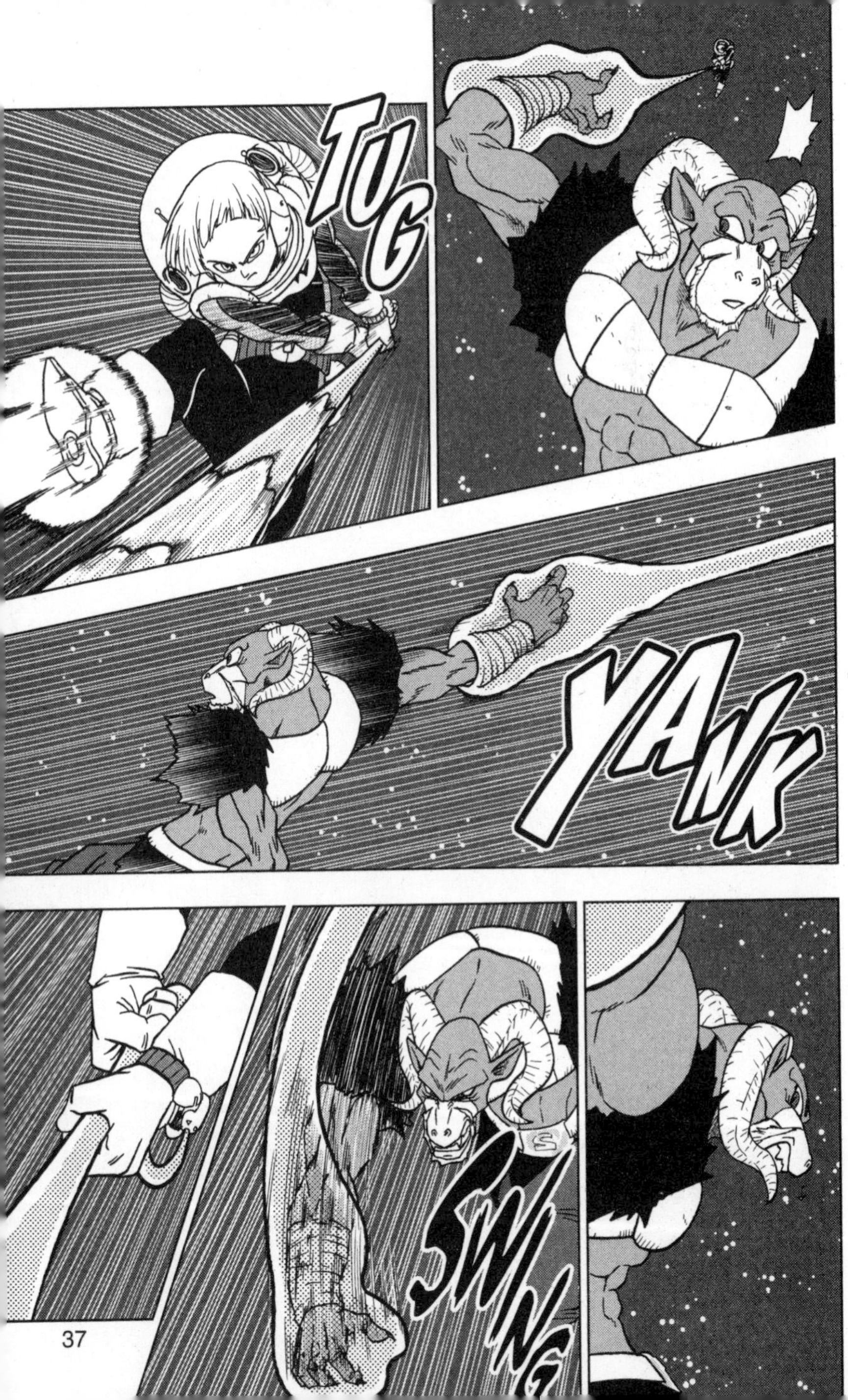
TUG
YANK
SWING

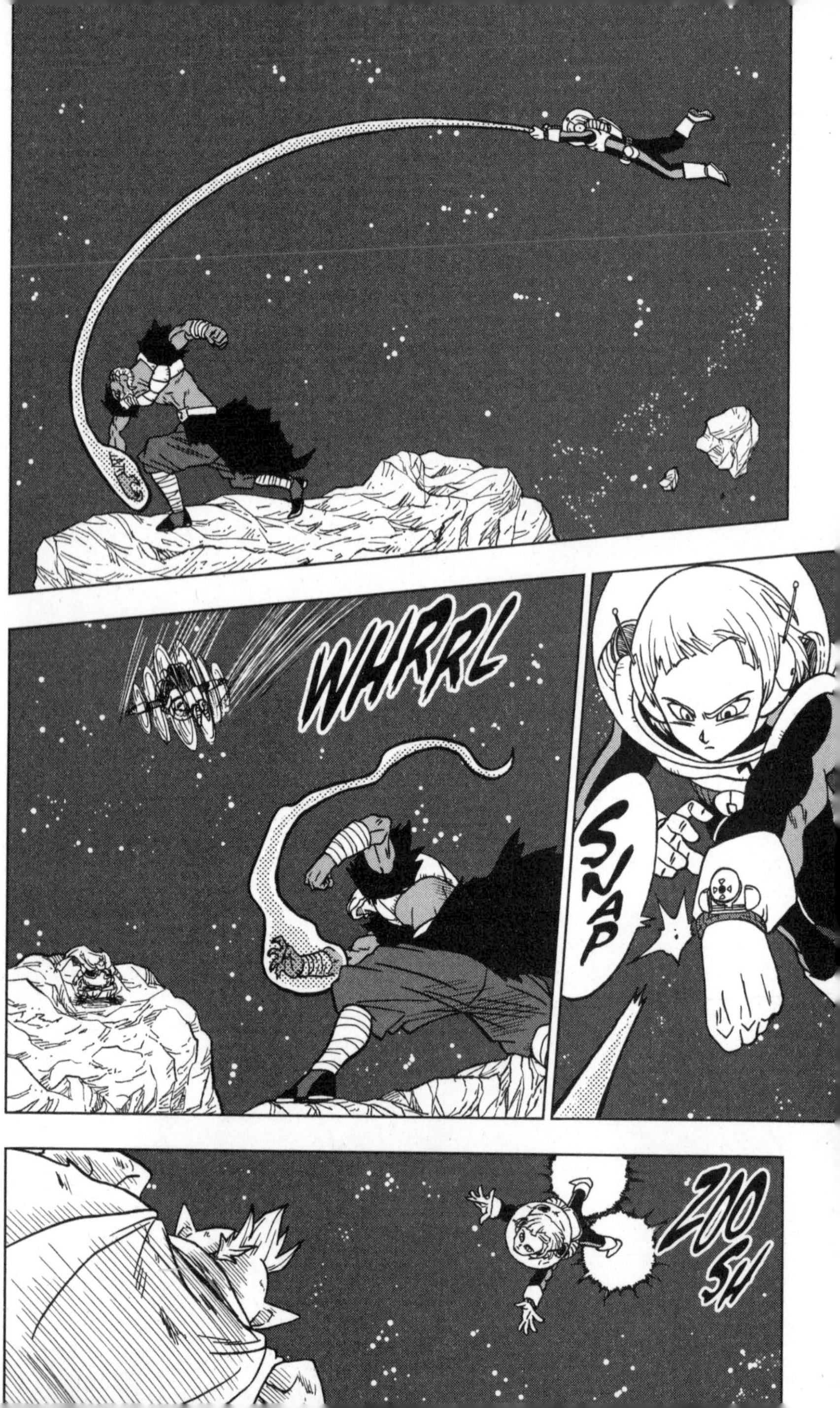
SNAP
WHRRL
ZOOSH

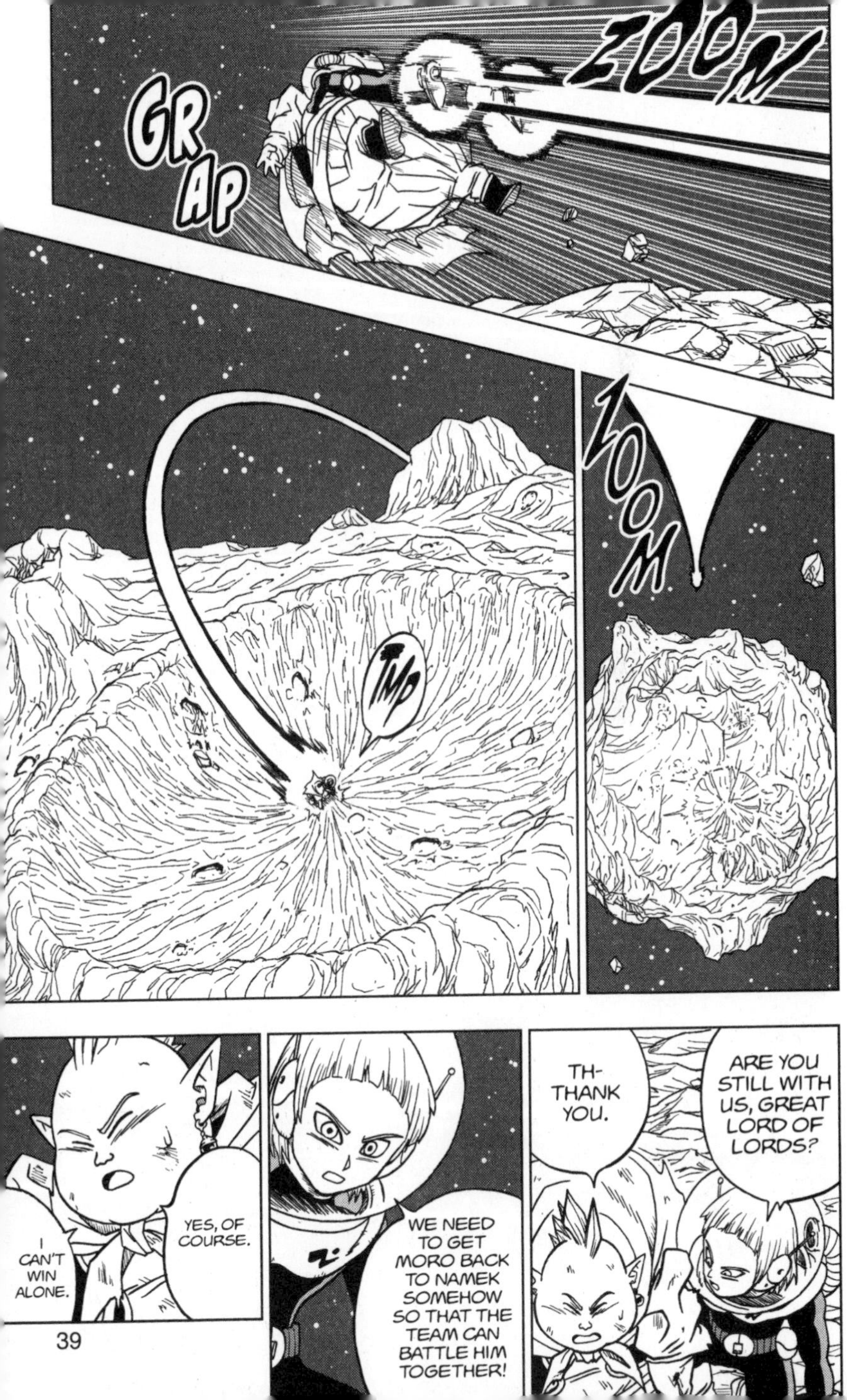
ZOOM
GRAP
ZOOM
TMP
ARE YOU STILL WITH US, GREAT LORD OF LORDS?
TH- THANK YOU.
WE NEED TO GET MORO BACK TO NAMEK SOMEHOW SO THAT THE TEAM CAN BATTLE HIM TOGETHER!
YES, OF COURSE.
I CAN'T WIN ALONE.

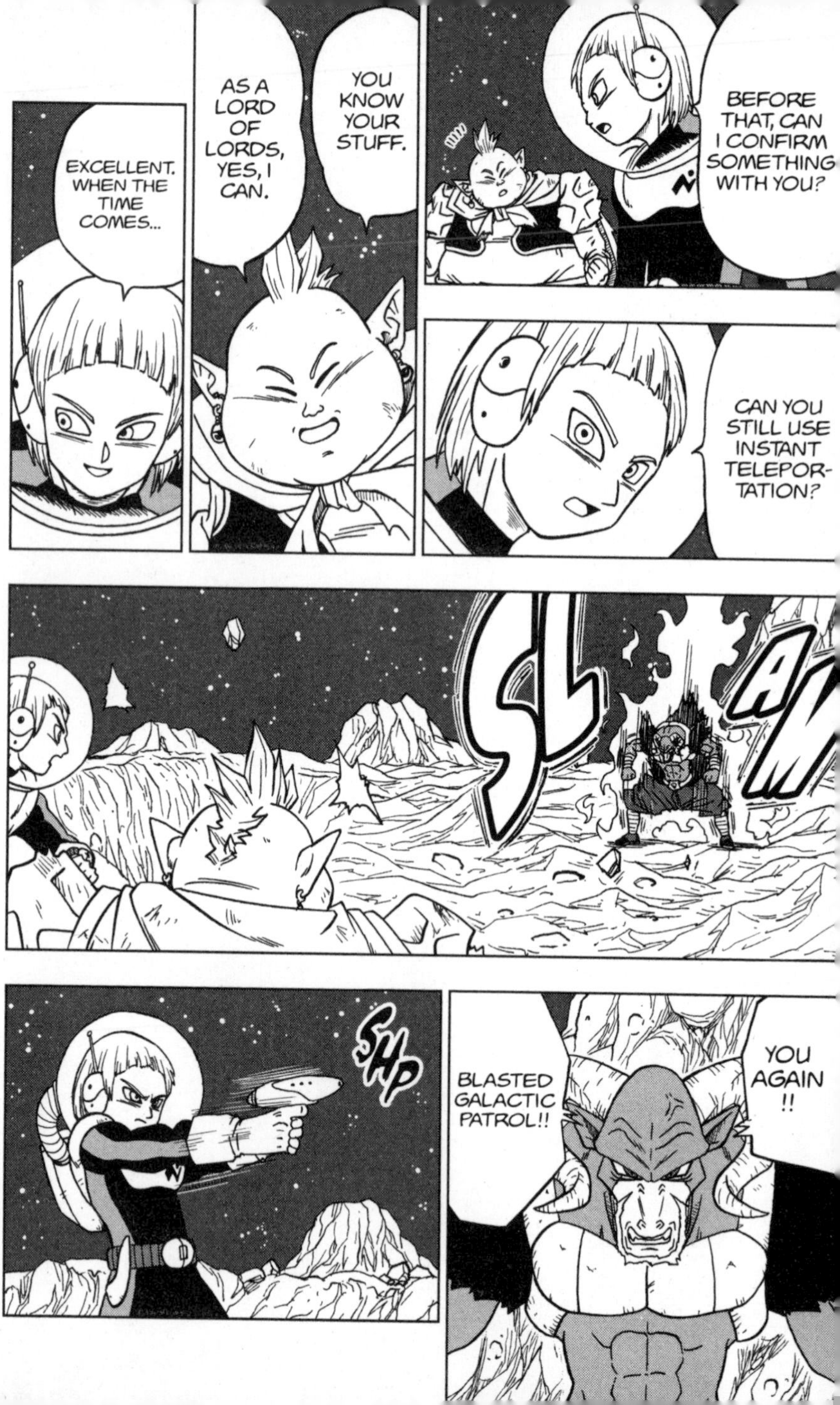
BEFORE THAT, CAN I CONFIRM SOMETHING WITH YOU?
CAN YOU STILL USE INSTANT TELEPOR-TATION?
YOU KNOW YOUR STUFF.
AS A LORD OF LORDS, YES, I CAN.
EXCELLENT. WHEN THE TIME COMES...
YOU AGAIN !!
BLASTED GALACTIC PATROL!!
SHP

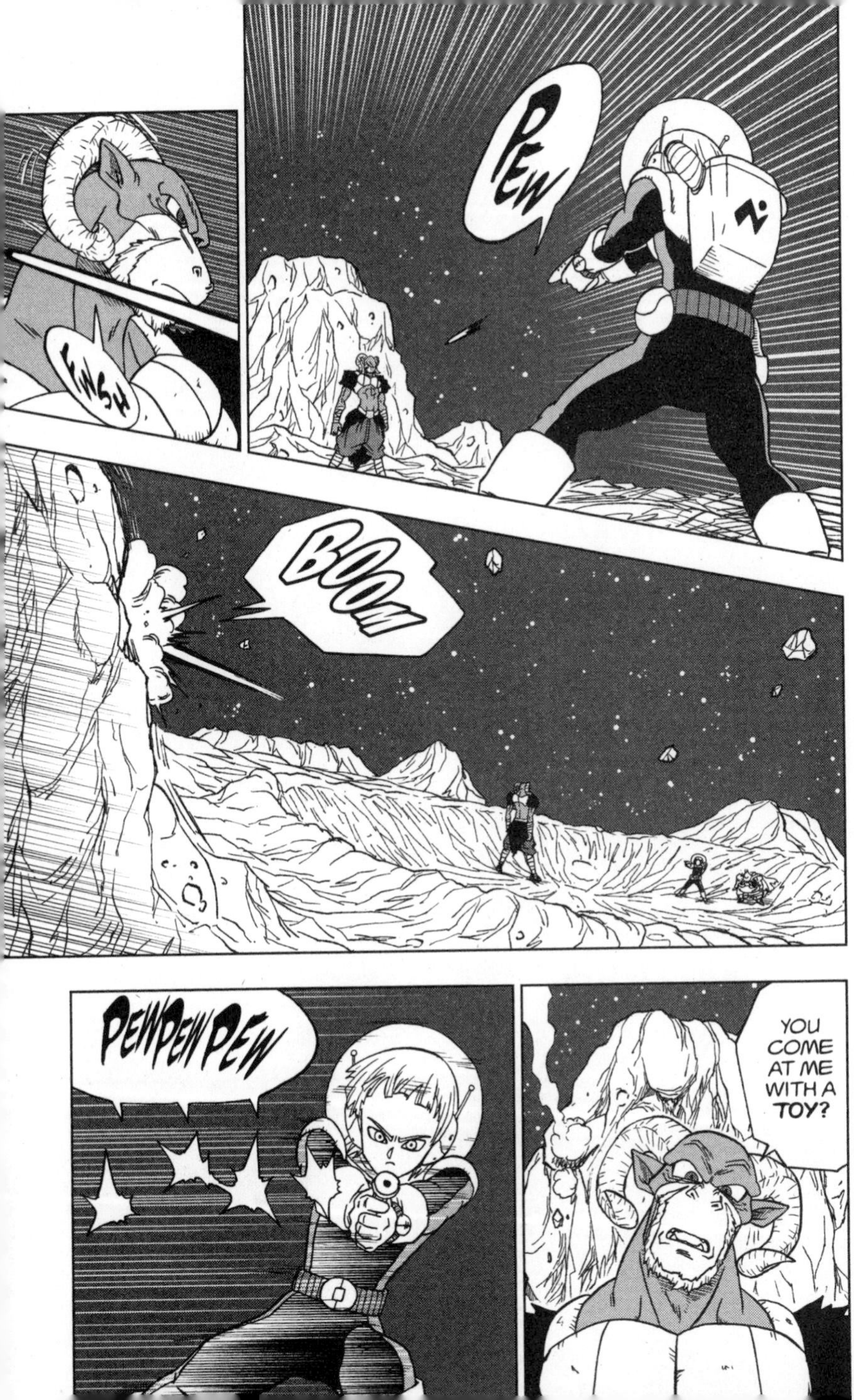
PEW
FWSH
BOOM
YOU COME AT ME WITH A TOY?
PEWPEWPEW

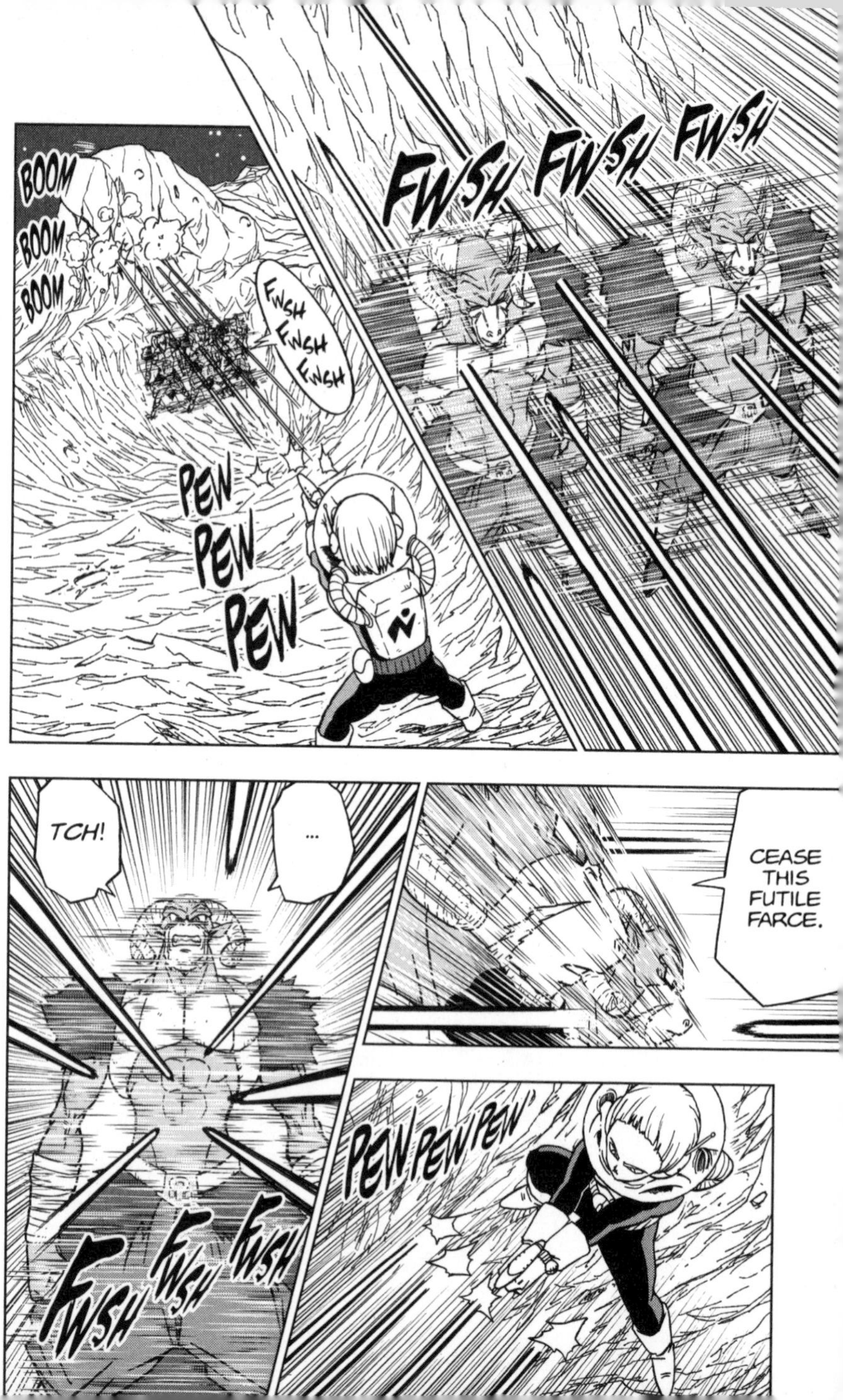
FWSH FWSH FWSH
FWSH FWSH FWSH
BOOM BOOM BOOM
PEW PEW PEW
CEASE THIS FUTILE FARCE.
PEW PEW PEW
...
TCH!
FWSH FWSH FWSH

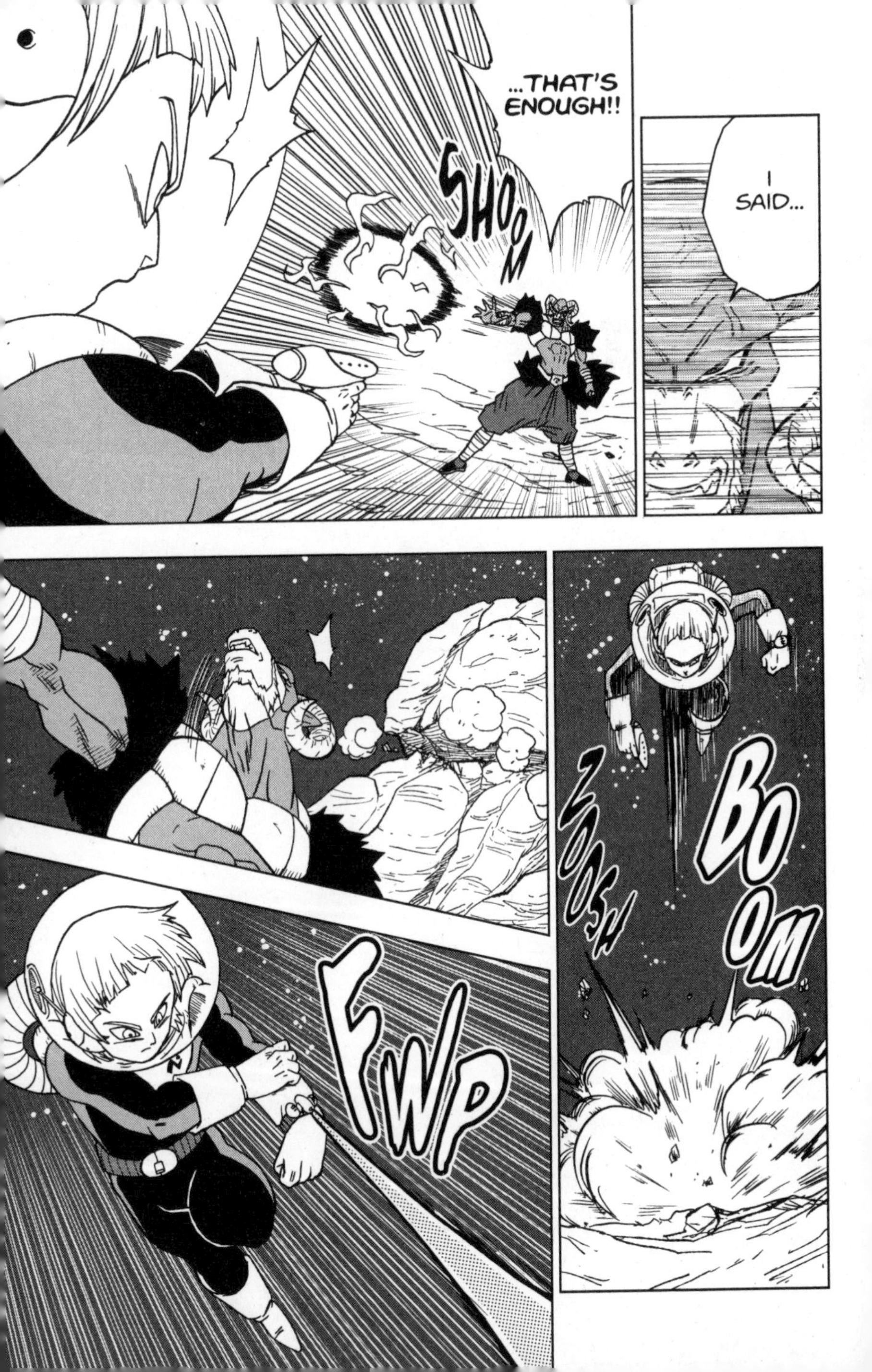

I SAID...
...THAT'S ENOUGH!!
SHOOOM
BOOM
ZOOSH
FWP

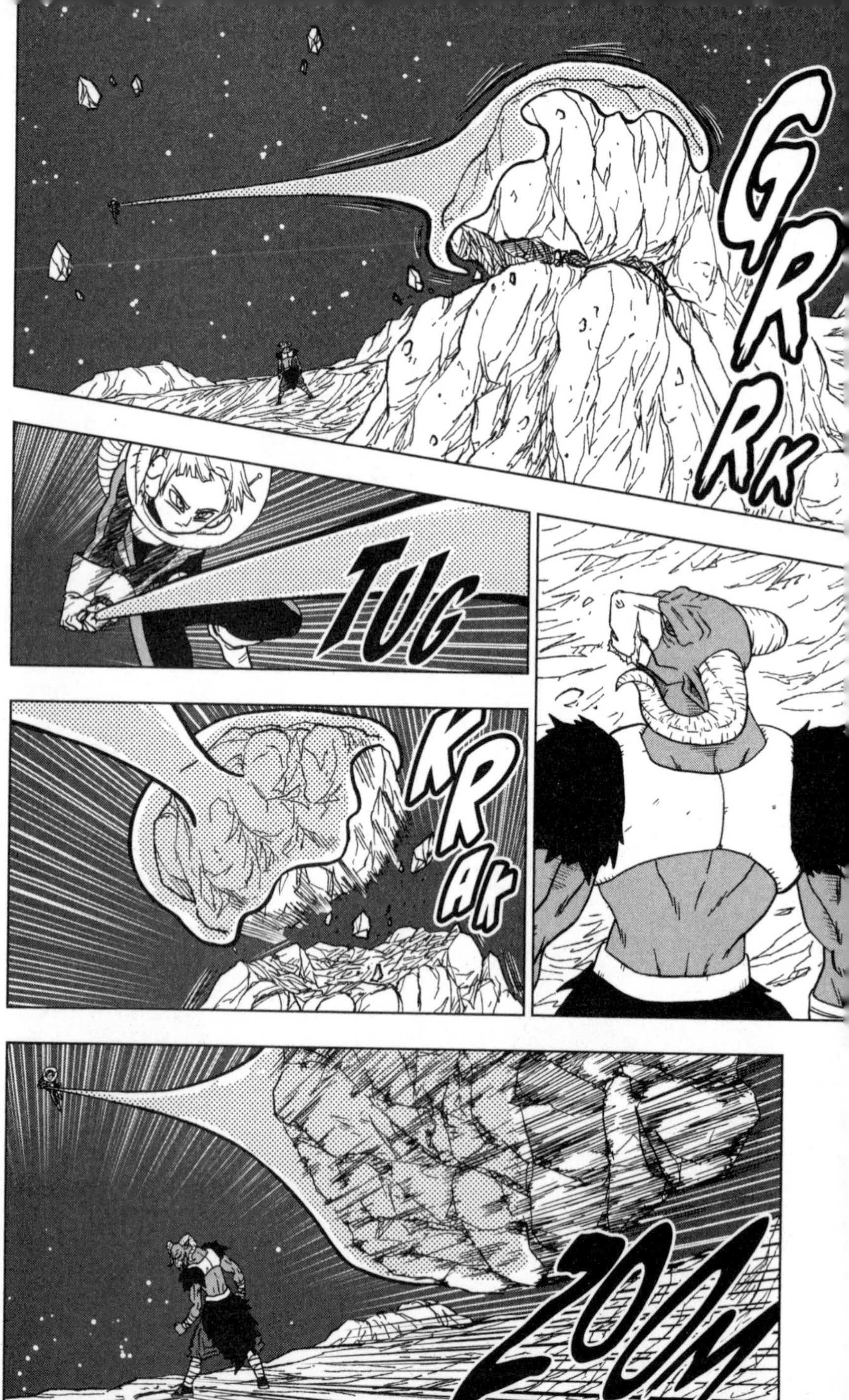
GRRK
TUG
KRAK
ZOOM

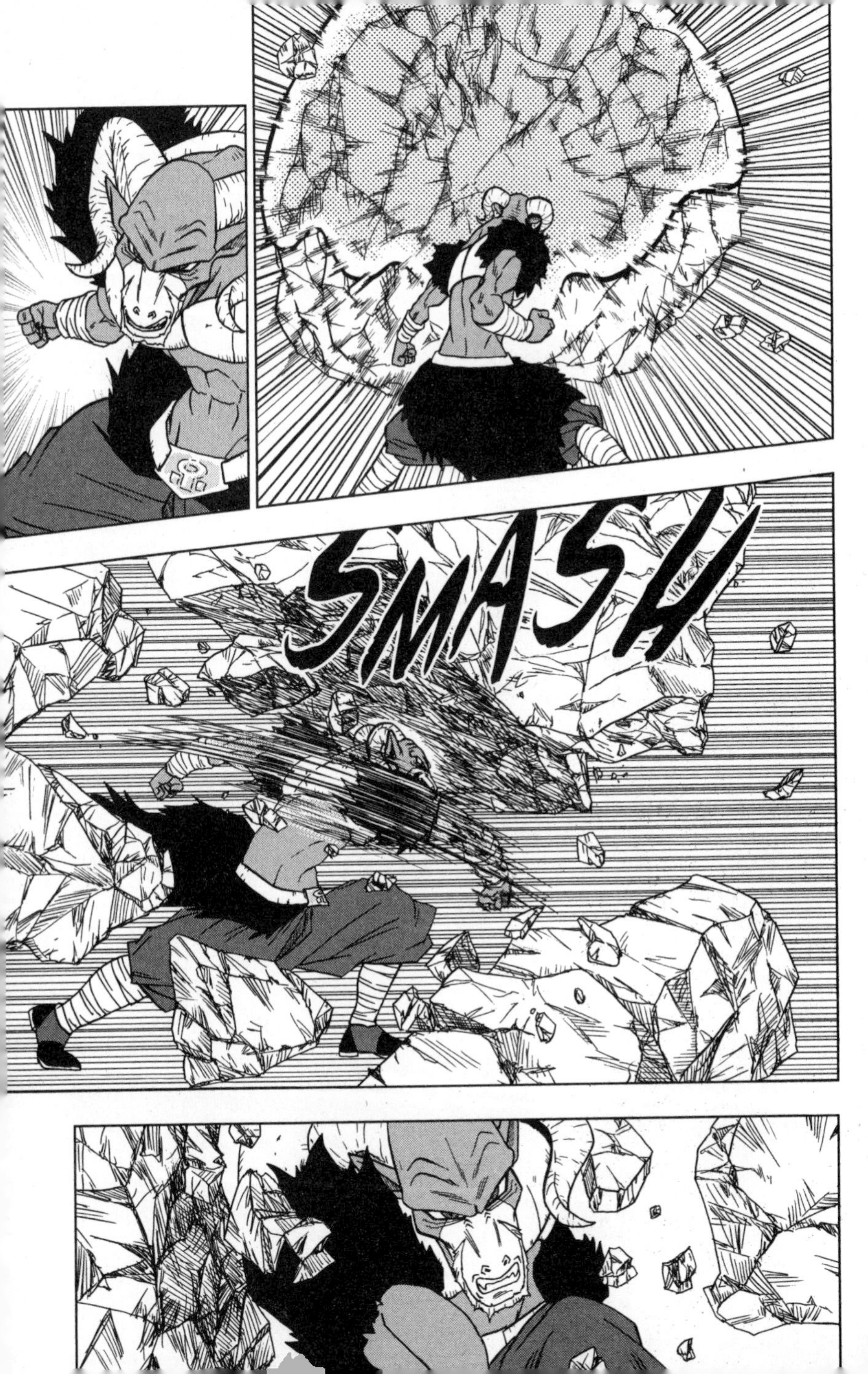
SMASH

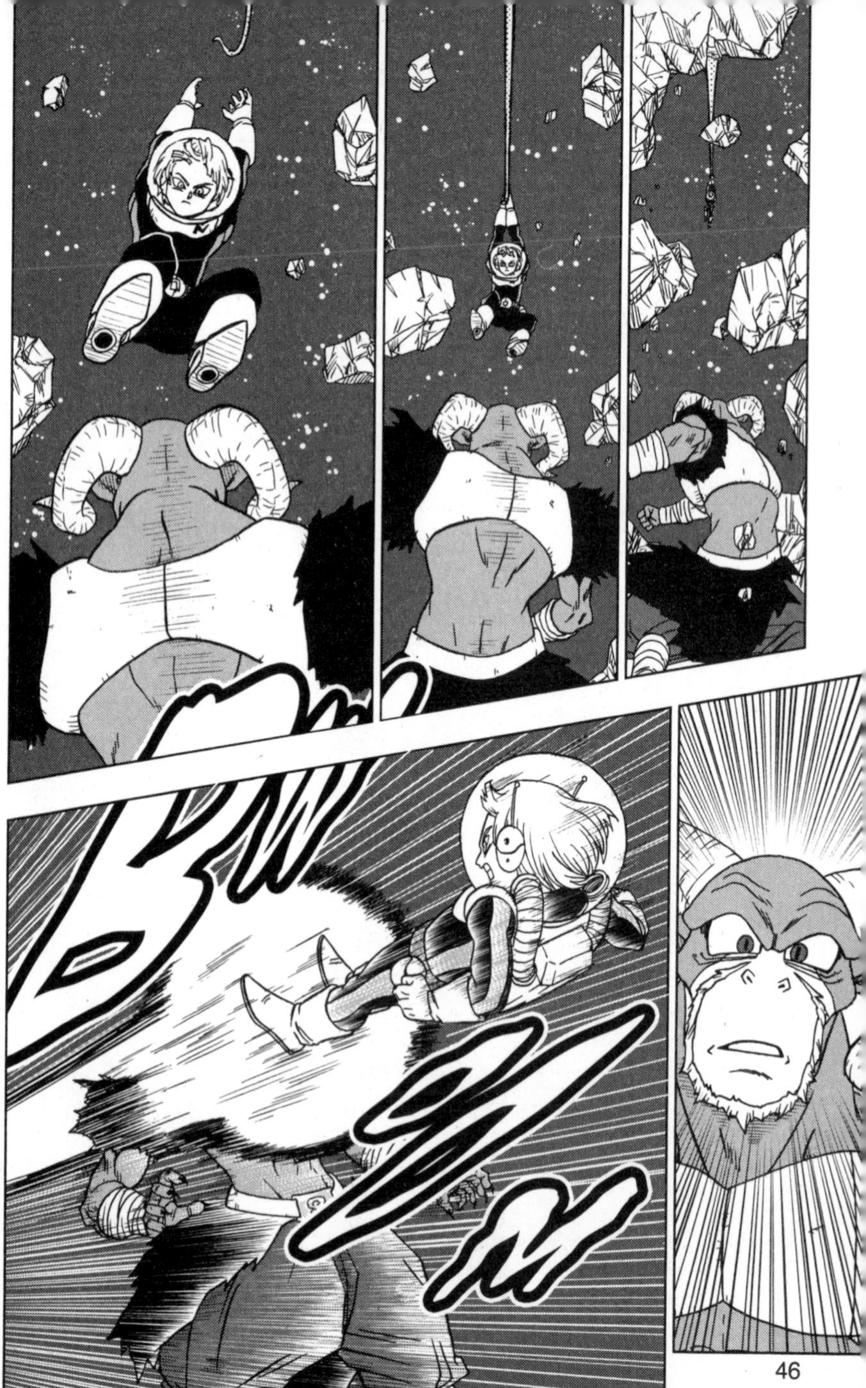

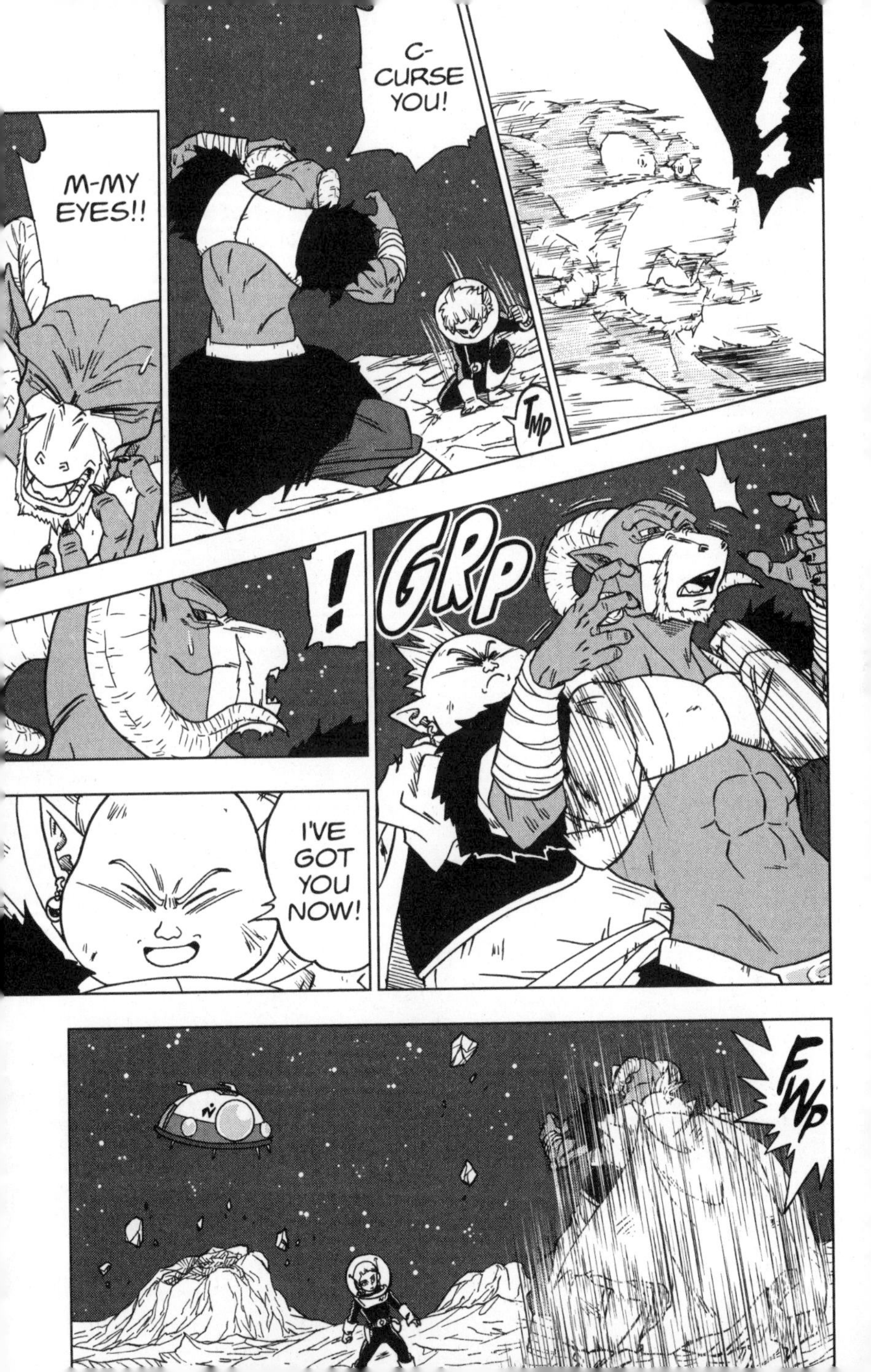
C-
CURSE
YOU!
TMP
M-MY
EYES!!
GRP
!
I'VE
GOT
YOU
NOW!
FWP

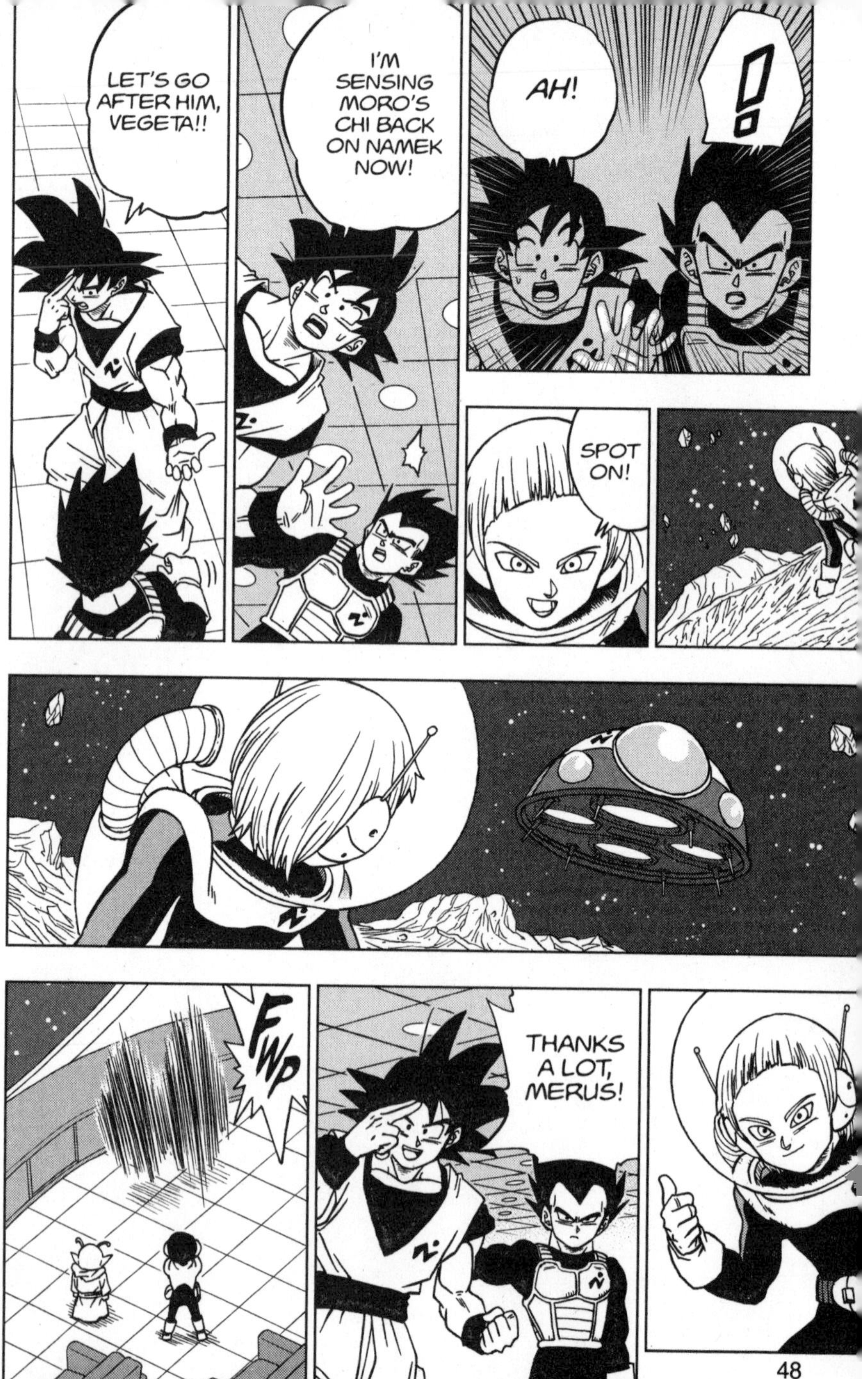

!
AH!
SPOT ON!
I'M SENSING MORO'S CHI BACK ON NAMEK NOW!
LET'S GO AFTER HIM, VEGETA!!
THANKS A LOT, MERUS!
FWP

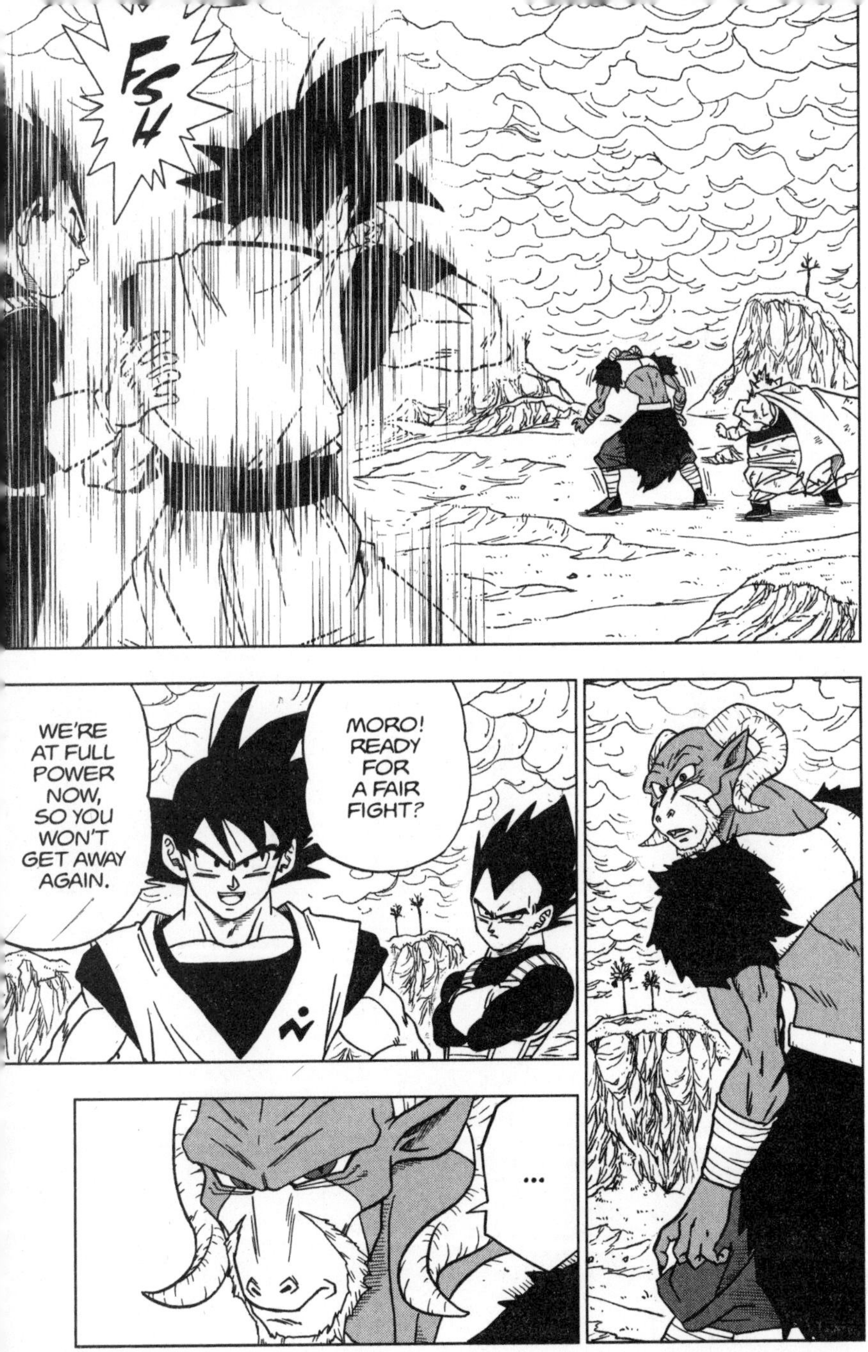
FSH
MORO! READY FOR A FAIR FIGHT?
WE'RE AT FULL POWER NOW, SO YOU WON'T GET AWAY AGAIN.
...

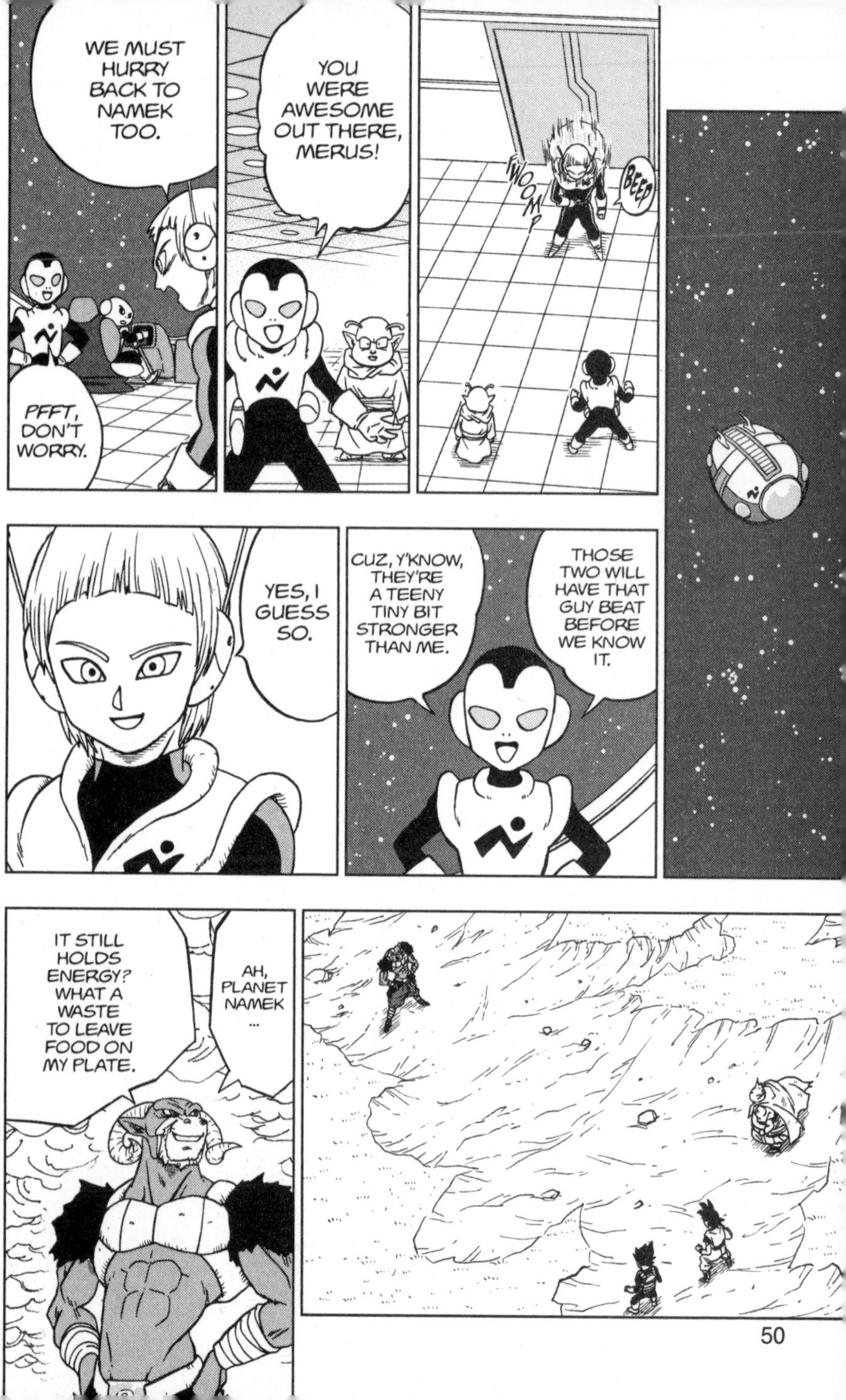
BEEP
FWOOMP
YOU WERE AWESOME OUT THERE, MERUS!
WE MUST HURRY BACK TO NAMEK TOO.
PFFT, DON'T WORRY.
THOSE TWO WILL HAVE THAT GUY BEAT BEFORE WE KNOW IT.
CUZ, Y'KNOW, THEY'RE A TEENY TINY BIT STRONGER THAN ME.
YES, I GUESS SO.
AH, PLANET NAMEK ...
IT STILL HOLDS ENERGY? WHAT A WASTE TO LEAVE FOOD ON MY PLATE.

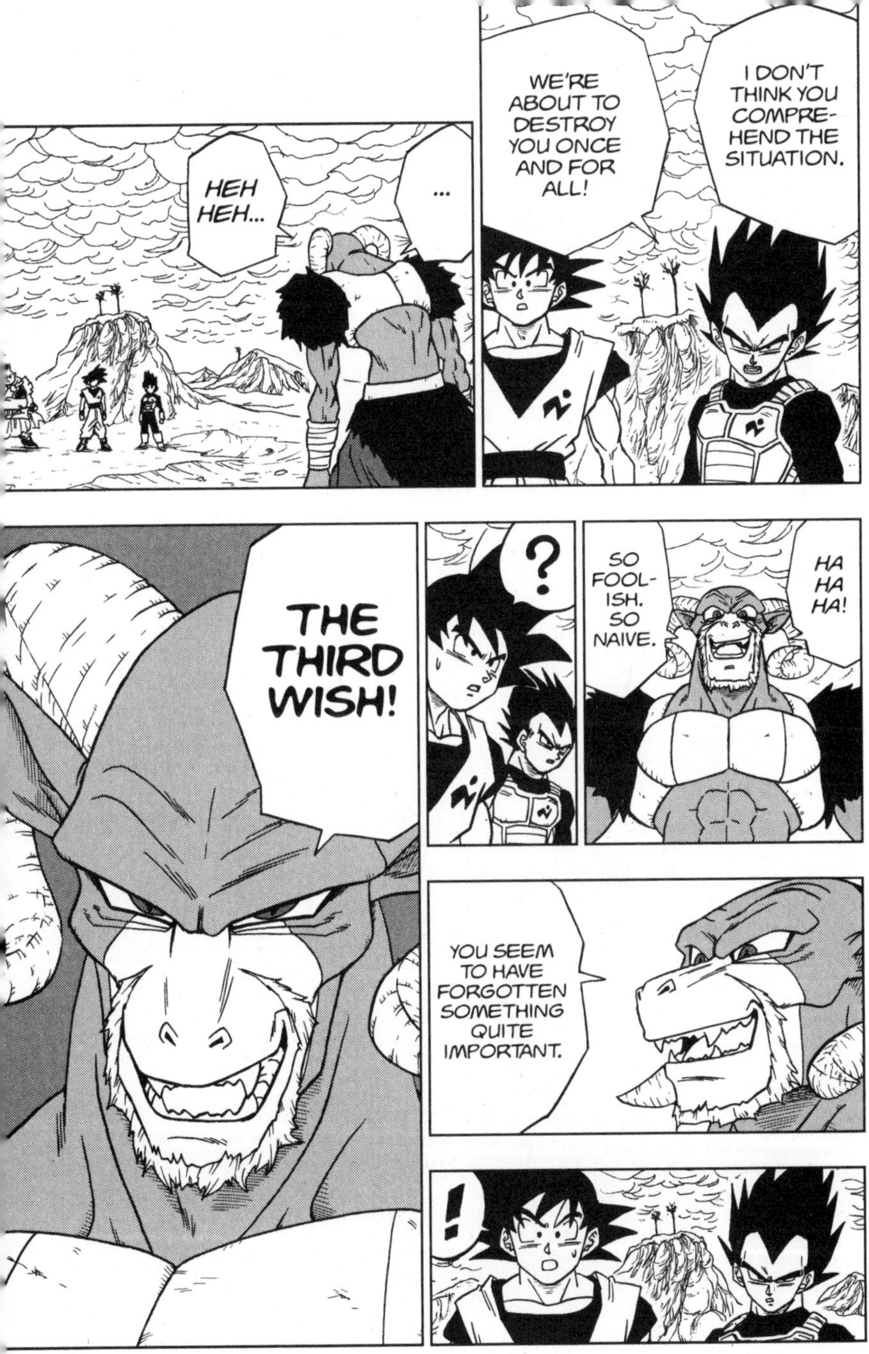
I DON'T THINK YOU COMPRE- HEND THE SITUATION.
WE'RE ABOUT TO DESTROY YOU ONCE AND FOR ALL!
...
HEH HEH...
HA HA HA!
SO FOOL- ISH. SO NAIVE.
?
YOU SEEM TO HAVE FORGOTTEN SOMETHING QUITE IMPORTANT.
!
THE THIRD WISH!

CHAPTER 50: GREAT ESCAPE

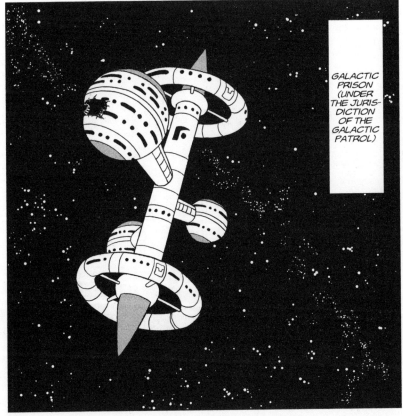

GALACTIC PRISON (UNDER THE JURISDICTION OF THE GALACTIC PATROL)

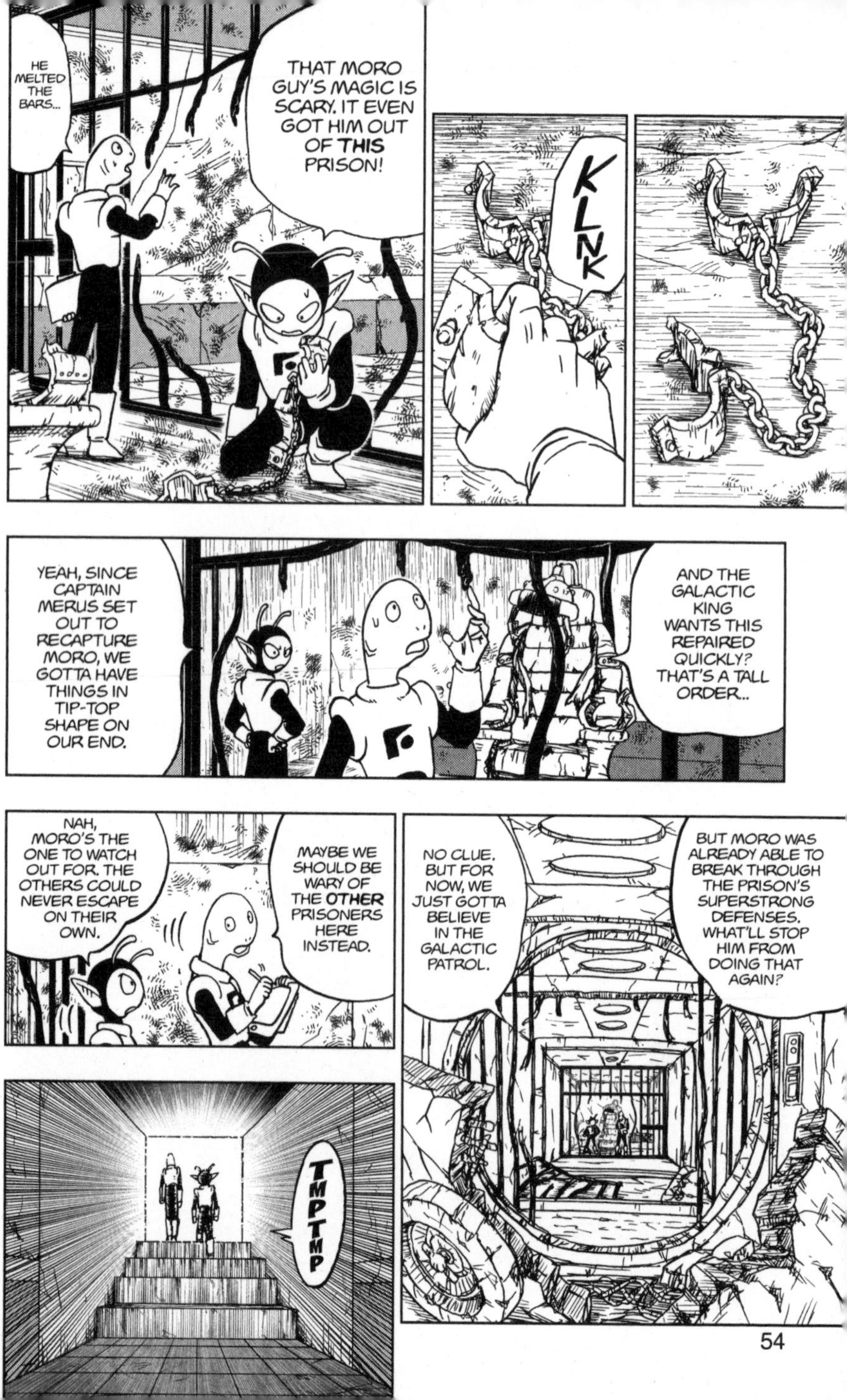
KLNK
THAT MORO GUY'S MAGIC IS SCARY. IT EVEN GOT HIM OUT OF **THIS** PRISON!
HE MELTED THE BARS...
AND THE GALACTIC KING WANTS THIS REPAIRED QUICKLY? THAT'S A TALL ORDER...
YEAH, SINCE CAPTAIN MERUS SET OUT TO RECAPTURE MORO, WE GOTTA HAVE THINGS IN TIP-TOP SHAPE ON OUR END.
BUT MORO WAS ALREADY ABLE TO BREAK THROUGH THE PRISON'S SUPERSTRONG DEFENSES. WHAT'LL STOP HIM FROM DOING THAT AGAIN?
NO CLUE. BUT FOR NOW, WE JUST GOTTA BELIEVE IN THE GALACTIC PATROL.
MAYBE WE SHOULD BE WARY OF THE **OTHER** PRISONERS HERE INSTEAD.
NAH, MORO'S THE ONE TO WATCH OUT FOR. THE OTHERS COULD NEVER ESCAPE ON THEIR OWN.
TMPTMP

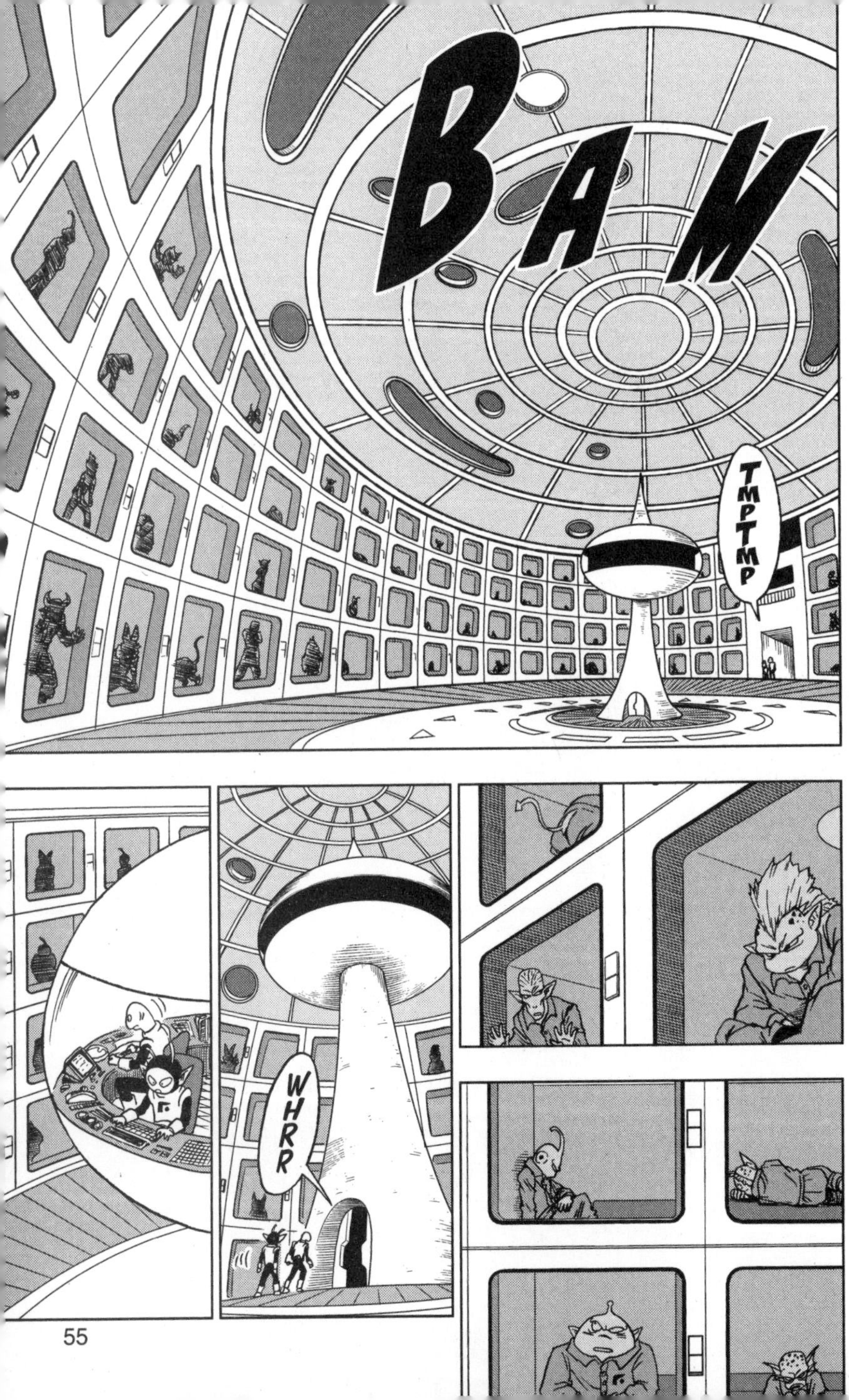
BAM
TMPTMP
WHRR

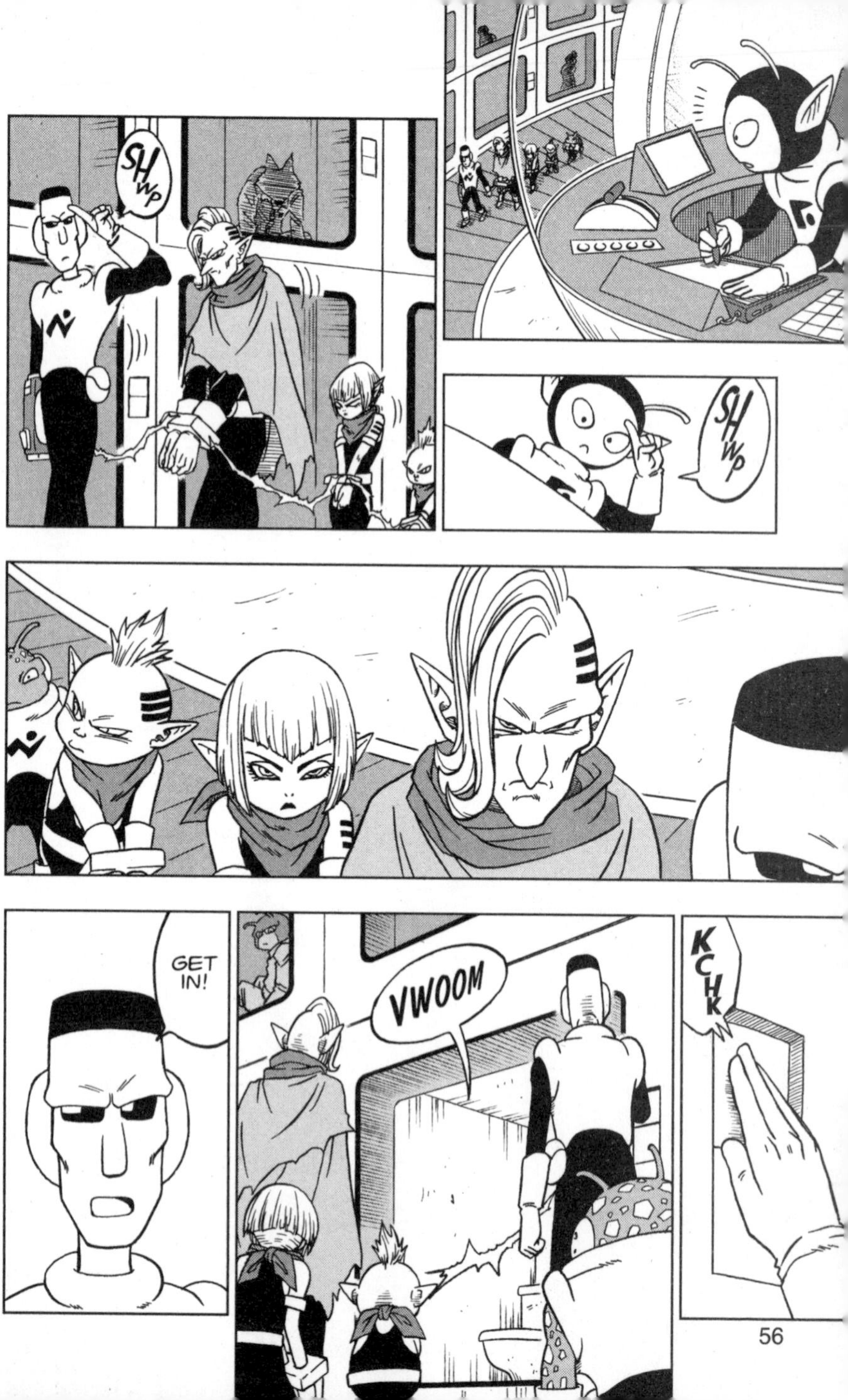
SHWP
SHWP
KCHK
VWOOM
GET IN!

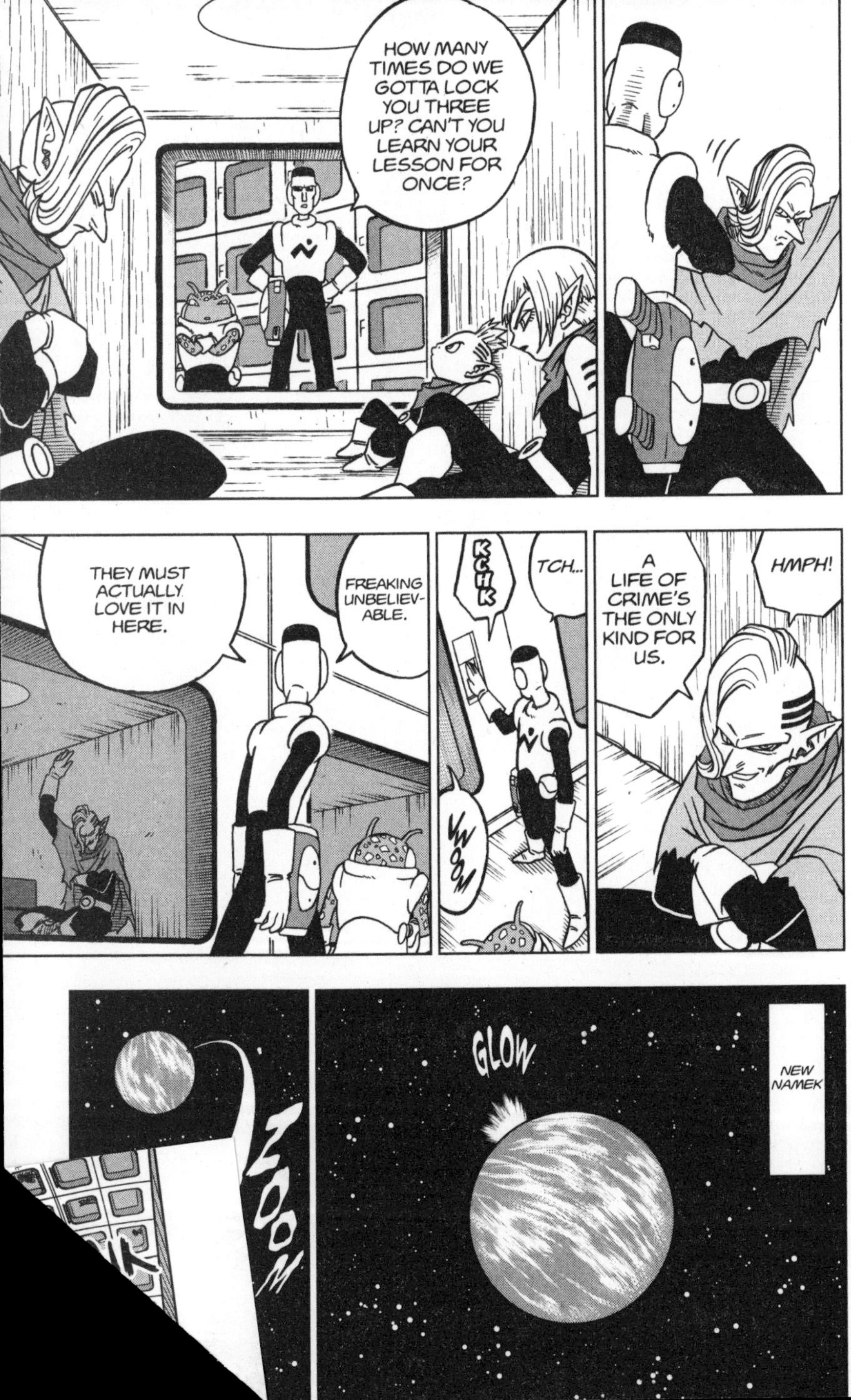
HOW MANY TIMES DO WE GOTTA LOCK YOU THREE UP? CAN'T YOU LEARN YOUR LESSON FOR ONCE?
HMPH!
A LIFE OF CRIME'S THE ONLY KIND FOR US.
TCH...
KCHK
VWOOM
FREAKING UNBELIEV-ABLE.
THEY MUST ACTUALLY LOVE IT IN HERE.
NEW NAMEK
GLOW

ZOOOM

GLINT

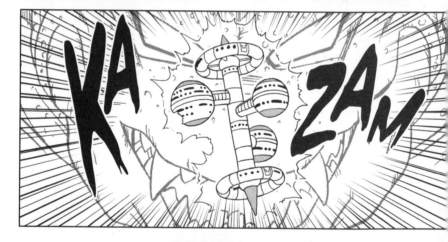

KA ZAM

HUH? WHAT'S HAPPENING?!

KZZT KZZT

KZZT KZZT

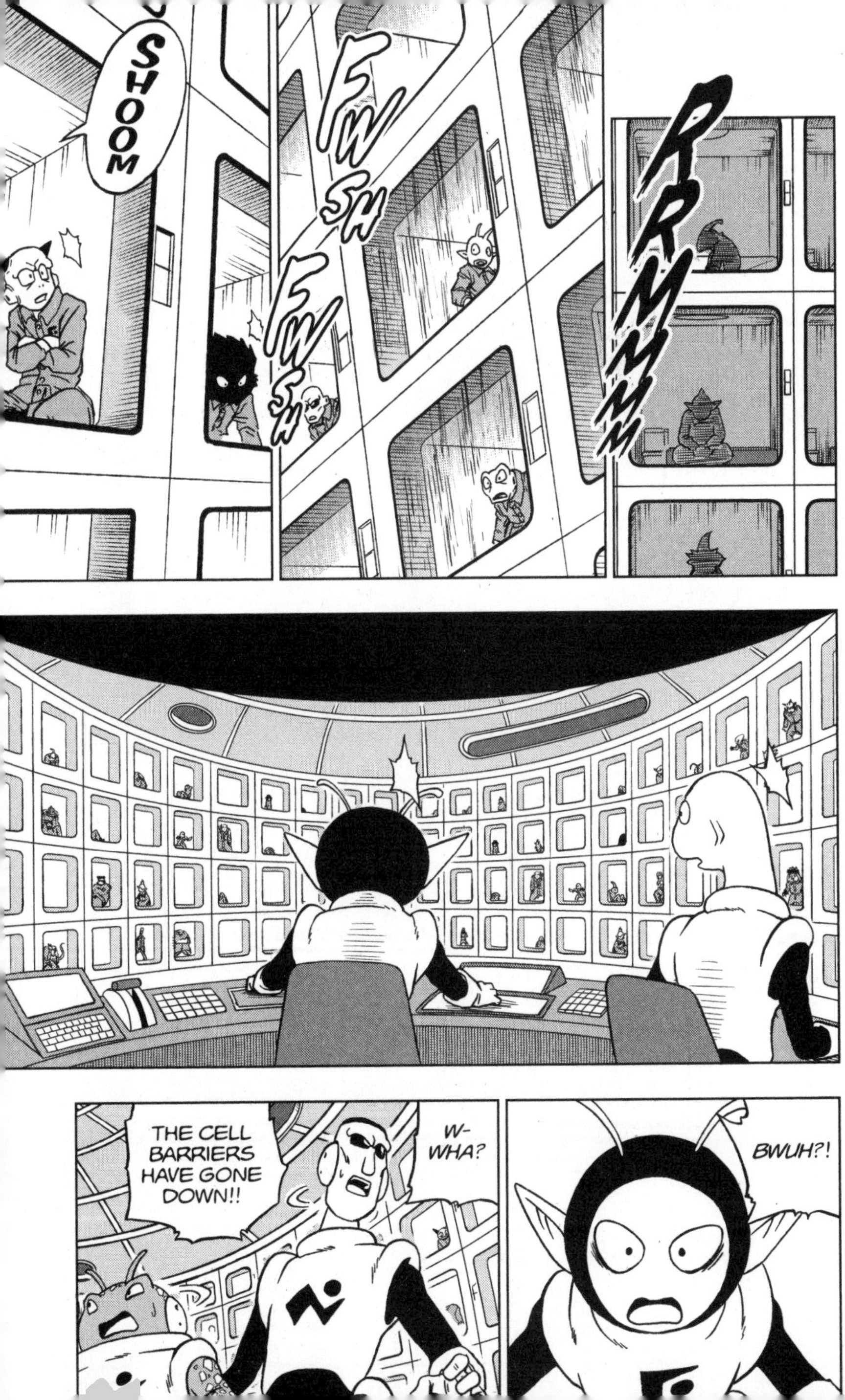
PRMMMM
FWSH
FWSH
SHOOM
BWUH?!
W-WHA?
THE CELL BARRIERS HAVE GONE DOWN!!

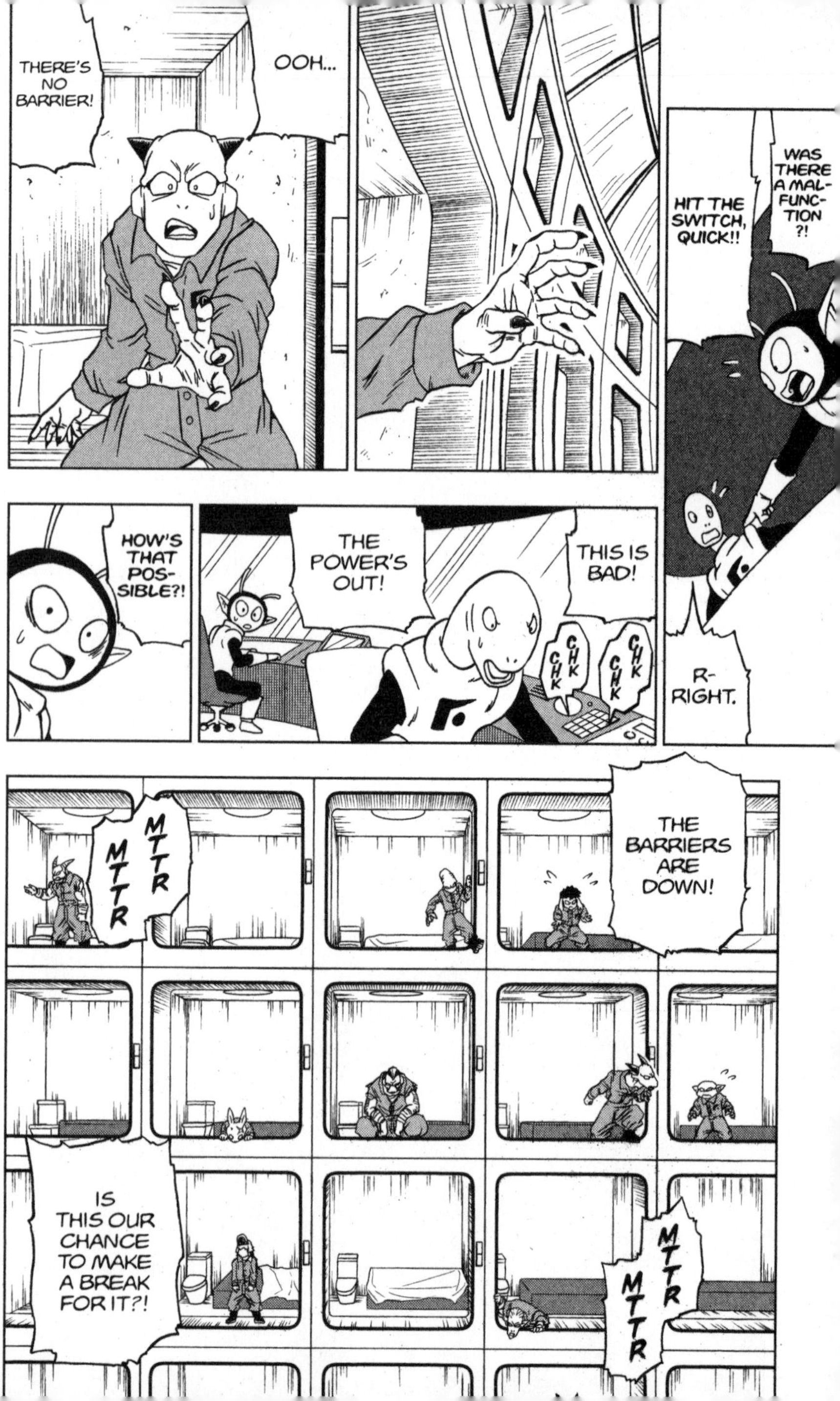
WAS THERE A MAL-FUNCTION ?!
HIT THE SWITCH, QUICK!!
R-RIGHT.
OOH...
THERE'S NO BARRIER!
THIS IS BAD!
CHK CHK
CHK CHK
THE POWER'S OUT!
HOW'S THAT POSSIBLE?!
THE BARRIERS ARE DOWN!
MTTR MTTR
MTTR MTTR
IS THIS OUR CHANCE TO MAKE A BREAK FOR IT?!

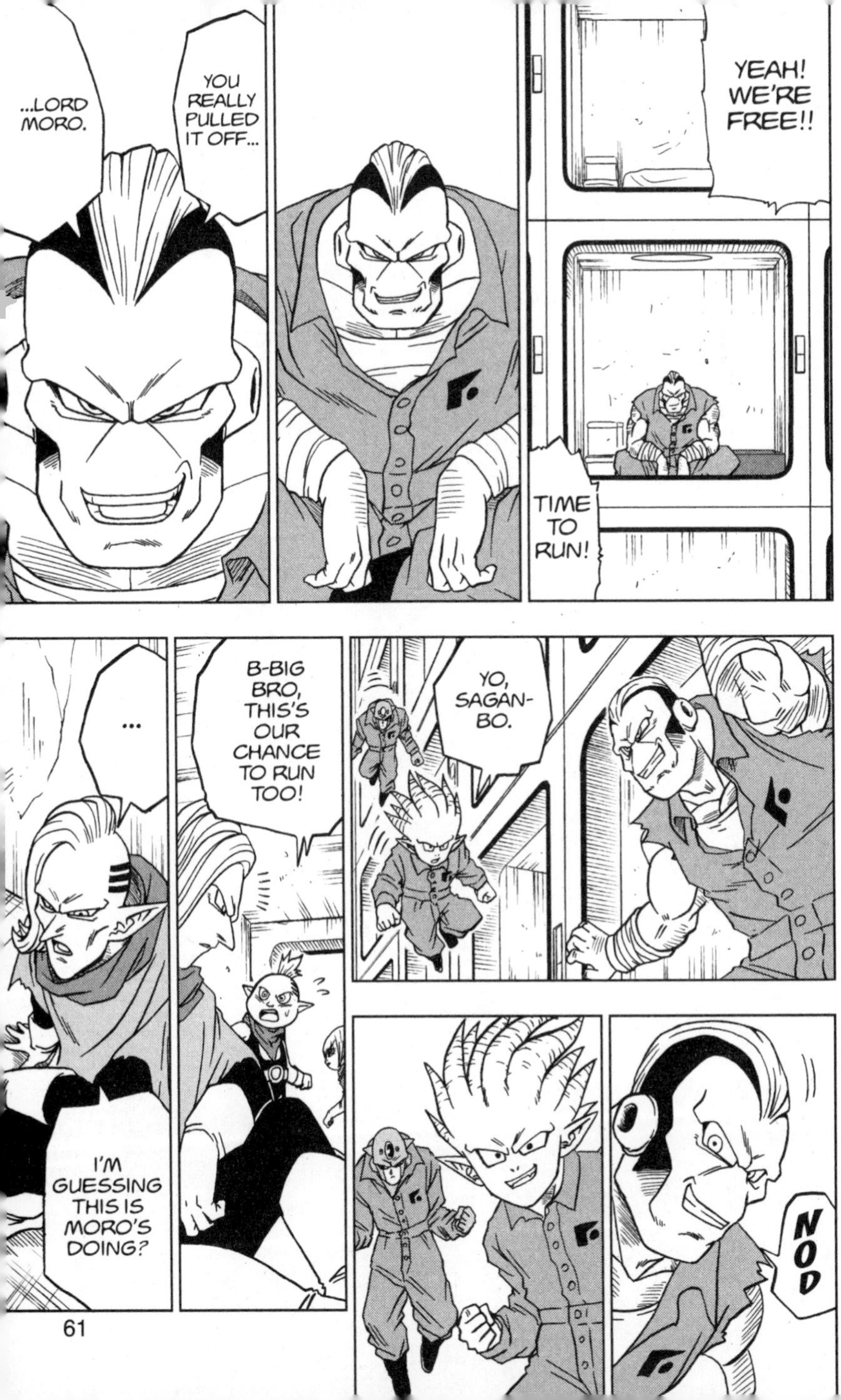
YEAH! WE'RE FREE!!
TIME TO RUN!
YOU REALLY PULLED IT OFF...
...LORD MORO.
YO, SAGAN-BO.
NOD
B-BIG BRO, THIS'S OUR CHANCE TO RUN TOO!
...
I'M GUESSING THIS IS MORO'S DOING?

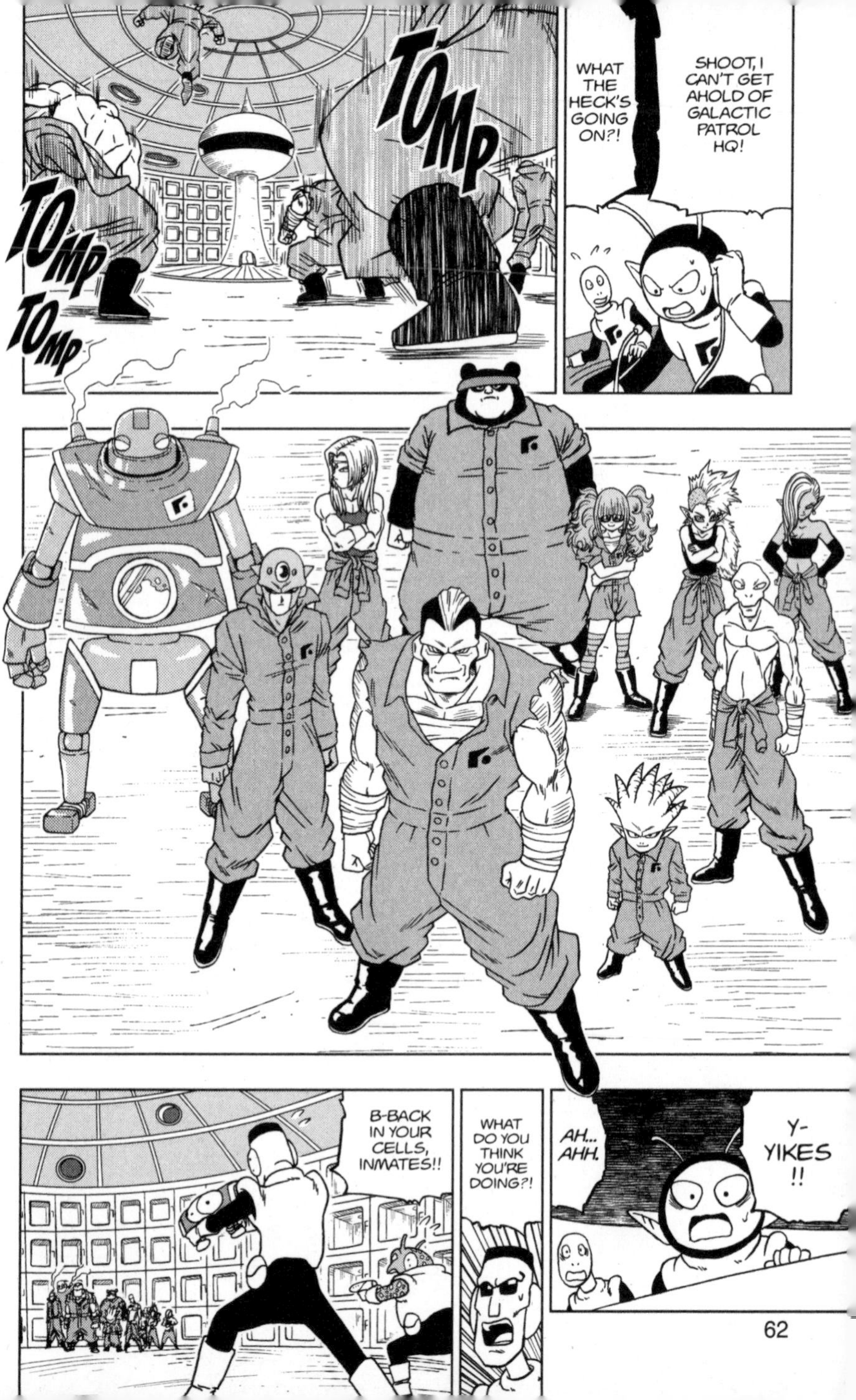
SHOOT, I CAN'T GET AHOLD OF GALACTIC PATROL HQ!
WHAT THE HECK'S GOING ON?!
TOMP
TOMP
TOMP
TOMP
Y-YIKES!!
AH... AHH.
WHAT DO YOU THINK YOU'RE DOING?!
B-BACK IN YOUR CELLS, INMATES!!

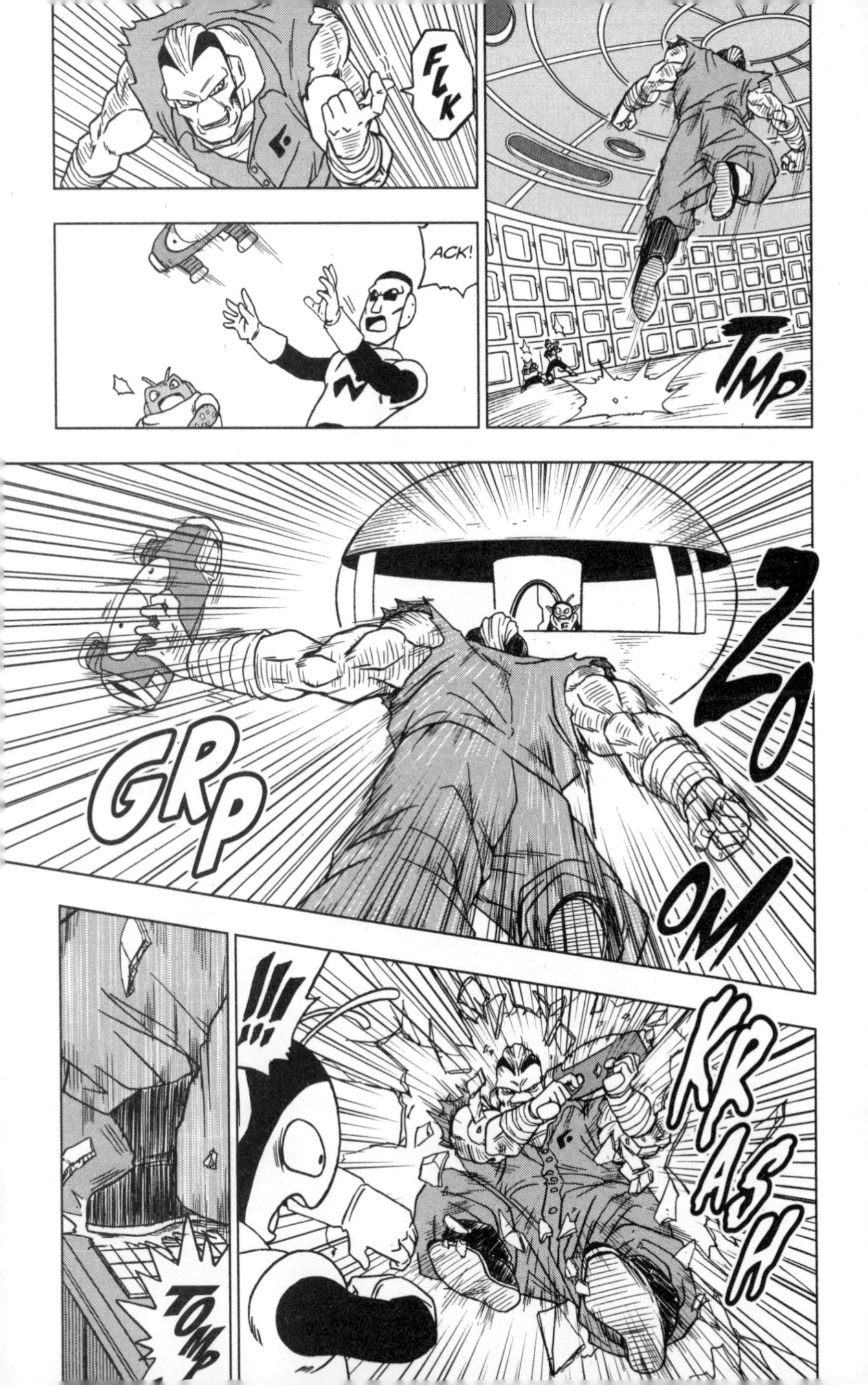
TMP
FLK
ACK!
ZOOM
GRP
KRASH
!!!
TOMP

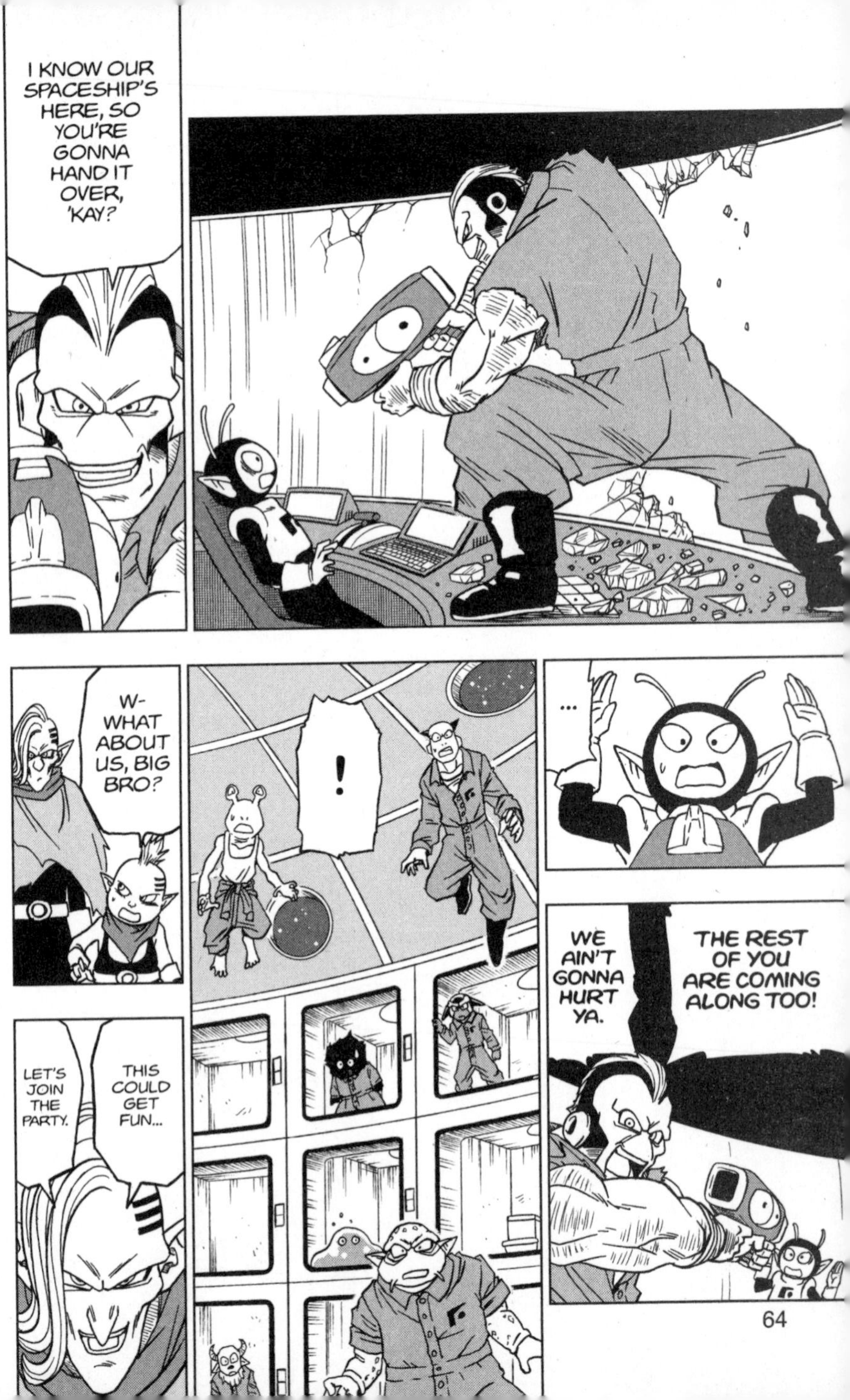
I KNOW OUR SPACESHIP'S HERE, SO YOU'RE GONNA HAND IT OVER, 'KAY?
...
THE REST OF YOU ARE COMING ALONG TOO!
WE AIN'T GONNA HURT YA.
!
W- WHAT ABOUT US, BIG BRO?
THIS COULD GET FUN...
LET'S JOIN THE PARTY.

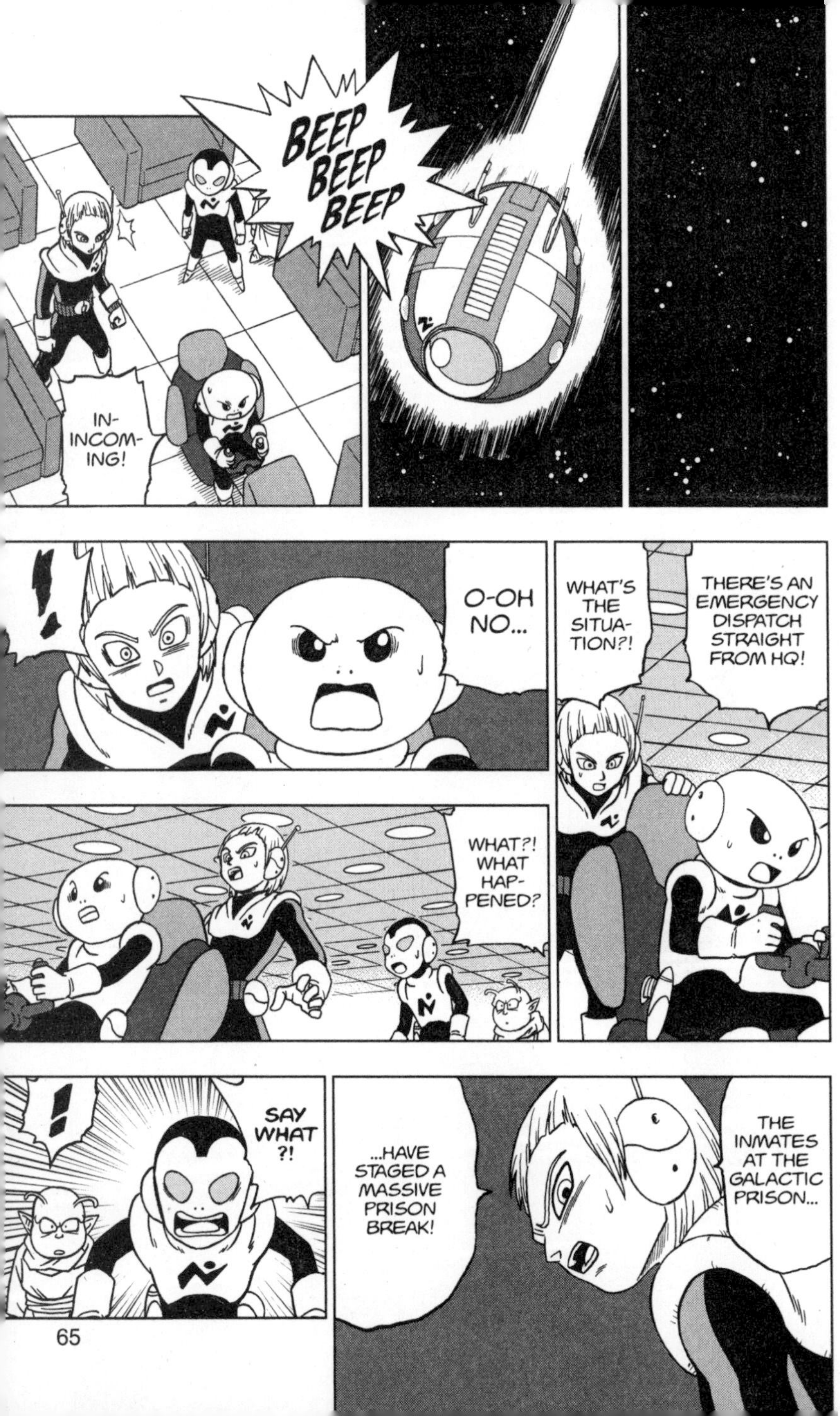
BEEP BEEP BEEP
IN- INCOMING!
THERE'S AN EMERGENCY DISPATCH STRAIGHT FROM HQ!
WHAT'S THE SITUATION?!
O-OH NO...
WHAT?! WHAT HAPPENED?
THE INMATES AT THE GALACTIC PRISON...
...HAVE STAGED A MASSIVE PRISON BREAK!
SAY WHAT?!

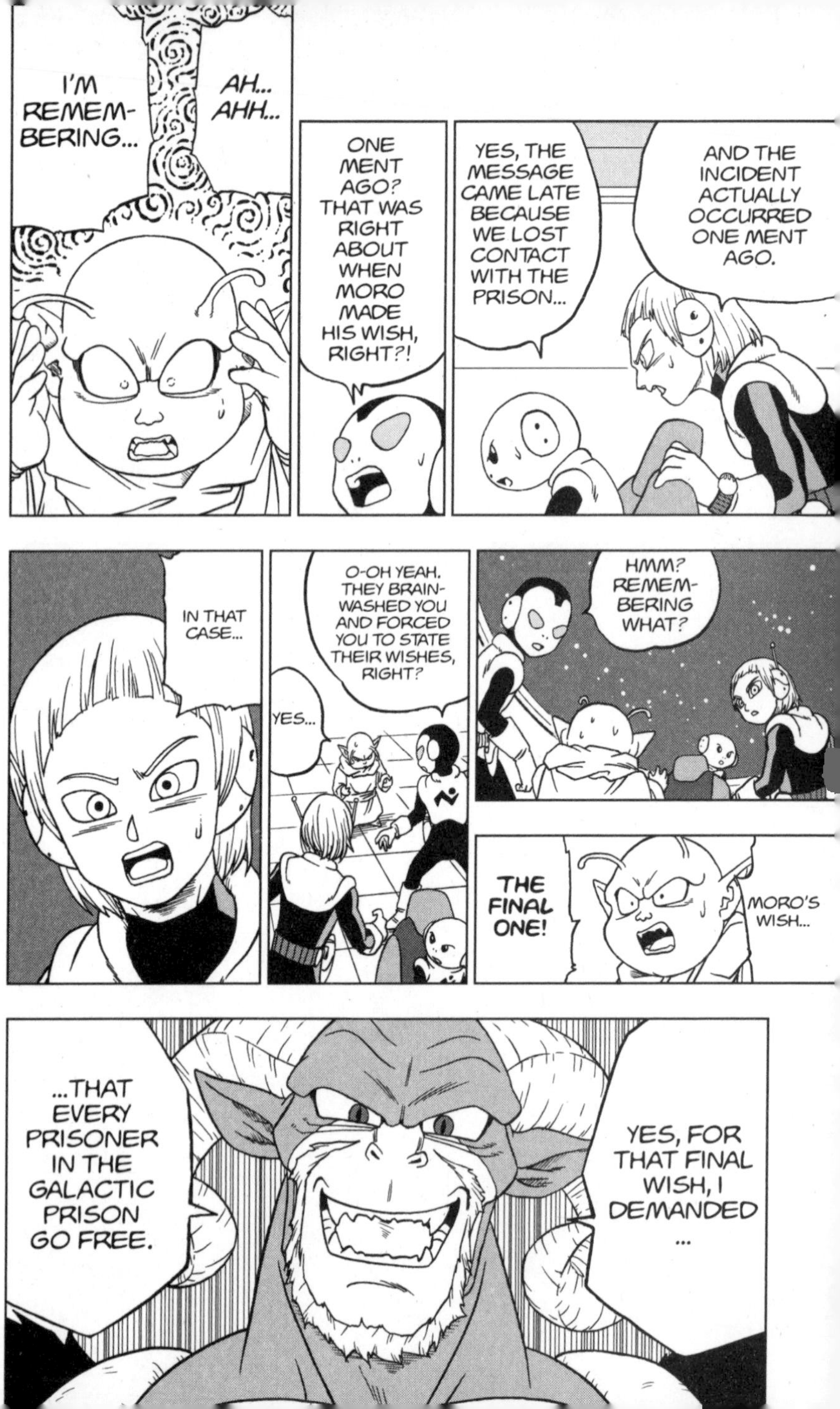
YES, THE MESSAGE CAME LATE BECAUSE WE LOST CONTACT WITH THE PRISON...
AND THE INCIDENT ACTUALLY OCCURRED ONE MENT AGO.
ONE MENT AGO? THAT WAS RIGHT ABOUT WHEN MORO MADE HIS WISH, RIGHT?!
AH... AHH...
I'M REMEMBERING...
HMM? REMEMBERING WHAT?
MORO'S WISH...
THE FINAL ONE!
O-OH YEAH. THEY BRAINWASHED YOU AND FORCED YOU TO STATE THEIR WISHES, RIGHT?
YES...
IN THAT CASE...
YES, FOR THAT FINAL WISH, I DEMANDED ...
...THAT EVERY PRISONER IN THE GALACTIC PRISON GO FREE.

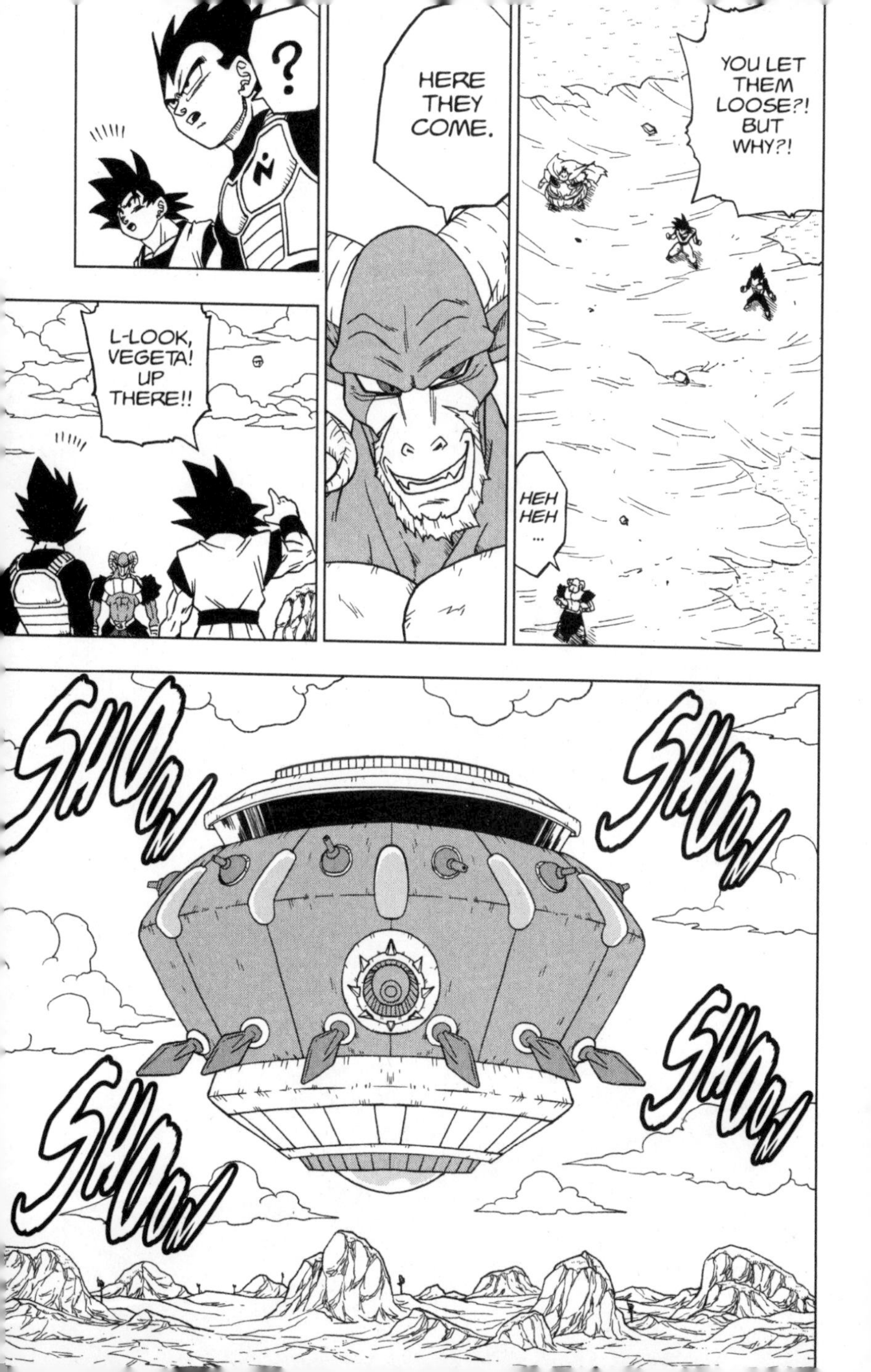
YOU LET THEM LOOSE?! BUT WHY?!
HEH HEH ...
HERE THEY COME.
?
L-LOOK, VEGETA! UP THERE!!
SHOOM
SHOOM
SHOOM
SHOOM

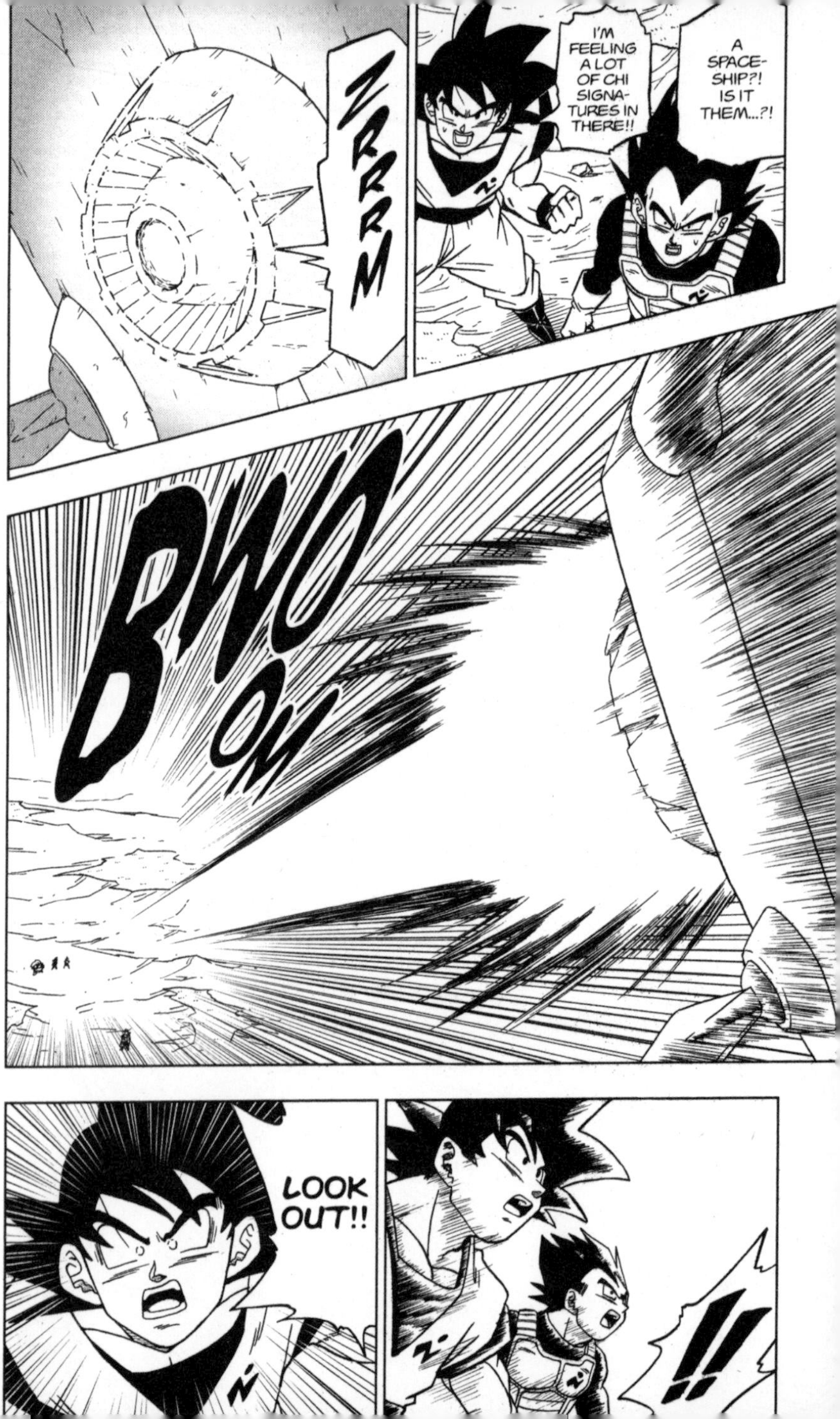
A SPACE-SHIP?! IS IT THEM...?!
I'M FEELING A LOT OF CHI SIGNA-TURES IN THERE!!
ZRRRM
BWOOOM
!!
LOOK OUT!!

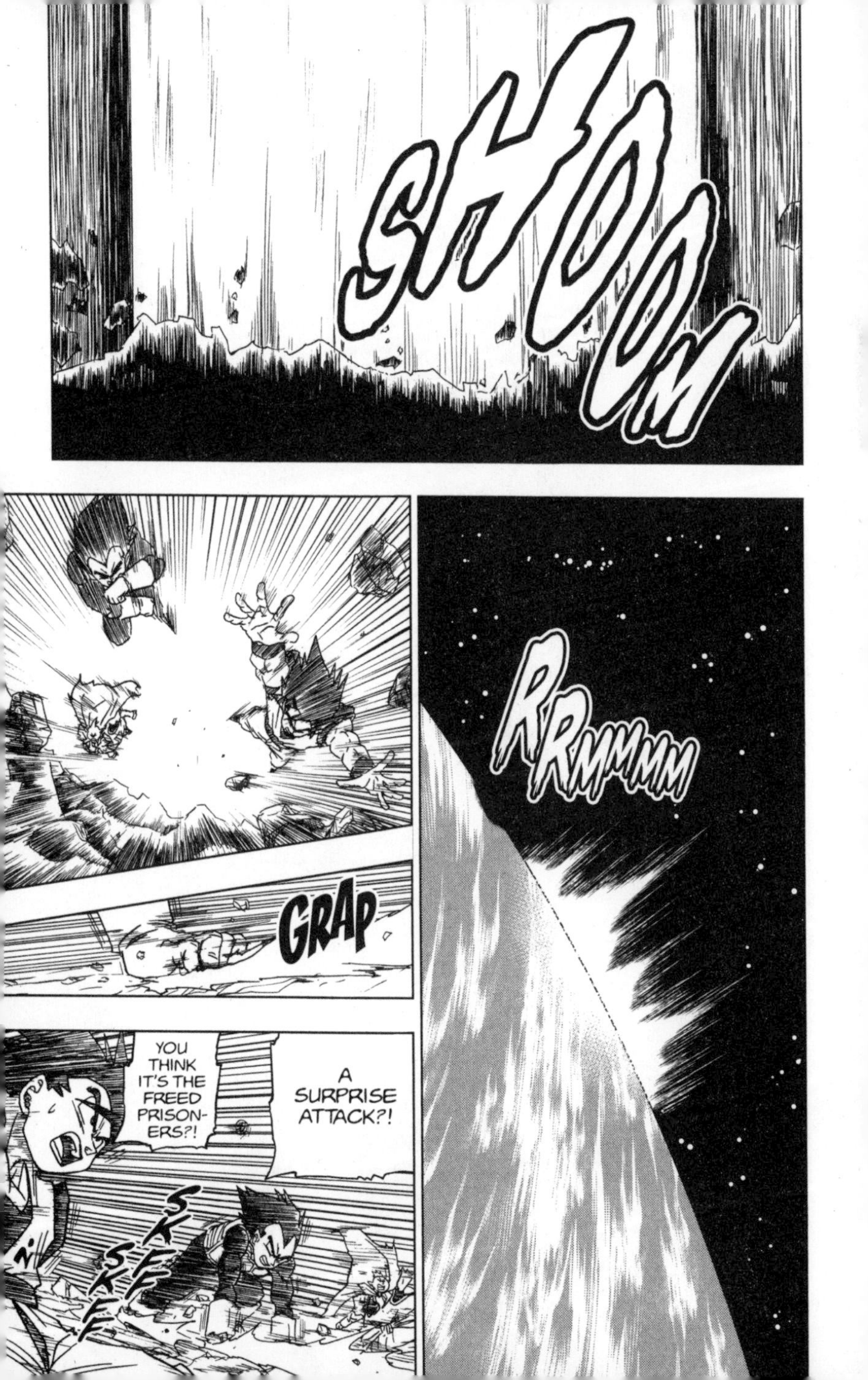
SHOOM
RRMMMMM
GRAP
A SURPRISE ATTACK?!
YOU THINK IT'S THE FREED PRISONERS?!
SKFF
SKFF
N

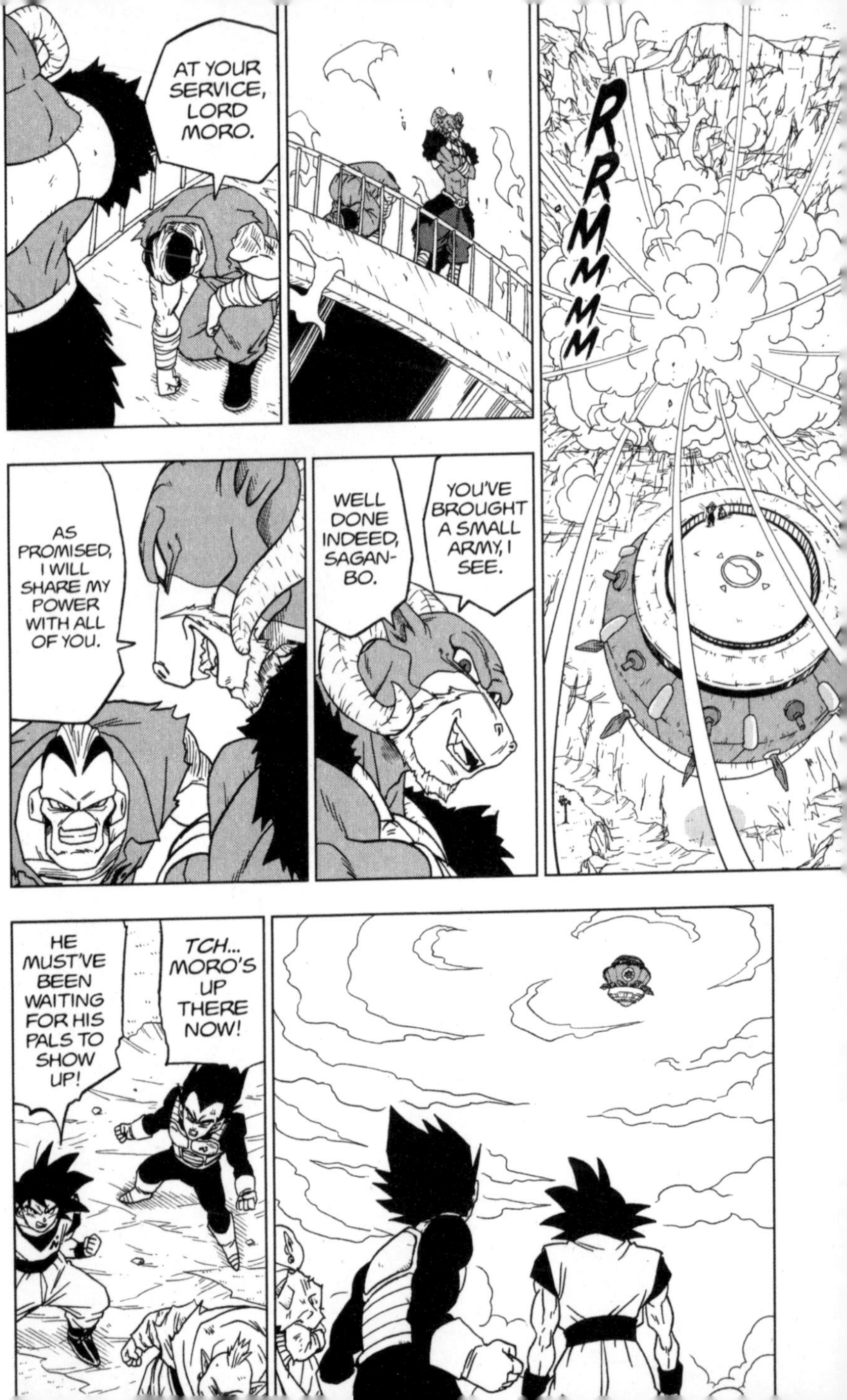
RRRMMMM
AT YOUR SERVICE, LORD MORO.
YOU'VE BROUGHT A SMALL ARMY, I SEE.
WELL DONE INDEED, SAGAN-BO.
AS PROMISED, I WILL SHARE MY POWER WITH ALL OF YOU.
TCH... MORO'S UP THERE NOW!
HE MUST'VE BEEN WAITING FOR HIS PALS TO SHOW UP!

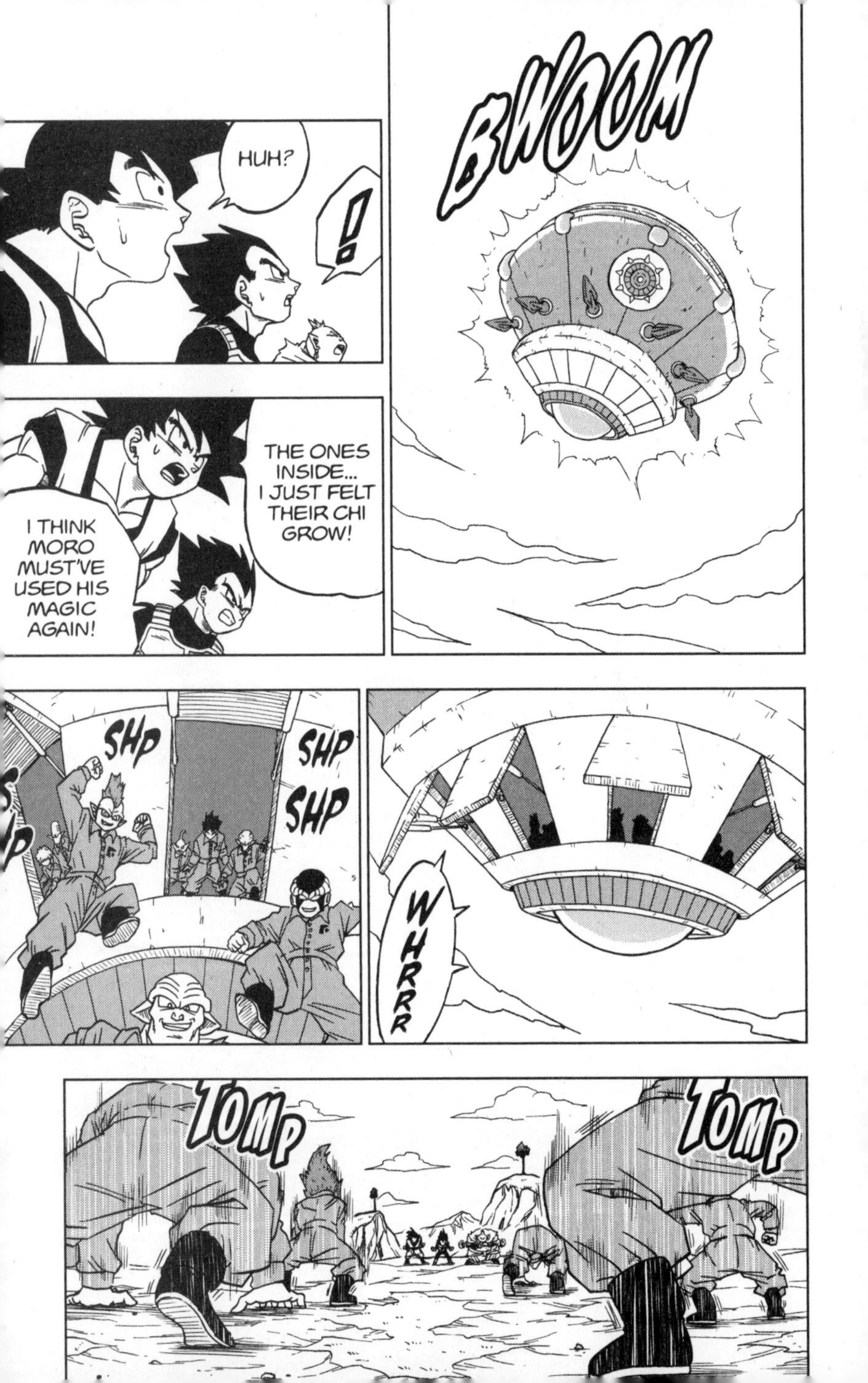
BWOOM
HUH?
!
THE ONES INSIDE... I JUST FELT THEIR CHI GROW!
I THINK MORO MUST'VE USED HIS MAGIC AGAIN!
WHRRR
SHP
SHP
SHP
TOMP
TOMP

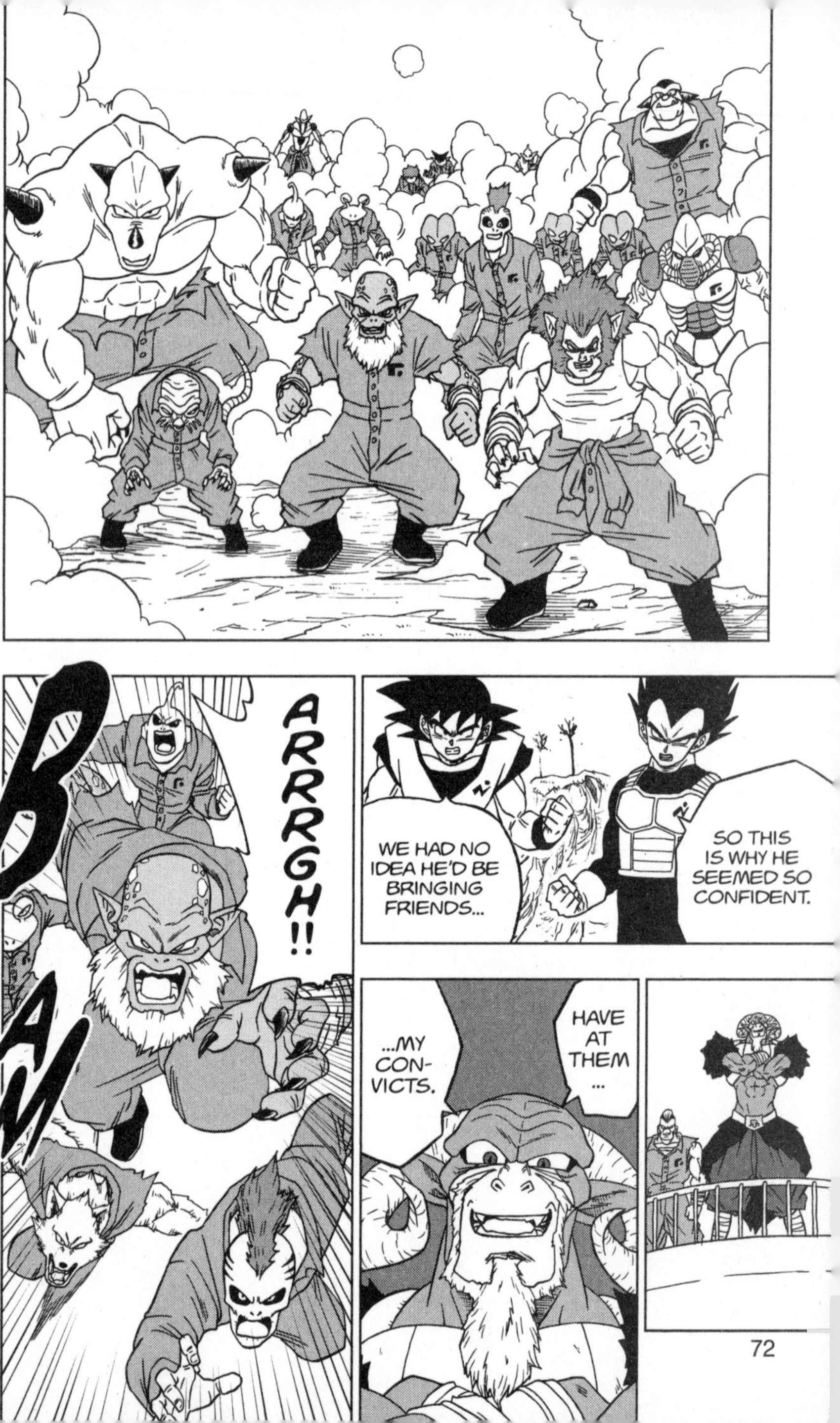
SO THIS IS WHY HE SEEMED SO CONFIDENT.
WE HAD NO IDEA HE'D BE BRINGING FRIENDS...
HAVE AT THEM ...
...MY CON-VICTS.
ARRRGH!!
BAM

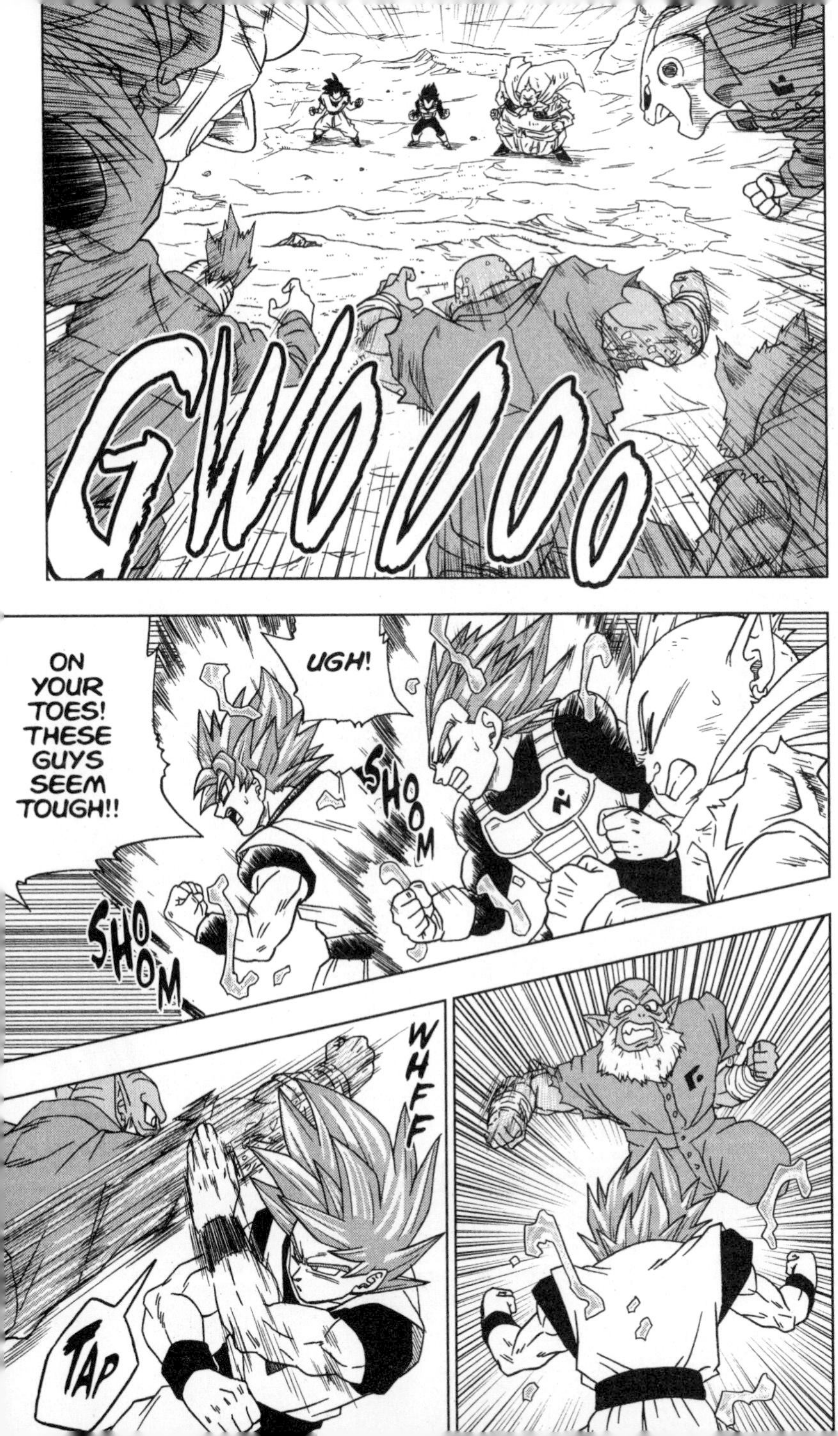
GWOOOOO
UGH!
ON YOUR TOES! THESE GUYS SEEM TOUGH!!
SHOOM
SHOOM
WHFF
TAP

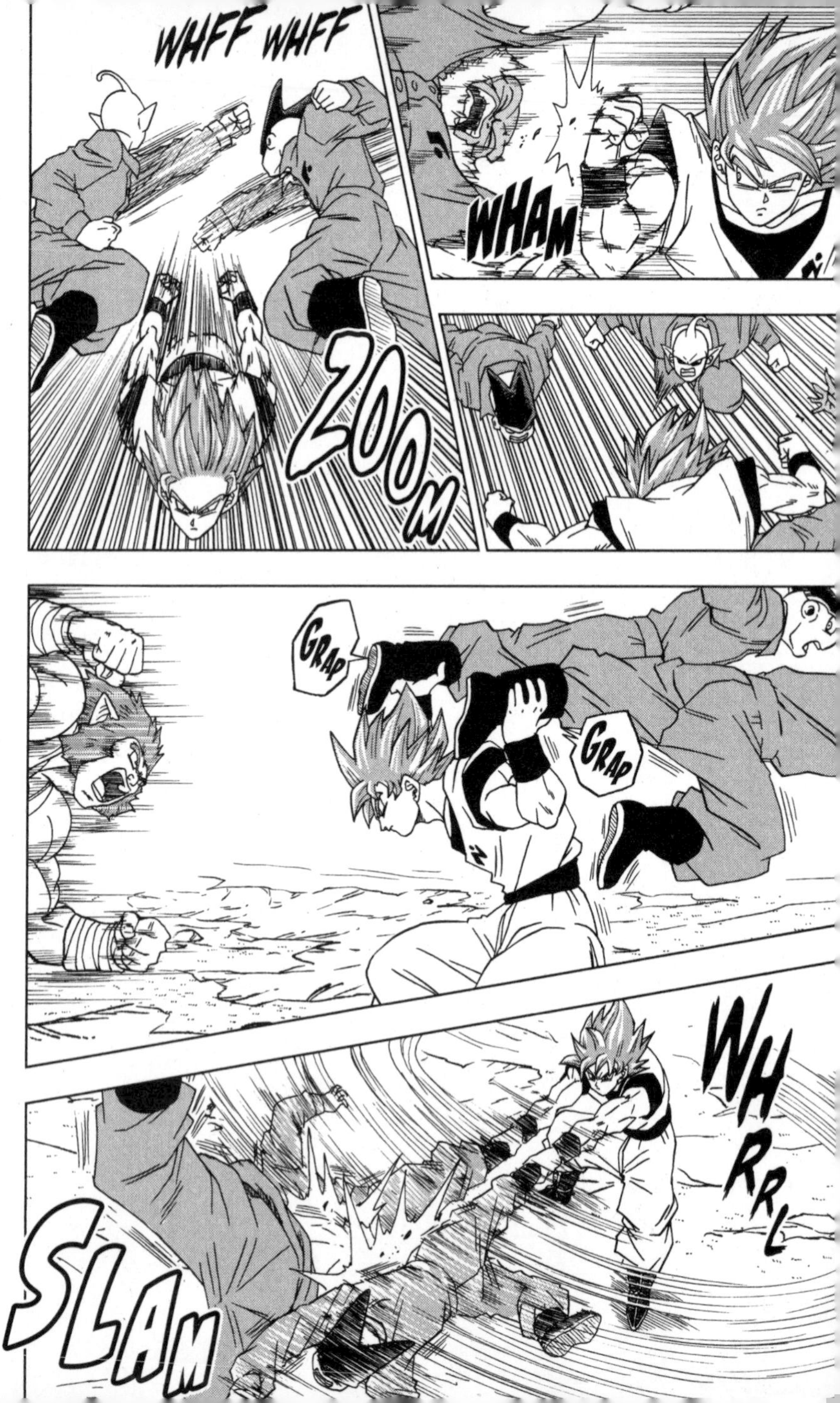
WHAM
WHFF WHFF
ZOOM
GRAP
GRAP
WHRRL
SLAM

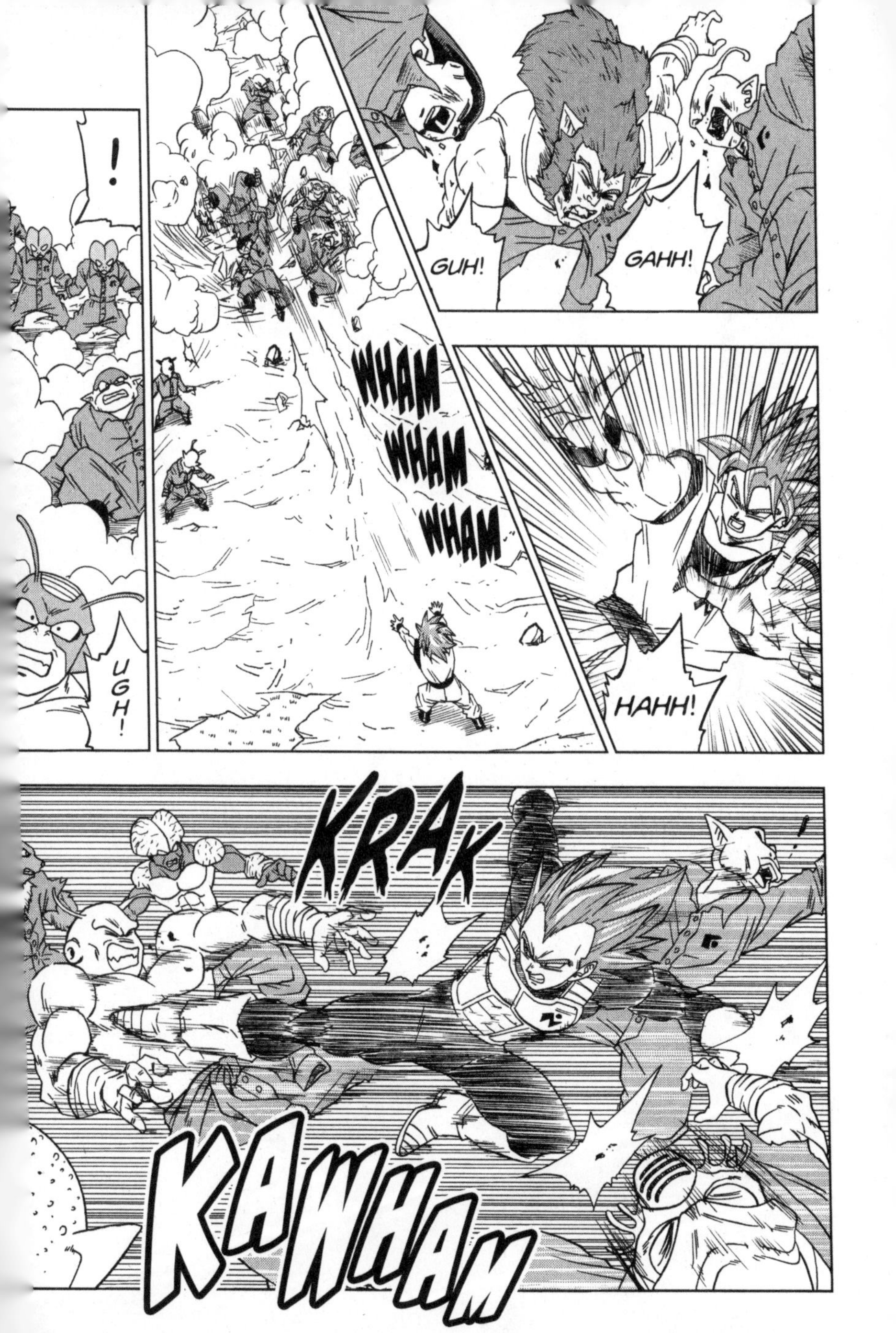
GAHH!
GUH!
HAHH!
WHAM WHAM WHAM
!
UGH!
KRAK
KAWHAM

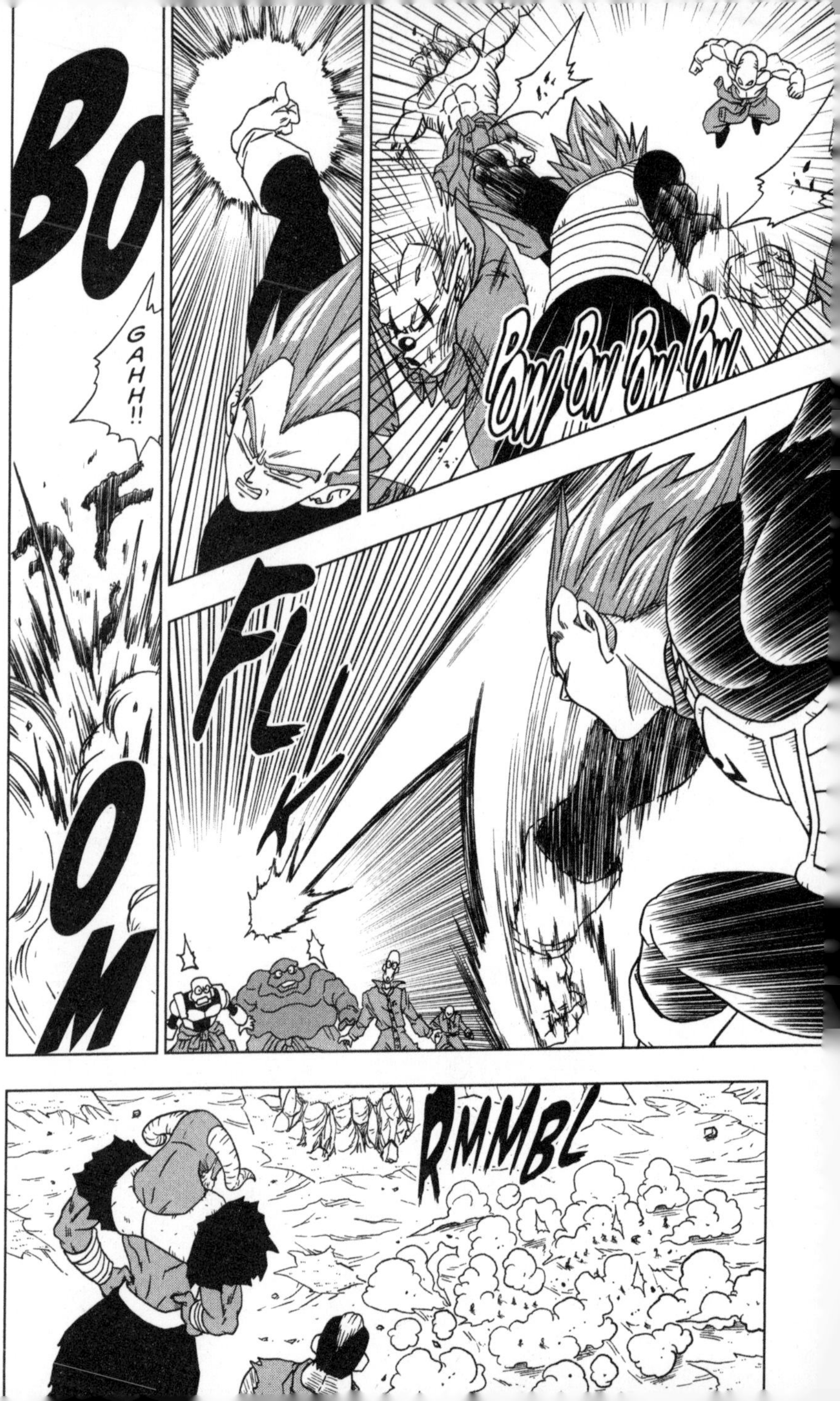
BWBWBWBW
FLIKK
GAHH!!
BOOOM
RMMBL

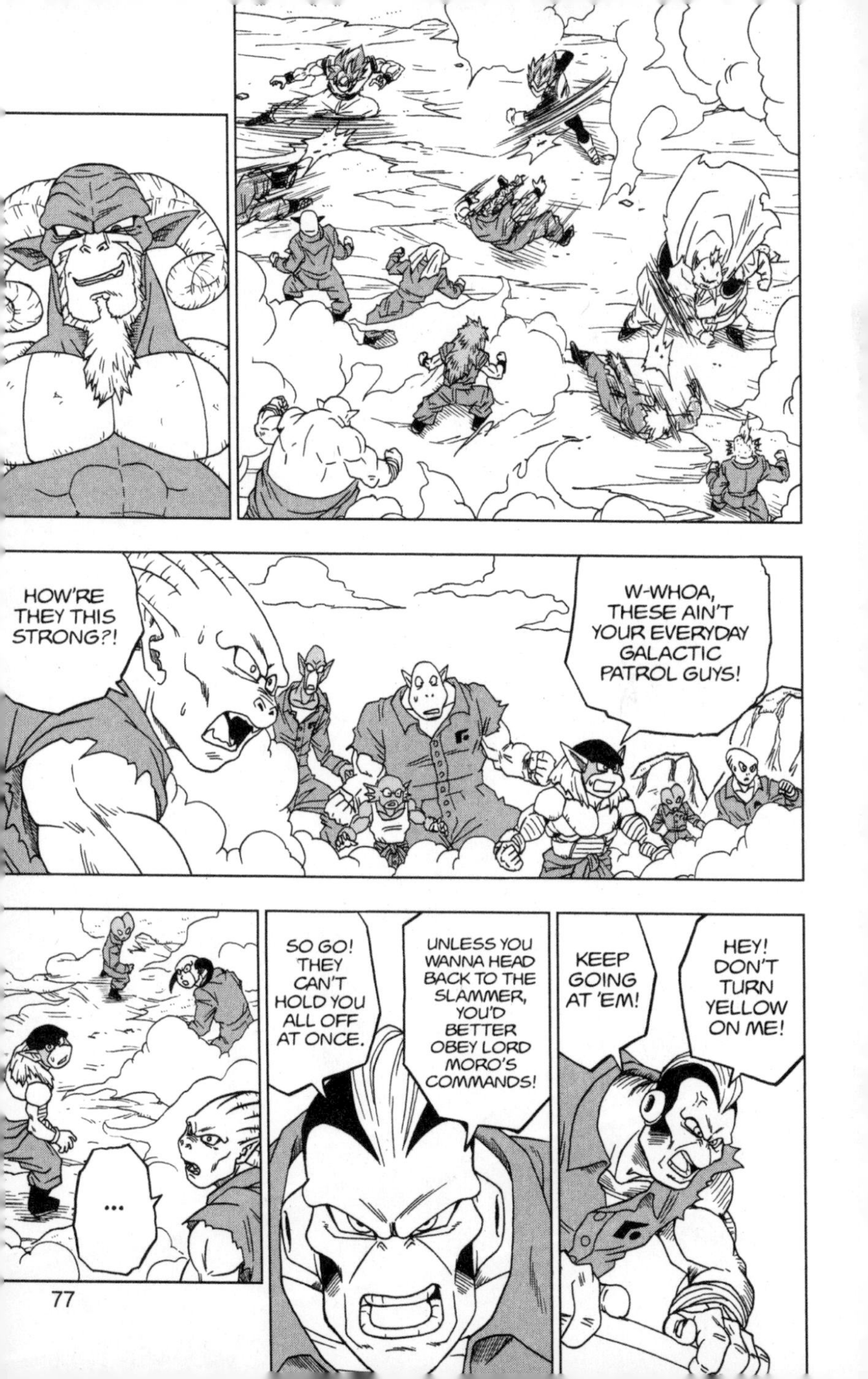
W-WHOA, THESE AIN'T YOUR EVERYDAY GALACTIC PATROL GUYS!
HOW'RE THEY THIS STRONG?!
HEY! DON'T TURN YELLOW ON ME!
KEEP GOING AT 'EM!
UNLESS YOU WANNA HEAD BACK TO THE SLAMMER, YOU'D BETTER OBEY LORD MORO'S COMMANDS!
SO GO! THEY CAN'T HOLD YOU ALL OFF AT ONCE.
...

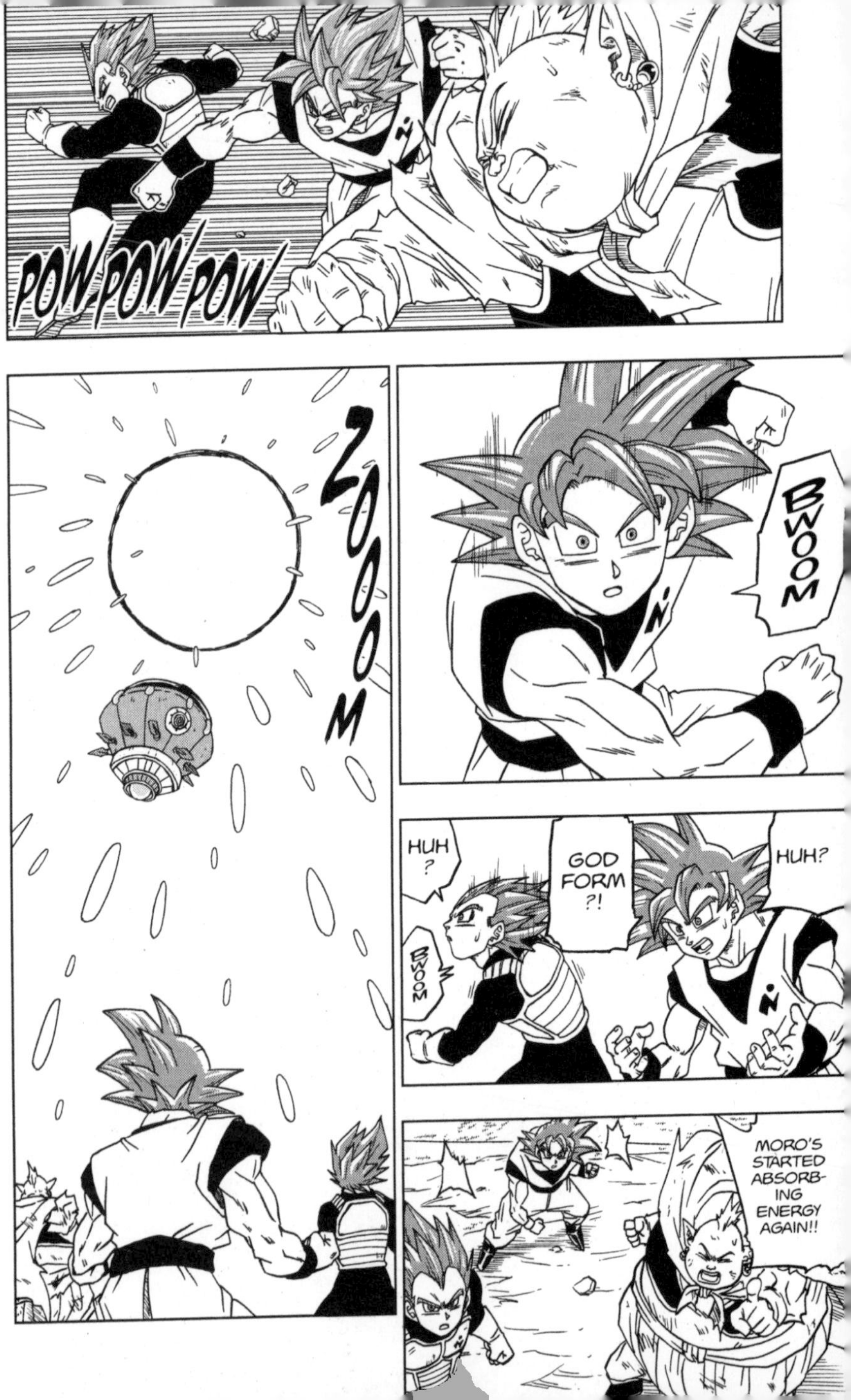
POW POW POW
BWOOM
HUH?
GOD FORM ?!
HUH ?
BWOOM
MORO'S STARTED ABSORBING ENERGY AGAIN!!
ZOOOOM

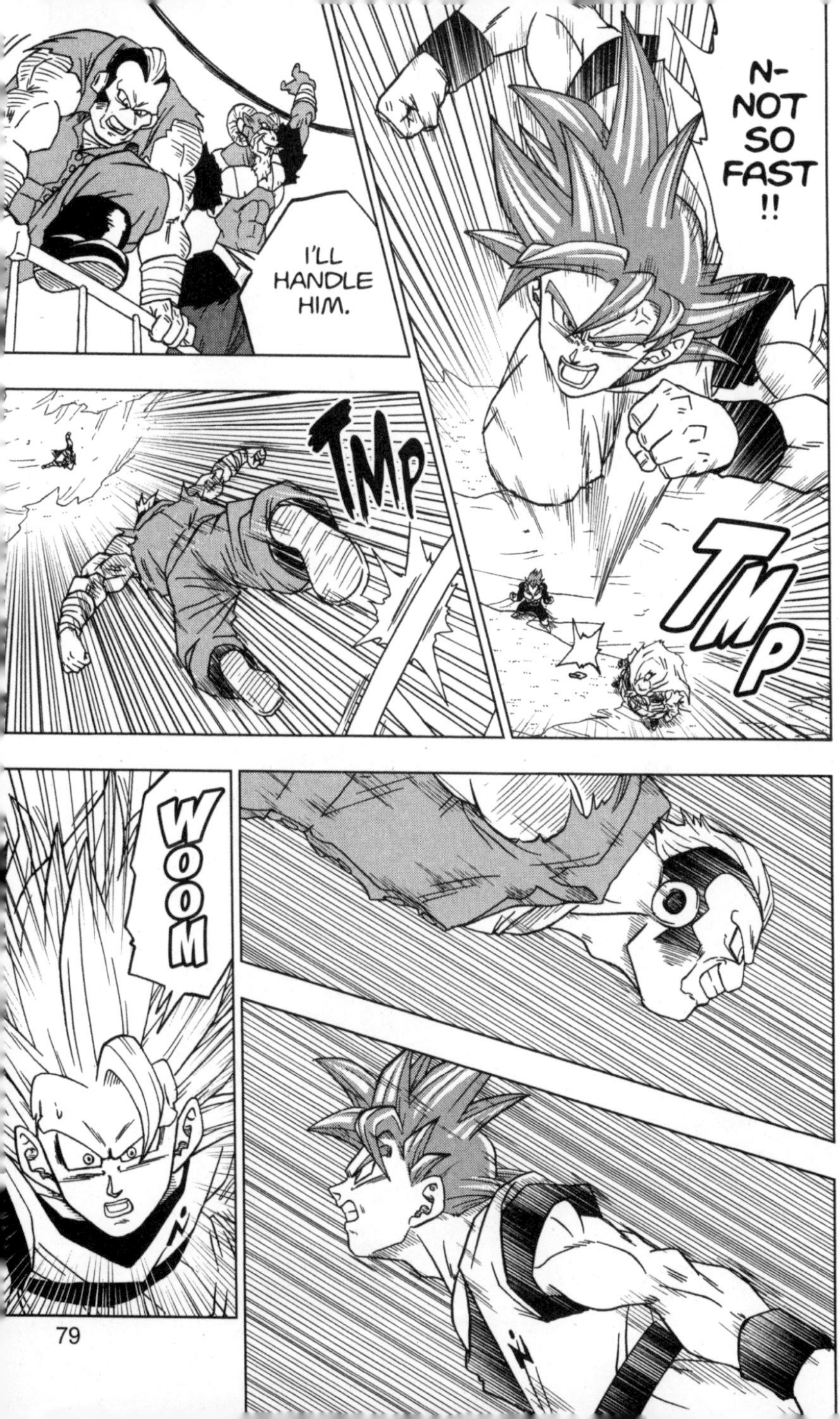
N-NOT SO FAST!!
TMP
I'LL HANDLE HIM.
TMP
WOOM

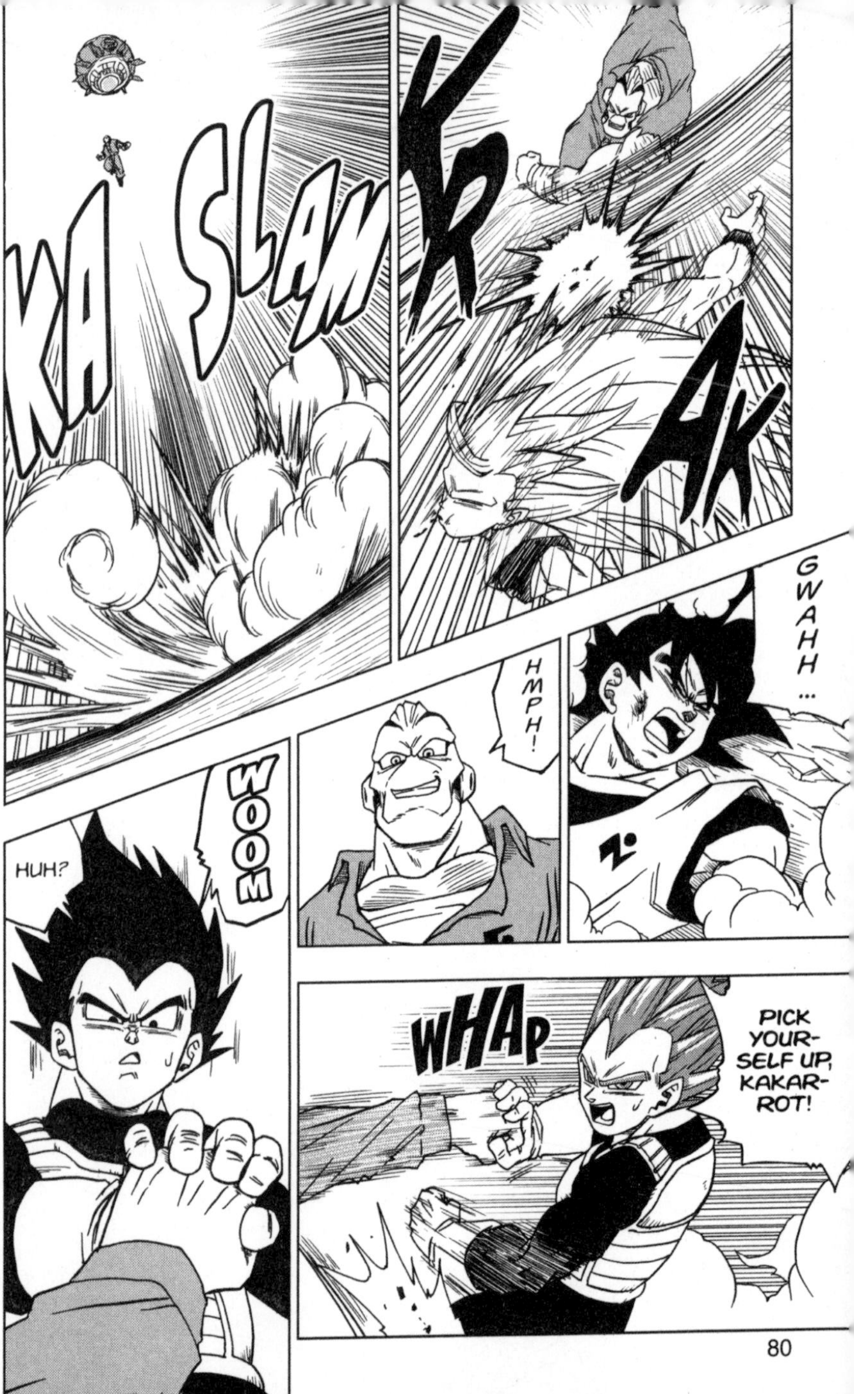
KA SLAM KRAK
GWAHH...
HMPH!
WHAP
PICK YOUR-SELF UP, KAKAR-ROT!
WOOOM
HUH?

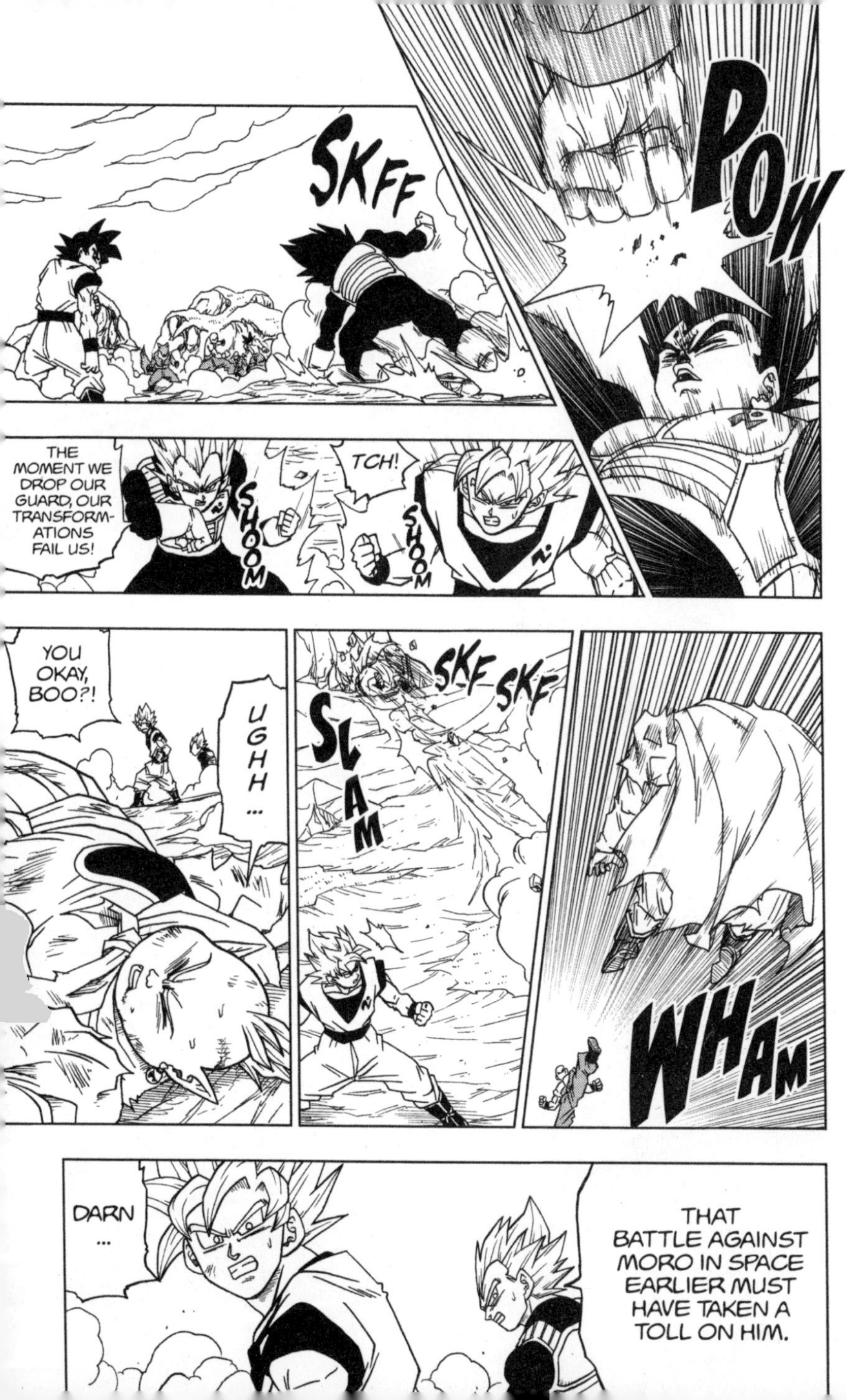
POW
SKFF
TCH!
SHOOM
SHOOM
THE MOMENT WE DROP OUR GUARD, OUR TRANSFORMATIONS FAIL US!
WHAM
SKF SKF
SLAM
UGHH ...
YOU OKAY, BOO?!
THAT BATTLE AGAINST MORO IN SPACE EARLIER MUST HAVE TAKEN A TOLL ON HIM.
DARN ...

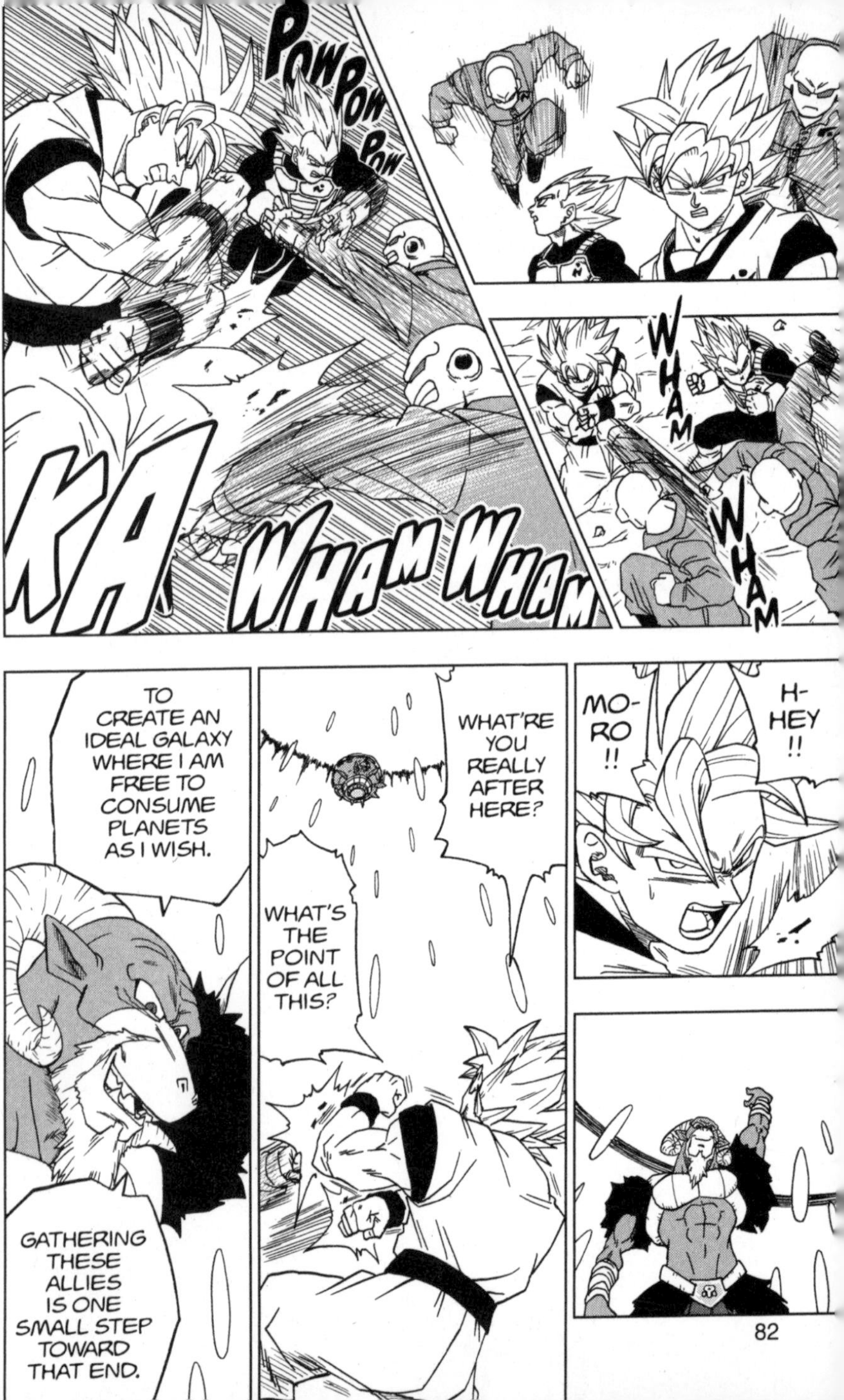
WHAM WHAM
WHAM WHAM
POW POW POW
KA
WHAM WHAM
H-HEY!!
MO-RO!!
WHAT'RE YOU REALLY AFTER HERE?
WHAT'S THE POINT OF ALL THIS?
TO CREATE AN IDEAL GALAXY WHERE I AM FREE TO CONSUME PLANETS AS I WISH.
GATHERING THESE ALLIES IS ONE SMALL STEP TOWARD THAT END.

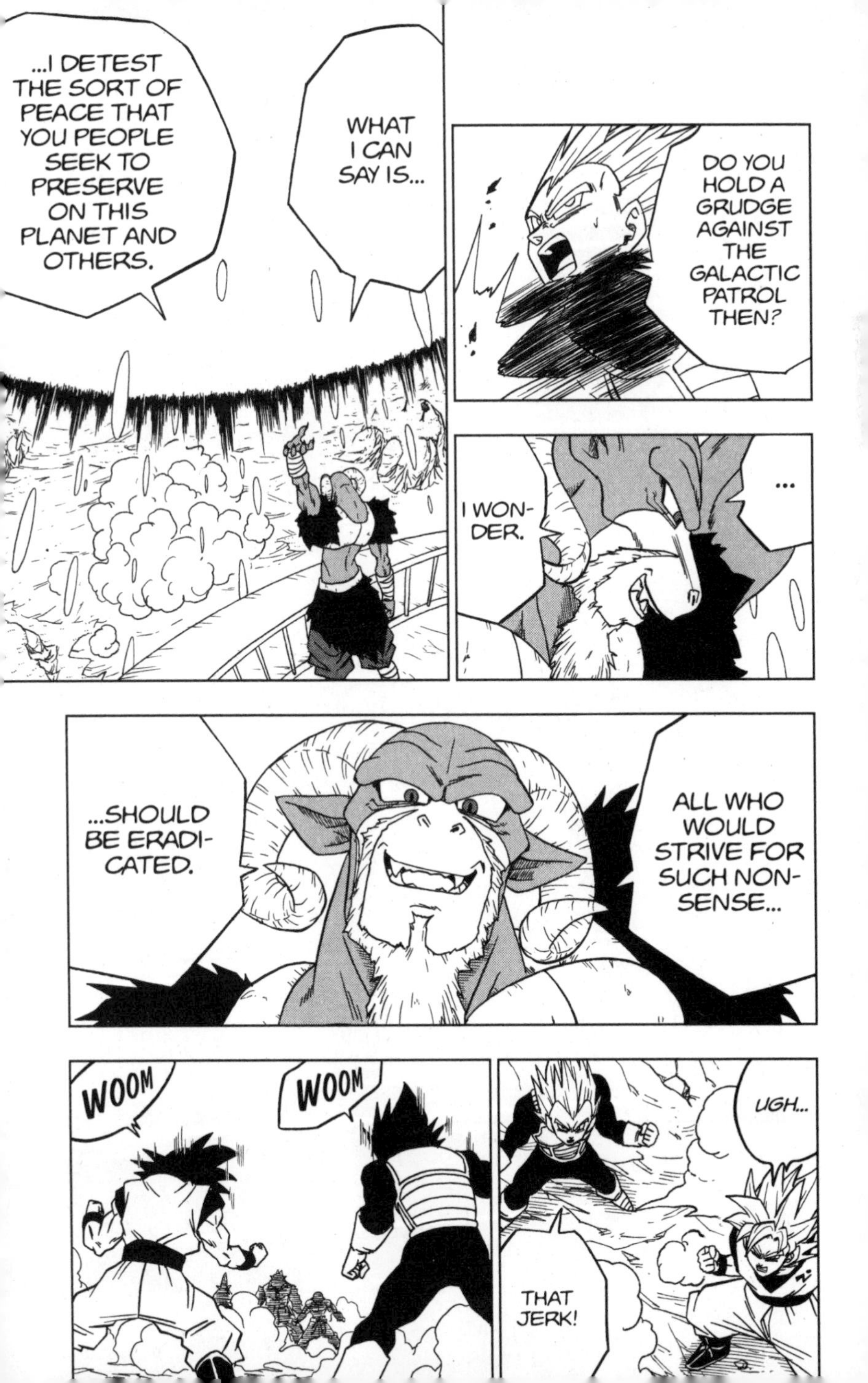
DO YOU HOLD A GRUDGE AGAINST THE GALACTIC PATROL THEN?
...
I WON-DER.
WHAT I CAN SAY IS...
...I DETEST THE SORT OF PEACE THAT YOU PEOPLE SEEK TO PRESERVE ON THIS PLANET AND OTHERS.
ALL WHO WOULD STRIVE FOR SUCH NON-SENSE...
...SHOULD BE ERADI-CATED.
UGH...
THAT JERK!
WOOM
WOOM

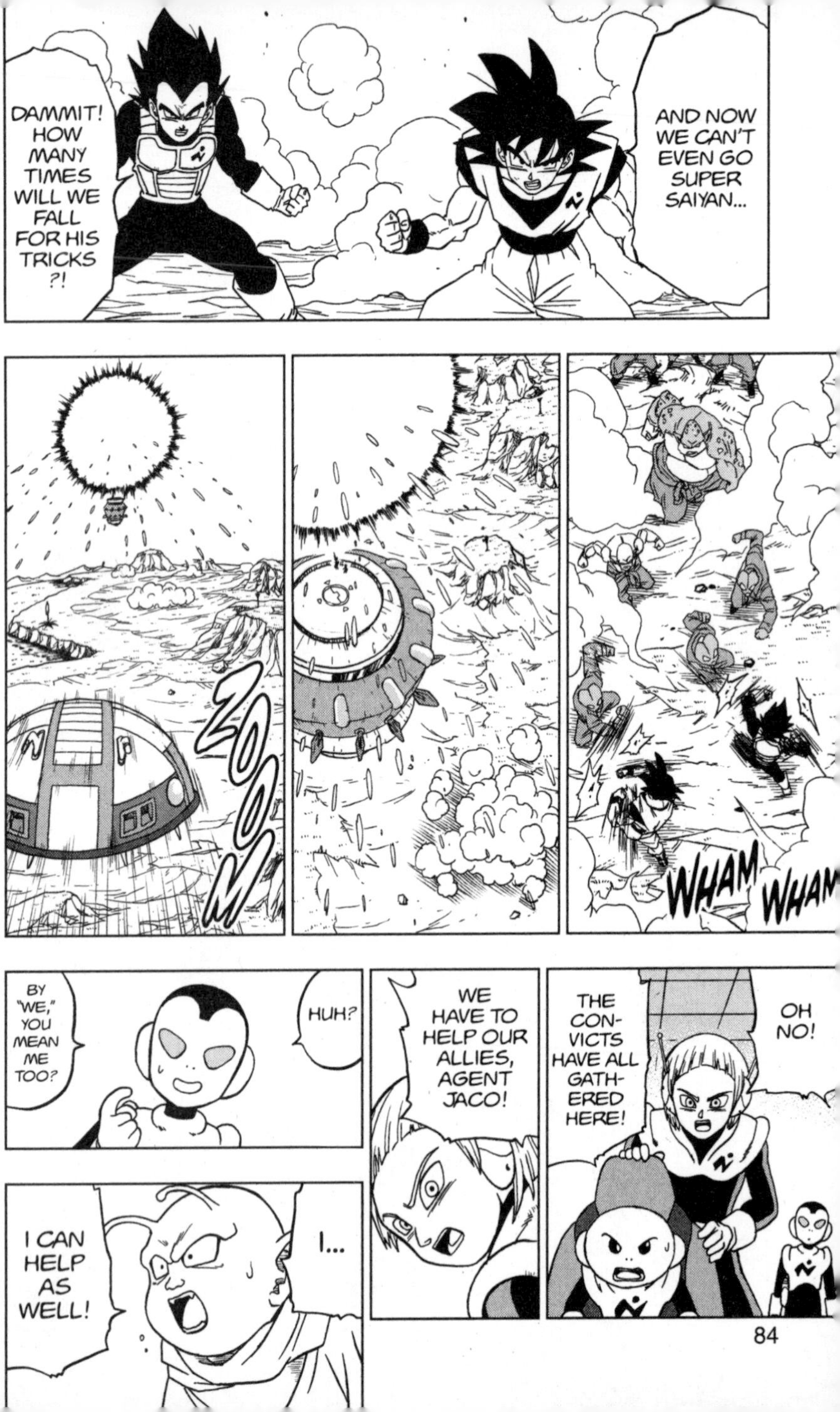
AND NOW WE CAN'T EVEN GO SUPER SAIYAN...
DAMMIT! HOW MANY TIMES WILL WE FALL FOR HIS TRICKS?!
WHAM WHAM
ZOOOM
OH NO!
THE CON-VICTS HAVE ALL GATH-ERED HERE!
WE HAVE TO HELP OUR ALLIES, AGENT JACO!
HUH?
BY "WE," YOU MEAN ME TOO?
I...
I CAN HELP AS WELL!

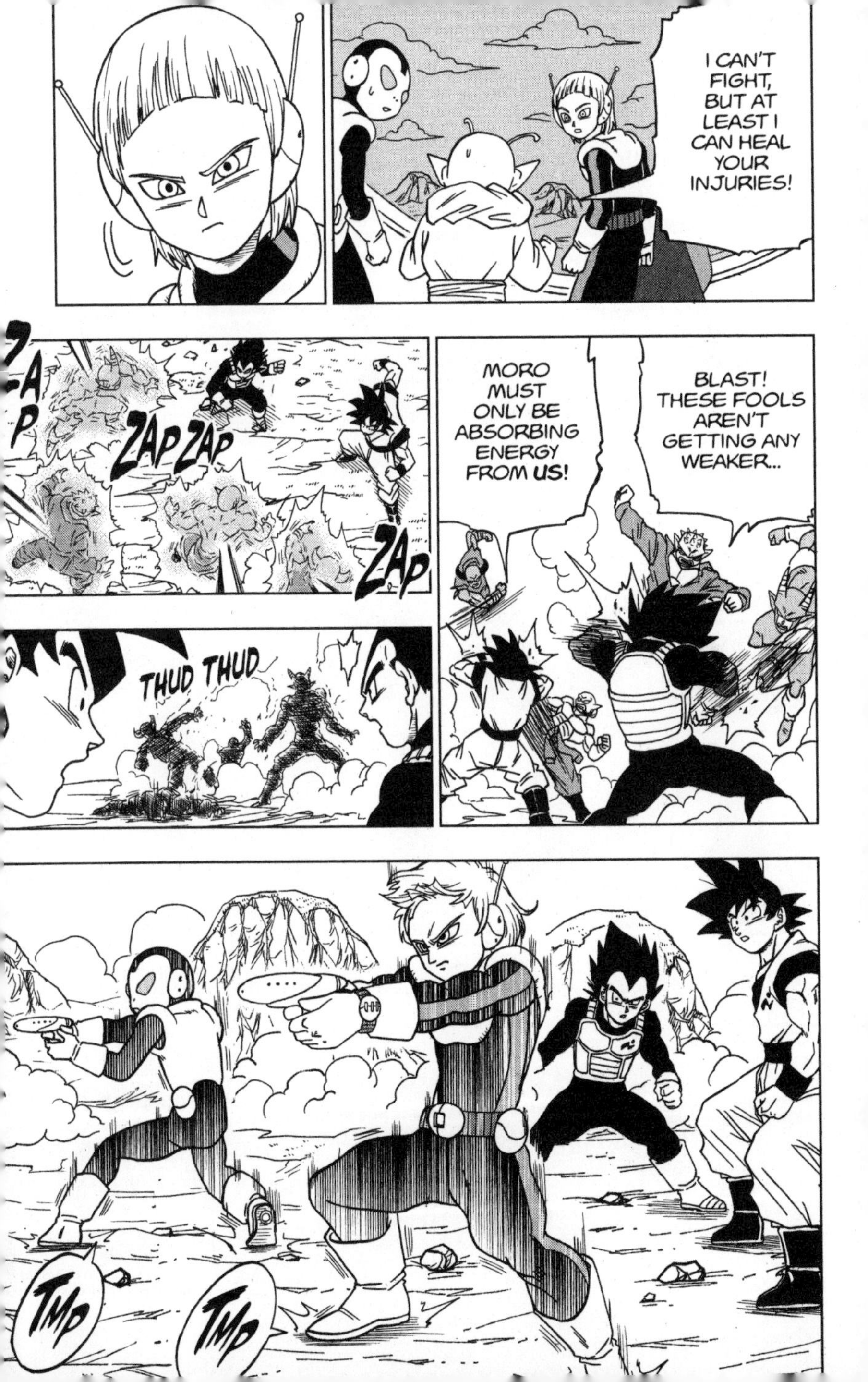
I CAN'T FIGHT, BUT AT LEAST I CAN HEAL YOUR INJURIES!
BLAST! THESE FOOLS AREN'T GETTING ANY WEAKER...
MORO MUST ONLY BE ABSORBING ENERGY FROM **US**!
ZAP
ZAP ZAP
THUD THUD
....
....
TMP
TMP

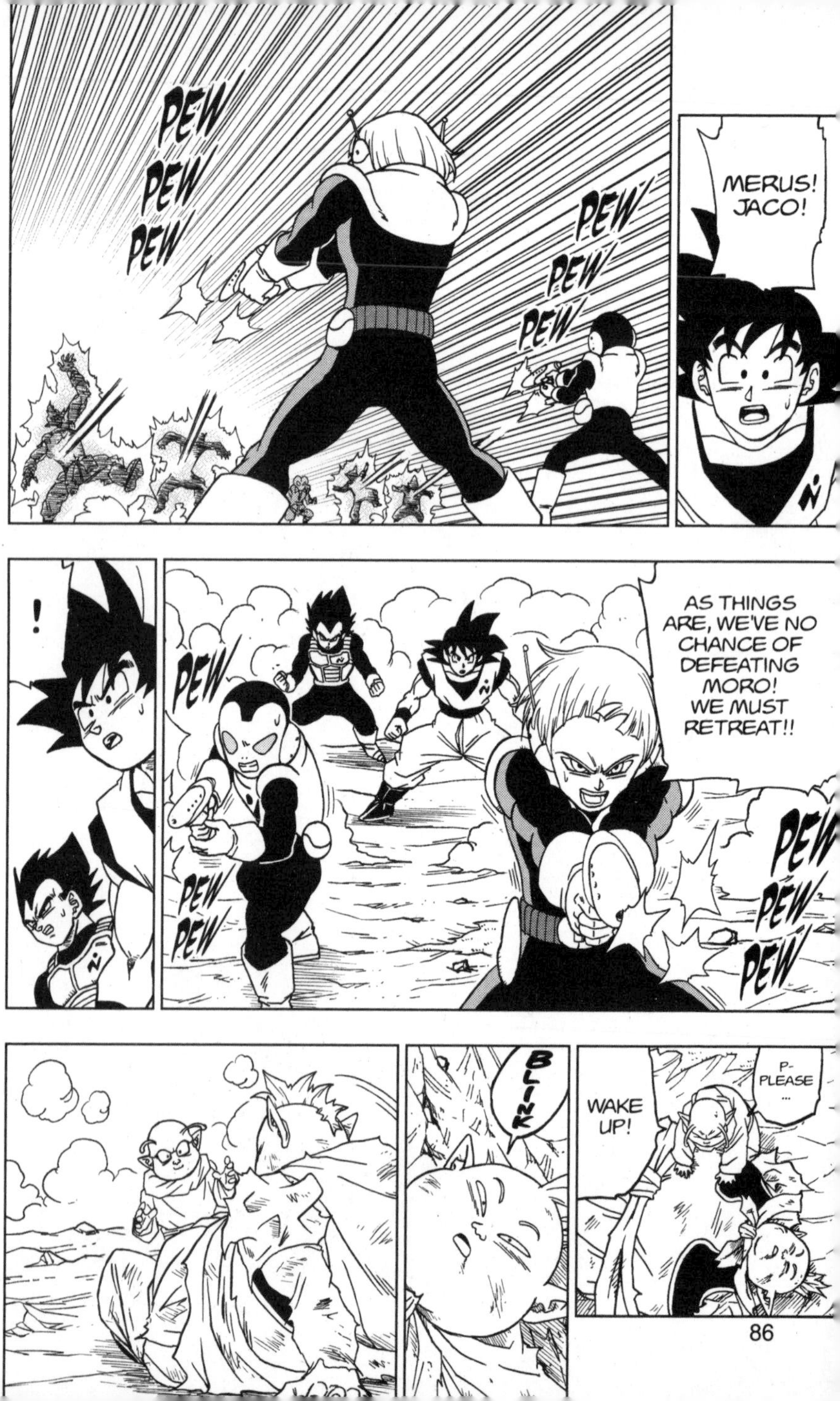
MERUS! JACO!
PEW PEW PEW
PEW PEW PEW
AS THINGS ARE, WE'VE NO CHANCE OF DEFEATING MORO! WE MUST RETREAT!!
PEW PEW PEW
PEW
PEW PEW
!
P- PLEASE ...
WAKE UP!
BLINK

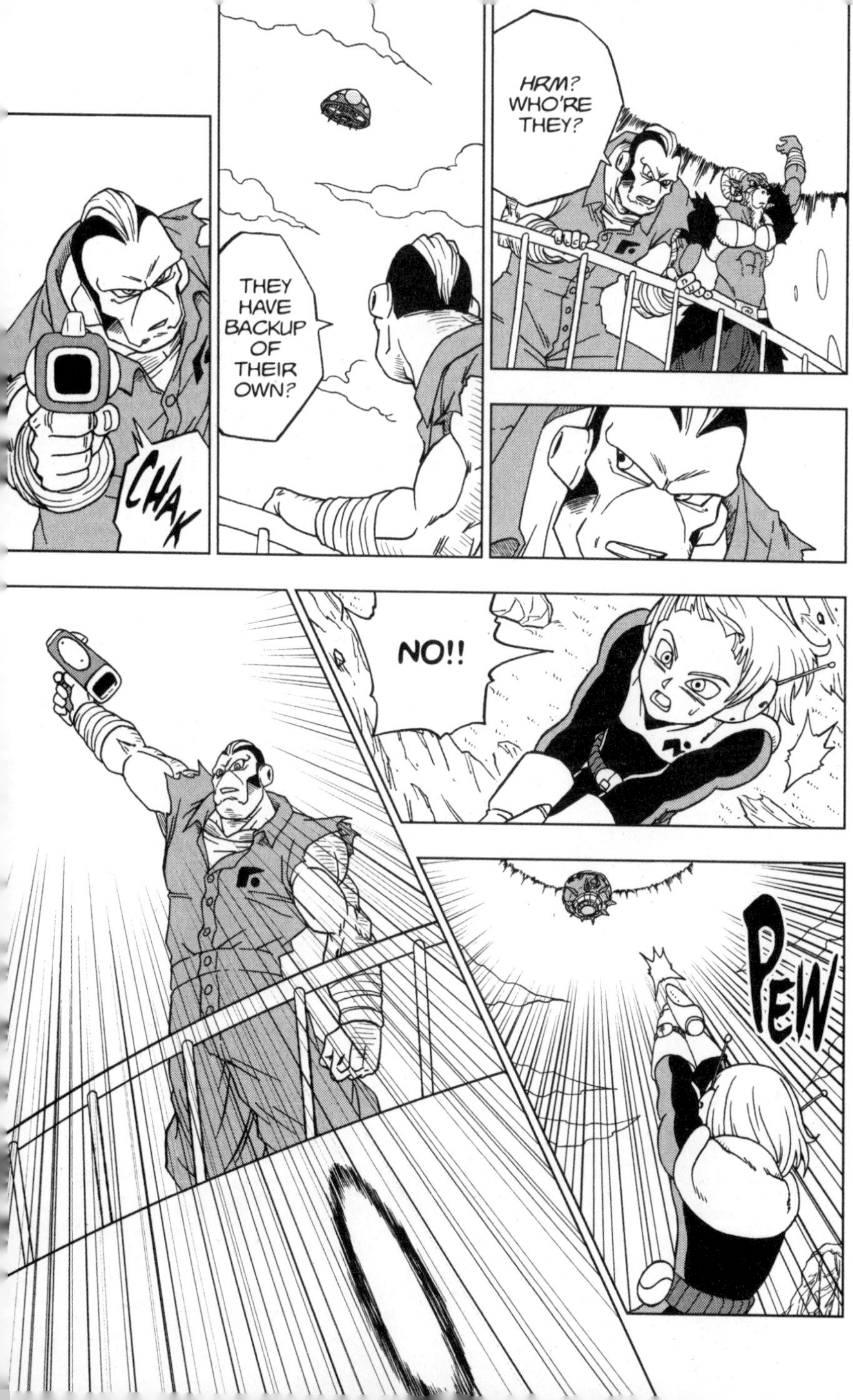
HRM? WHO'RE THEY?
THEY HAVE BACKUP OF THEIR OWN?
CHAK
NO!!
PEW

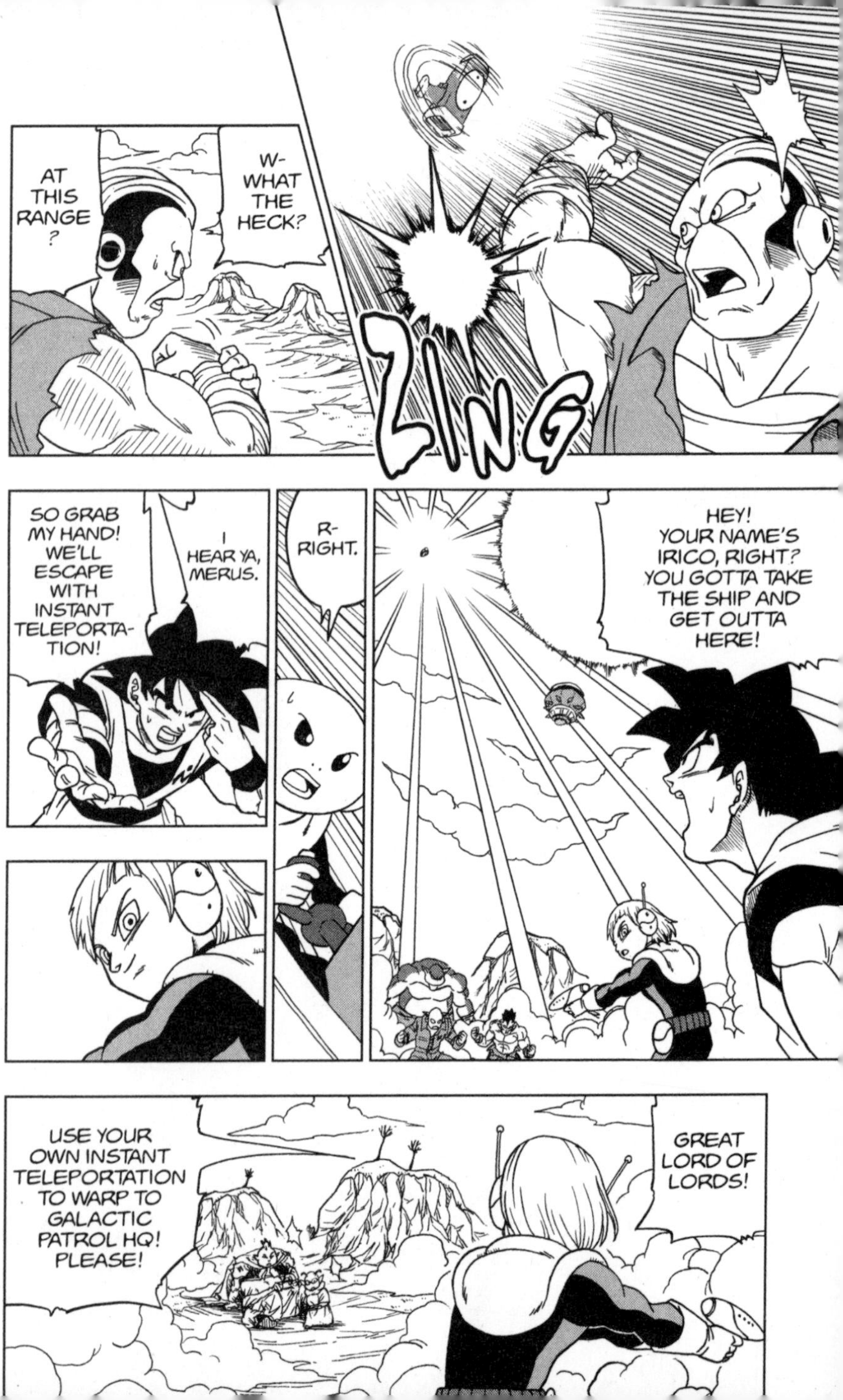
ZING
W- WHAT THE HECK?
AT THIS RANGE?
HEY! YOUR NAME'S IRICO, RIGHT? YOU GOTTA TAKE THE SHIP AND GET OUTTA HERE!
R- RIGHT.
I HEAR YA, MERUS.
SO GRAB MY HAND! WE'LL ESCAPE WITH INSTANT TELEPORTA-TION!
GREAT LORD OF LORDS!
USE YOUR OWN INSTANT TELEPORTATION TO WARP TO GALACTIC PATROL HQ! PLEASE!

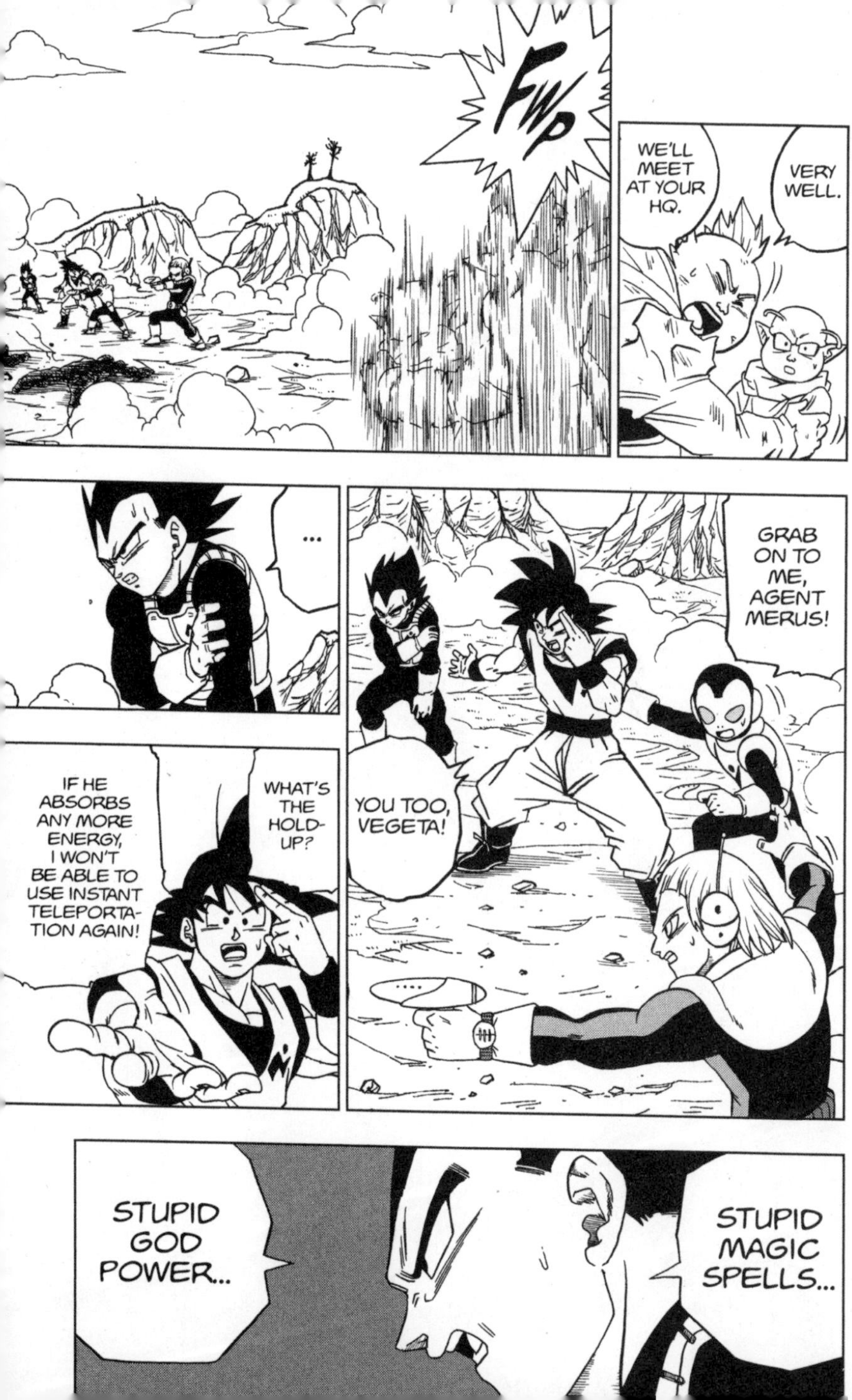

WE'LL MEET AT YOUR HQ.
VERY WELL.
FWP
GRAB ON TO ME, AGENT MERUS!
YOU TOO, VEGETA!
...
WHAT'S THE HOLD-UP?
IF HE ABSORBS ANY MORE ENERGY, I WON'T BE ABLE TO USE INSTANT TELEPORTATION AGAIN!
STUPID MAGIC SPELLS...
STUPID GOD POWER...

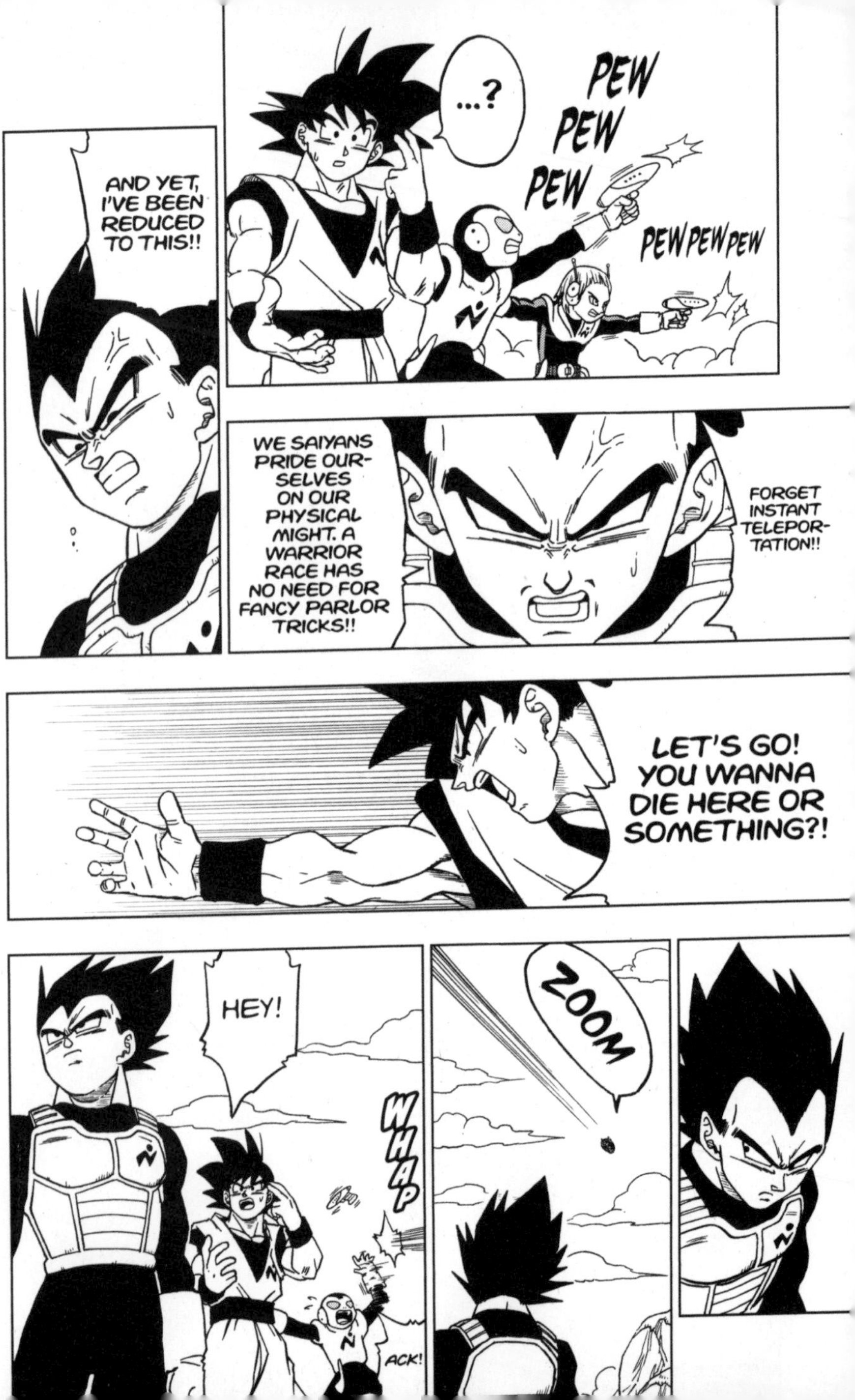
PEW
PEW
PEW
...?
PEW PEW PEW
FORGET INSTANT TELEPORTATION!!
WE SAIYANS PRIDE OURSELVES ON OUR PHYSICAL MIGHT. A WARRIOR RACE HAS NO NEED FOR FANCY PARLOR TRICKS!!
AND YET, I'VE BEEN REDUCED TO THIS!!
LET'S GO! YOU WANNA DIE HERE OR SOMETHING?!
ZOOM
HEY!
WHAP
ACK!

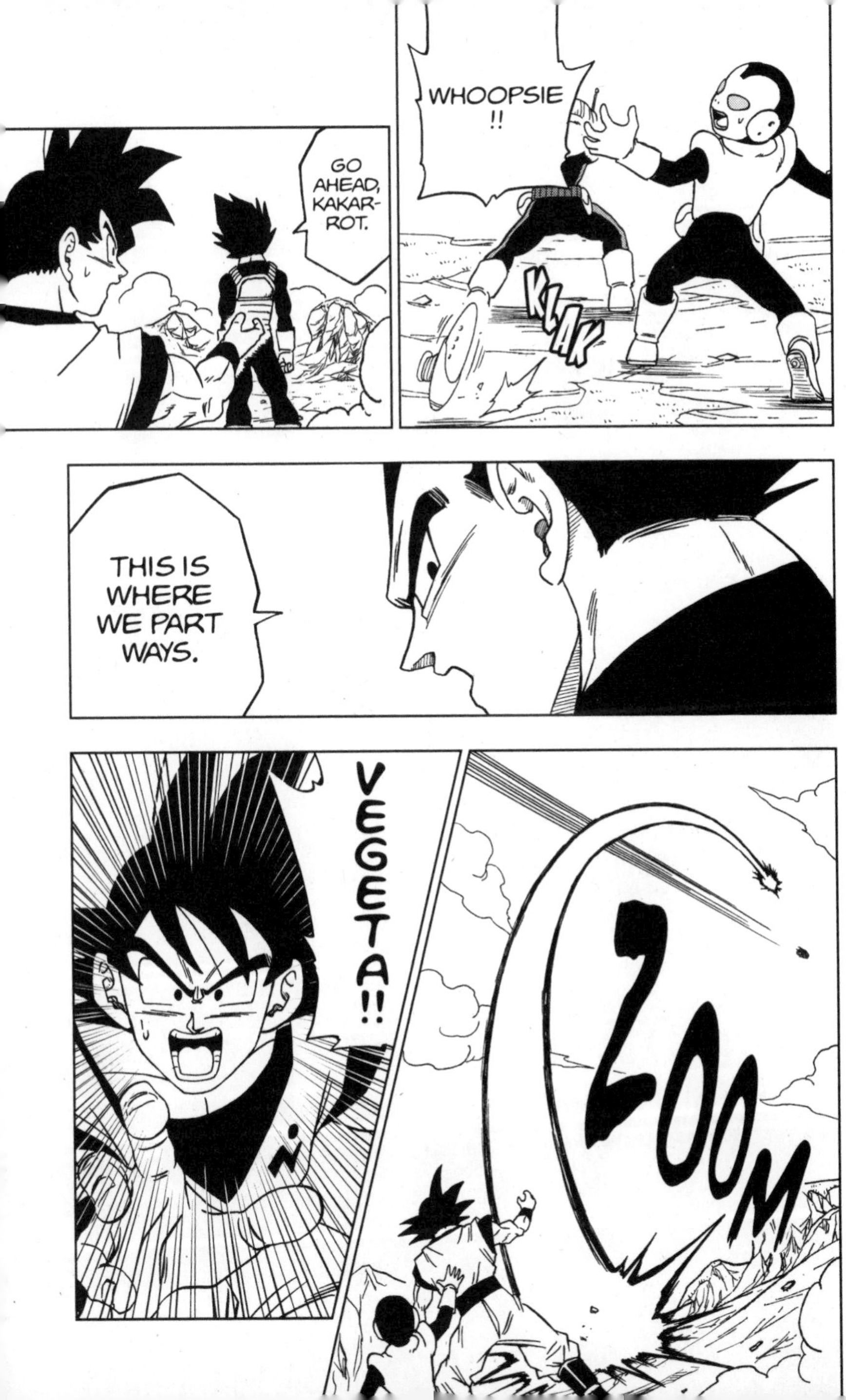
WHOOPSIE !!
KLAK
GO AHEAD, KAKAR-ROT.
THIS IS WHERE WE PART WAYS.
ZOOM
VEGETA!!

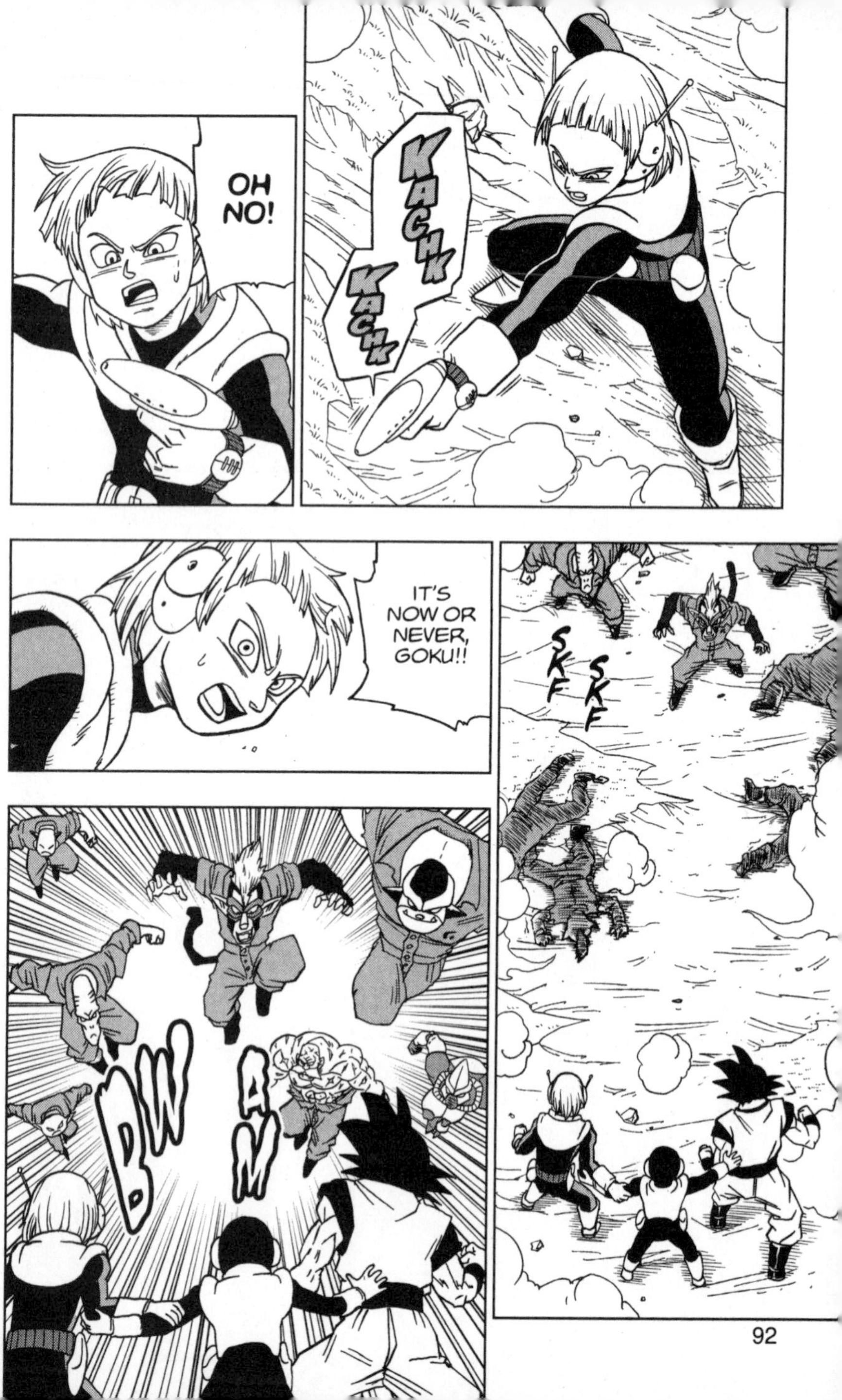
KACHK KACHK
OH NO!
SKF SKF
IT'S NOW OR NEVER, GOKU!!
BWAM

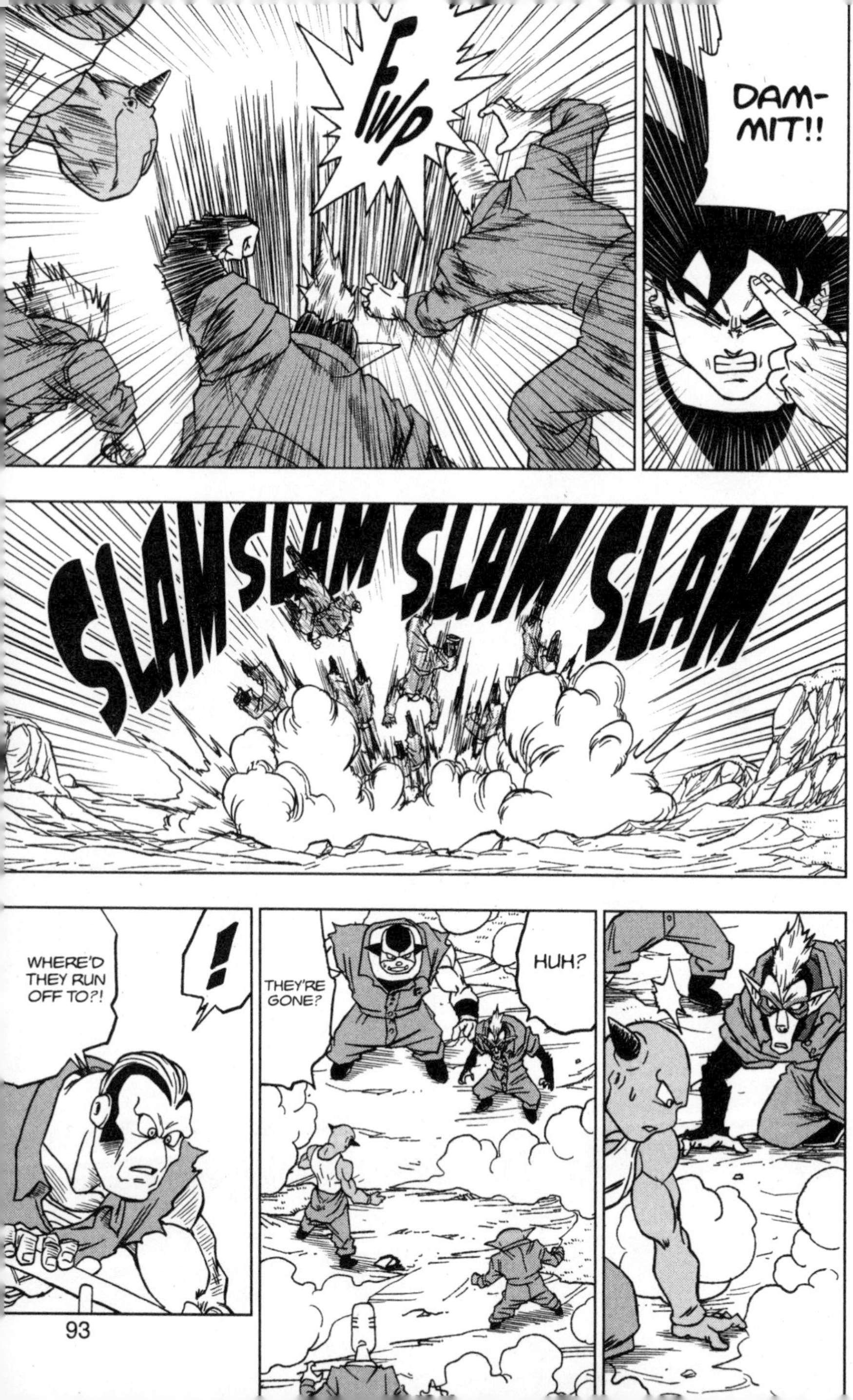
DAM-MIT!!
FWP
SLAM SLAM SLAM SLAM
HUH?
THEY'RE GONE?
!
WHERE'D THEY RUN OFF TO?!

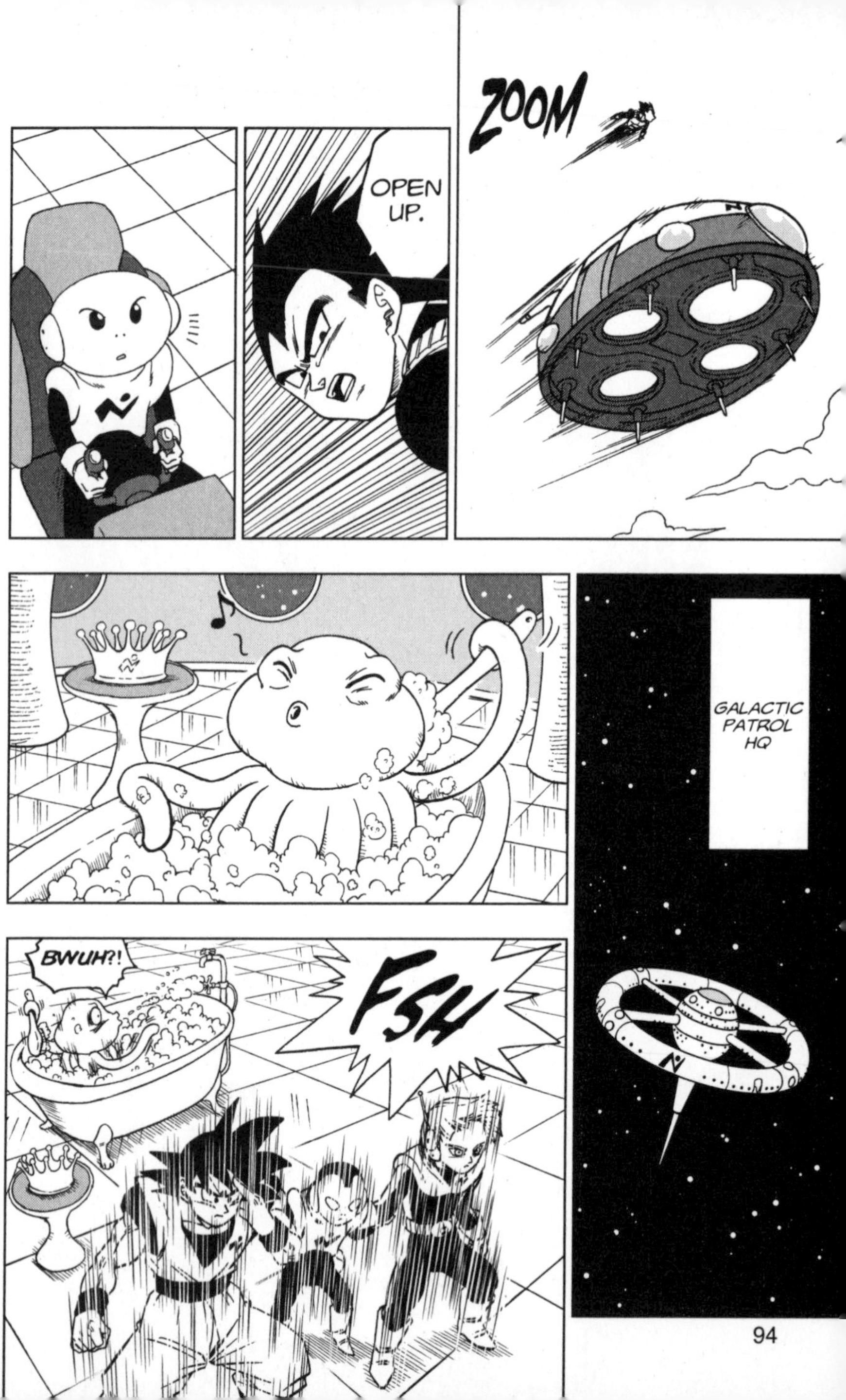
ZOOM
OPEN UP.
GALACTIC PATROL HQ
FSH
BWUH?!

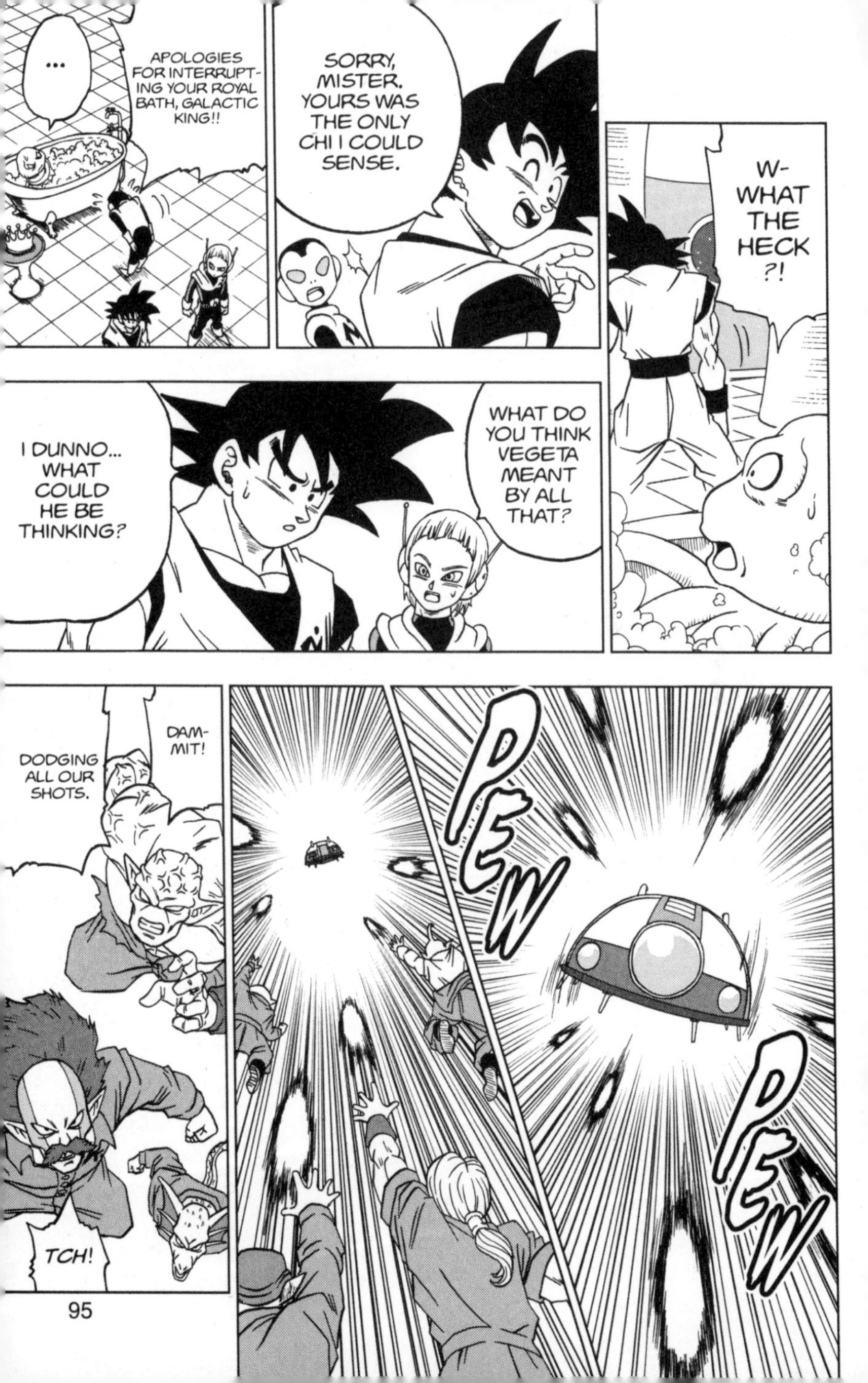

W-WHAT THE HECK?!
SORRY, MISTER. YOURS WAS THE ONLY CHI I COULD SENSE.
APOLOGIES FOR INTERRUPTING YOUR ROYAL BATH, GALACTIC KING!!
...
WHAT DO YOU THINK VEGETA MEANT BY ALL THAT?
I DUNNO... WHAT COULD HE BE THINKING?
PEW
PEW
DAM-MIT!
DODGING ALL OUR SHOTS.
TCH!

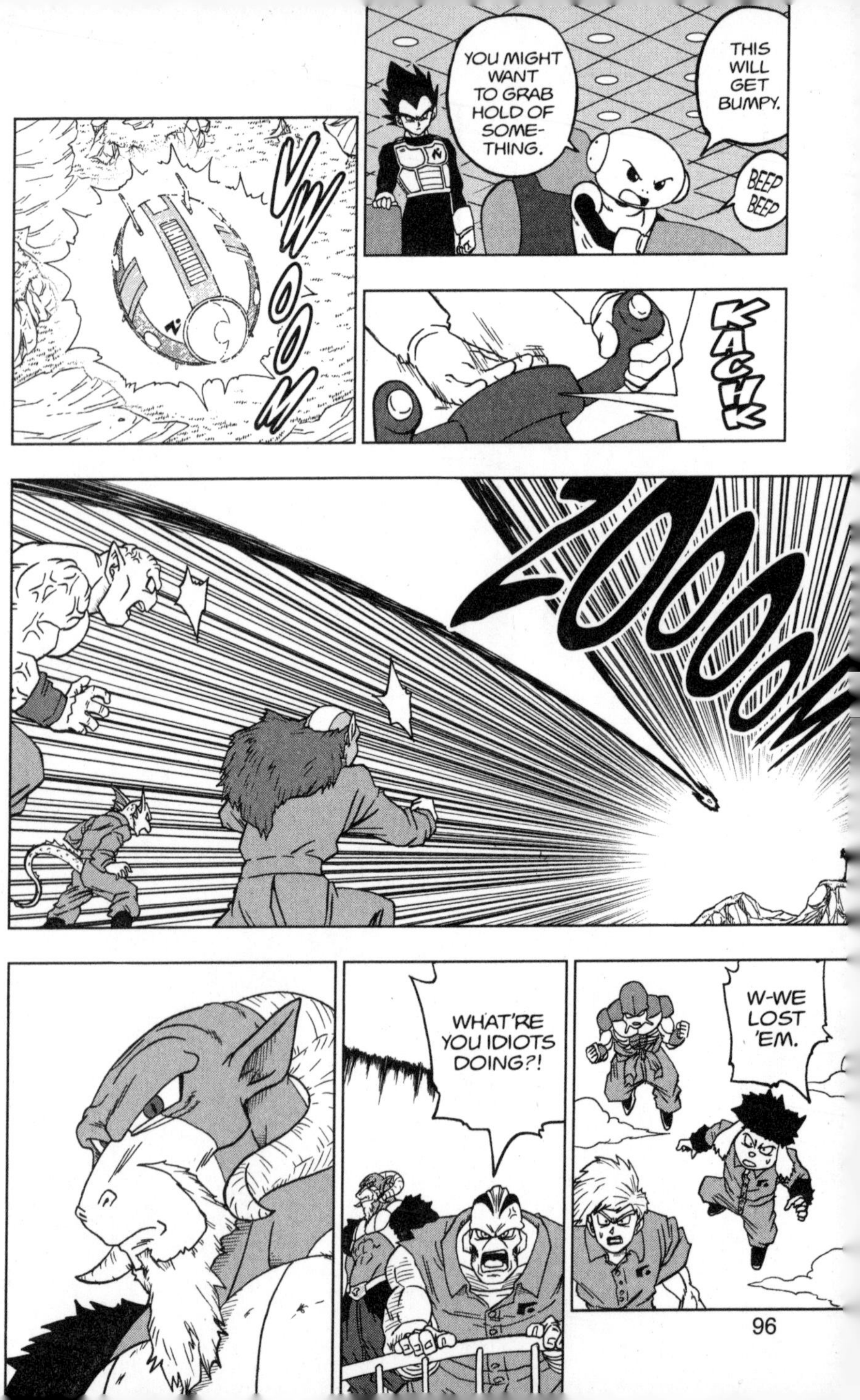
THIS WILL GET BUMPY.
BEEP BEEP
YOU MIGHT WANT TO GRAB HOLD OF SOME-THING.
KACHIK
VWOOOOM
ZOOOOM
W-WE LOST 'EM.
WHAT'RE YOU IDIOTS DOING?!

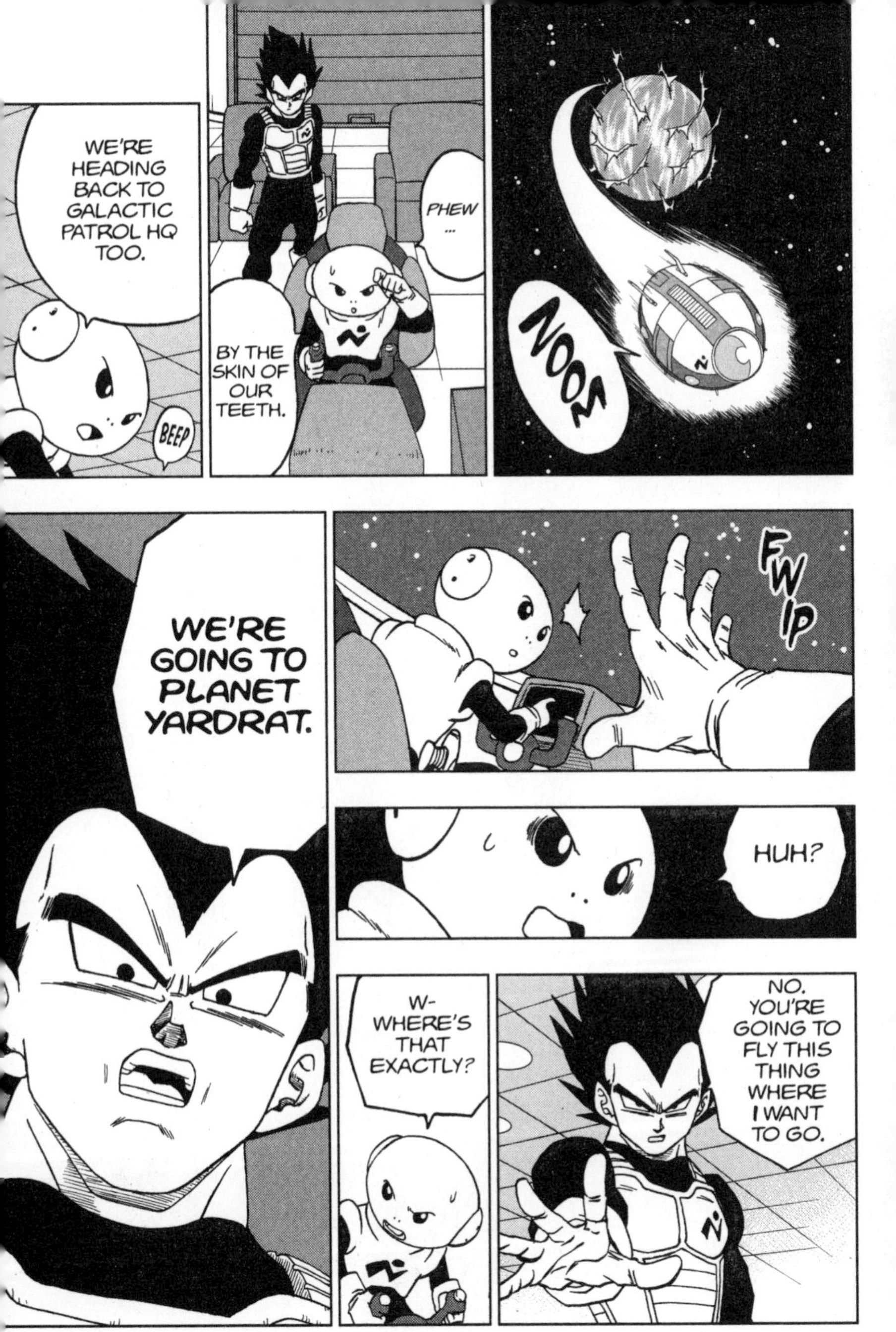
NOOM
PHEW ...
BY THE SKIN OF OUR TEETH.
WE'RE HEADING BACK TO GALACTIC PATROL HQ TOO.
BEEP
FWIP
HUH?
NO. YOU'RE GOING TO FLY THIS THING WHERE I WANT TO GO.
W- WHERE'S THAT EXACTLY?
WE'RE GOING TO PLANET YARDRAT.

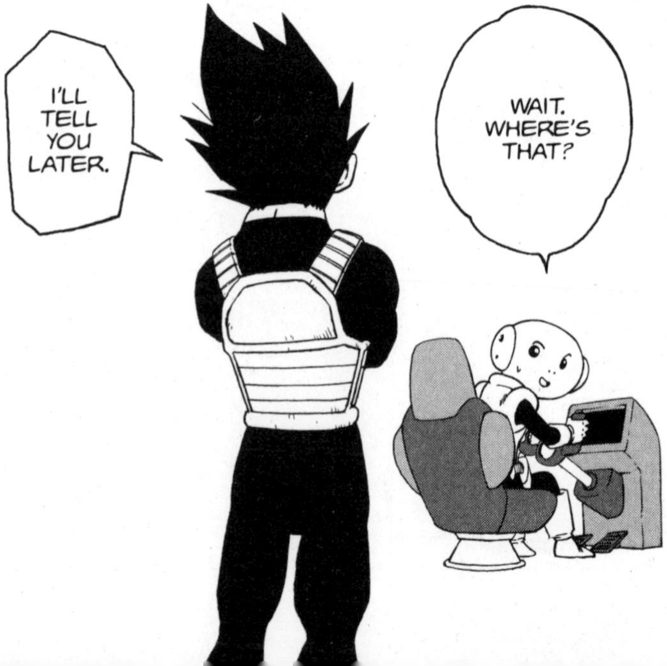
WAIT. WHERE'S THAT?
I'LL TELL YOU LATER.

CHAPTER 51: TO EACH THEIR OWN PLANS

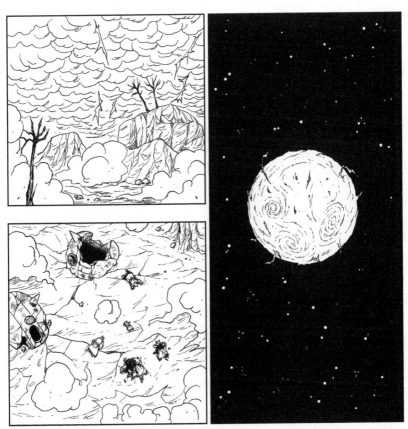

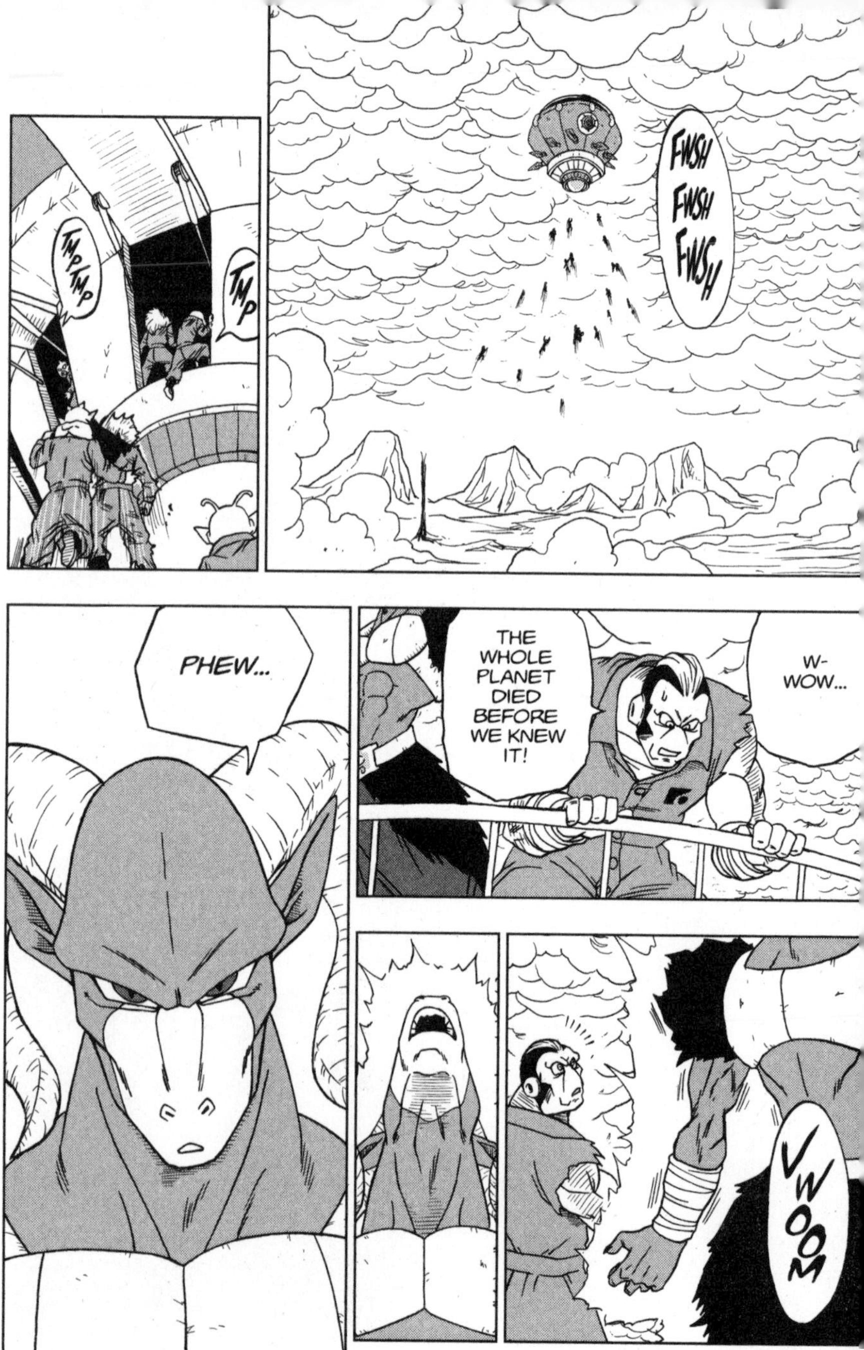
FWSH FWSH FWSH
TMP
TMPTMP
W-WOW...
THE WHOLE PLANET DIED BEFORE WE KNEW IT!
VWOOM
PHEW...

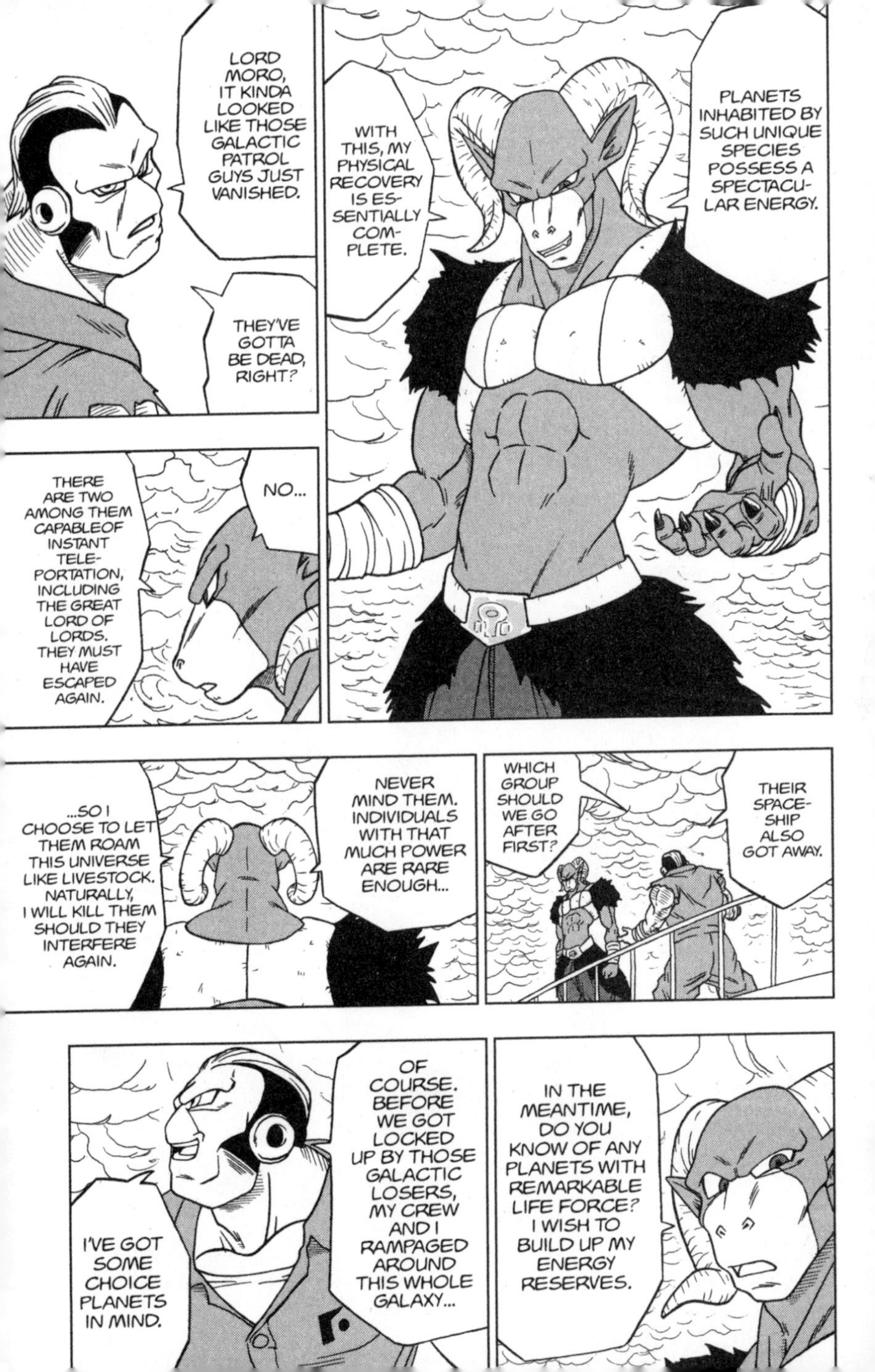
PLANETS INHABITED BY SUCH UNIQUE SPECIES POSSESS A SPECTACU-LAR ENERGY.
WITH THIS, MY PHYSICAL RECOVERY IS ES-SENTIALLY COM-PLETE.
LORD MORO, IT KINDA LOOKED LIKE THOSE GALACTIC PATROL GUYS JUST VANISHED.
THEY'VE GOTTA BE DEAD, RIGHT?
NO...
THERE ARE TWO AMONG THEM CAPABLEOF INSTANT TELE-PORTATION, INCLUDING THE GREAT LORD OF LORDS. THEY MUST HAVE ESCAPED AGAIN.
THEIR SPACE-SHIP ALSO GOT AWAY.
WHICH GROUP SHOULD WE GO AFTER FIRST?
NEVER MIND THEM. INDIVIDUALS WITH THAT MUCH POWER ARE RARE ENOUGH...
...SO I CHOOSE TO LET THEM ROAM THIS UNIVERSE LIKE LIVESTOCK. NATURALLY, I WILL KILL THEM SHOULD THEY INTERFERE AGAIN.
IN THE MEANTIME, DO YOU KNOW OF ANY PLANETS WITH REMARKABLE LIFE FORCE? I WISH TO BUILD UP MY ENERGY RESERVES.
OF COURSE. BEFORE WE GOT LOCKED UP BY THOSE GALACTIC LOSERS, MY CREW AND I RAMPAGED AROUND THIS WHOLE GALAXY...
I'VE GOT SOME CHOICE PLANETS IN MIND.

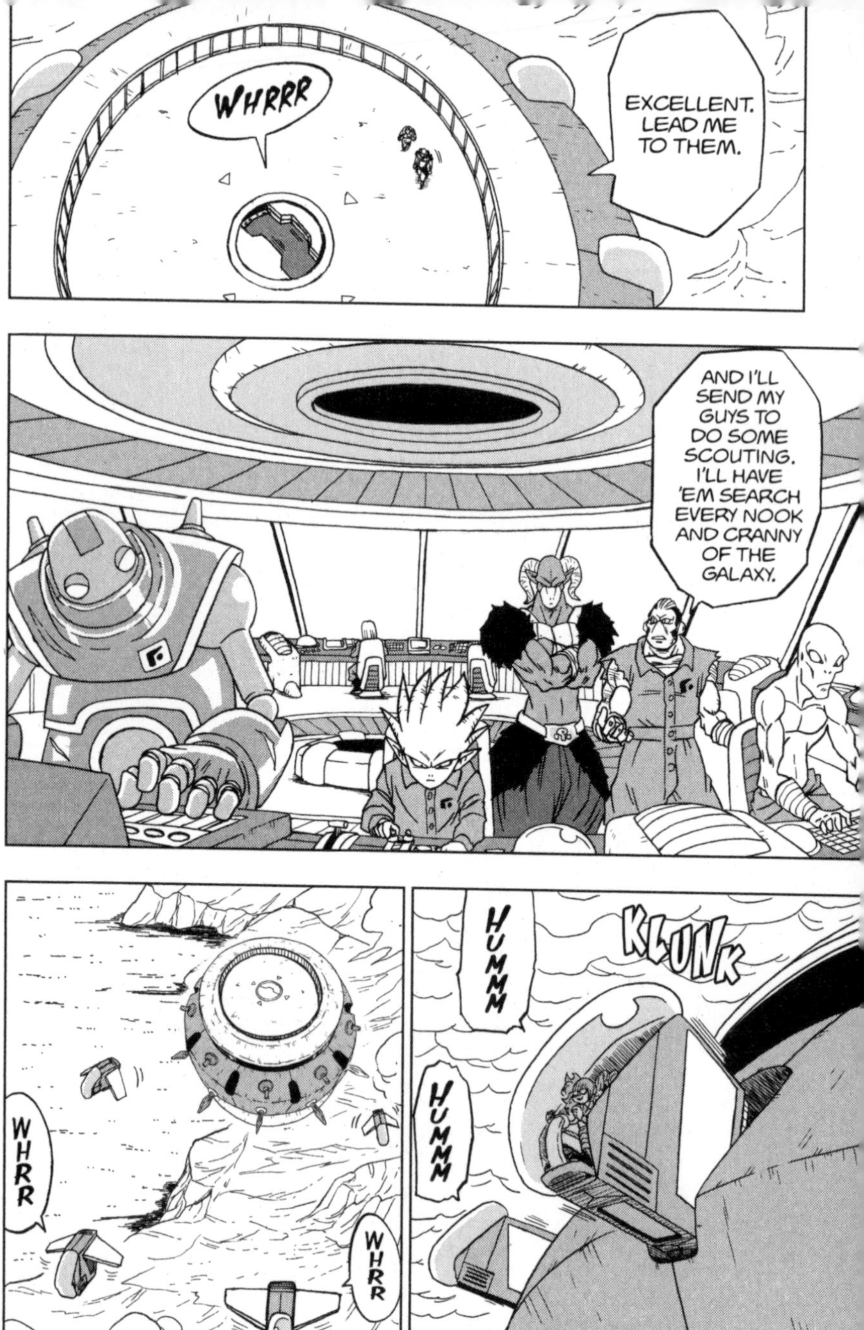
EXCELLENT. LEAD ME TO THEM.
WHRRR
AND I'LL SEND MY GUYS TO DO SOME SCOUTING. I'LL HAVE 'EM SEARCH EVERY NOOK AND CRANNY OF THE GALAXY.
KLUNK
HUMMM
HUMMM
WHRR
WHRR

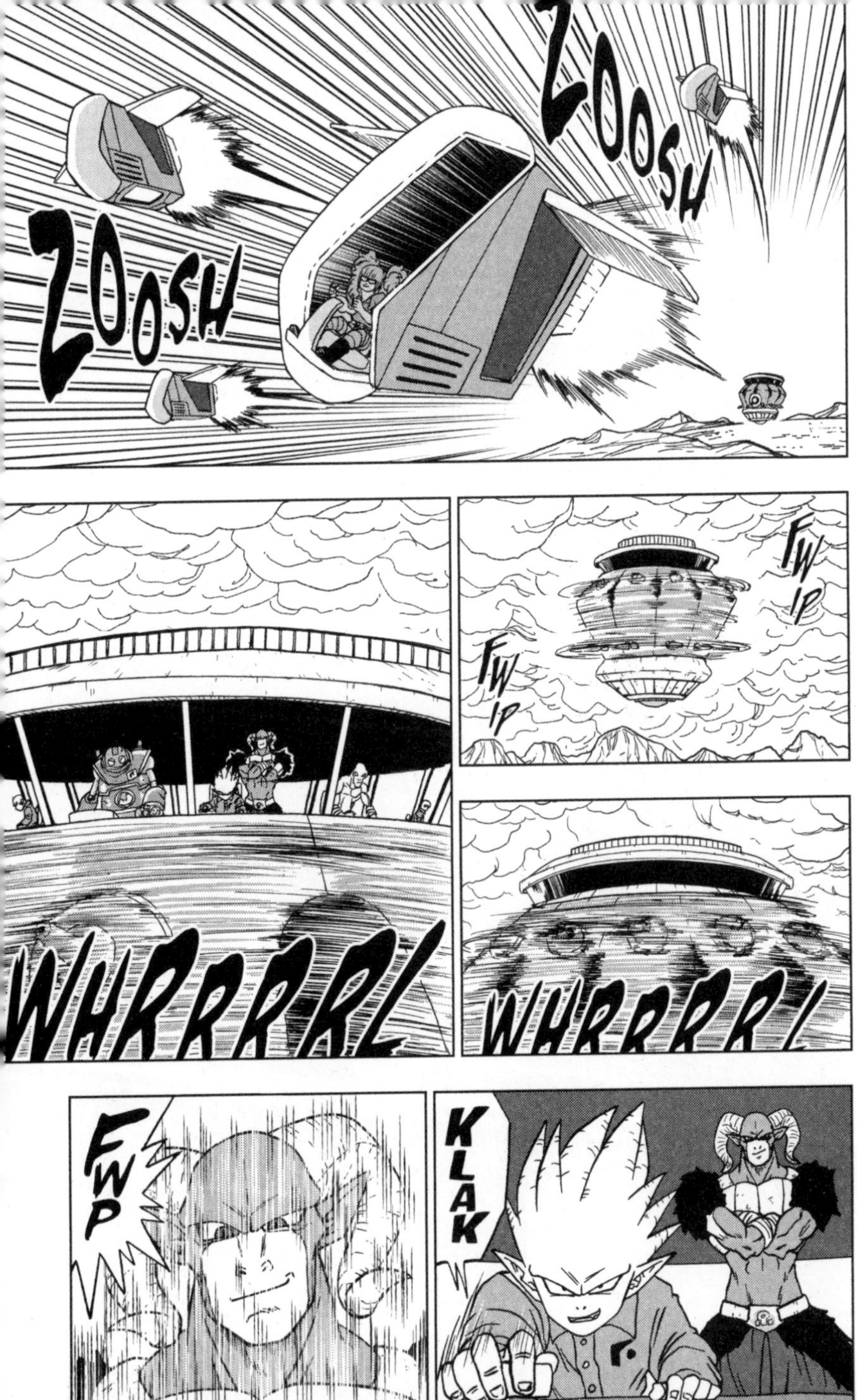
ZOOSH
ZOOSH
FWIP
FWIP
WHRRRRL
WHRRRRL
KLAK
FWP

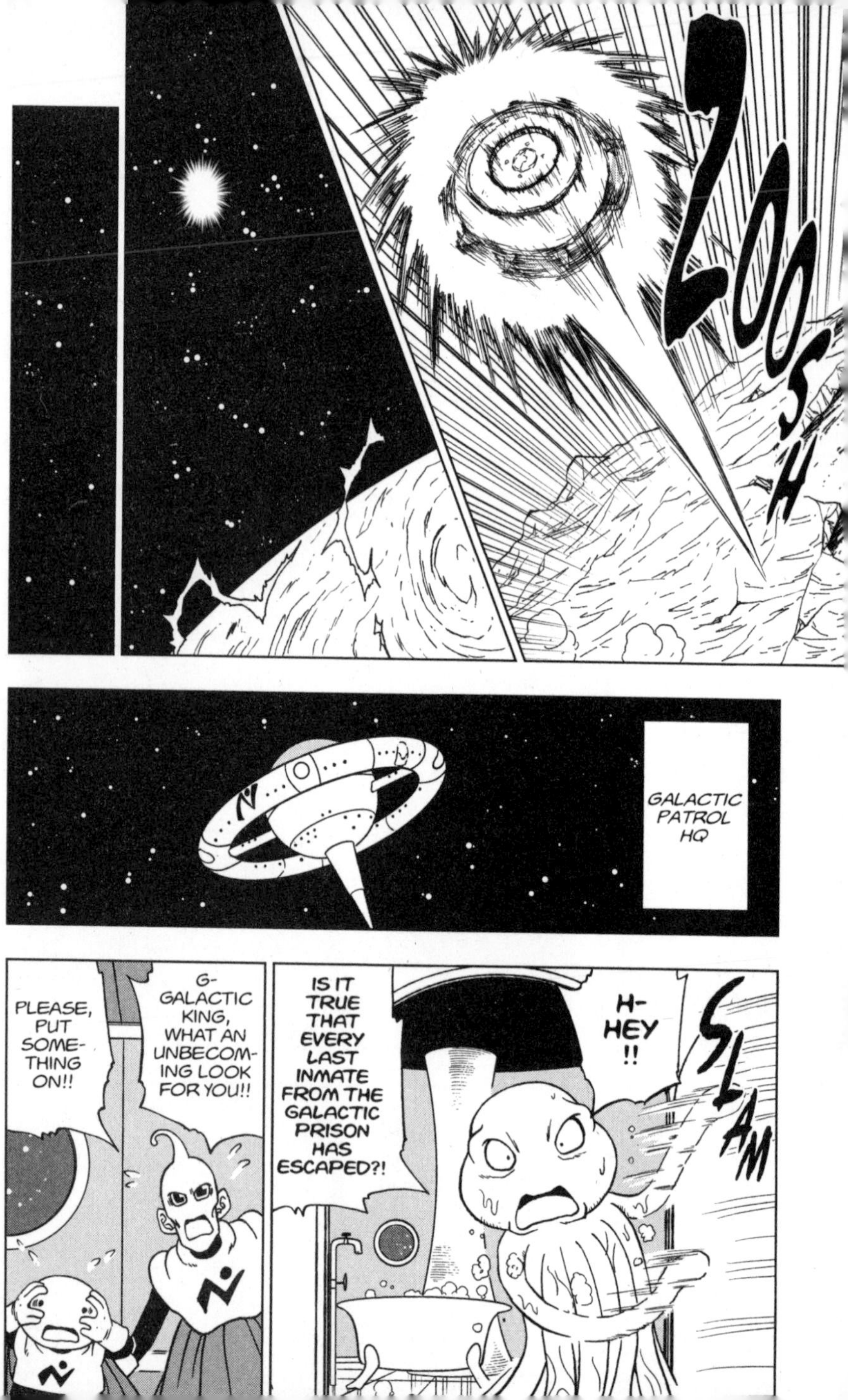
ZOOSH
GALACTIC PATROL HQ
SLAM
H-HEY!!
IS IT TRUE THAT EVERY LAST INMATE FROM THE GALACTIC PRISON HAS ESCAPED?!
G-GALACTIC KING, WHAT AN UNBECOMING LOOK FOR YOU!!
PLEASE, PUT SOMETHING ON!!

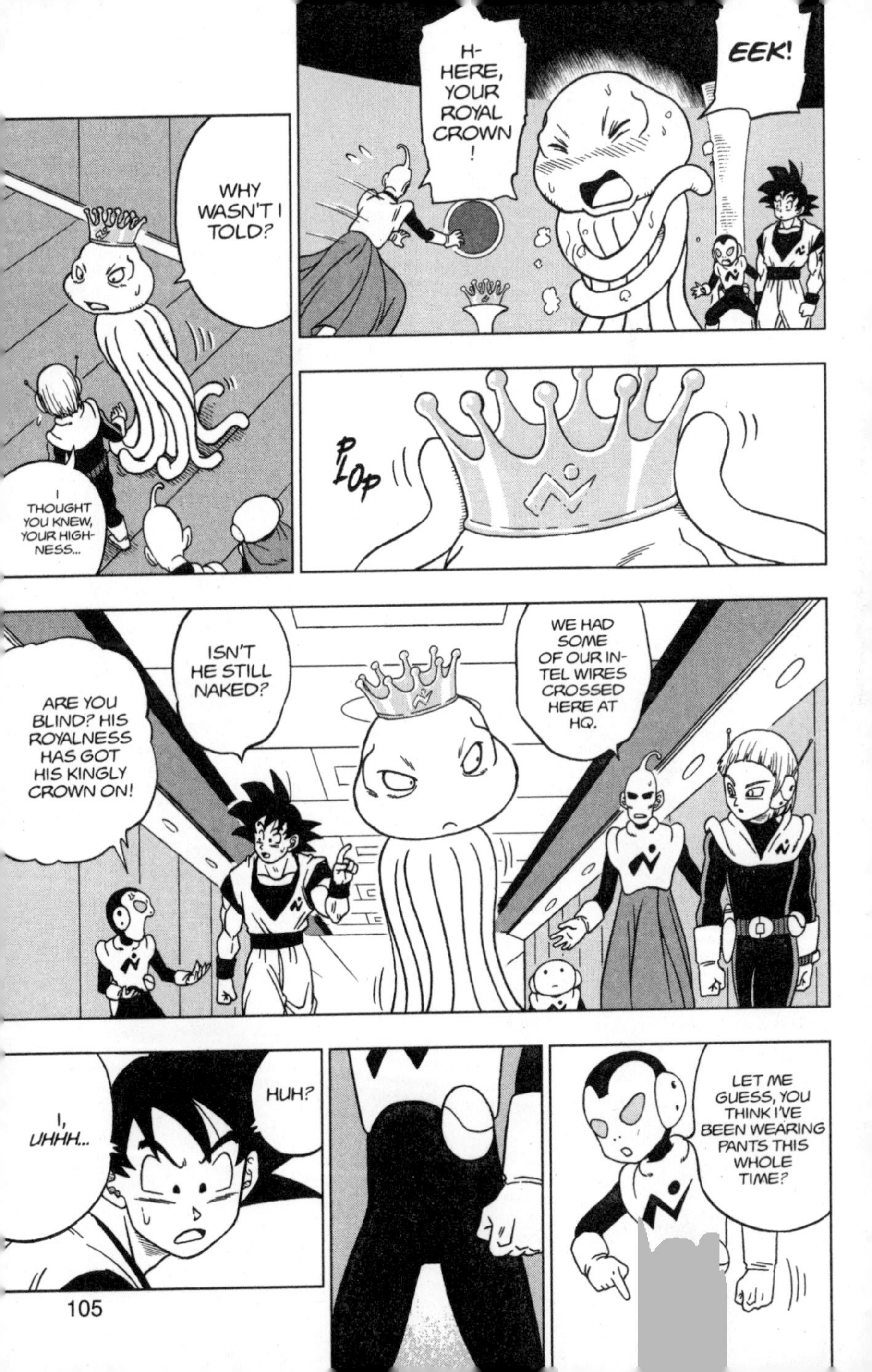
EEK!
H-HERE, YOUR ROYAL CROWN!
PLOP
WHY WASN'T I TOLD?
I THOUGHT YOU KNEW, YOUR HIGHNESS...
WE HAD SOME OF OUR IN-TEL WIRES CROSSED HERE AT HQ.
ISN'T HE STILL NAKED?
ARE YOU BLIND? HIS ROYALNESS HAS GOT HIS KINGLY CROWN ON!
LET ME GUESS, YOU THINK I'VE BEEN WEARING PANTS THIS WHOLE TIME?
HUH?
I, UHHH...

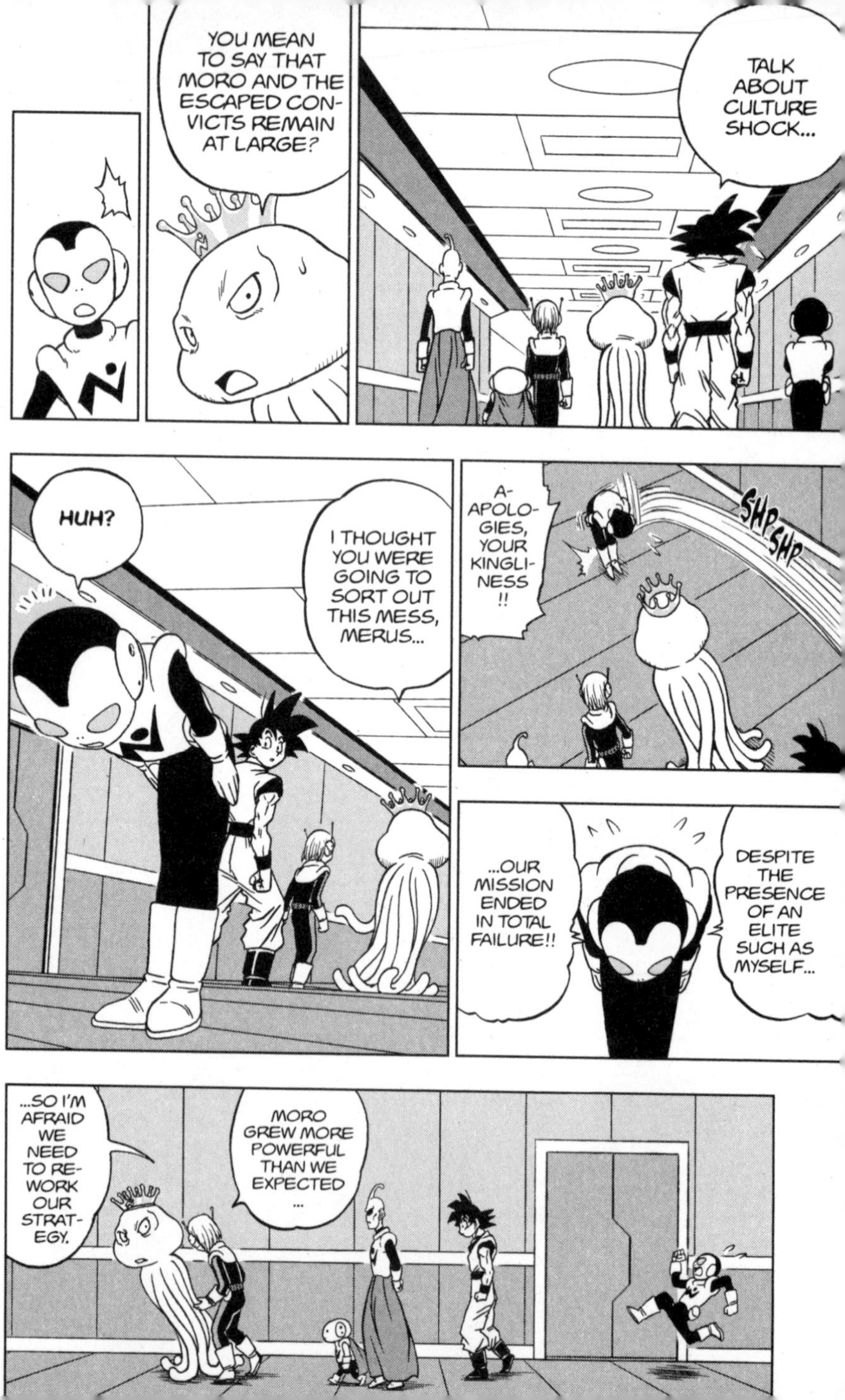
TALK ABOUT CULTURE SHOCK...
YOU MEAN TO SAY THAT MORO AND THE ESCAPED CONVICTS REMAIN AT LARGE?
SHP SHP
A-APOLOGIES, YOUR KINGLINESS!!
DESPITE THE PRESENCE OF AN ELITE SUCH AS MYSELF...
...OUR MISSION ENDED IN TOTAL FAILURE!!
I THOUGHT YOU WERE GOING TO SORT OUT THIS MESS, MERUS...
HUH?
MORO GREW MORE POWERFUL THAN WE EXPECTED...
...SO I'M AFRAID WE NEED TO REWORK OUR STRATEGY.

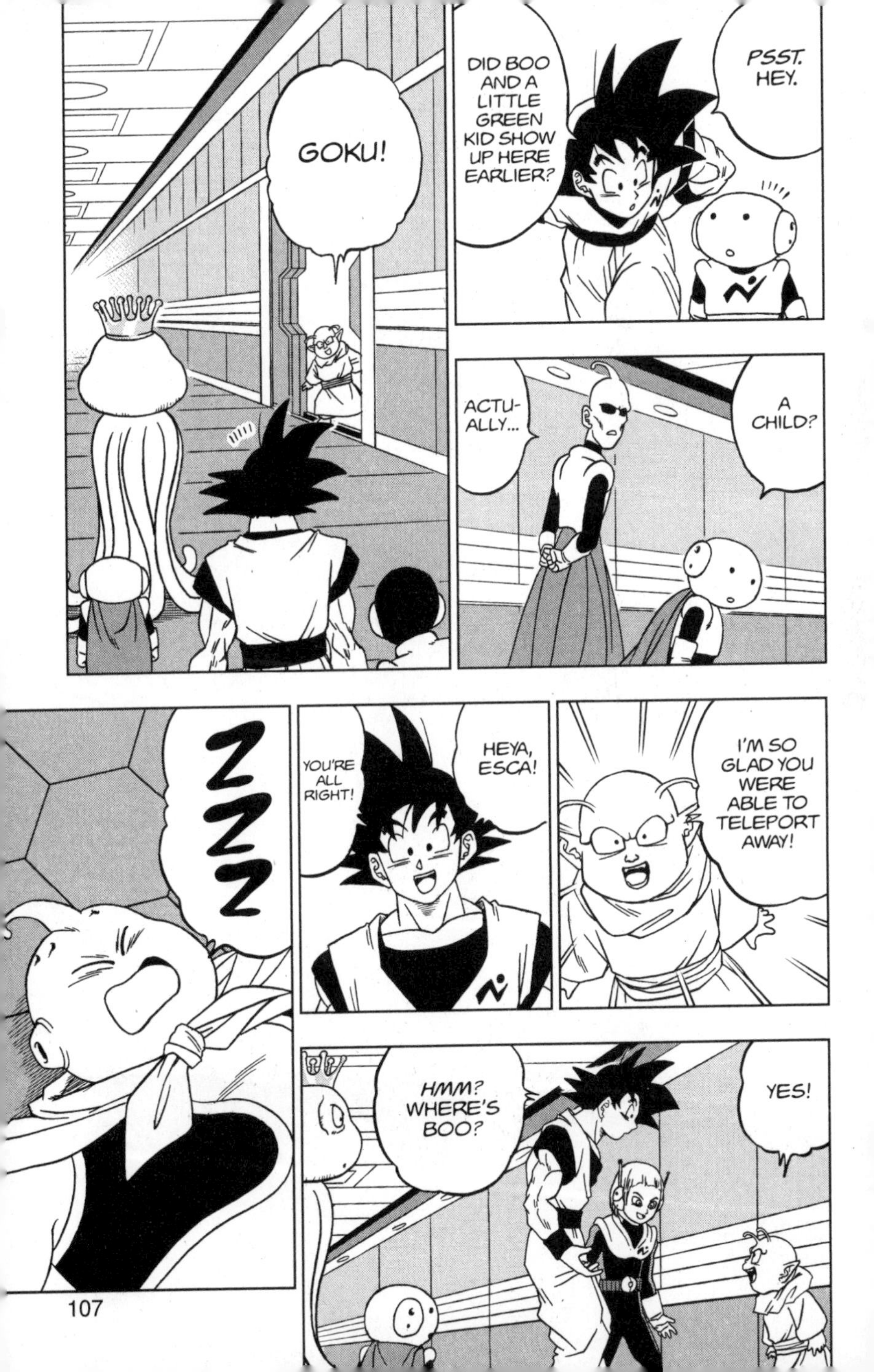
PSST. HEY.
DID BOO AND A LITTLE GREEN KID SHOW UP HERE EARLIER?
A CHILD?
ACTU-ALLY...
GOKU!
I'M SO GLAD YOU WERE ABLE TO TELEPORT AWAY!
HEYA, ESCA!
YOU'RE ALL RIGHT!
YES!
HMM? WHERE'S BOO?
ZZZ

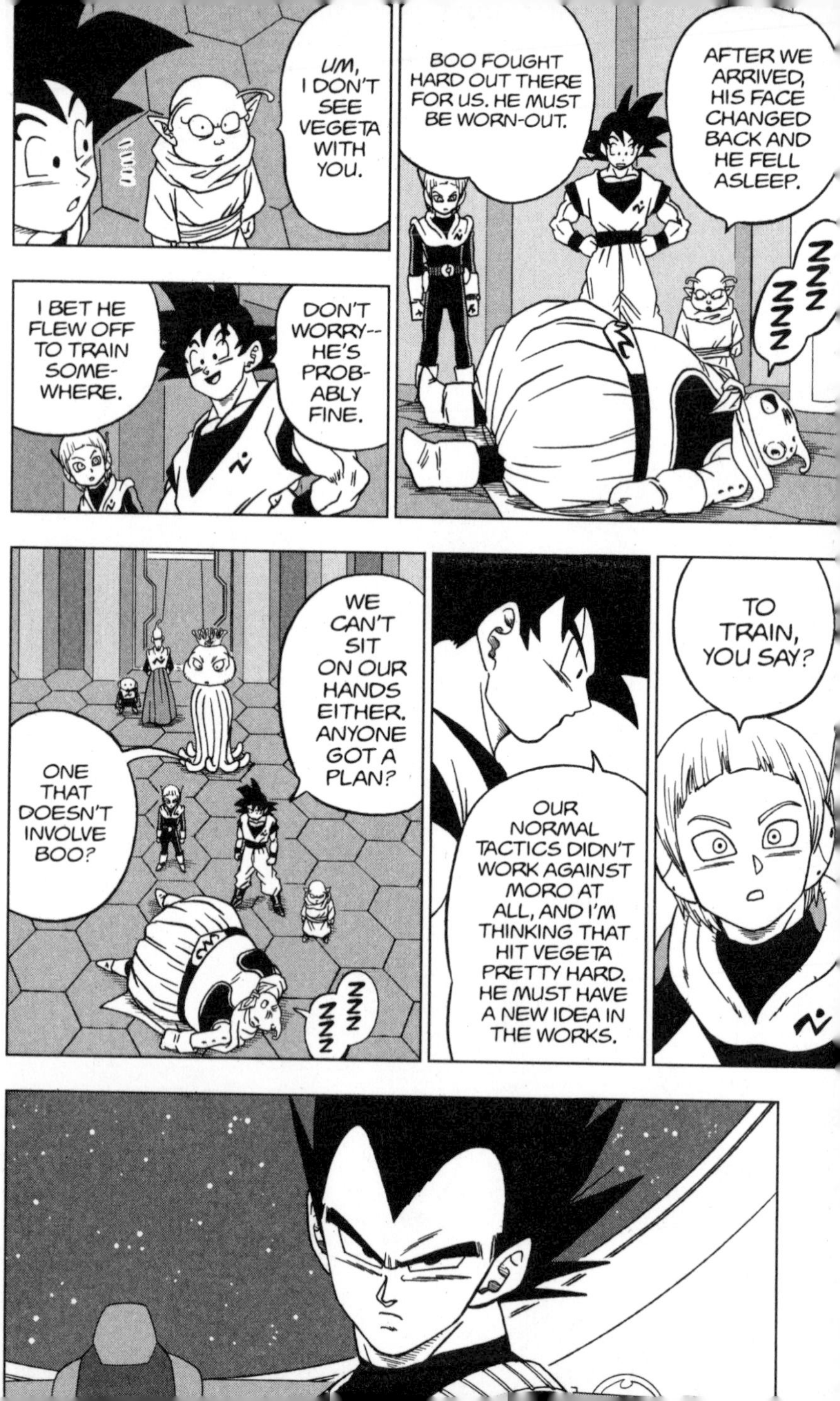
AFTER WE ARRIVED, HIS FACE CHANGED BACK AND HE FELL ASLEEP.
BOO FOUGHT HARD OUT THERE FOR US. HE MUST BE WORN-OUT.
ZZZ ZZZ
UM, I DON'T SEE VEGETA WITH YOU.
DON'T WORRY-- HE'S PROBABLY FINE.
I BET HE FLEW OFF TO TRAIN SOMEWHERE.
TO TRAIN, YOU SAY?
OUR NORMAL TACTICS DIDN'T WORK AGAINST MORO AT ALL, AND I'M THINKING THAT HIT VEGETA PRETTY HARD. HE MUST HAVE A NEW IDEA IN THE WORKS.
WE CAN'T SIT ON OUR HANDS EITHER. ANYONE GOT A PLAN?
ONE THAT DOESN'T INVOLVE BOO?
ZZZ ZZZ

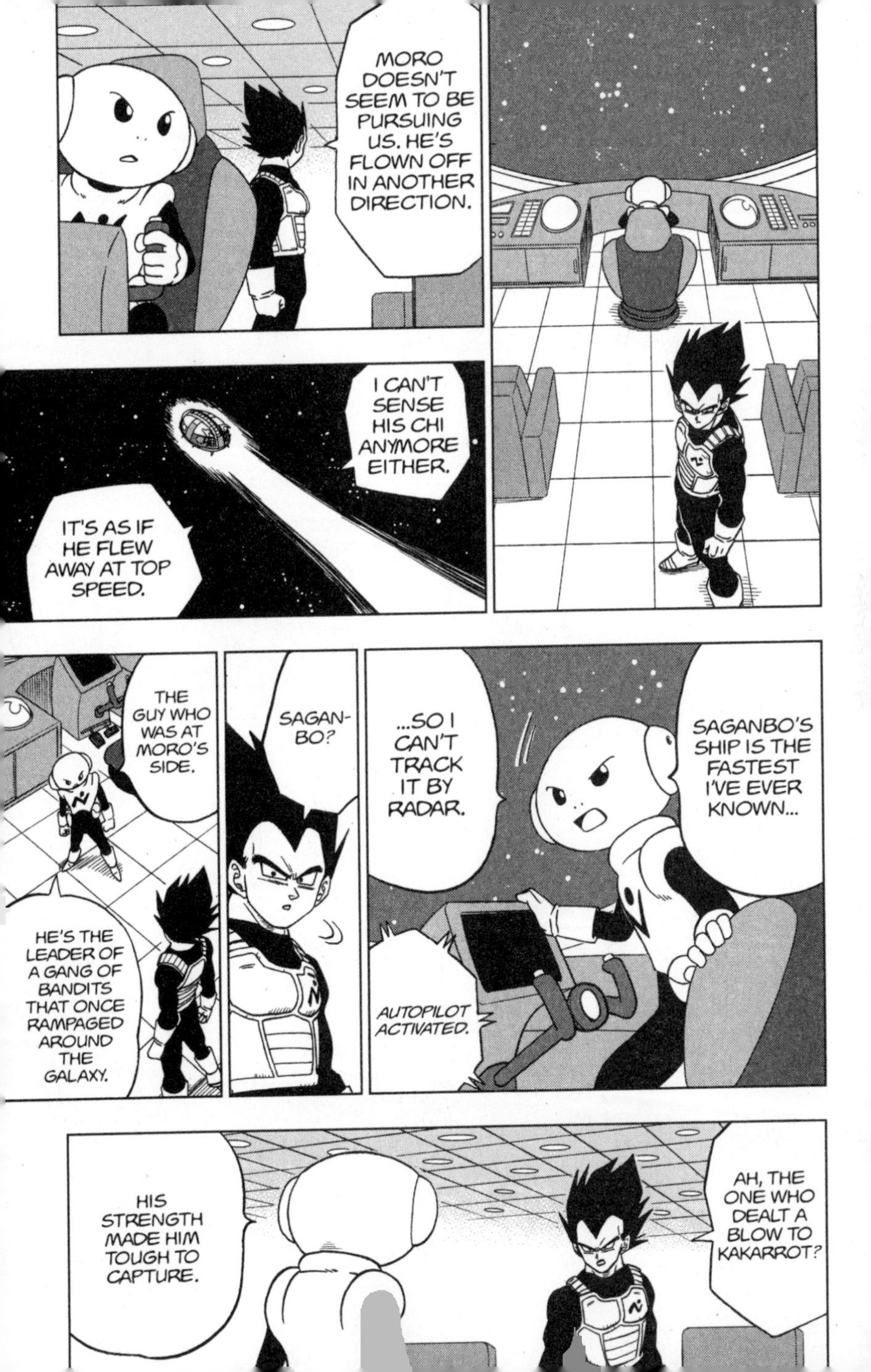
MORO DOESN'T SEEM TO BE PURSUING US. HE'S FLOWN OFF IN ANOTHER DIRECTION.
I CAN'T SENSE HIS CHI ANYMORE EITHER.
IT'S AS IF HE FLEW AWAY AT TOP SPEED.
SAGANBO'S SHIP IS THE FASTEST I'VE EVER KNOWN...
...SO I CAN'T TRACK IT BY RADAR.
AUTOPILOT ACTIVATED.
SAGAN-BO?
THE GUY WHO WAS AT MORO'S SIDE.
HE'S THE LEADER OF A GANG OF BANDITS THAT ONCE RAMPAGED AROUND THE GALAXY.
AH, THE ONE WHO DEALT A BLOW TO KAKARROT?
HIS STRENGTH MADE HIM TOUGH TO CAPTURE.

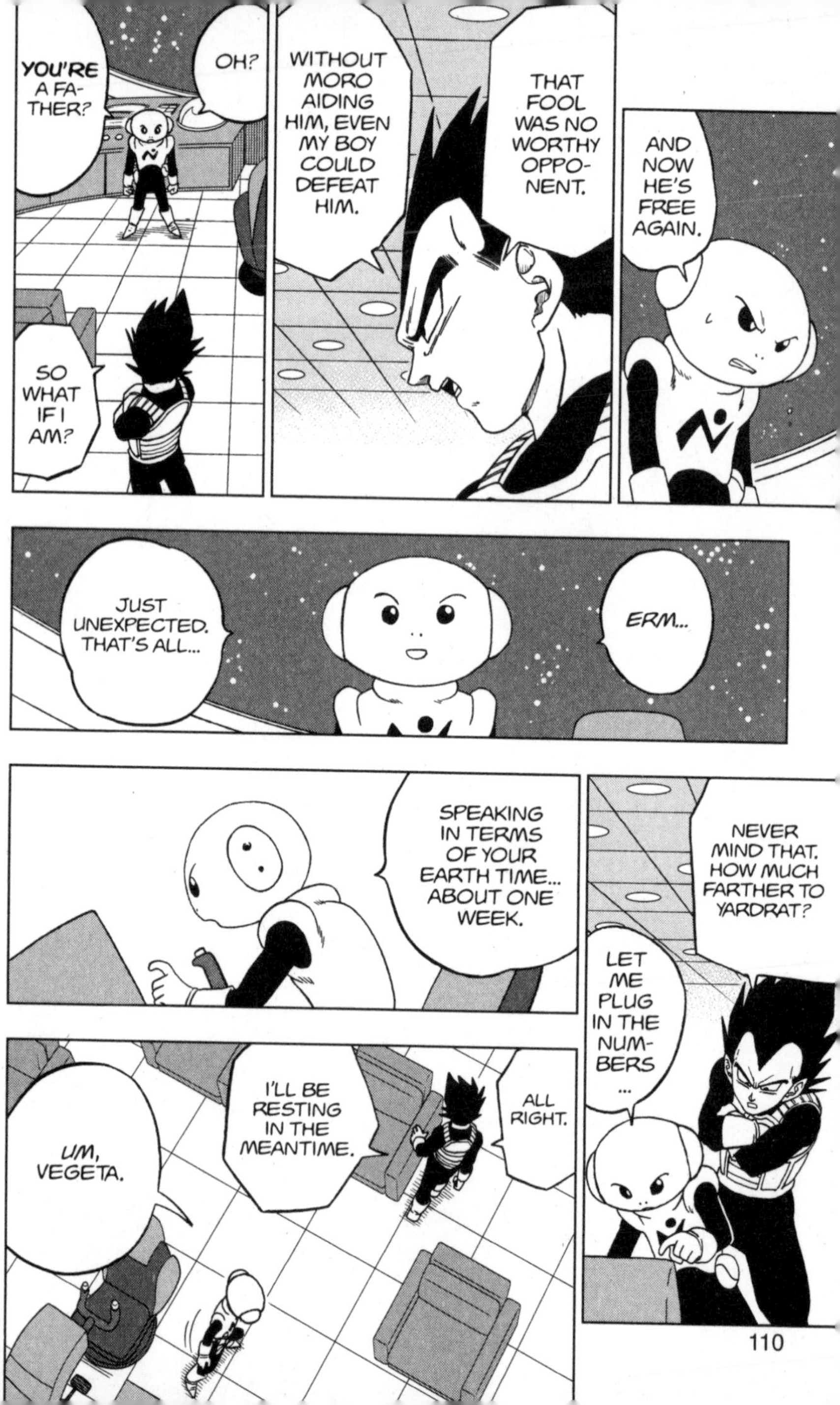
AND NOW HE'S FREE AGAIN.
THAT FOOL WAS NO WORTHY OPPONENT.
WITHOUT MORO AIDING HIM, EVEN MY BOY COULD DEFEAT HIM.
OH?
YOU'RE A FATHER?
SO WHAT IF I AM?
ERM...
JUST UNEXPECTED. THAT'S ALL...
NEVER MIND THAT. HOW MUCH FARTHER TO YARDRAT?
LET ME PLUG IN THE NUMBERS...
SPEAKING IN TERMS OF YOUR EARTH TIME... ABOUT ONE WEEK.
ALL RIGHT.
I'LL BE RESTING IN THE MEANTIME.
UM, VEGETA.

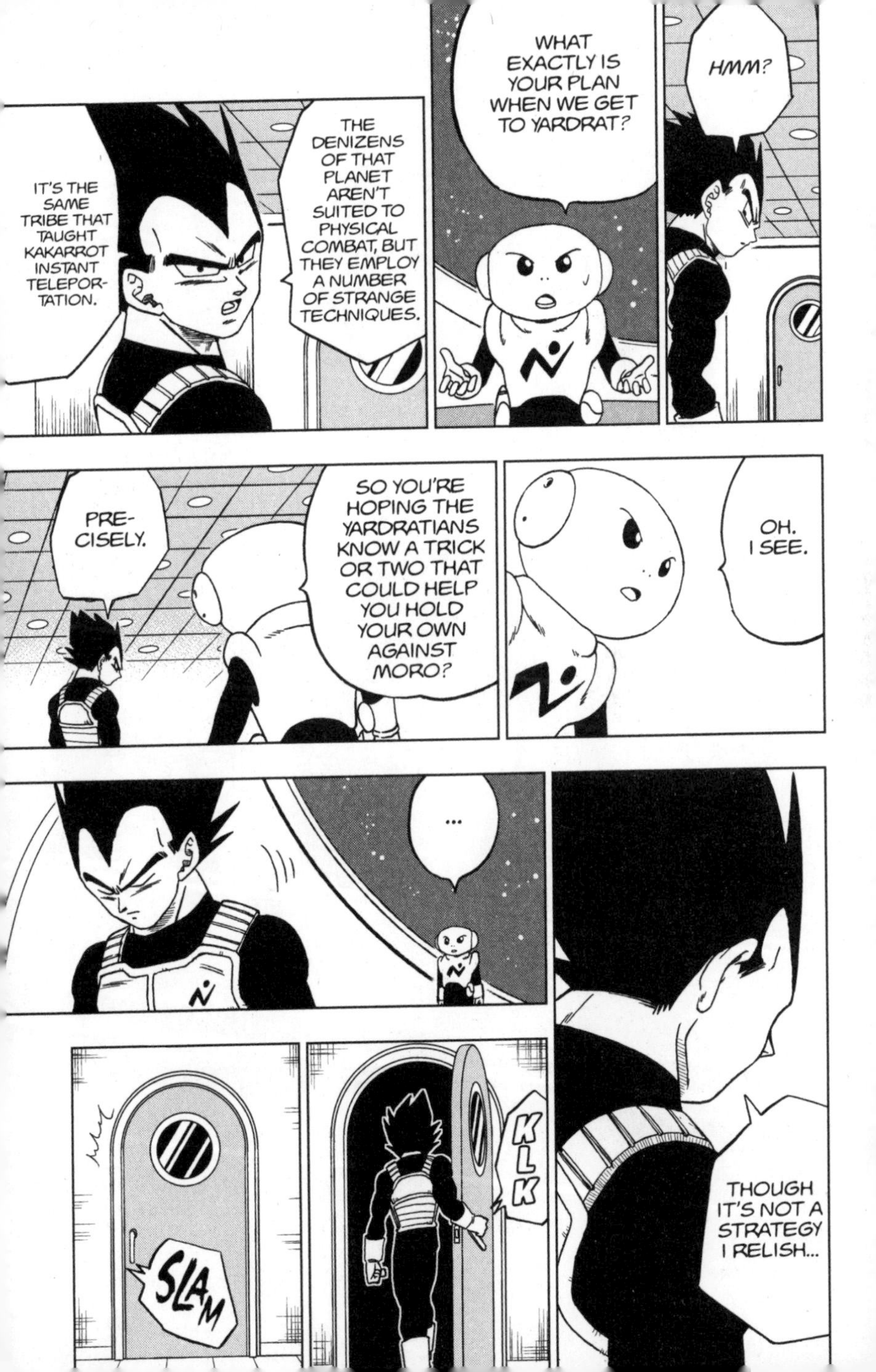
HMM?
WHAT EXACTLY IS YOUR PLAN WHEN WE GET TO YARDRAT?
THE DENIZENS OF THAT PLANET AREN'T SUITED TO PHYSICAL COMBAT, BUT THEY EMPLOY A NUMBER OF STRANGE TECHNIQUES.
IT'S THE SAME TRIBE THAT TAUGHT KAKARROT INSTANT TELEPOR-TATION.
OH. I SEE.
SO YOU'RE HOPING THE YARDRATIANS KNOW A TRICK OR TWO THAT COULD HELP YOU HOLD YOUR OWN AGAINST MORO?
PRE-CISELY.
THOUGH IT'S NOT A STRATEGY I RELISH...
...
KLK
SLAM

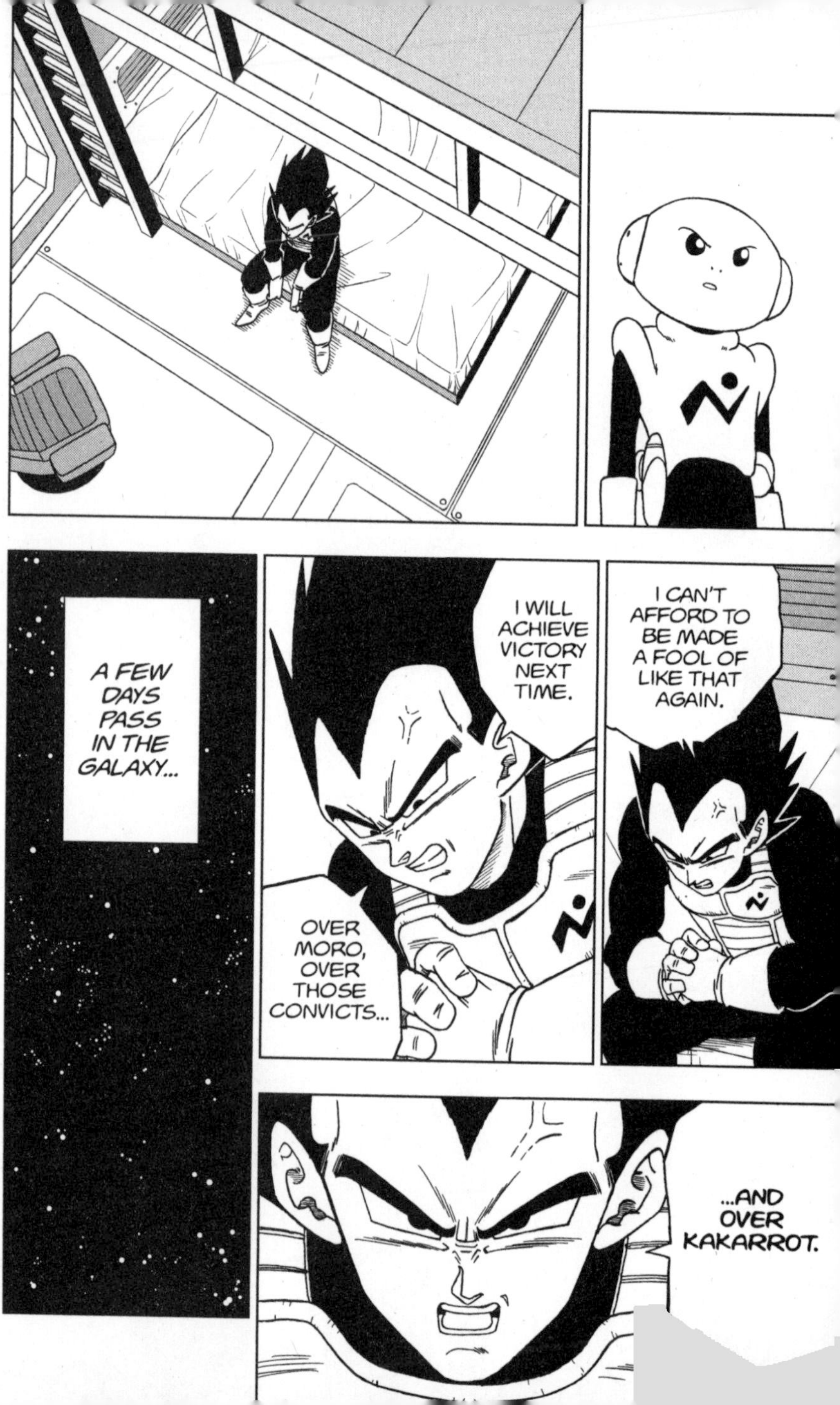
I CAN'T AFFORD TO BE MADE A FOOL OF LIKE THAT AGAIN.
I WILL ACHIEVE VICTORY NEXT TIME.
OVER MORO, OVER THOSE CONVICTS...
...AND OVER KAKARROT.
A FEW DAYS PASS IN THE GALAXY...

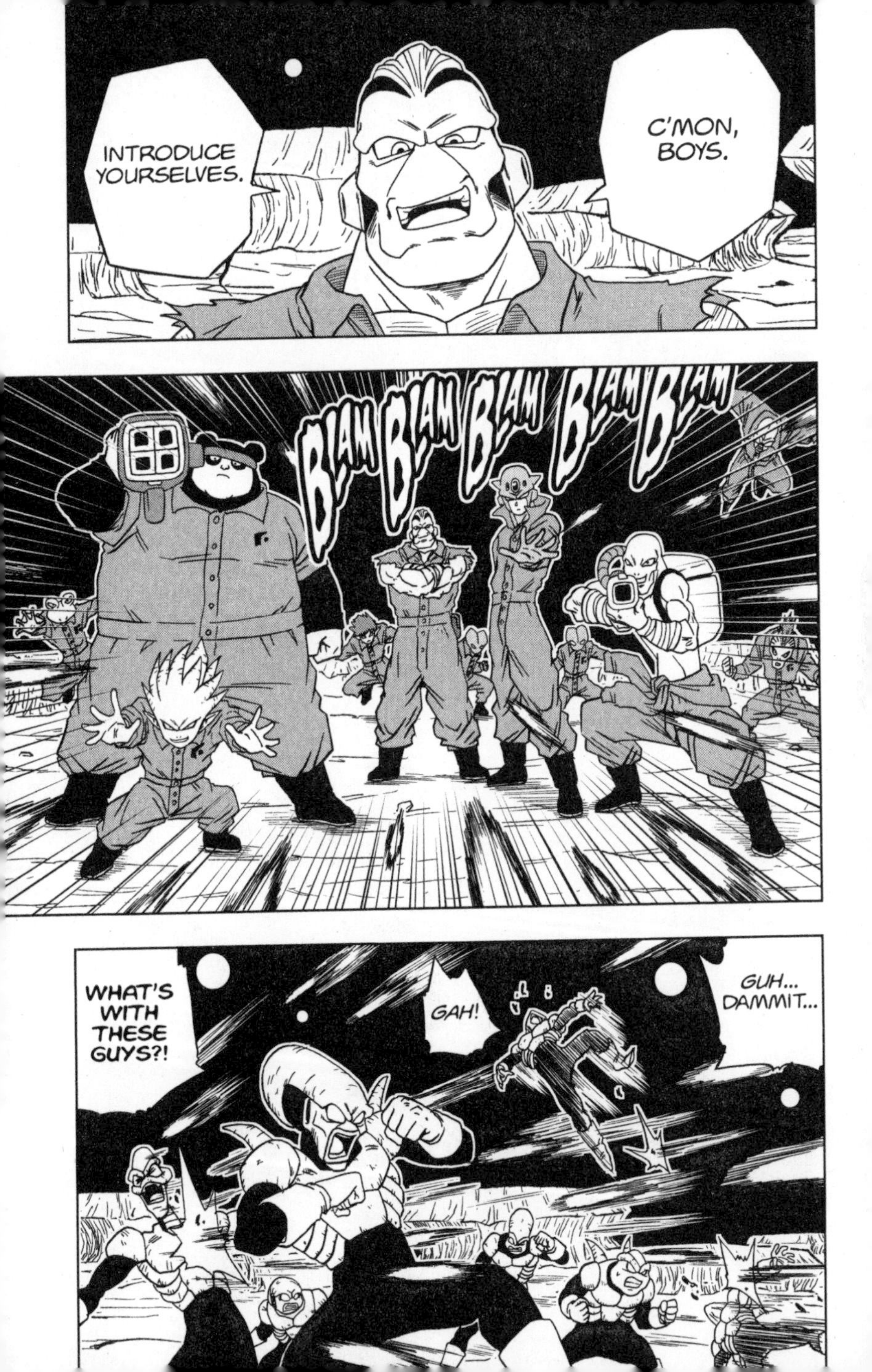
C'MON, BOYS.
INTRODUCE YOURSELVES.
BLAM BLAM BLAM BLAM BLAM
GUH... DAMMIT...
GAH!
WHAT'S WITH THESE GUYS?!

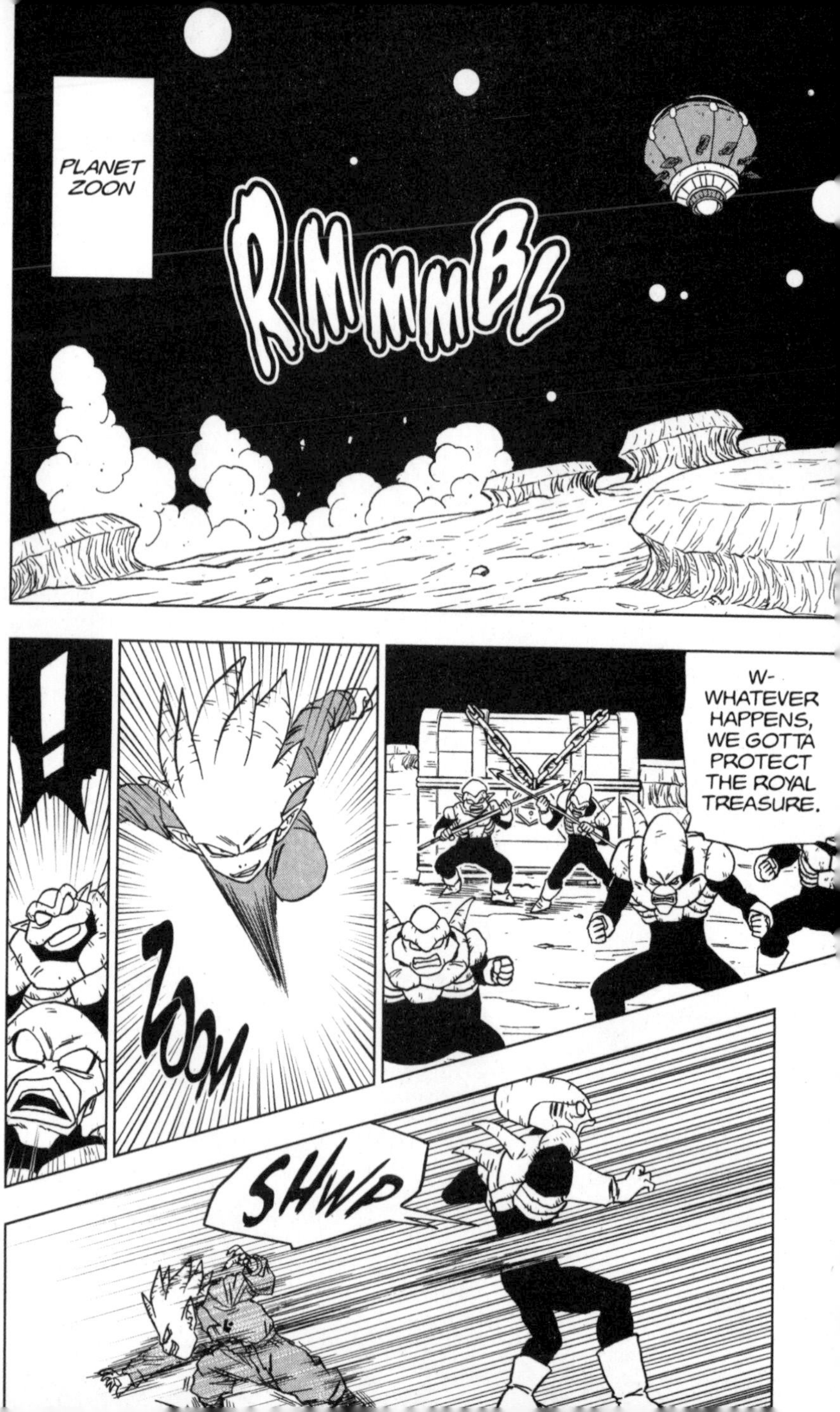
PLANET ZOON
RMMMBL
W-WHATEVER HAPPENS, WE GOTTA PROTECT THE ROYAL TREASURE.
ZOOM
!
SHWP

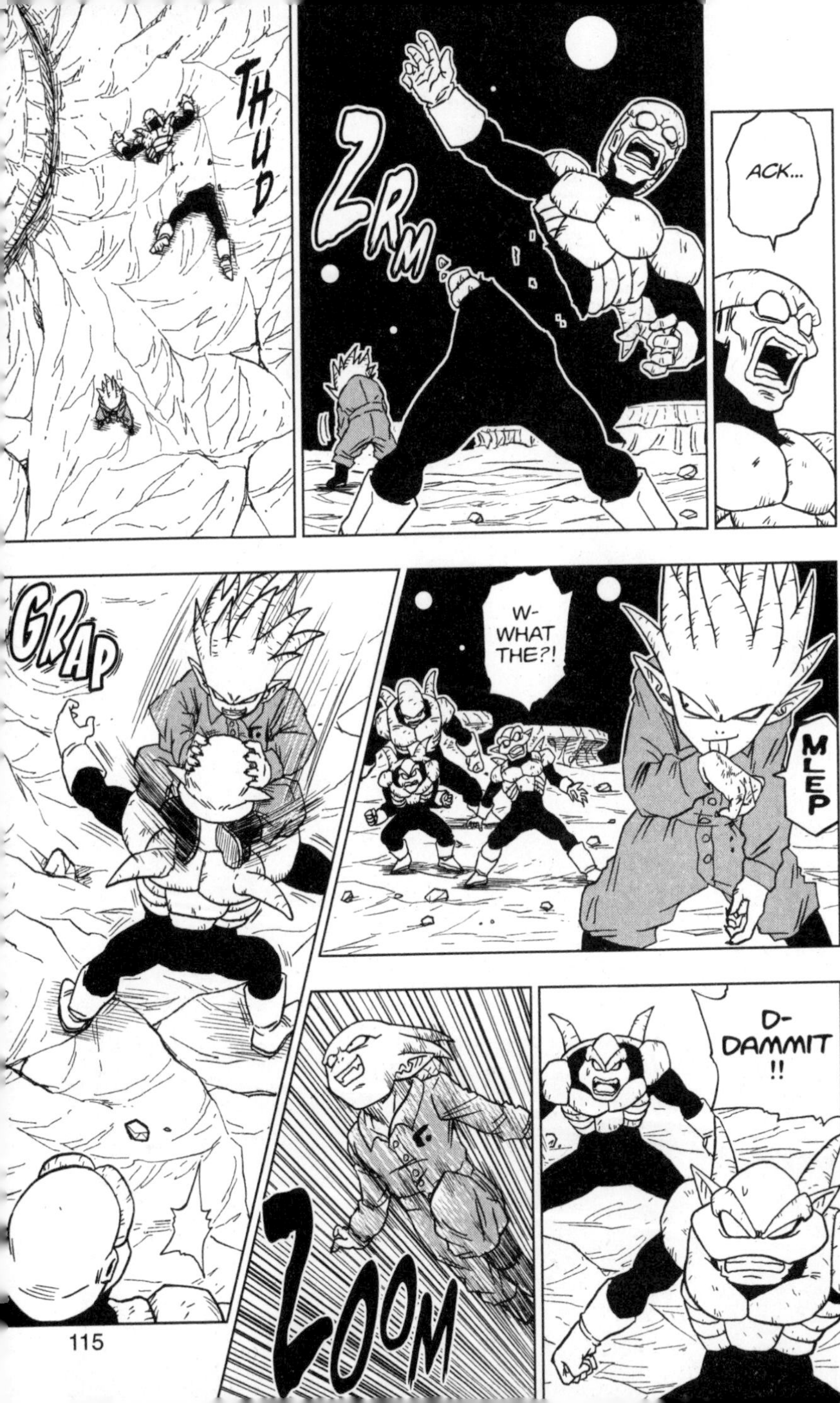
ACK...
ZRM
THUD
MLEP
W- WHAT THE?!
GRAP
D- DAMMIT !!
ZOOM

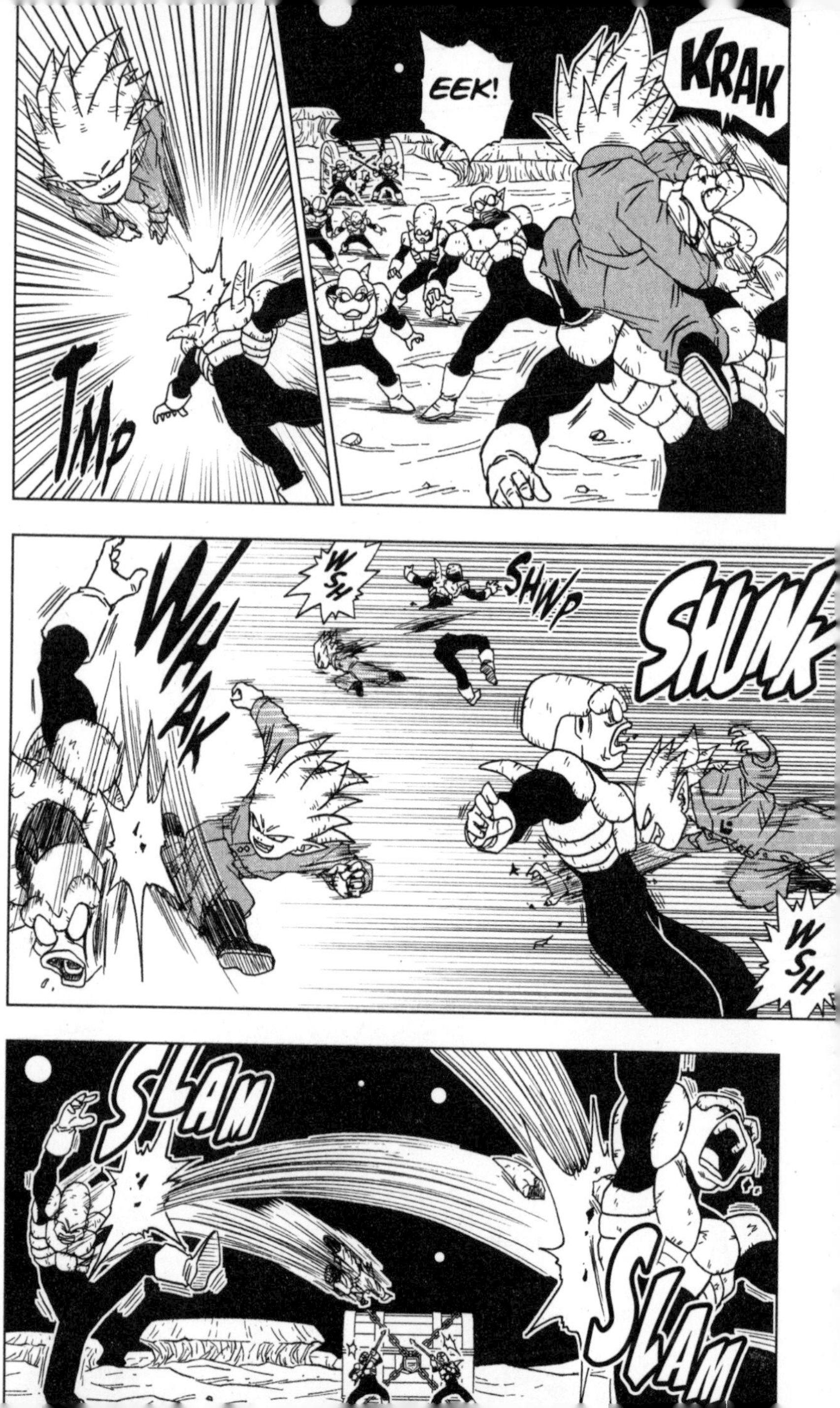
EEK!
KRAK
TMP
SHUNK
WSH
SHWP
WSH
WHAAK
SLAM
SLAM

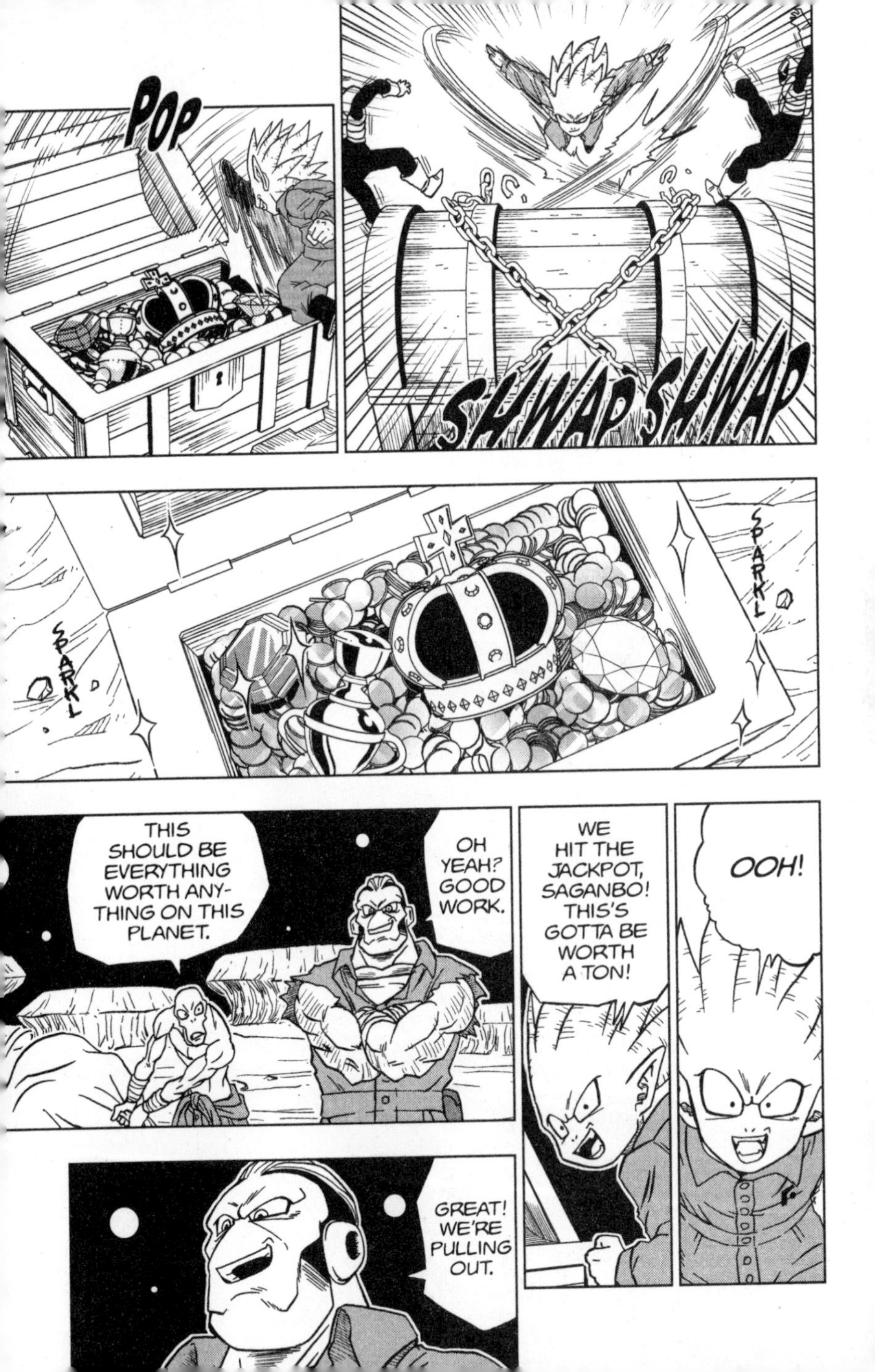
SHWAP SHWAP
POP
SPARKL
SPARKL
OOH!
WE HIT THE JACKPOT, SAGANBO! THIS'S GOTTA BE WORTH A TON!
THIS SHOULD BE EVERYTHING WORTH ANY-THING ON THIS PLANET.
OH YEAH? GOOD WORK.
GREAT! WE'RE PULLING OUT.

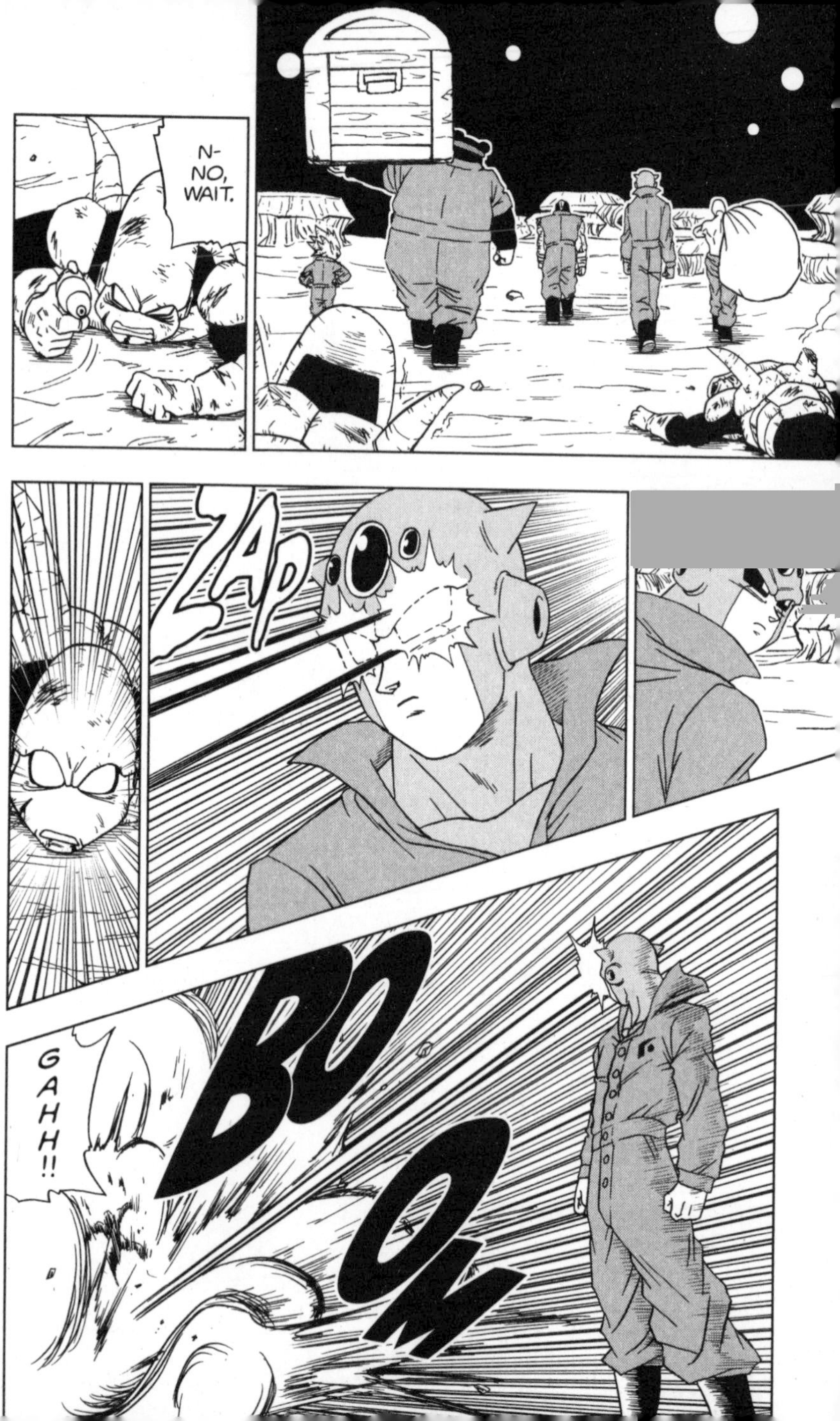
N- NO, WAIT.
ZAP
BOOOM
GAHH!!

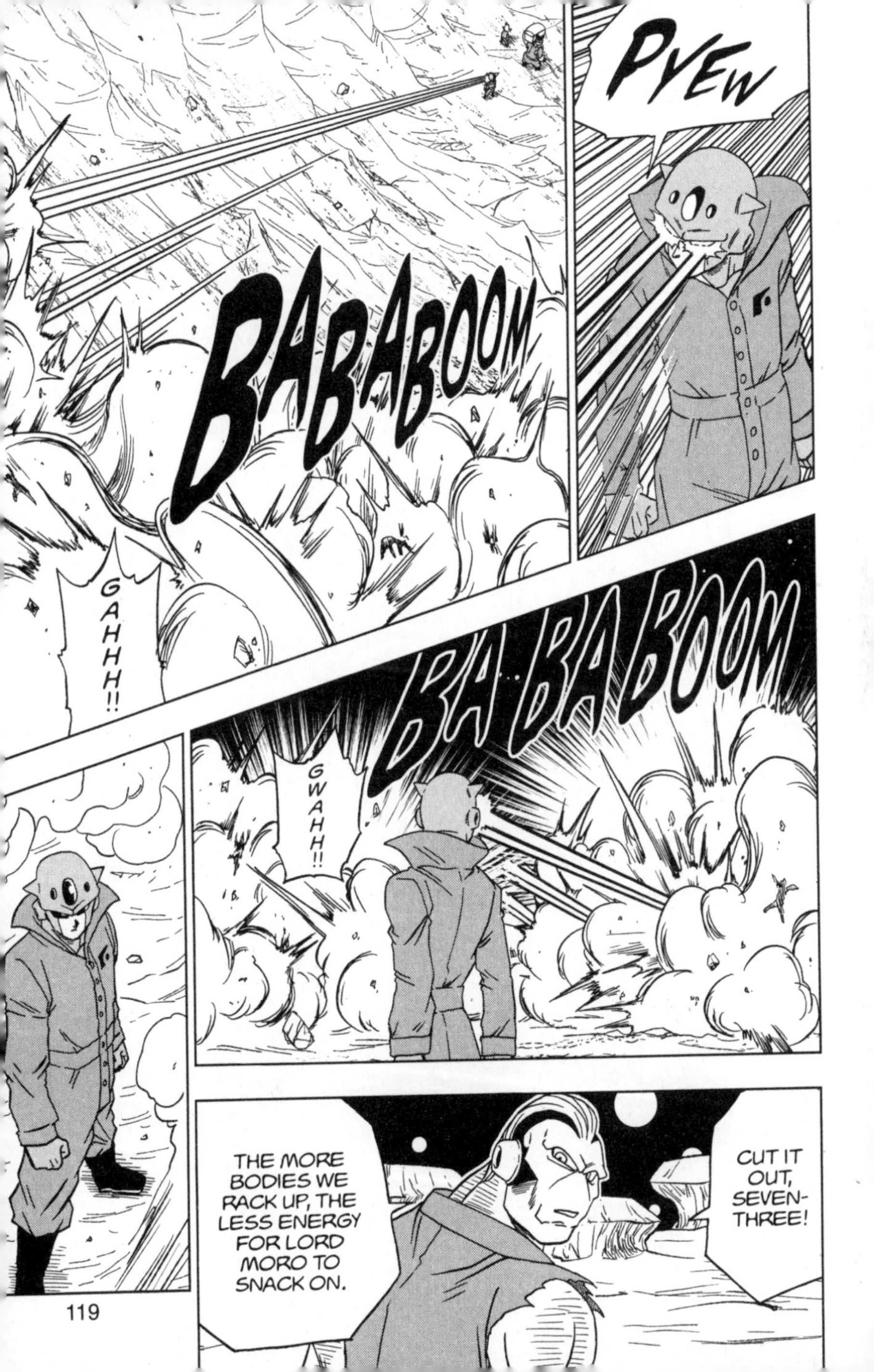
PYEW
BABABOOM
GAHHH!!
BA BA BOOM
GWAHH!!
CUT IT OUT, SEVEN-THREE!
THE MORE BODIES WE RACK UP, THE LESS ENERGY FOR LORD MORO TO SNACK ON.

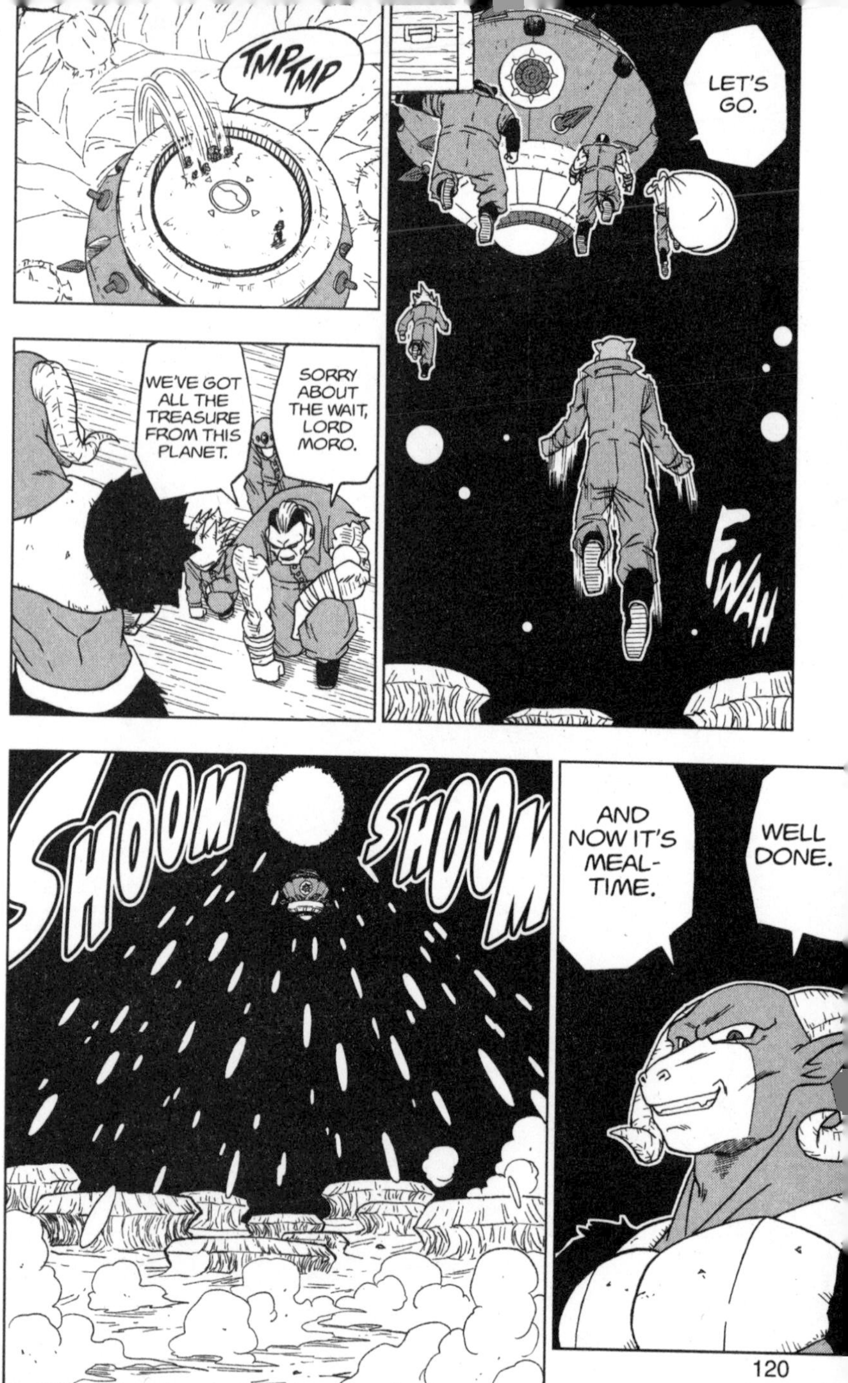
LET'S GO.
FWAH
TMP TMP
SORRY ABOUT THE WAIT, LORD MORO.
WE'VE GOT ALL THE TREASURE FROM THIS PLANET.
WELL DONE.
AND NOW IT'S MEAL-TIME.
SHOOM
SHOOM

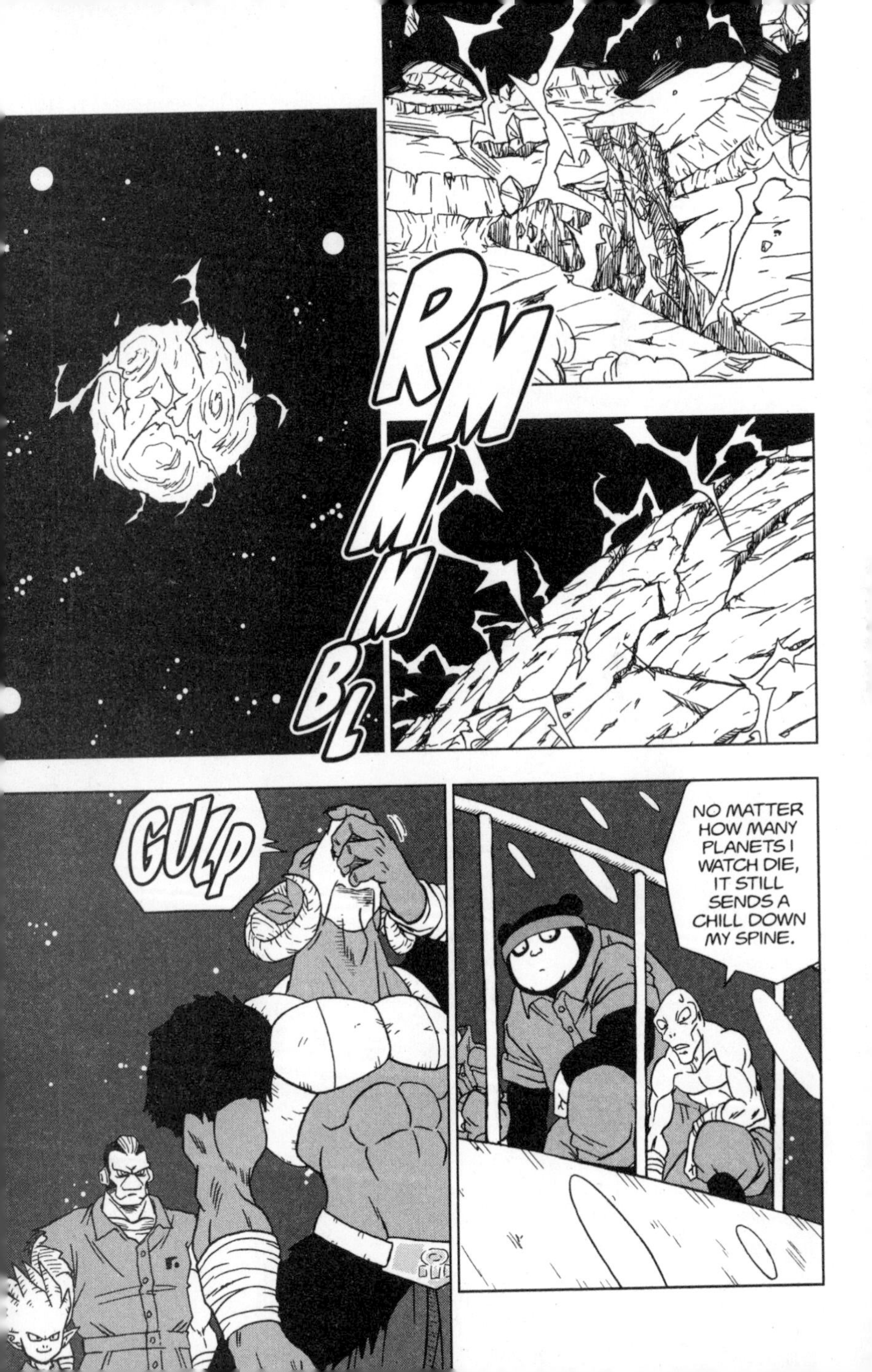
RMMMMBL
NO MATTER HOW MANY PLANETS I WATCH DIE, IT STILL SENDS A CHILL DOWN MY SPINE.
GULP

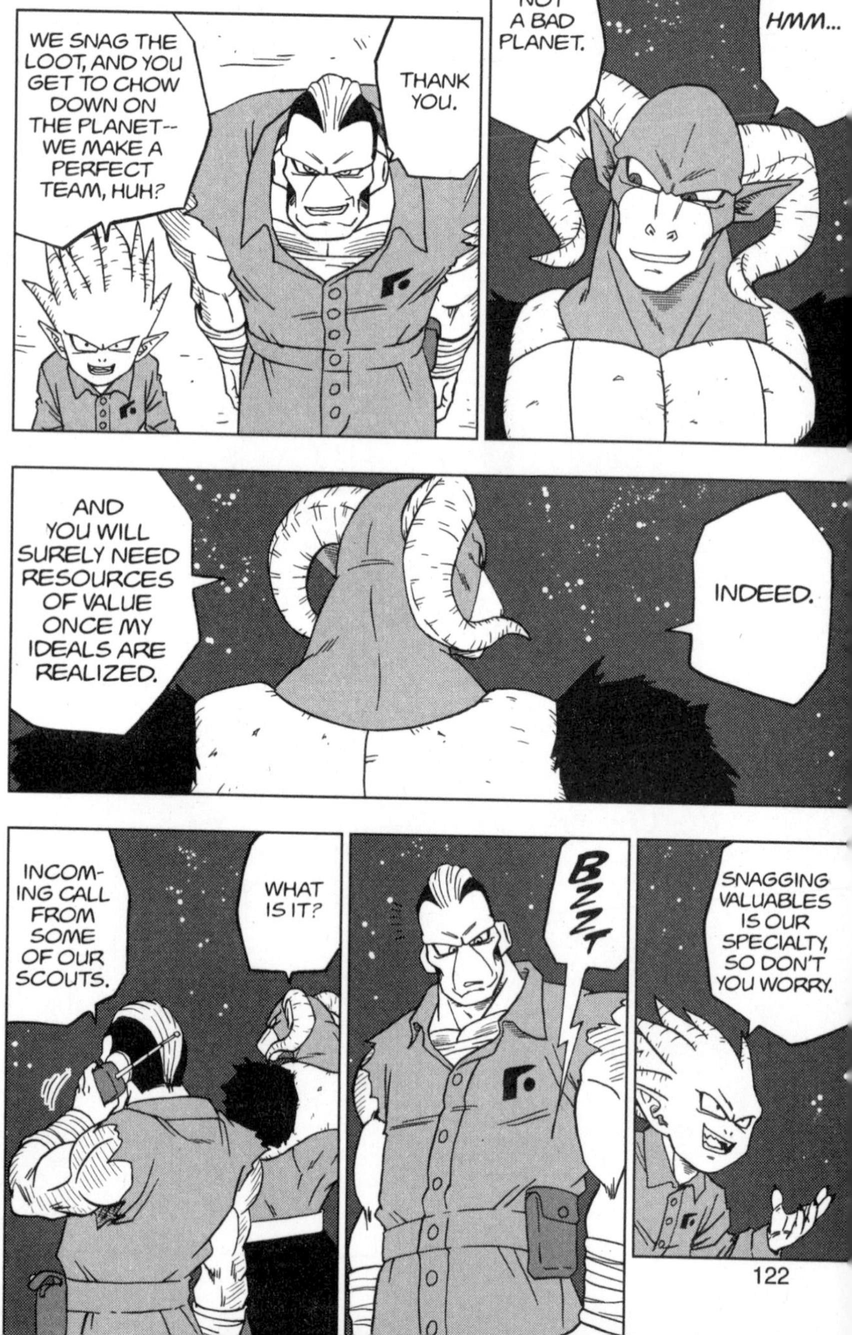
HMM...
NOT A BAD PLANET.
THANK YOU.
WE SNAG THE LOOT, AND YOU GET TO CHOW DOWN ON THE PLANET-- WE MAKE A PERFECT TEAM, HUH?
INDEED.
AND YOU WILL SURELY NEED RESOURCES OF VALUE ONCE MY IDEALS ARE REALIZED.
SNAGGING VALUABLES IS OUR SPECIALTY, SO DON'T YOU WORRY.
BZZZT
WHAT IS IT?
INCOMING CALL FROM SOME OF OUR SCOUTS.

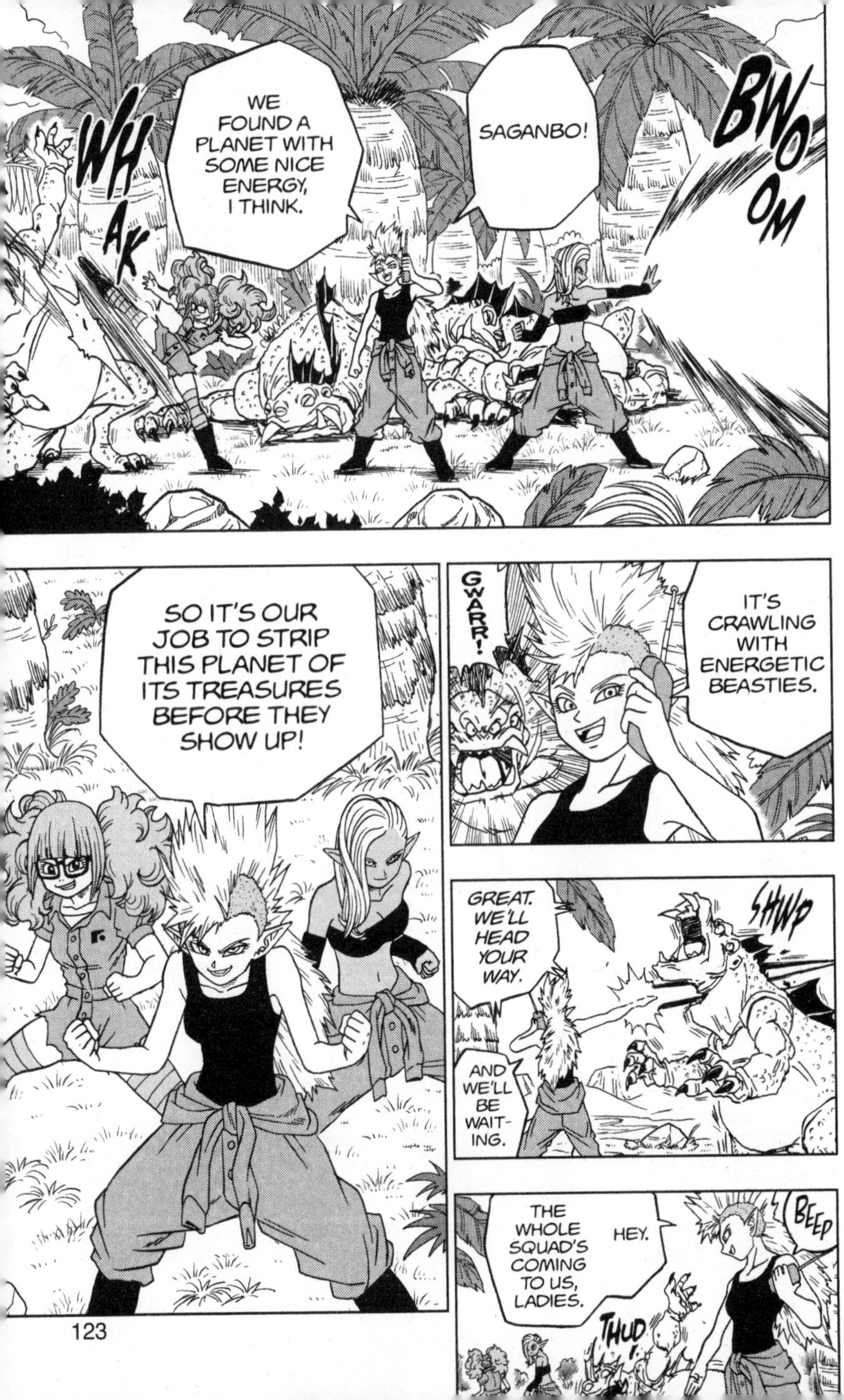
BWOOOM
SAGANBO!
WE FOUND A PLANET WITH SOME NICE ENERGY, I THINK.
WHAK
IT'S CRAWLING WITH ENERGETIC BEASTIES.
GWARR!
SHWP
GREAT. WE'LL HEAD YOUR WAY.
AND WE'LL BE WAIT-ING.
BEEP
HEY.
THE WHOLE SQUAD'S COMING TO US, LADIES.
THUD!
SO IT'S OUR JOB TO STRIP THIS PLANET OF ITS TREASURES BEFORE THEY SHOW UP!

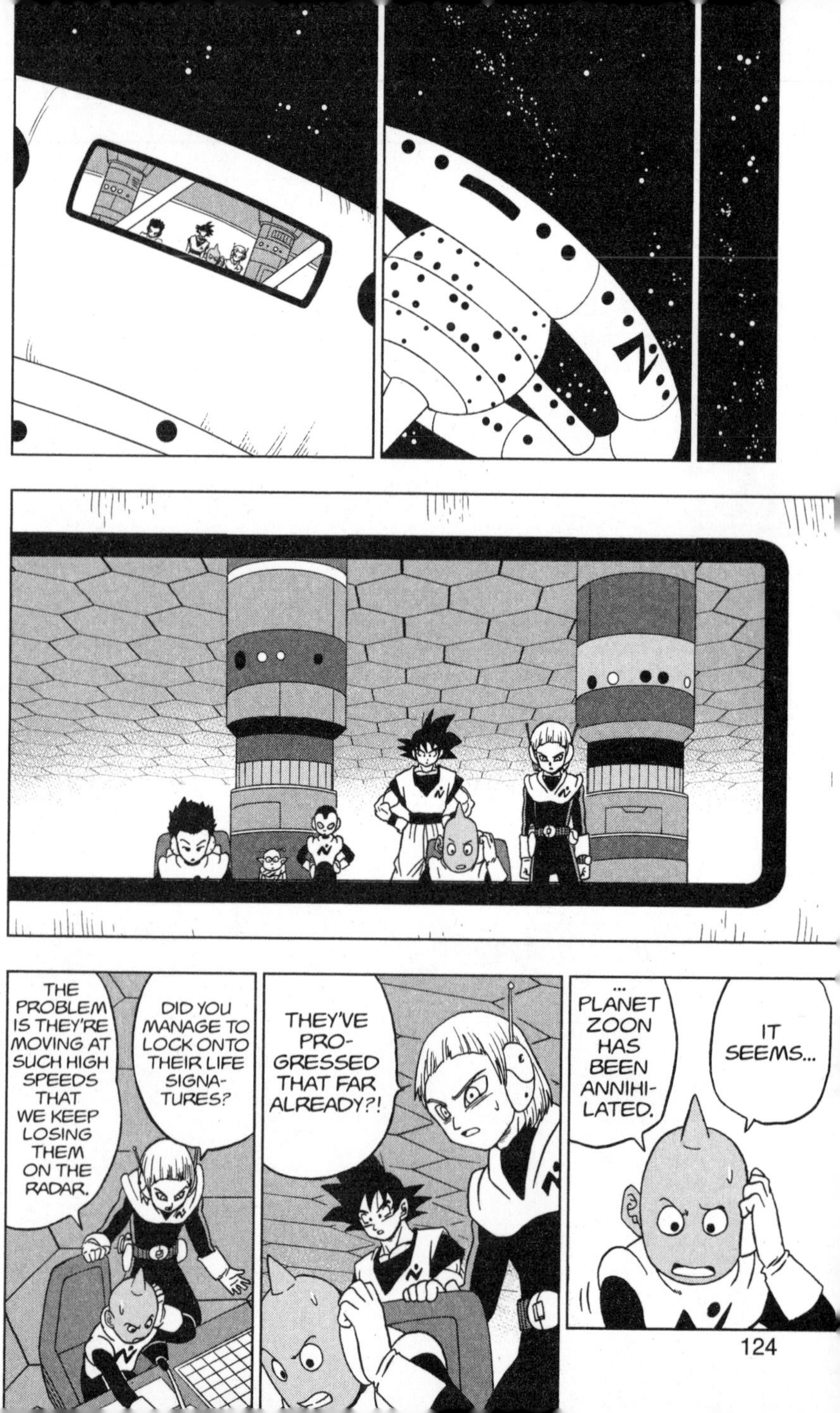
IT SEEMS...
...PLANET ZOON HAS BEEN ANNIHILATED.
THEY'VE PROGRESSED THAT FAR ALREADY?!
DID YOU MANAGE TO LOCK ONTO THEIR LIFE SIGNATURES?
THE PROBLEM IS THEY'RE MOVING AT SUCH HIGH SPEEDS THAT WE KEEP LOSING THEM ON THE RADAR.

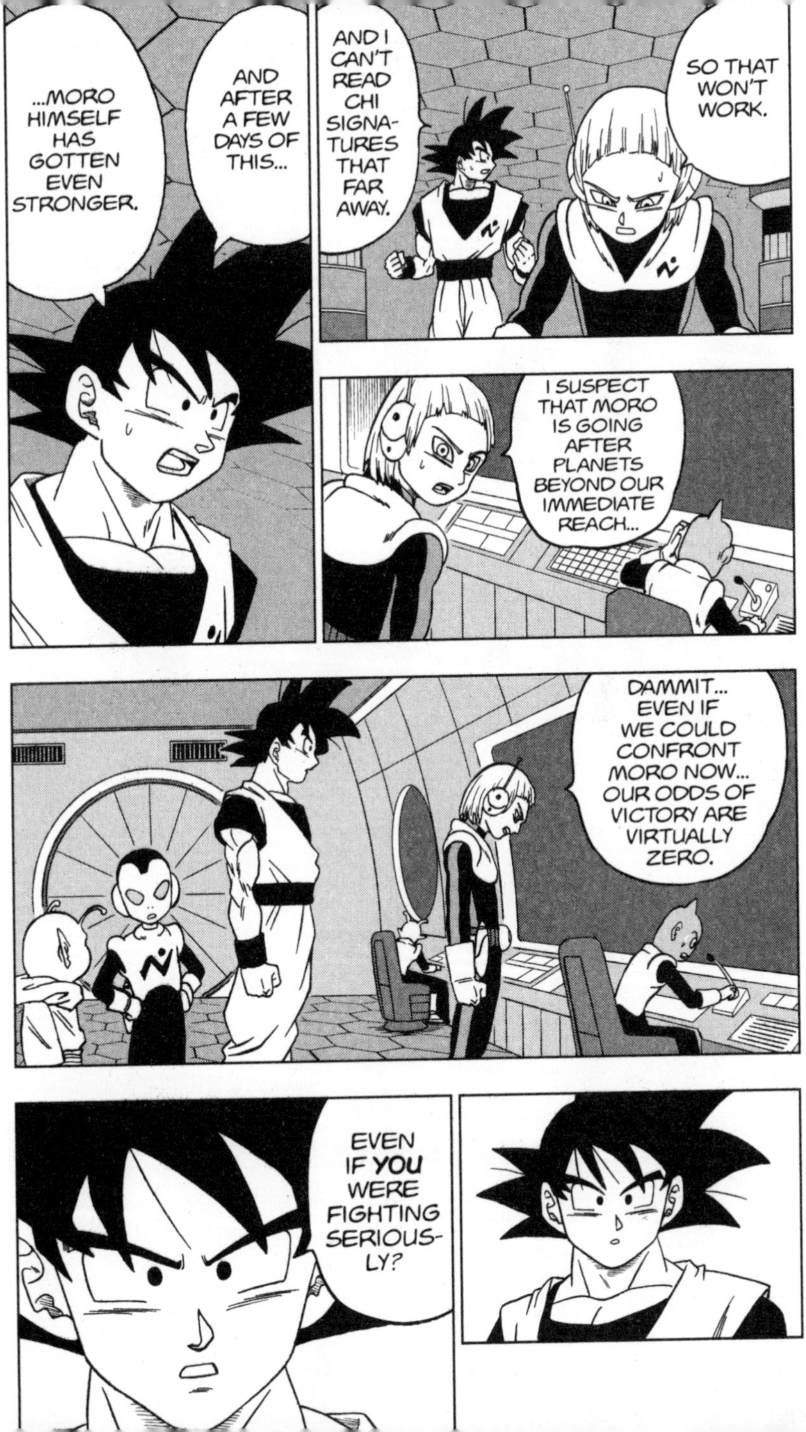
SO THAT WON'T WORK.
AND I CAN'T READ CHI SIGNATURES THAT FAR AWAY.
I SUSPECT THAT MORO IS GOING AFTER PLANETS BEYOND OUR IMMEDIATE REACH...
AND AFTER A FEW DAYS OF THIS...
...MORO HIMSELF HAS GOTTEN EVEN STRONGER.
DAMMIT... EVEN IF WE COULD CONFRONT MORO NOW... OUR ODDS OF VICTORY ARE VIRTUALLY ZERO.
EVEN IF **YOU** WERE FIGHTING SERIOUSLY?

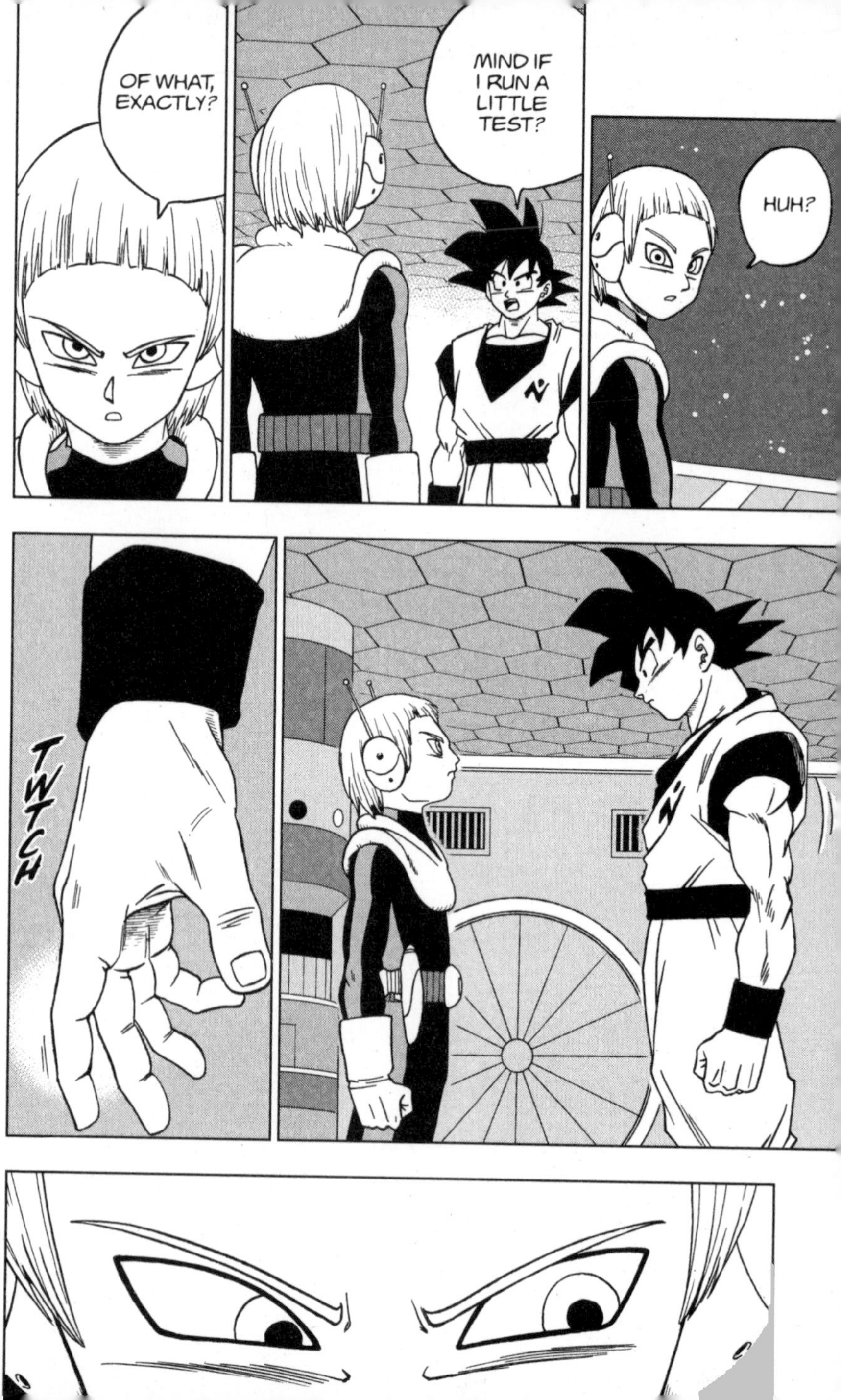
HUH?
MIND IF I RUN A LITTLE TEST?
OF WHAT, EXACTLY?
TWTCH

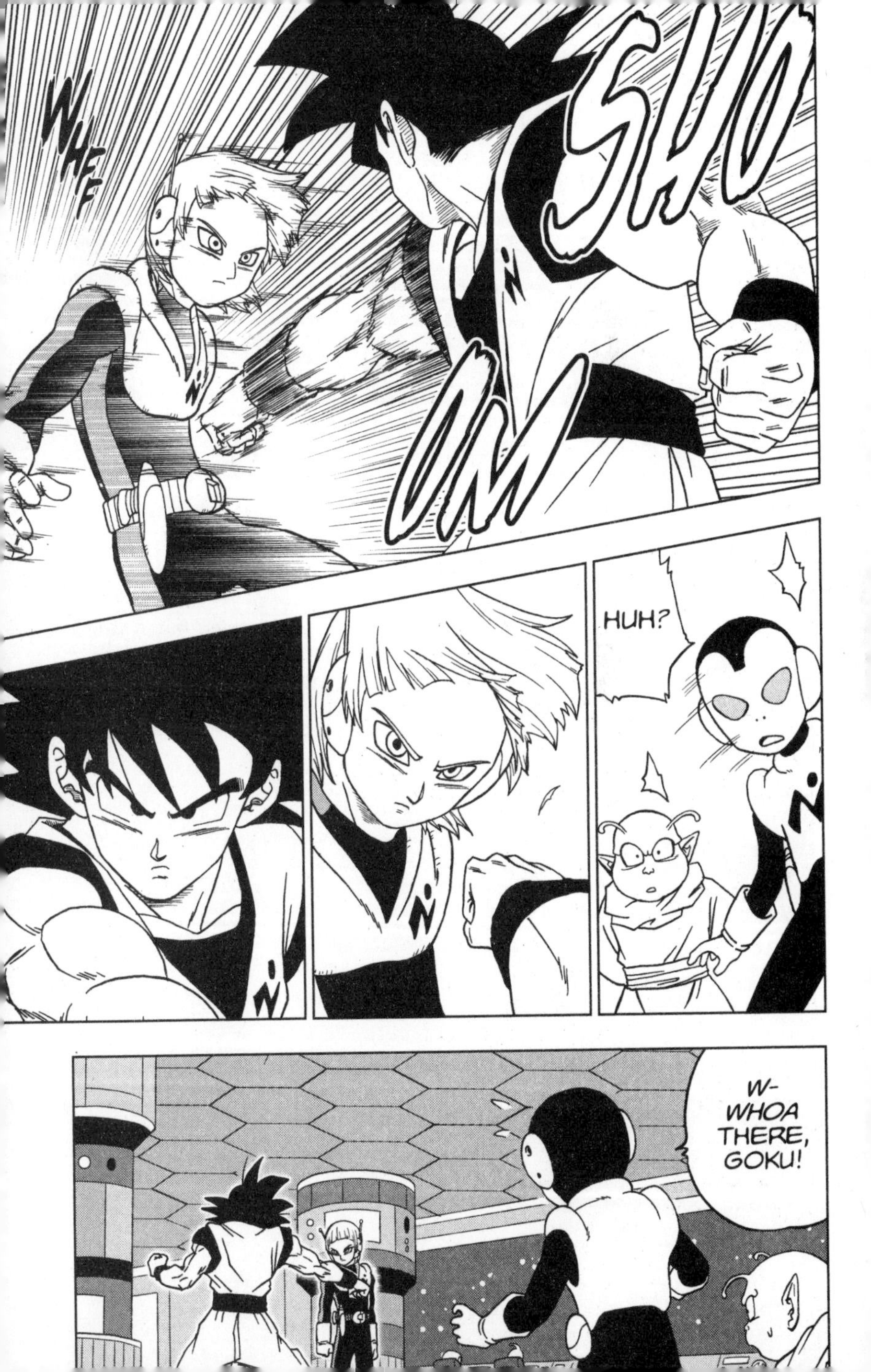
SHOOM
WHFF
HUH?
W-WHOA THERE, GOKU!

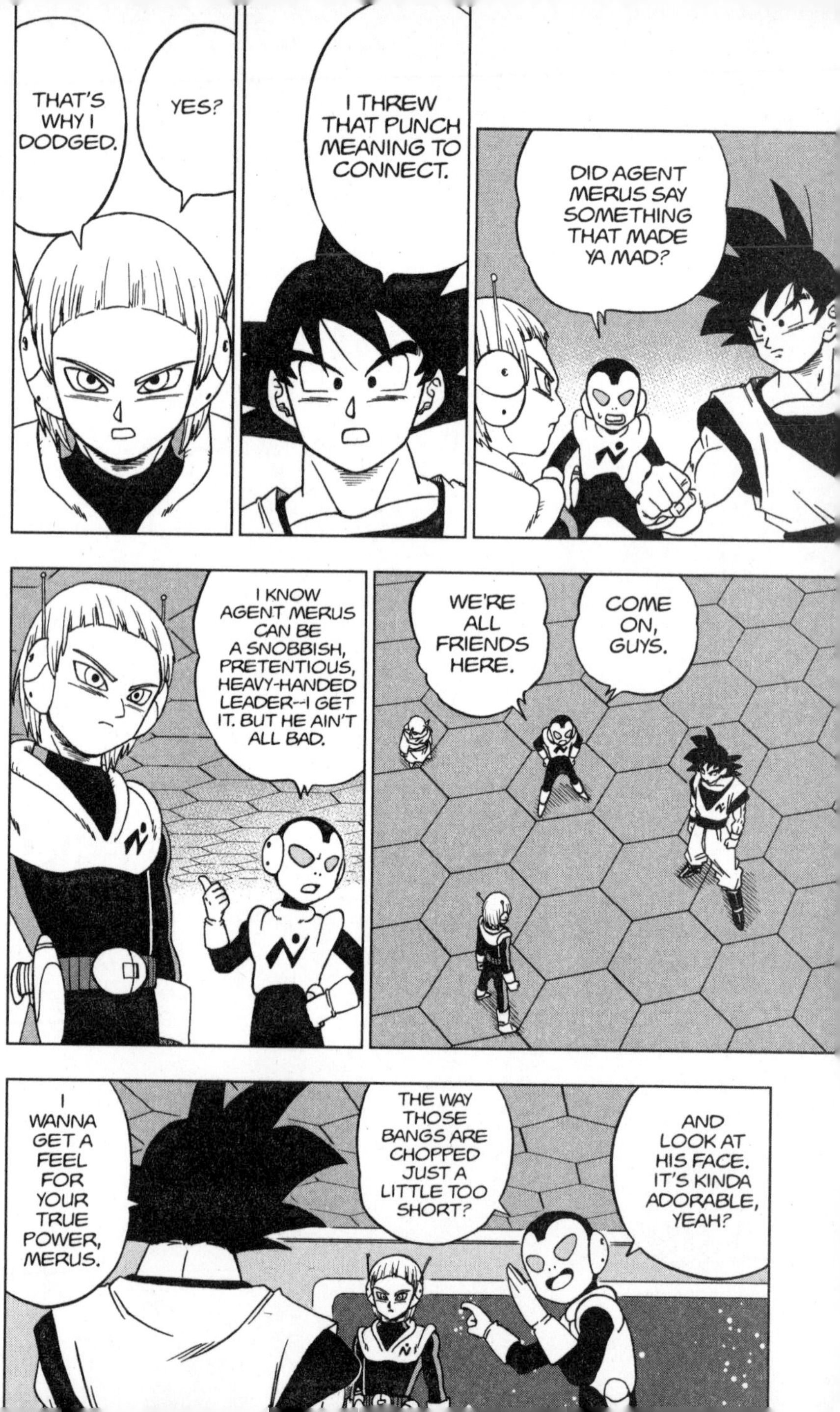
DID AGENT MERUS SAY SOMETHING THAT MADE YA MAD?
I THREW THAT PUNCH MEANING TO CONNECT.
YES?
THAT'S WHY I DODGED.
COME ON, GUYS.
WE'RE ALL FRIENDS HERE.
I KNOW AGENT MERUS CAN BE A SNOBBISH, PRETENTIOUS, HEAVY-HANDED LEADER--I GET IT. BUT HE AIN'T ALL BAD.
AND LOOK AT HIS FACE. IT'S KINDA ADORABLE, YEAH?
THE WAY THOSE BANGS ARE CHOPPED JUST A LITTLE TOO SHORT?
I WANNA GET A FEEL FOR YOUR TRUE POWER, MERUS.

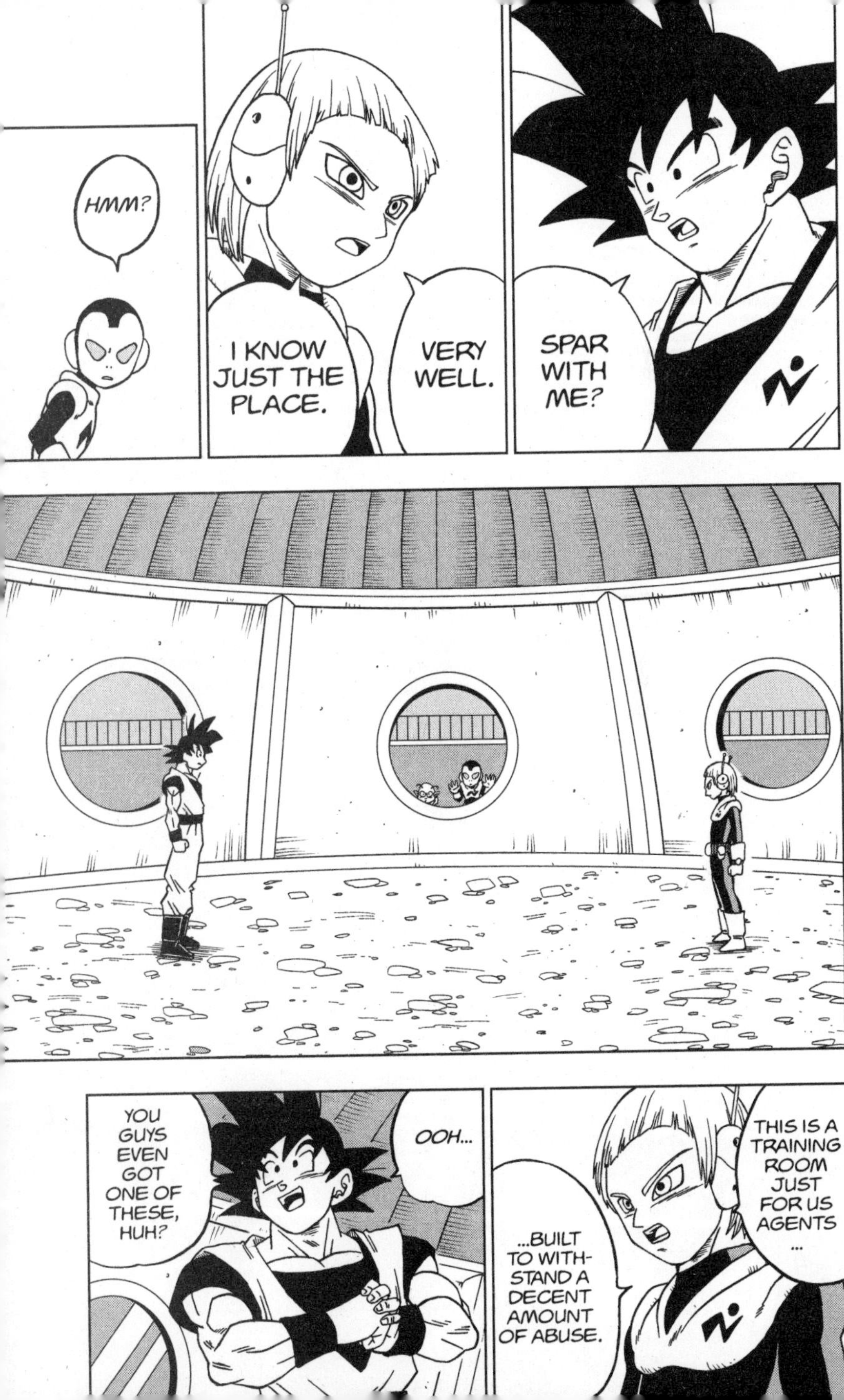
SPAR WITH ME?
VERY WELL.
I KNOW JUST THE PLACE.
HMM?
THIS IS A TRAINING ROOM JUST FOR US AGENTS ...
...BUILT TO WITH-STAND A DECENT AMOUNT OF ABUSE.
OOH...
YOU GUYS EVEN GOT ONE OF THESE, HUH?

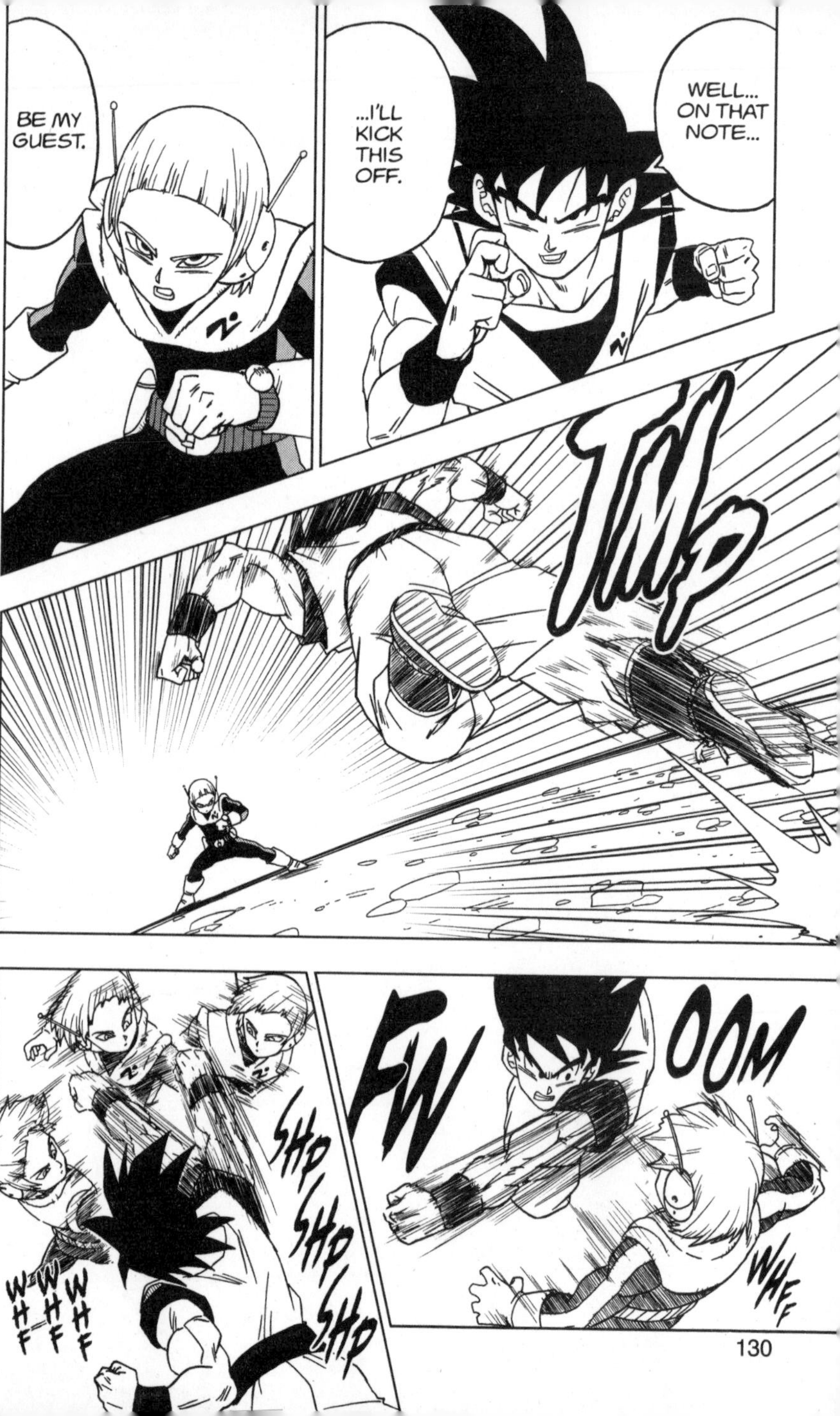
WELL... ON THAT NOTE...
...I'LL KICK THIS OFF.
BE MY GUEST.
TMP
FWOOM
WHFF
SHP SHP SHP
WHF WHF WHF

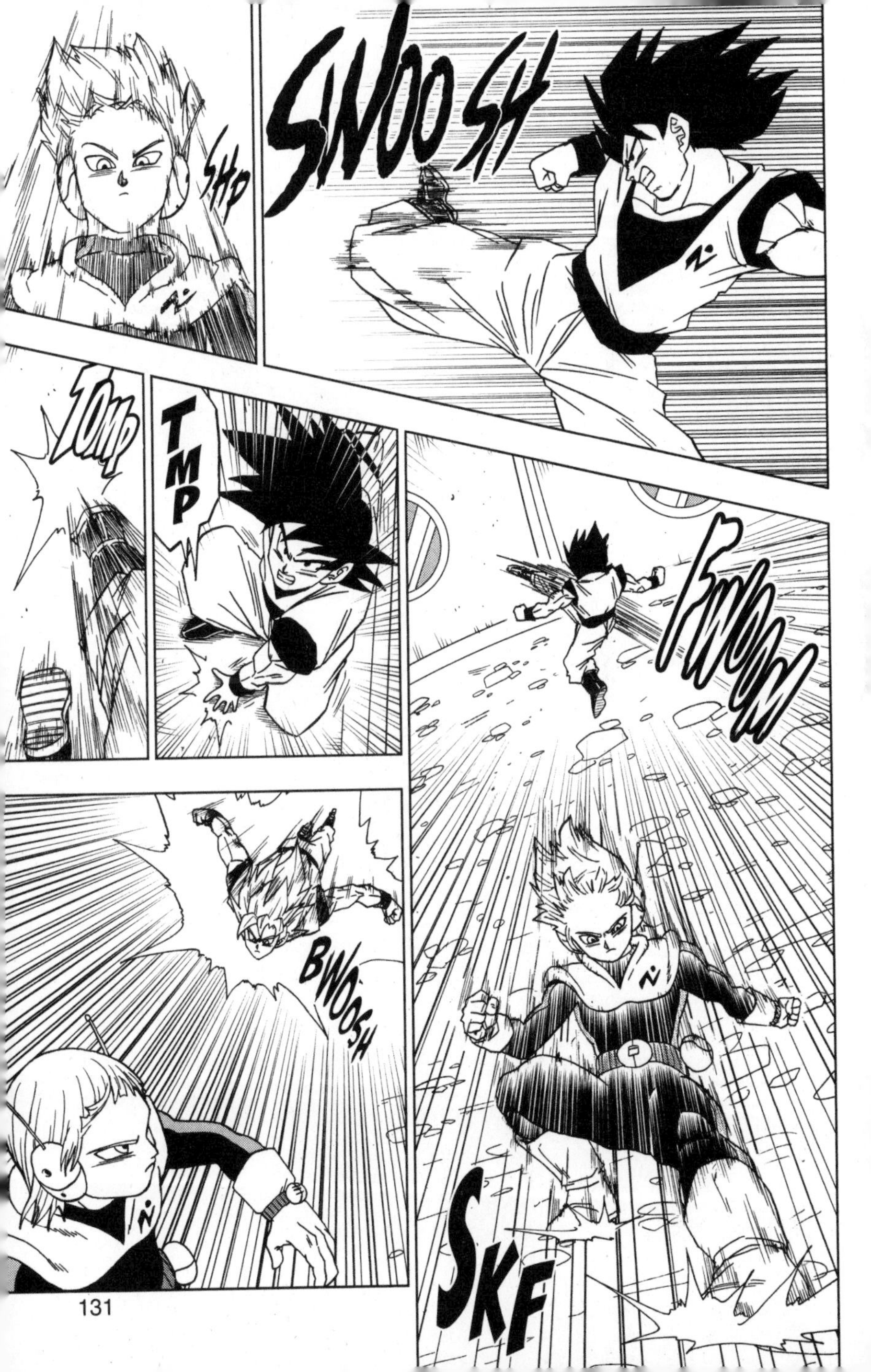
SWOOSH
SHP
FWOOM
SKF
TMP
TOMP
BWOOSH

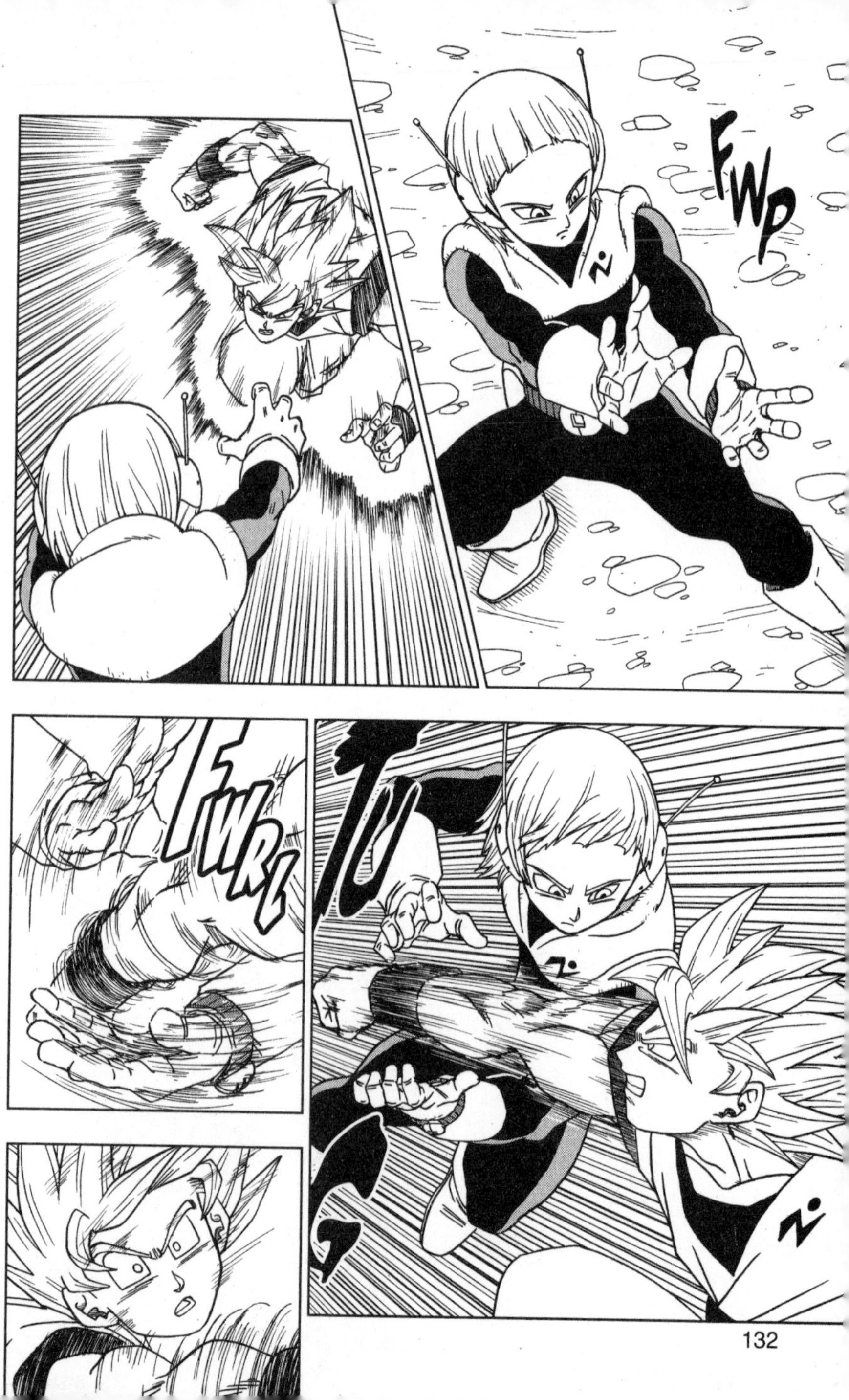
FWP
FWRL

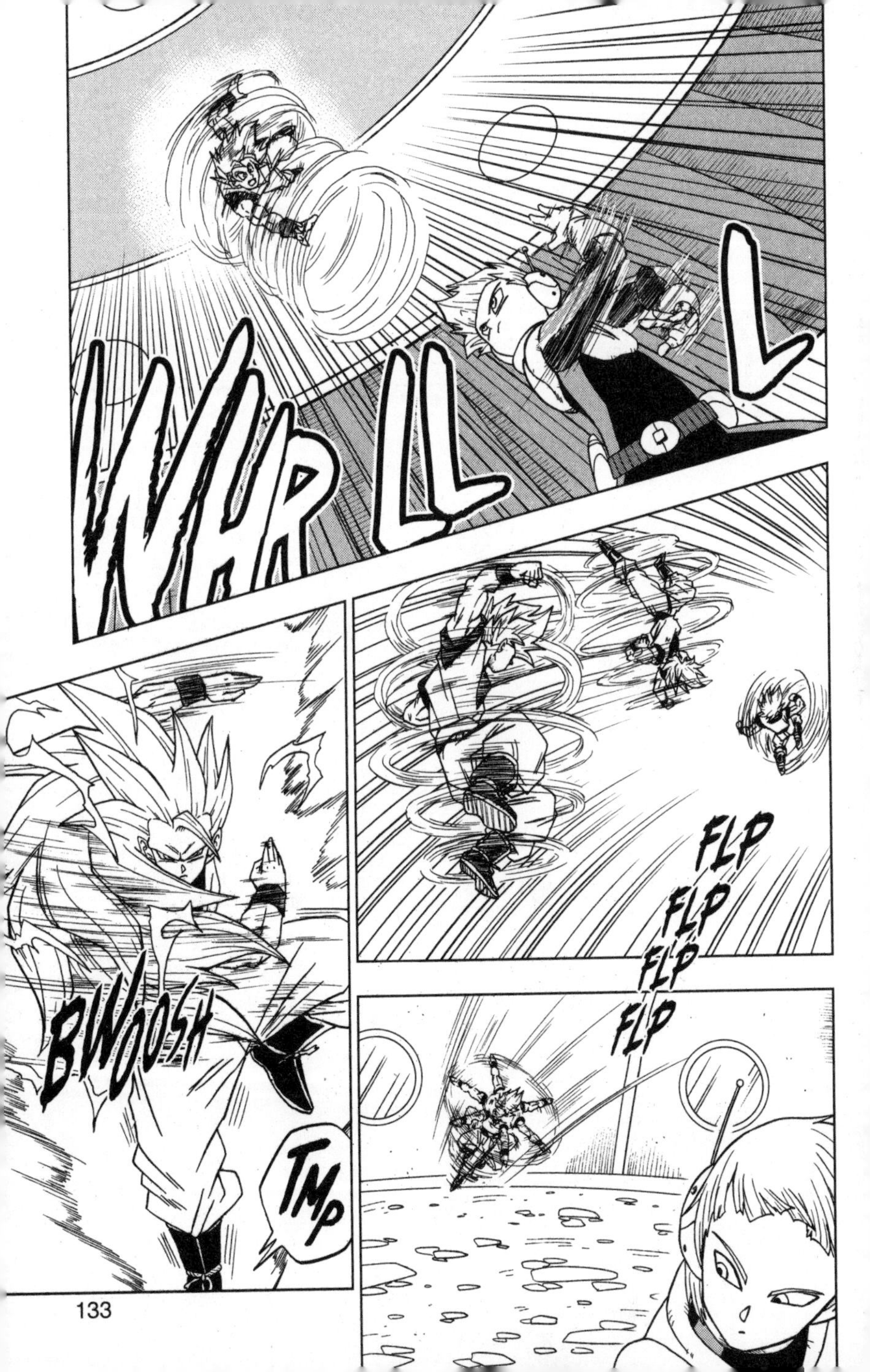
WHRLLL
FLP
FLP
FLP
FLP
BWOOSH
TMP

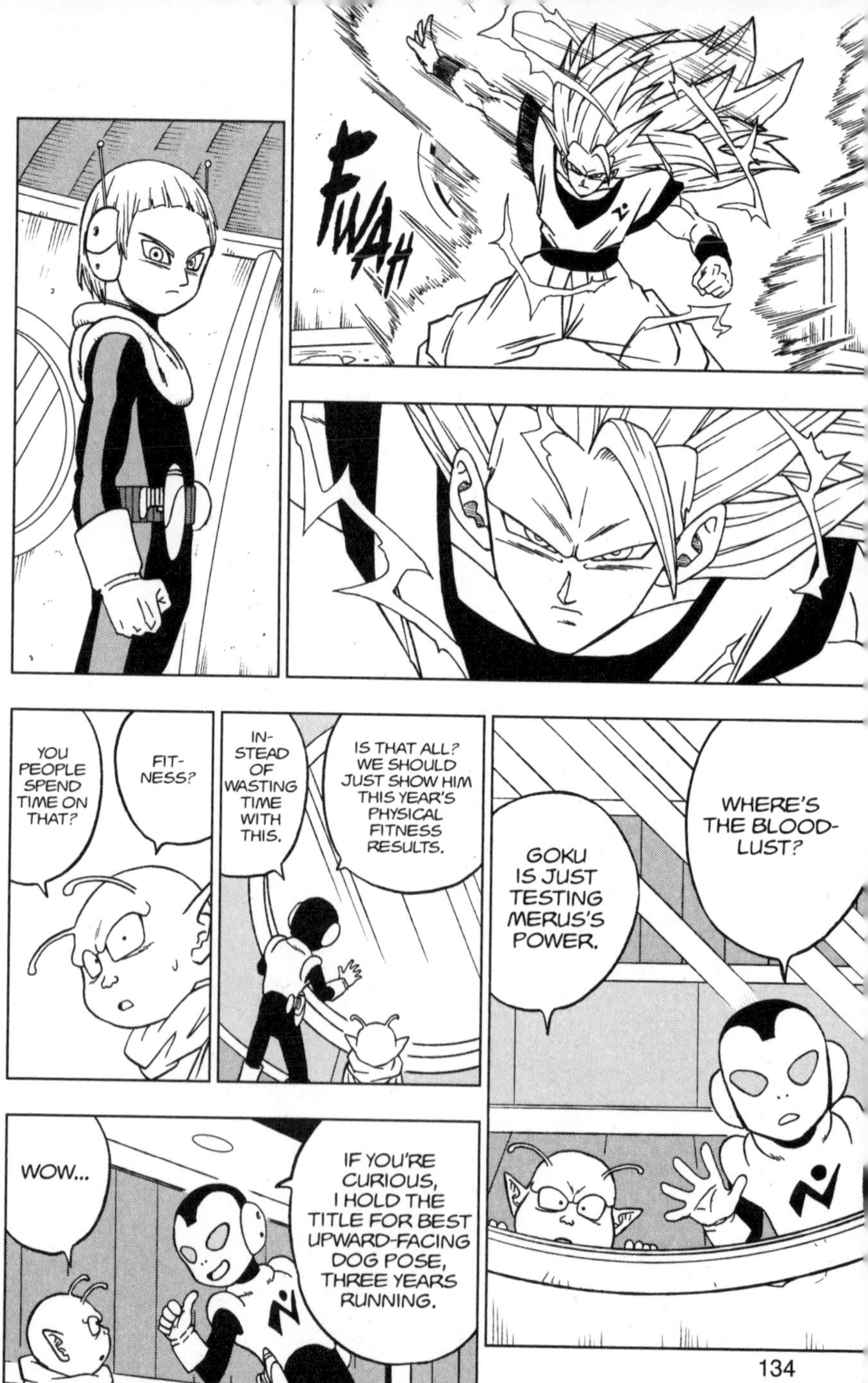
FWAH
WHERE'S THE BLOOD-LUST?
GOKU IS JUST TESTING MERUS'S POWER.
IS THAT ALL? WE SHOULD JUST SHOW HIM THIS YEAR'S PHYSICAL FITNESS RESULTS.
IN-STEAD OF WASTING TIME WITH THIS.
FIT-NESS?
YOU PEOPLE SPEND TIME ON THAT?
IF YOU'RE CURIOUS, I HOLD THE TITLE FOR BEST UPWARD-FACING DOG POSE, THREE YEARS RUNNING.
WOW...

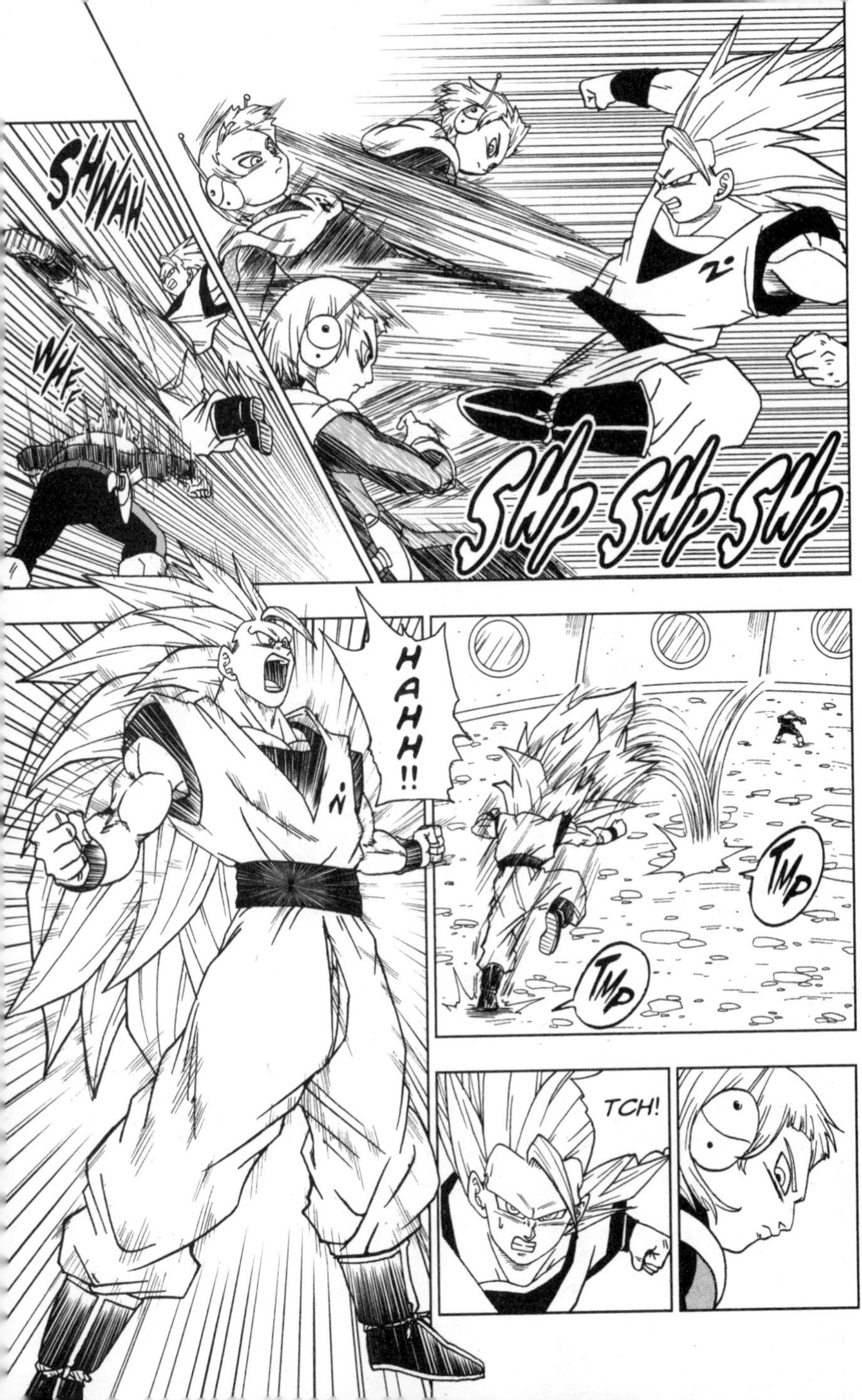
SHP SHP SHP
SHWAH
WHF
TMP
TMP
TCH!
HAHHH!!

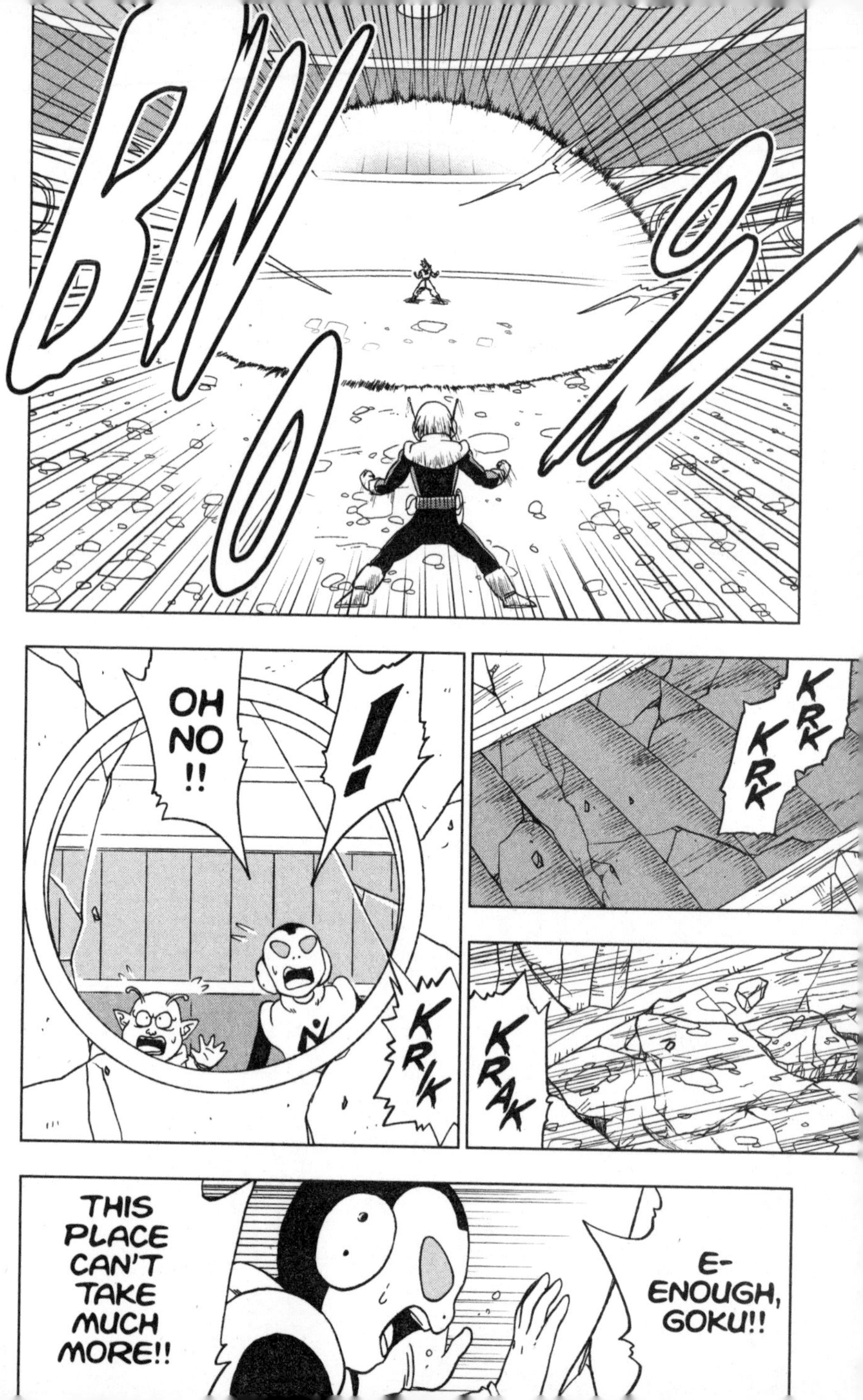
BWOOOM
KRK KRK
KRAK
!
OH NO!!
KRIK
E-ENOUGH, GOKU!!
THIS PLACE CAN'T TAKE MUCH MORE!!

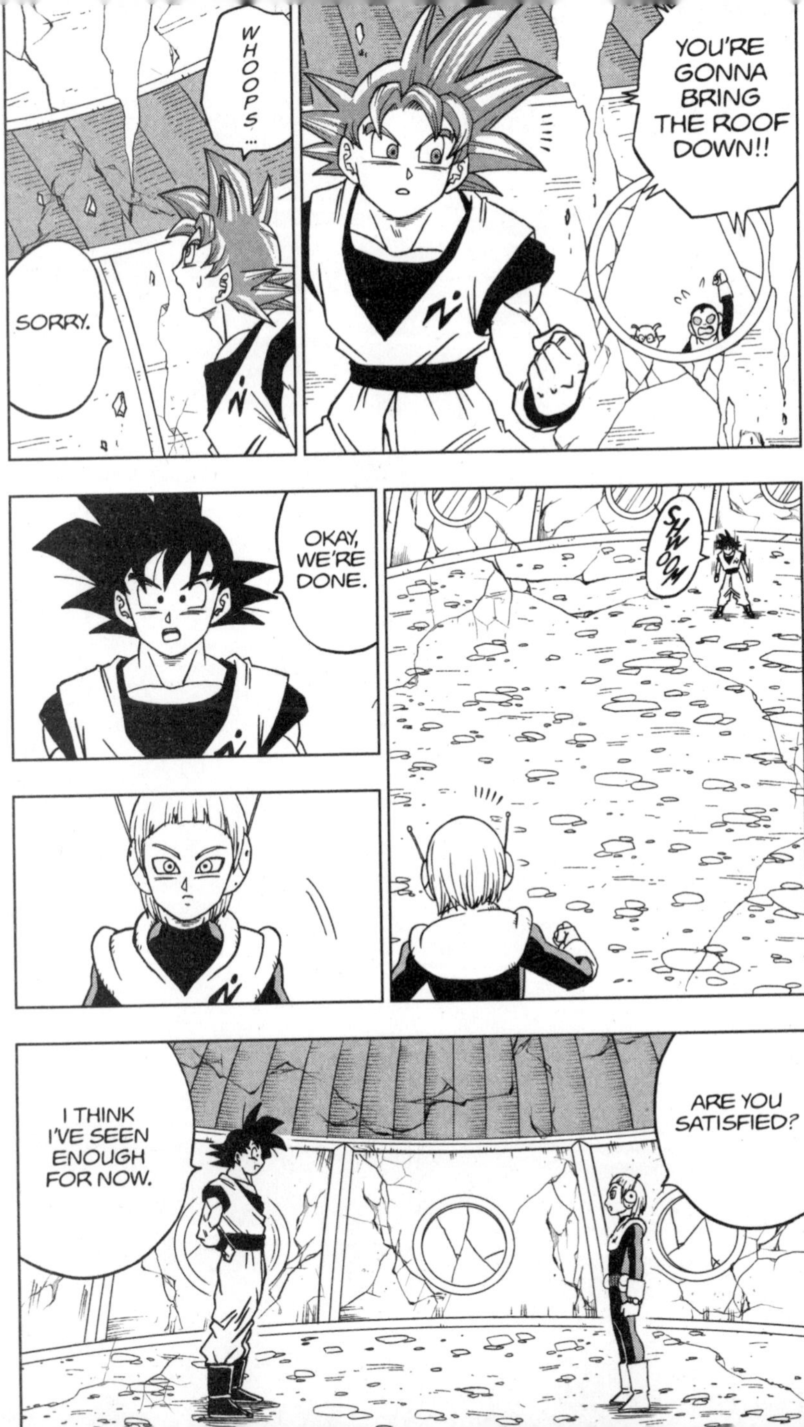
YOU'RE GONNA BRING THE ROOF DOWN!!
WHOOPS...
SORRY.
SHWOOM
OKAY, WE'RE DONE.
ARE YOU SATISFIED?
I THINK I'VE SEEN ENOUGH FOR NOW.

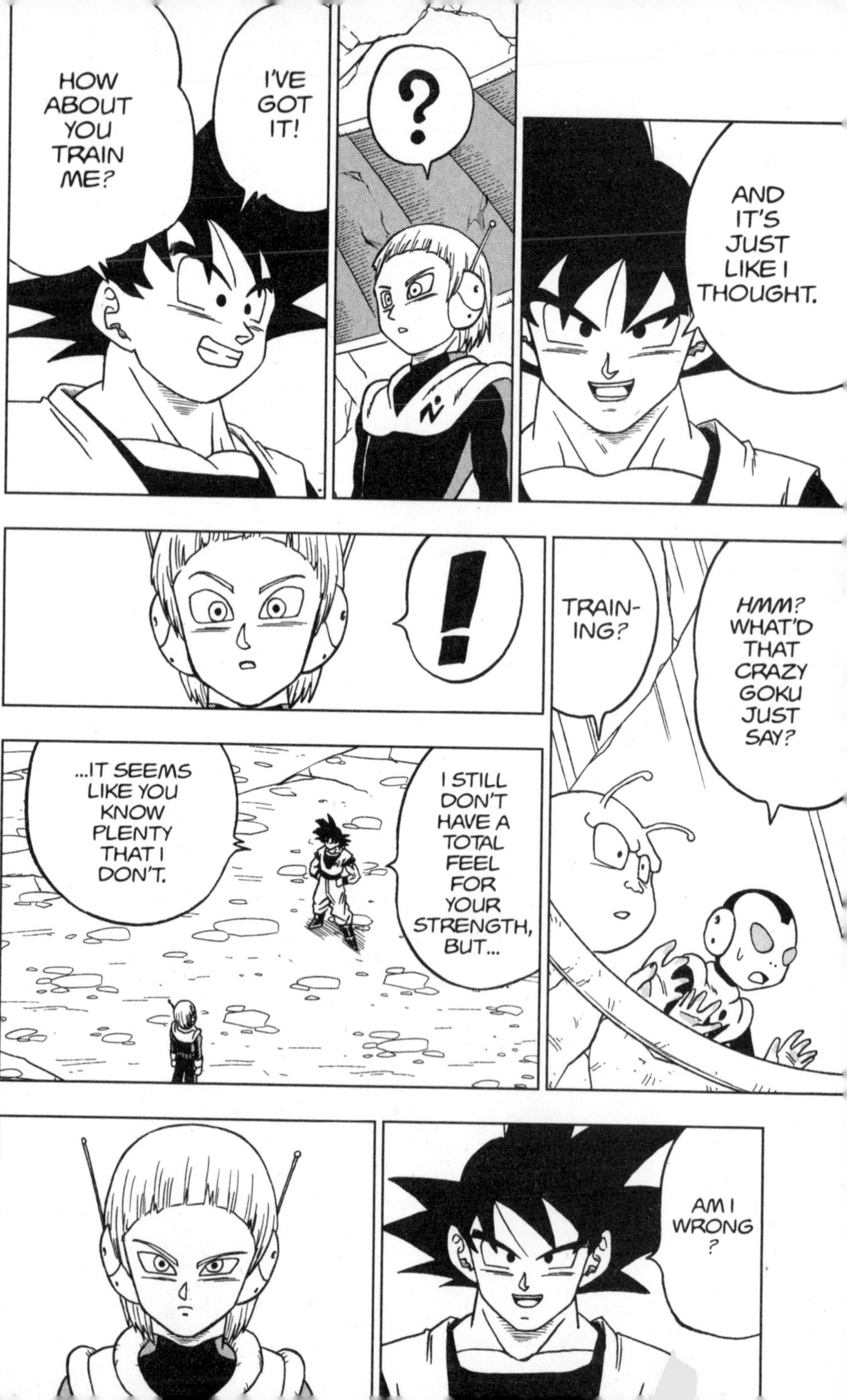
AND IT'S JUST LIKE I THOUGHT.
?
I'VE GOT IT!
HOW ABOUT YOU TRAIN ME?
HMM? WHAT'D THAT CRAZY GOKU JUST SAY?
TRAIN-ING?
!
I STILL DON'T HAVE A TOTAL FEEL FOR YOUR STRENGTH, BUT...
...IT SEEMS LIKE YOU KNOW PLENTY THAT I DON'T.
AM I WRONG?

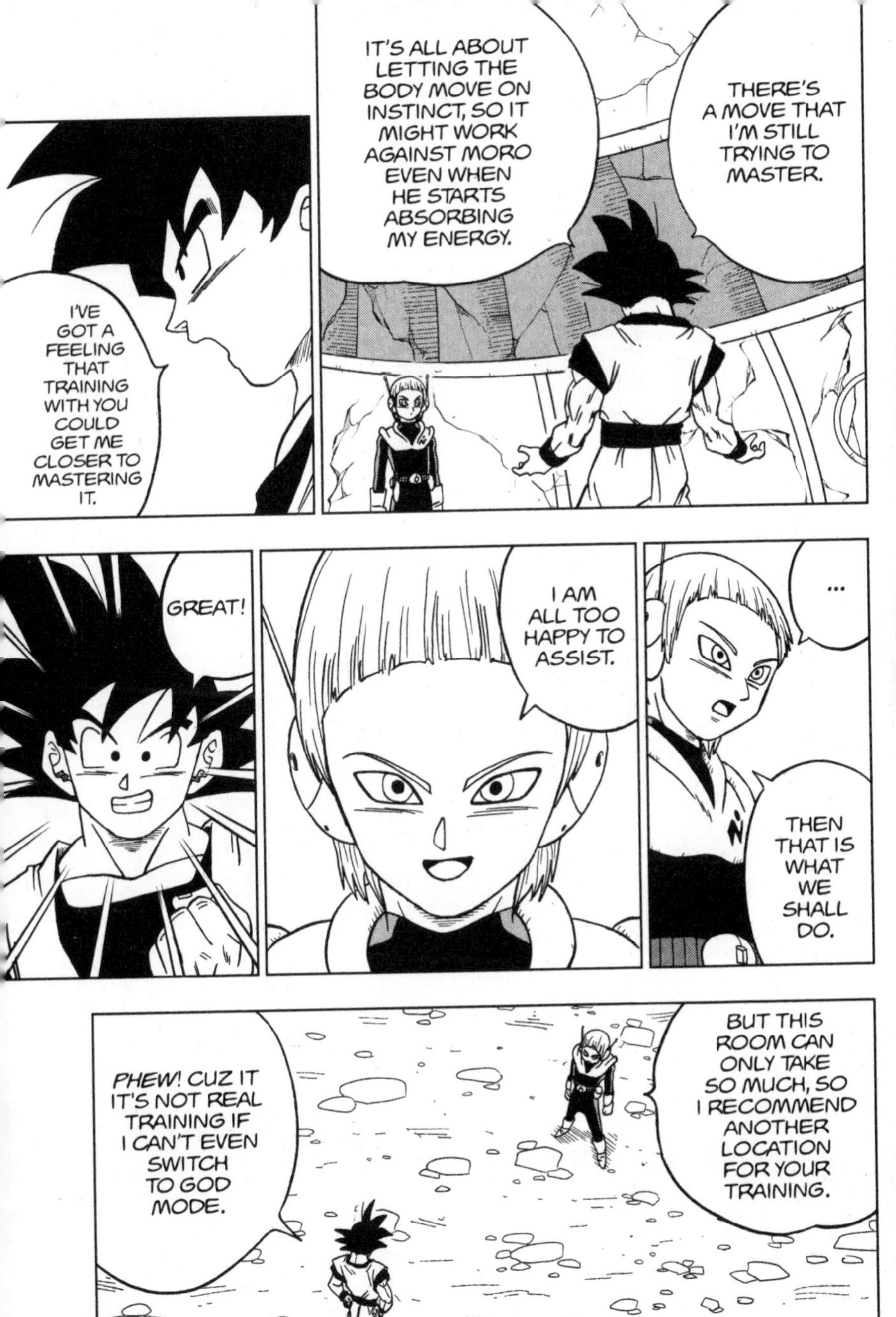
THERE'S A MOVE THAT I'M STILL TRYING TO MASTER.
IT'S ALL ABOUT LETTING THE BODY MOVE ON INSTINCT, SO IT MIGHT WORK AGAINST MORO EVEN WHEN HE STARTS ABSORBING MY ENERGY.
I'VE GOT A FEELING THAT TRAINING WITH YOU COULD GET ME CLOSER TO MASTERING IT.
...
THEN THAT IS WHAT WE SHALL DO.
I AM ALL TOO HAPPY TO ASSIST.
GREAT!
BUT THIS ROOM CAN ONLY TAKE SO MUCH, SO I RECOMMEND ANOTHER LOCATION FOR YOUR TRAINING.
PHEW! CUZ IT IT'S NOT REAL TRAINING IF I CAN'T EVEN SWITCH TO GOD MODE.

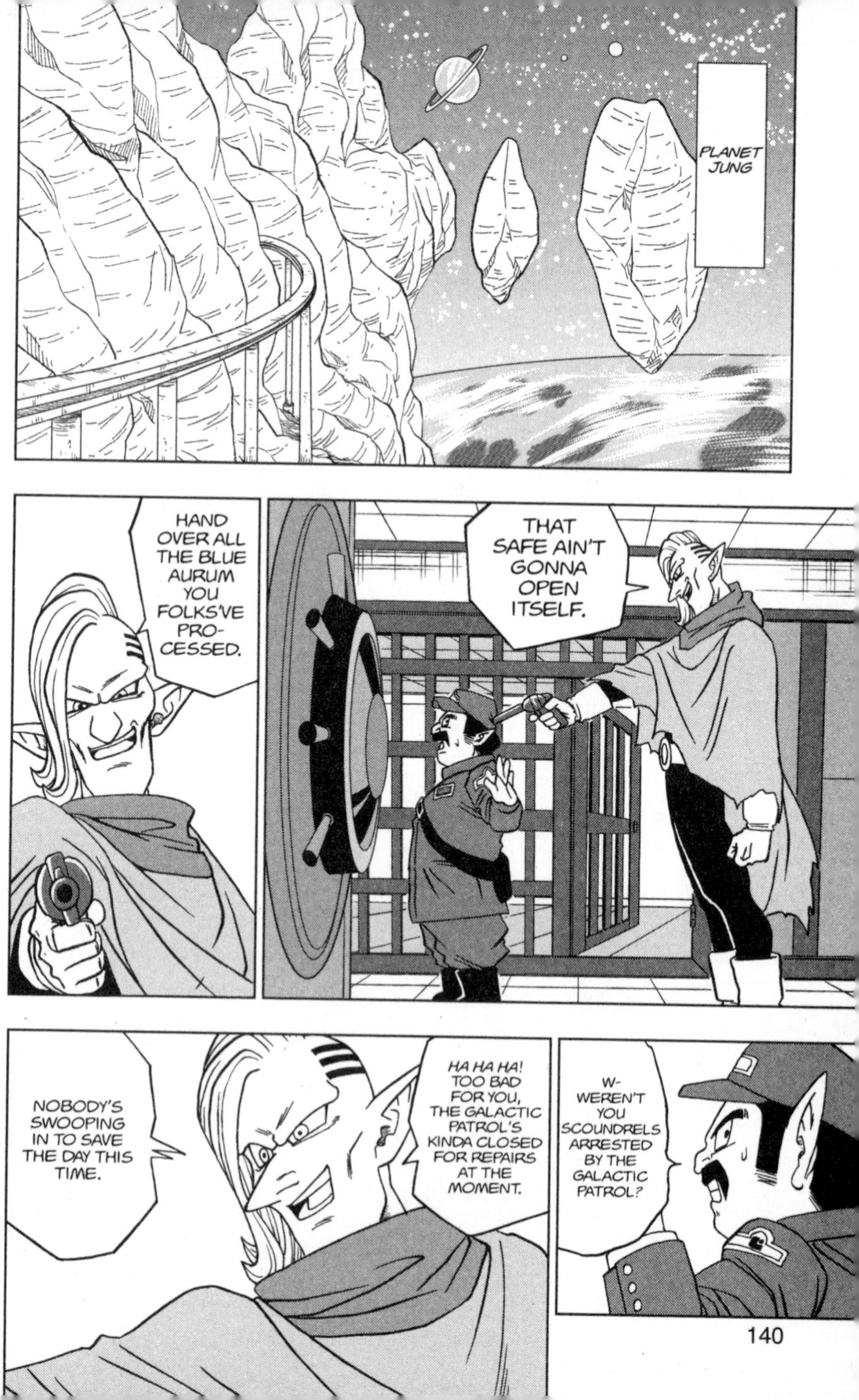
PLANET JUNG
THAT SAFE AIN'T GONNA OPEN ITSELF.
HAND OVER ALL THE BLUE AURUM YOU FOLKS'VE PRO-CESSED.
W-WEREN'T YOU SCOUNDRELS ARRESTED BY THE GALACTIC PATROL?
HA HA HA! TOO BAD FOR YOU, THE GALACTIC PATROL'S KINDA CLOSED FOR REPAIRS AT THE MOMENT.
NOBODY'S SWOOPING IN TO SAVE THE DAY THIS TIME.

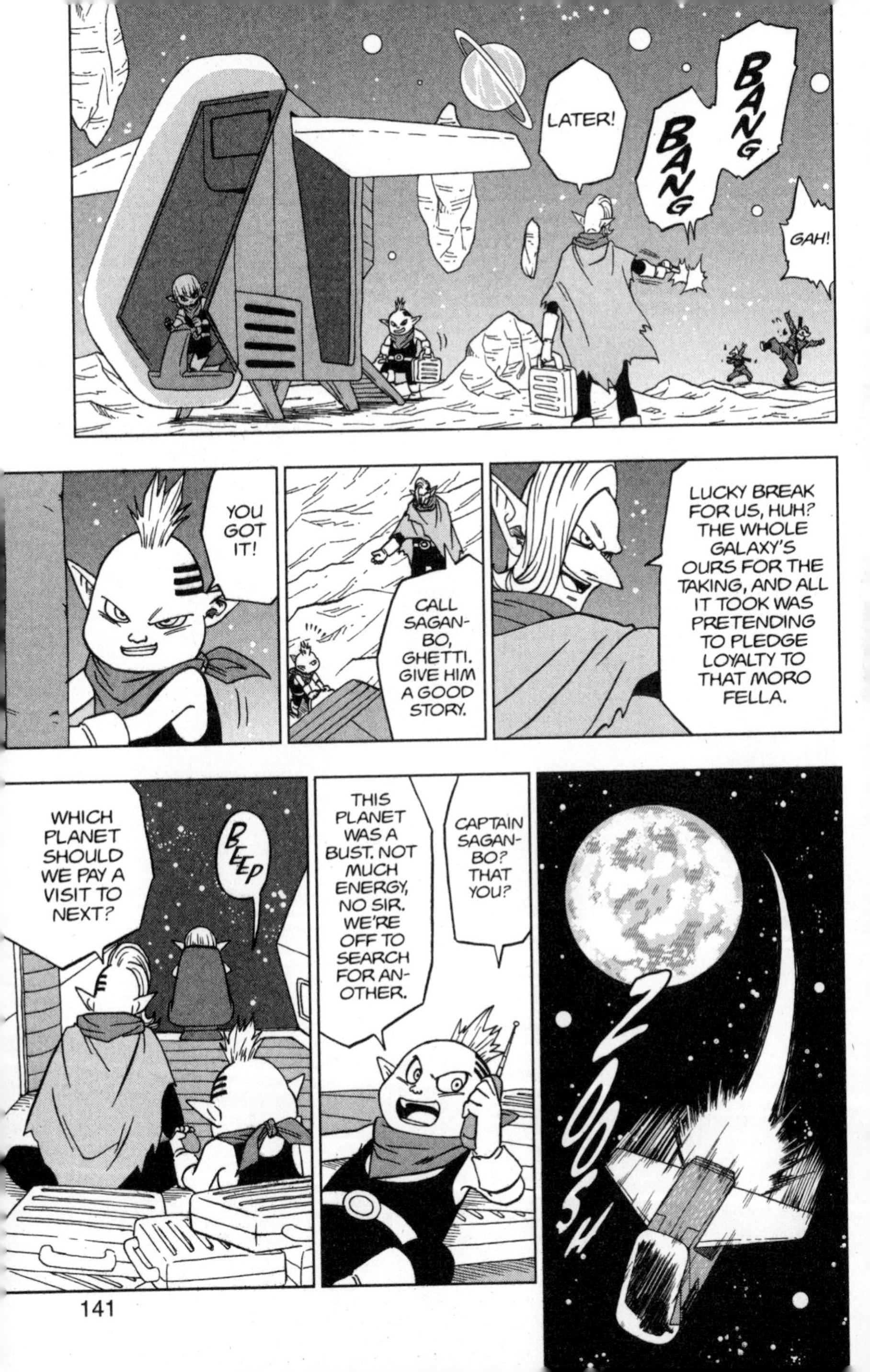
BANG
BANG
LATER!
GAH!
LUCKY BREAK FOR US, HUH? THE WHOLE GALAXY'S OURS FOR THE TAKING, AND ALL IT TOOK WAS PRETENDING TO PLEDGE LOYALTY TO THAT MORO FELLA.
CALL SAGAN-BO, GHETTI. GIVE HIM A GOOD STORY.
YOU GOT IT!
ZOOSH
CAPTAIN SAGAN-BO? THAT YOU?
THIS PLANET WAS A BUST. NOT MUCH ENERGY, NO SIR. WE'RE OFF TO SEARCH FOR AN-OTHER.
BEEP
WHICH PLANET SHOULD WE PAY A VISIT TO NEXT?

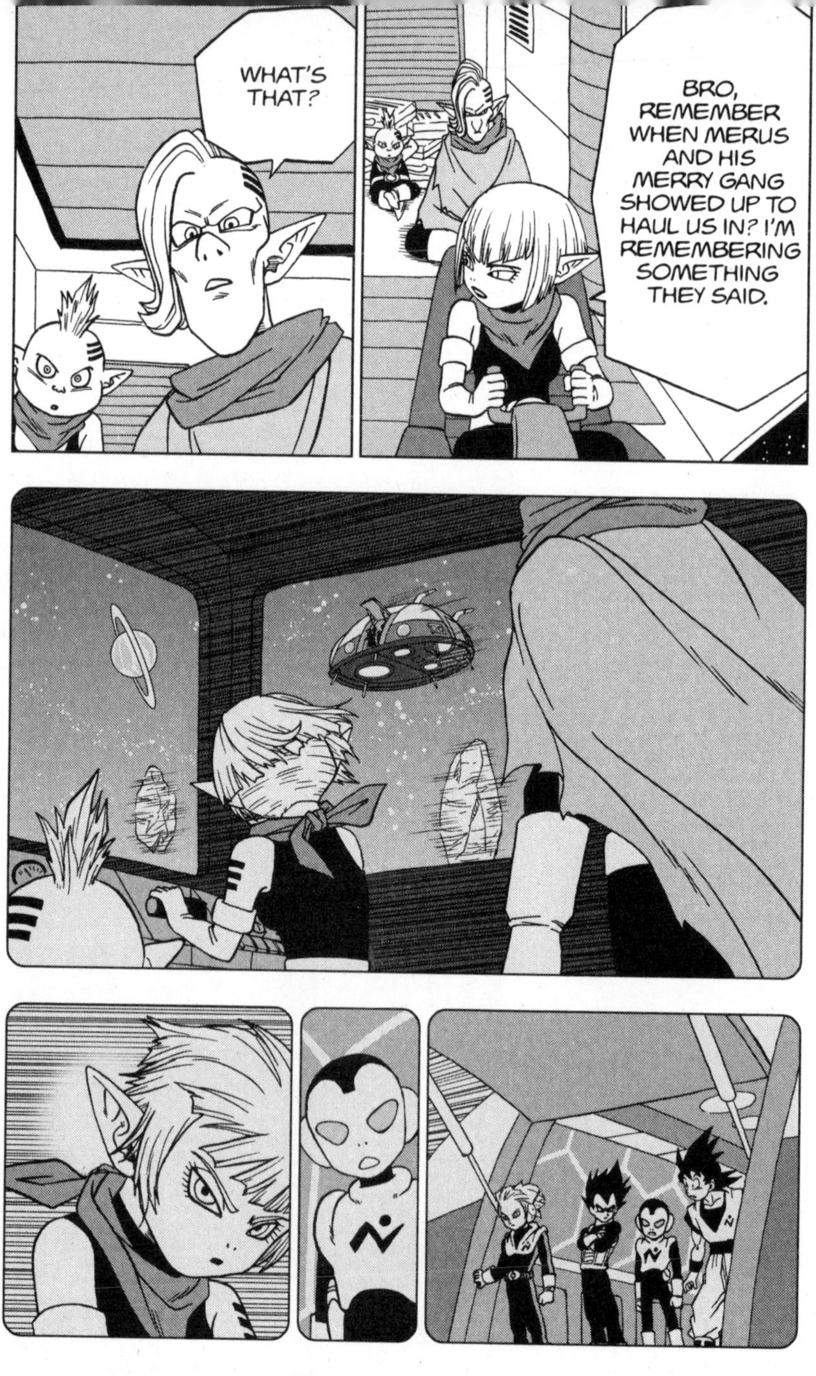
BRO, REMEMBER WHEN MERUS AND HIS MERRY GANG SHOWED UP TO HAUL US IN? I'M REMEMBERING SOMETHING THEY SAID.
WHAT'S THAT?

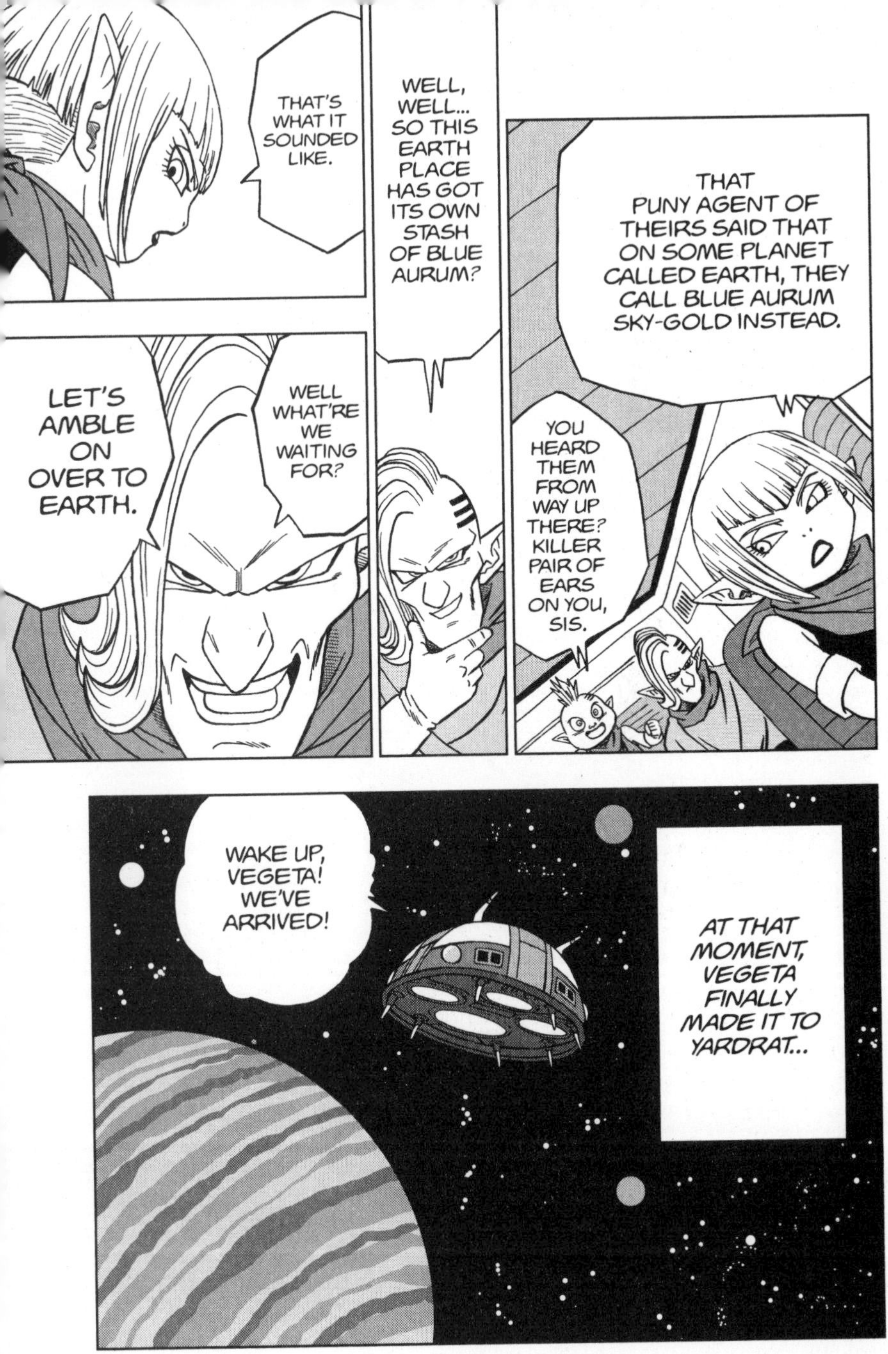
THAT PUNY AGENT OF THEIRS SAID THAT ON SOME PLANET CALLED EARTH, THEY CALL BLUE AURUM SKY-GOLD INSTEAD.
YOU HEARD THEM FROM WAY UP THERE? KILLER PAIR OF EARS ON YOU, SIS.
WELL, WELL... SO THIS EARTH PLACE HAS GOT ITS OWN STASH OF BLUE AURUM?
THAT'S WHAT IT SOUNDED LIKE.
WELL WHAT'RE WE WAITING FOR?
LET'S AMBLE ON OVER TO EARTH.
AT THAT MOMENT, VEGETA FINALLY MADE IT TO YARDRAT...
WAKE UP, VEGETA! WE'VE ARRIVED!

CHAPTER 52: GOKU AND VEGETA'S TRAINING

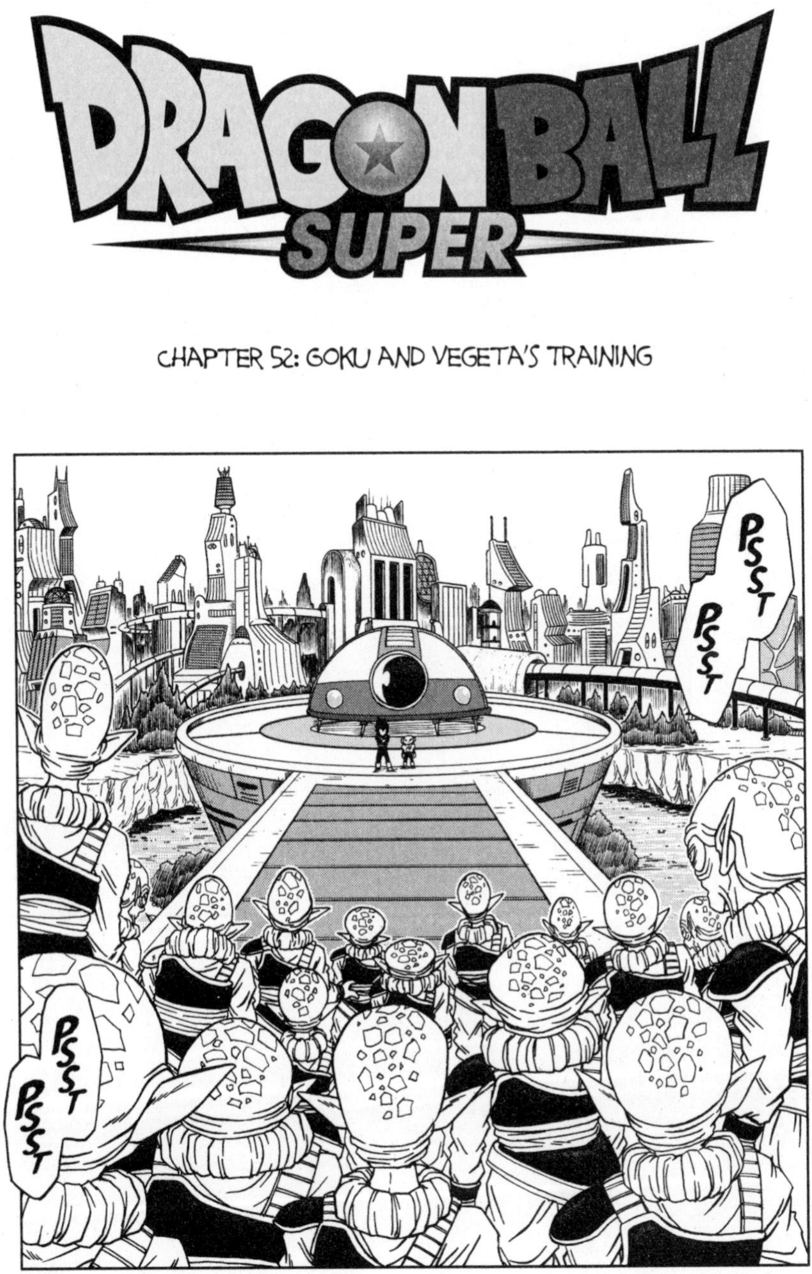
PSST PSST
PSST PSST

So these are the Yardratians. I've never encountered them before.

I hear they come in multiple types.

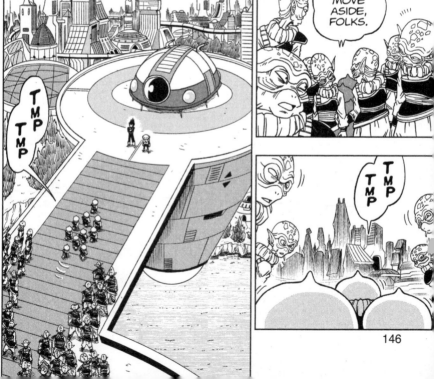

Move aside, folks.

TMP TMP

TMP TMP

146

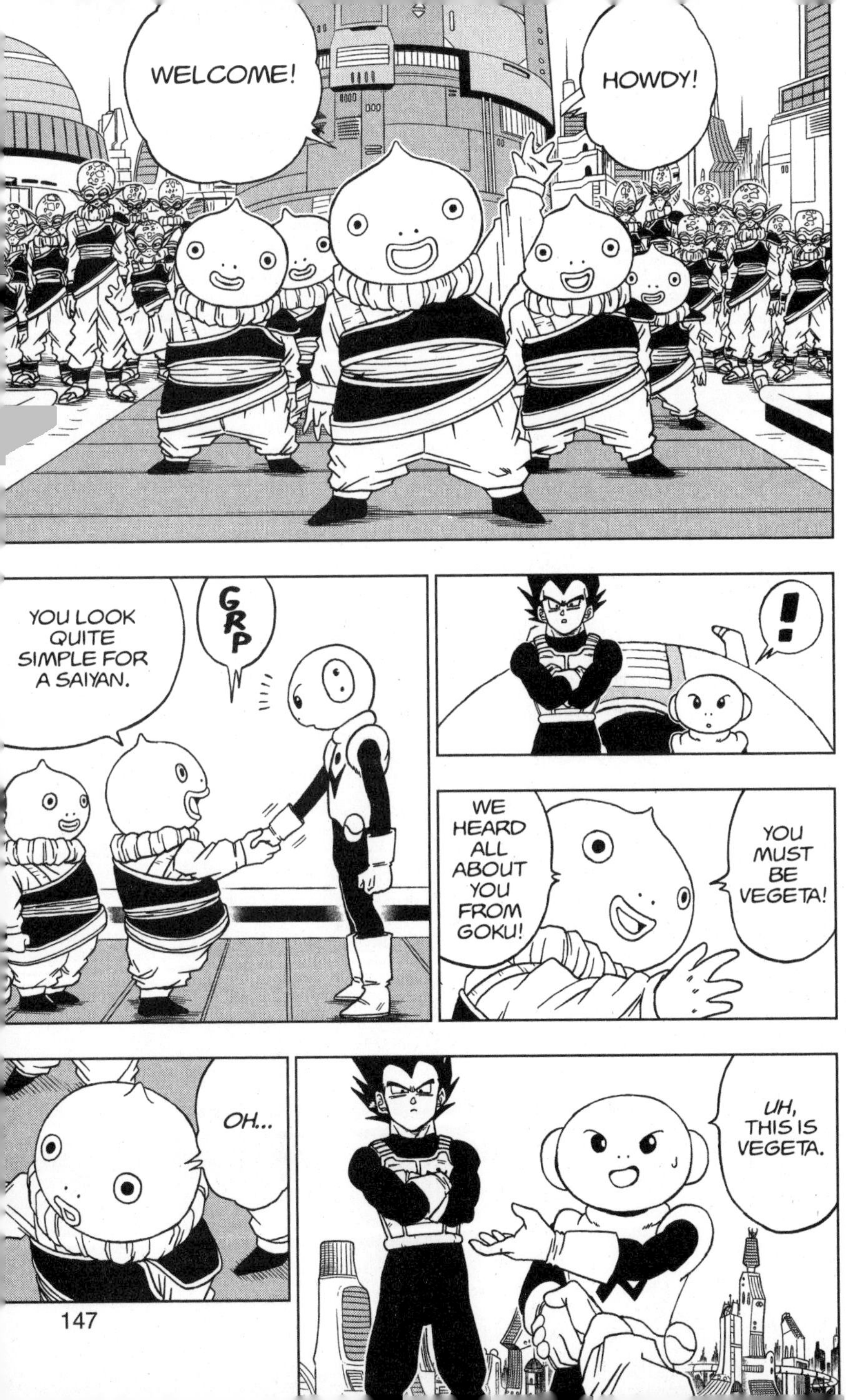
HOWDY!
WELCOME!
!
YOU MUST BE VEGETA!
WE HEARD ALL ABOUT YOU FROM GOKU!
GRP
YOU LOOK QUITE SIMPLE FOR A SAIYAN.
UH, THIS IS VEGETA.
OH...

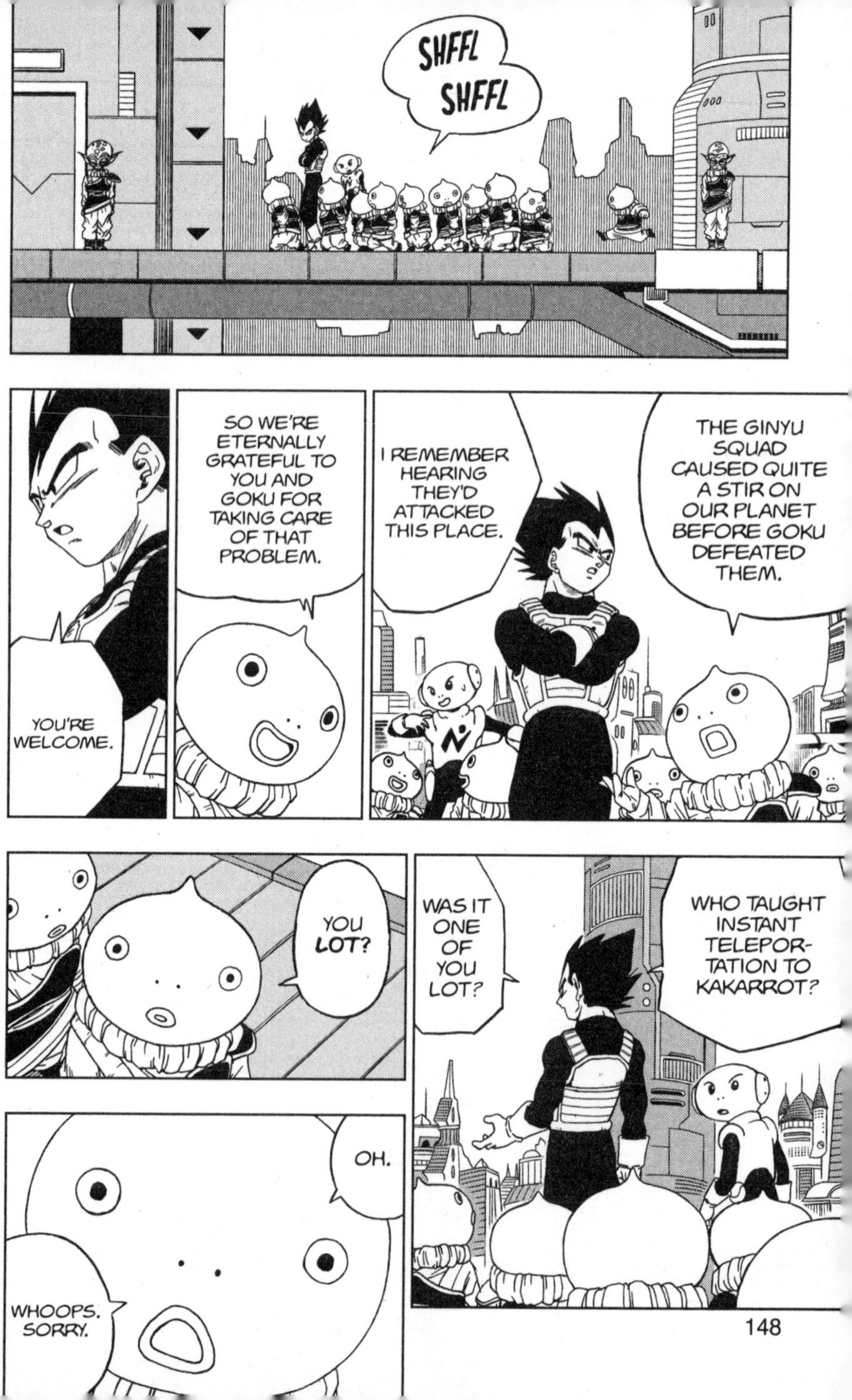
SHFFL SHFFL
THE GINYU SQUAD CAUSED QUITE A STIR ON OUR PLANET BEFORE GOKU DEFEATED THEM.
I REMEMBER HEARING THEY'D ATTACKED THIS PLACE.
SO WE'RE ETERNALLY GRATEFUL TO YOU AND GOKU FOR TAKING CARE OF THAT PROBLEM.
YOU'RE WELCOME.
WHO TAUGHT INSTANT TELEPORTATION TO KAKARROT?
WAS IT ONE OF YOU LOT?
YOU **LOT?**
OH.
WHOOPS. SORRY.

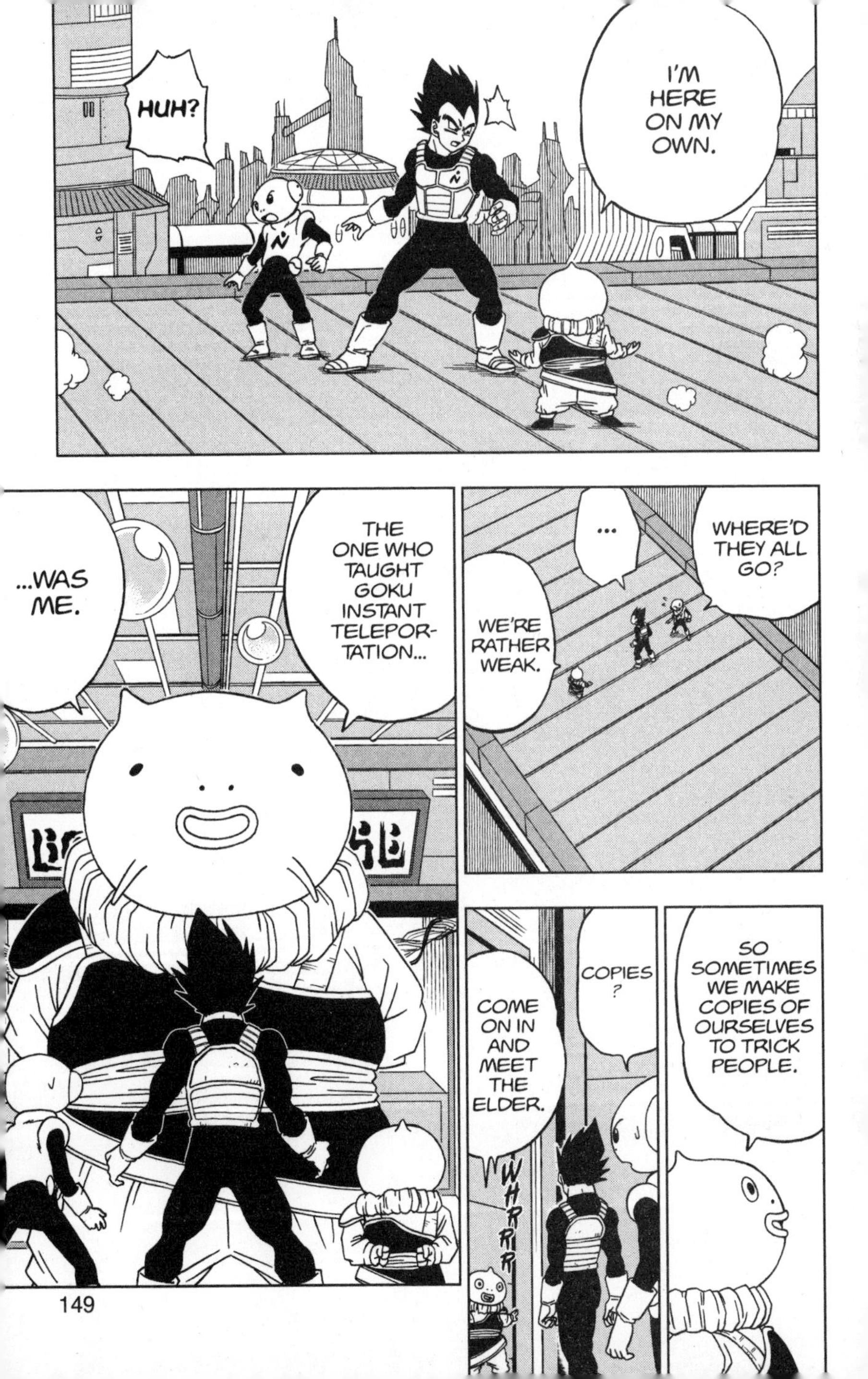

I'M HERE ON MY OWN.
HUH?
WHERE'D THEY ALL GO?
...
WE'RE RATHER WEAK.
SO SOMETIMES WE MAKE COPIES OF OURSELVES TO TRICK PEOPLE.
COPIES?
COME ON IN AND MEET THE ELDER.
WHRRRR
THE ONE WHO TAUGHT GOKU INSTANT TELEPORTATION...
...WAS ME.

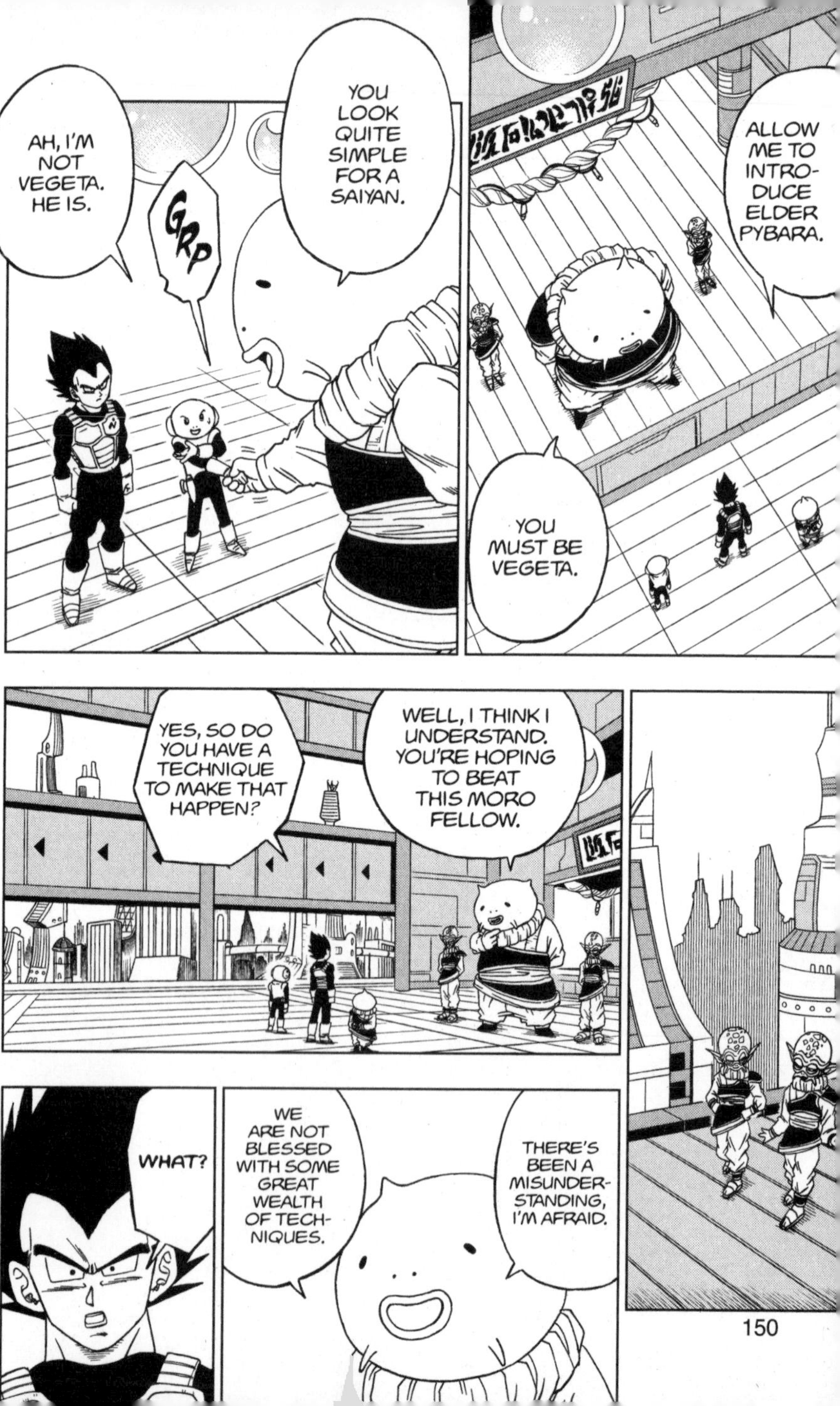
ALLOW ME TO INTRODUCE ELDER PYBARA.
YOU MUST BE VEGETA.
YOU LOOK QUITE SIMPLE FOR A SAIYAN.
GRP
AH, I'M NOT VEGETA. HE IS.
WELL, I THINK I UNDERSTAND. YOU'RE HOPING TO BEAT THIS MORO FELLOW.
YES, SO DO YOU HAVE A TECHNIQUE TO MAKE THAT HAPPEN?
THERE'S BEEN A MISUNDERSTANDING, I'M AFRAID.
WE ARE NOT BLESSED WITH SOME GREAT WEALTH OF TECHNIQUES.
WHAT?

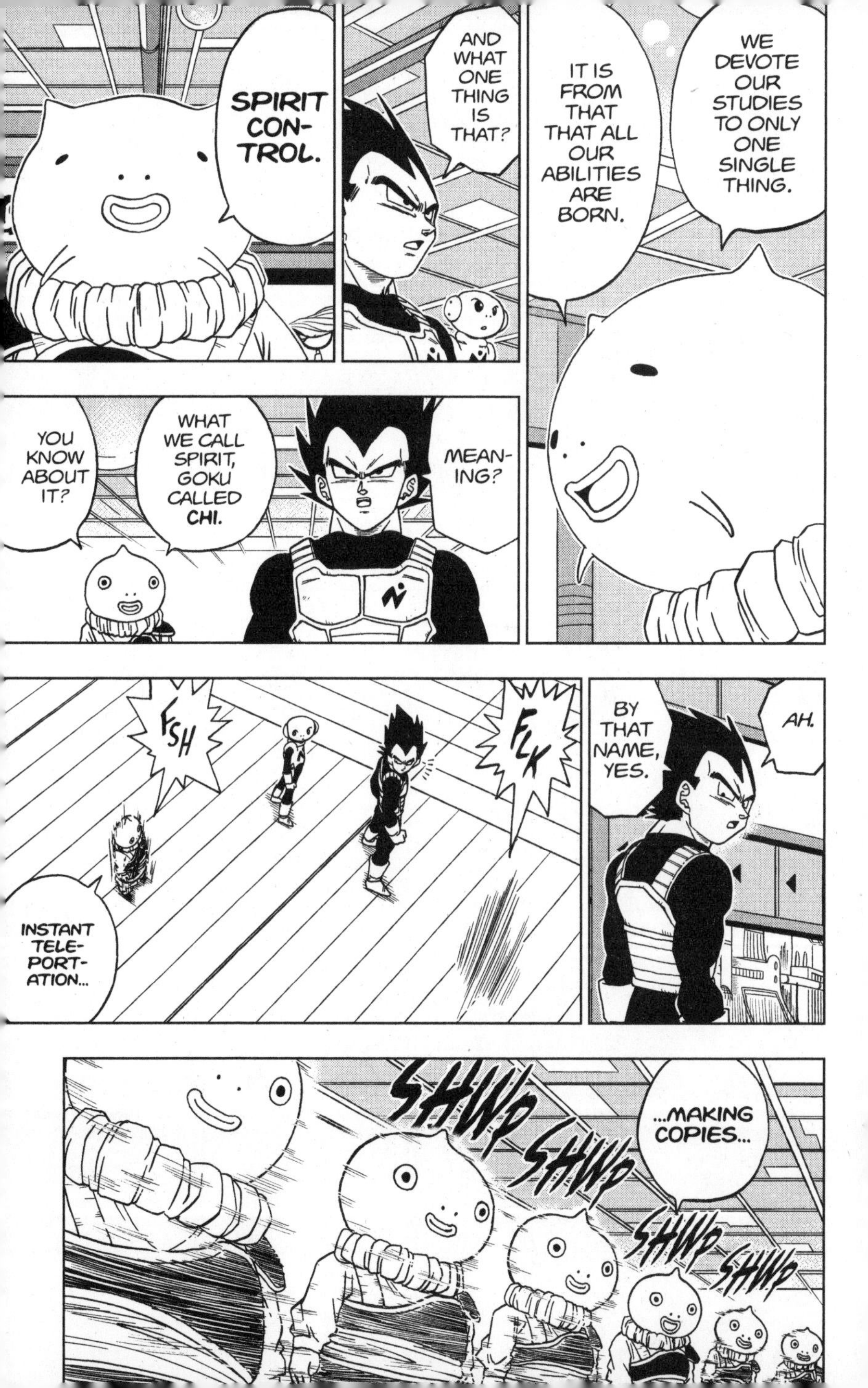
WE DEVOTE OUR STUDIES TO ONLY ONE SINGLE THING.
IT IS FROM THAT THAT ALL OUR ABILITIES ARE BORN.
AND WHAT ONE THING IS THAT?
SPIRIT CONTROL.
MEANING?
WHAT WE CALL SPIRIT, GOKU CALLED CHI.
YOU KNOW ABOUT IT?
AH.
BY THAT NAME, YES.
FLK
FSH
INSTANT TELEPORTATION...
SHWP
SHWP
...MAKING COPIES...
SHWP
SHWP

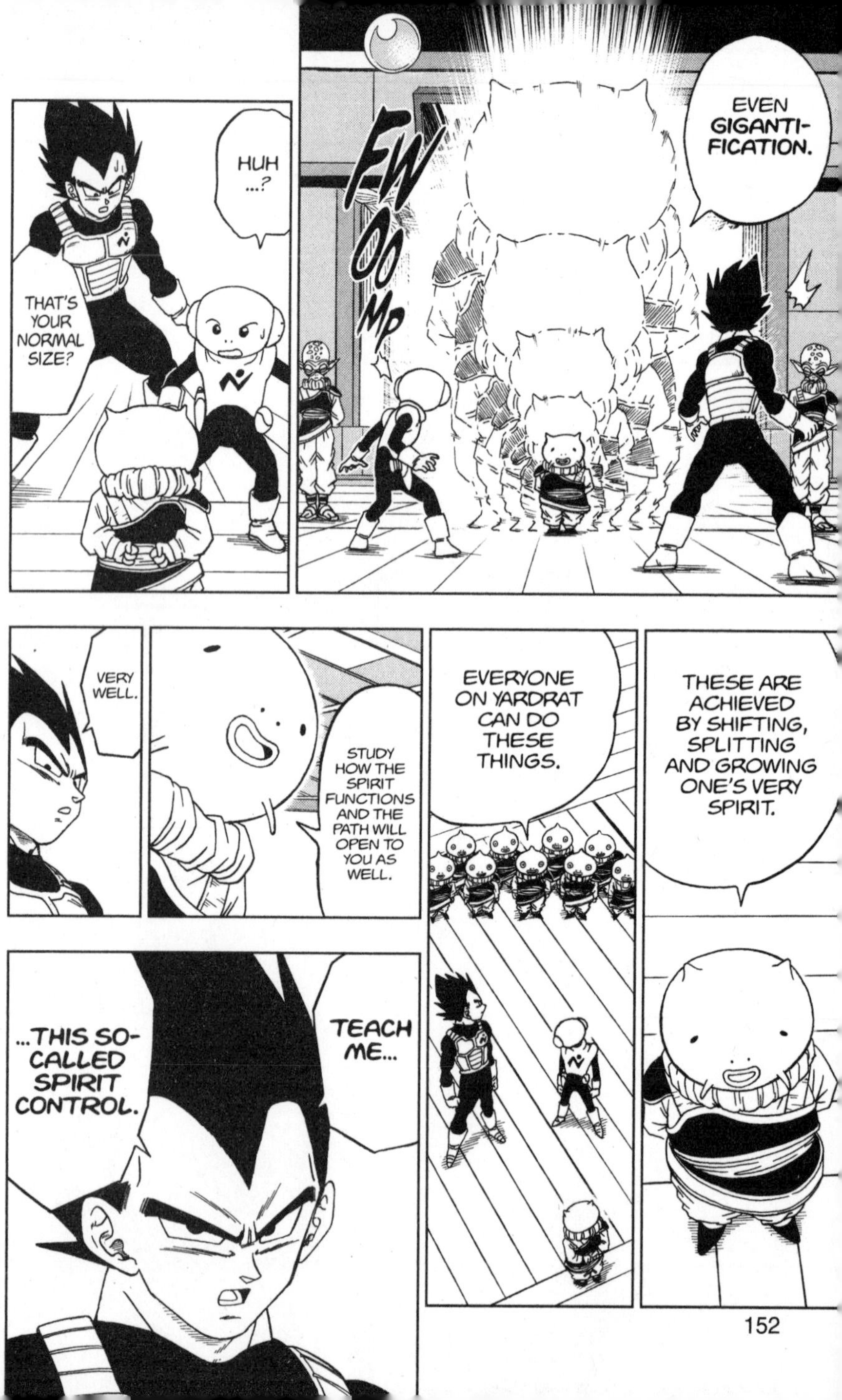
FWOOMP
EVEN GIGANTI-FICATION.
HUH ...?
THAT'S YOUR NORMAL SIZE?
THESE ARE ACHIEVED BY SHIFTING, SPLITTING AND GROWING ONE'S VERY SPIRIT.
EVERYONE ON YARDRAT CAN DO THESE THINGS.
STUDY HOW THE SPIRIT FUNCTIONS AND THE PATH WILL OPEN TO YOU AS WELL.
VERY WELL.
TEACH ME...
...THIS SO-CALLED SPIRIT CONTROL.

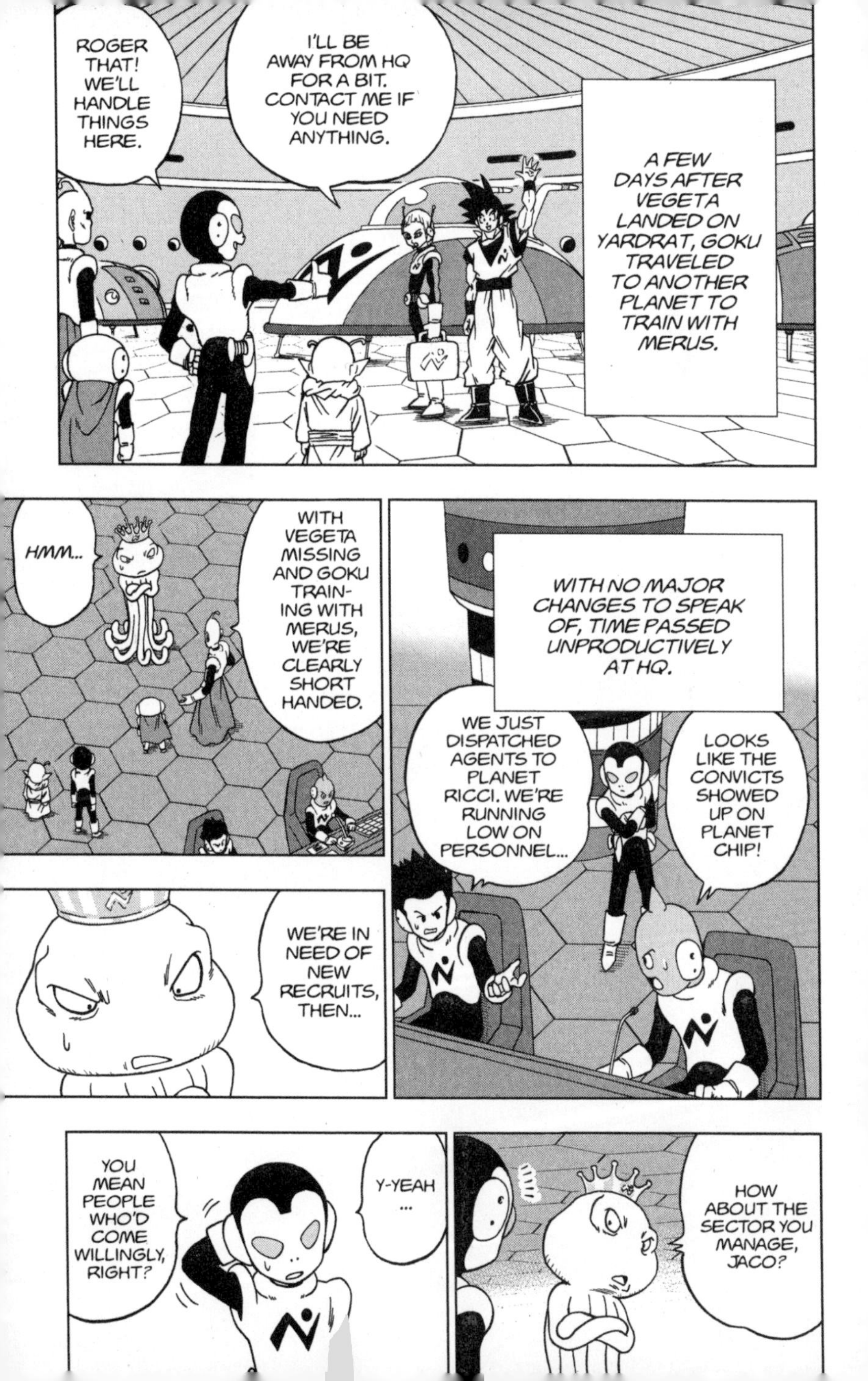
A FEW DAYS AFTER VEGETA LANDED ON YARDRAT, GOKU TRAVELED TO ANOTHER PLANET TO TRAIN WITH MERUS.
I'LL BE AWAY FROM HQ FOR A BIT. CONTACT ME IF YOU NEED ANYTHING.
ROGER THAT! WE'LL HANDLE THINGS HERE.
WITH NO MAJOR CHANGES TO SPEAK OF, TIME PASSED UNPRODUCTIVELY AT HQ.
LOOKS LIKE THE CONVICTS SHOWED UP ON PLANET CHIP!
WE JUST DISPATCHED AGENTS TO PLANET RICCI. WE'RE RUNNING LOW ON PERSONNEL...
WITH VEGETA MISSING AND GOKU TRAIN-ING WITH MERUS, WE'RE CLEARLY SHORT HANDED.
HMM...
WE'RE IN NEED OF NEW RECRUITS, THEN...
HOW ABOUT THE SECTOR YOU MANAGE, JACO?
Y-YEAH ...
YOU MEAN PEOPLE WHO'D COME WILLINGLY, RIGHT?

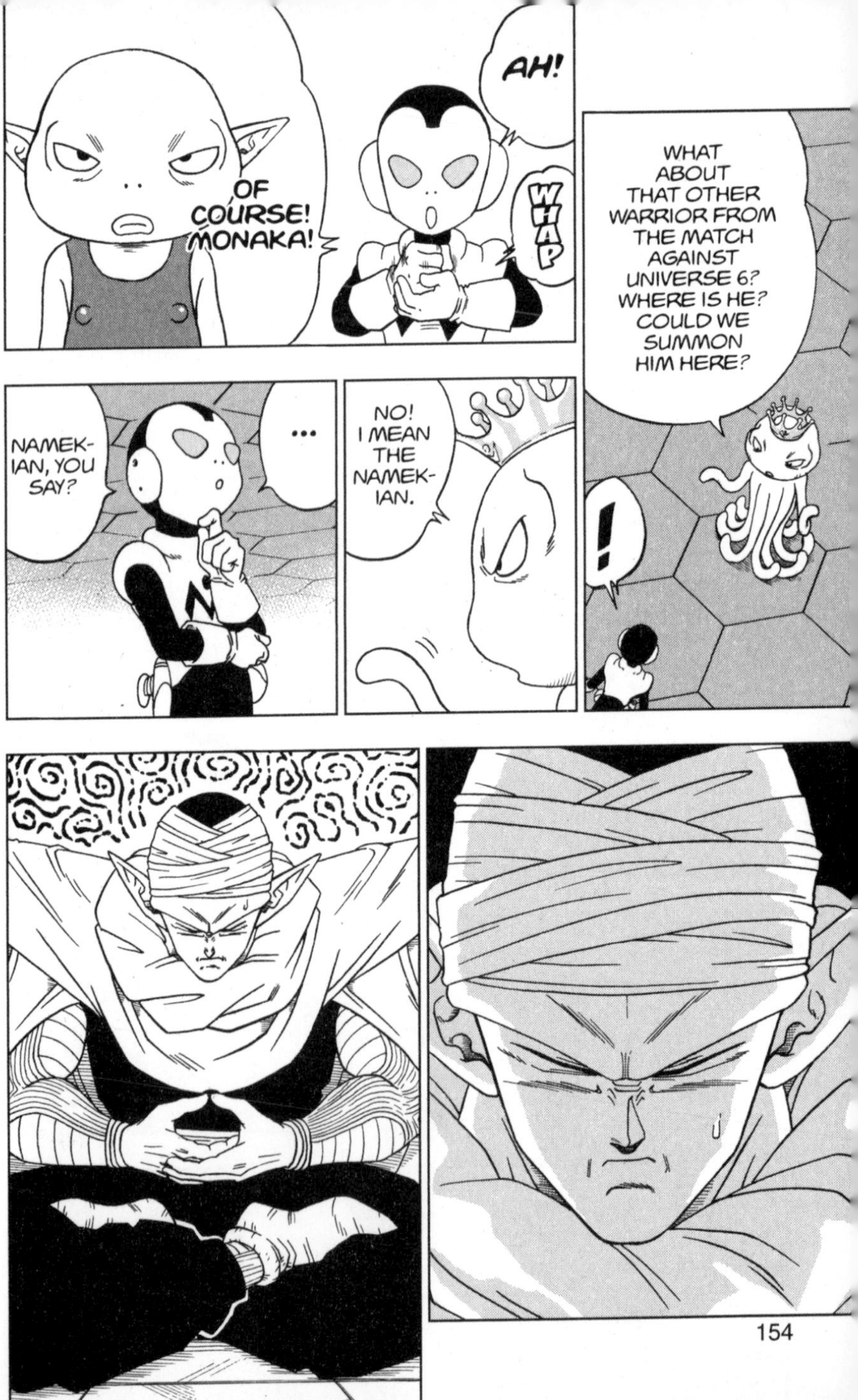
WHAT ABOUT THAT OTHER WARRIOR FROM THE MATCH AGAINST UNIVERSE 6? WHERE IS HE? COULD WE SUMMON HIM HERE?
!
AH!
WHAP
OF COURSE! MONAKA!
NO! I MEAN THE NAMEK-IAN.
...
NAMEK-IAN, YOU SAY?

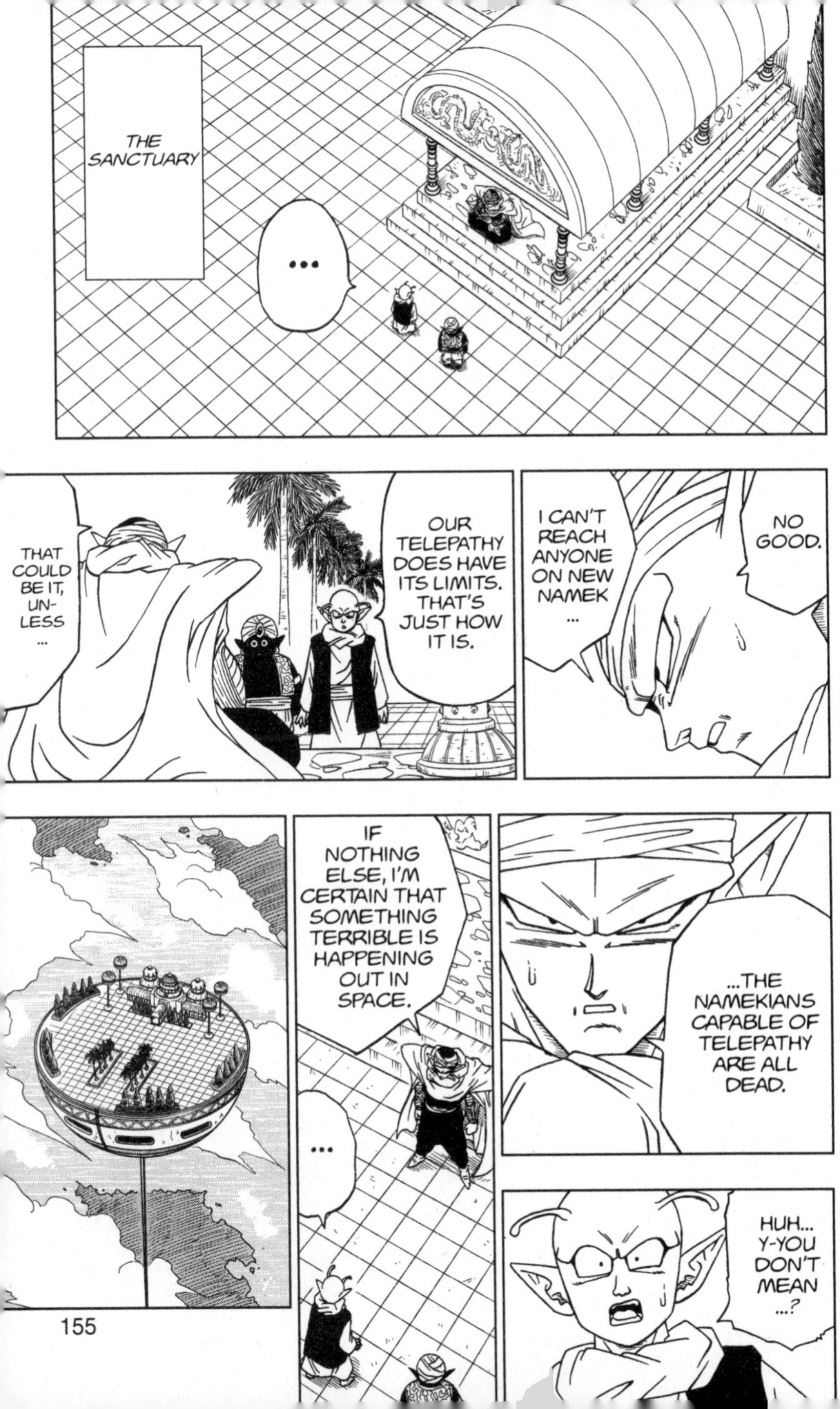
THE SANCTUARY
...
NO GOOD.
I CAN'T REACH ANYONE ON NEW NAMEK...
OUR TELEPATHY DOES HAVE ITS LIMITS. THAT'S JUST HOW IT IS.
THAT COULD BE IT, UN-LESS...
...THE NAMEKIANS CAPABLE OF TELEPATHY ARE ALL DEAD.
HUH... Y-YOU DON'T MEAN...?
IF NOTHING ELSE, I'M CERTAIN THAT SOMETHING TERRIBLE IS HAPPENING OUT IN SPACE.
...

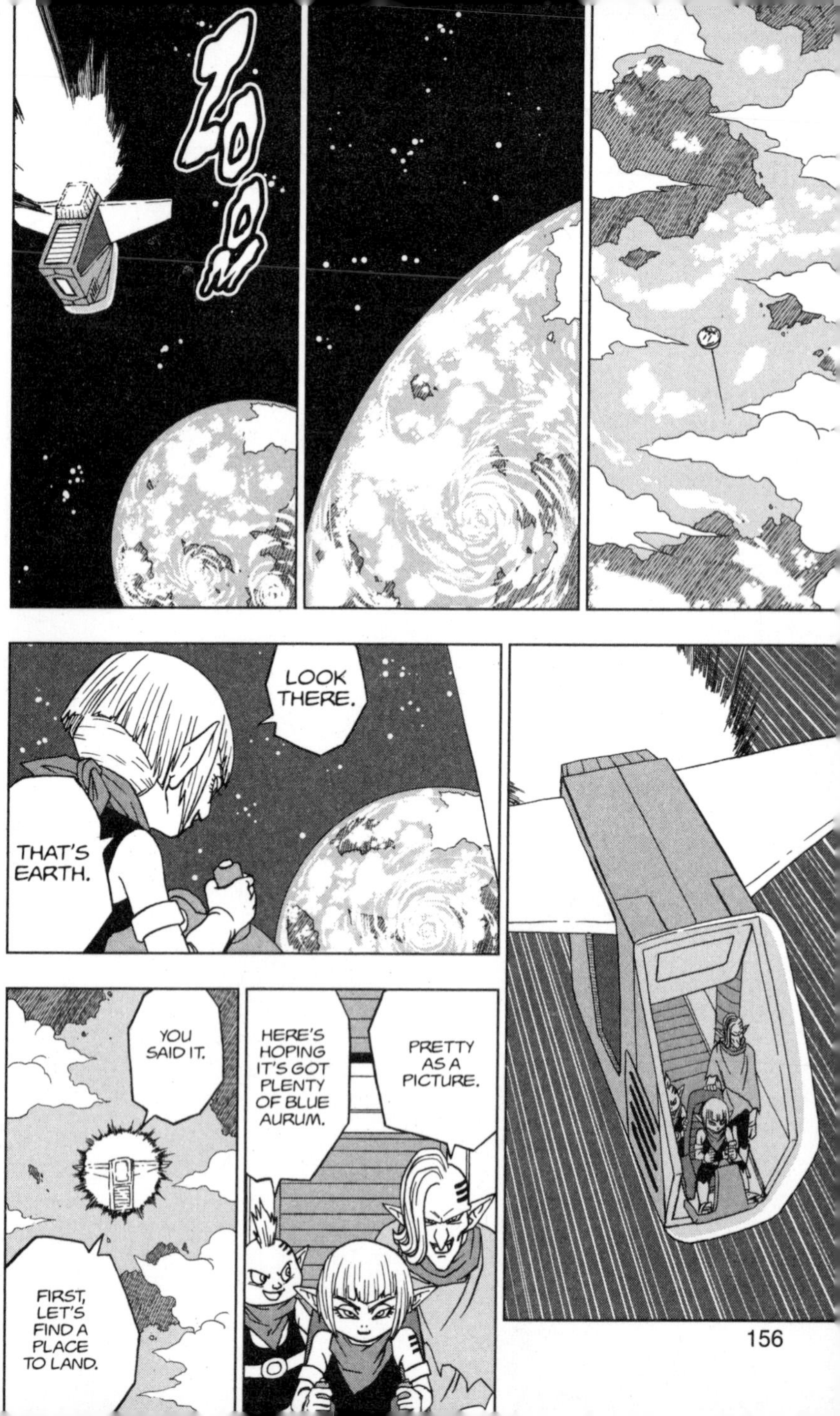
ZOOM
LOOK THERE.
THAT'S EARTH.
PRETTY AS A PICTURE.
HERE'S HOPING IT'S GOT PLENTY OF BLUE AURUM.
YOU SAID IT.
FIRST, LET'S FIND A PLACE TO LAND.

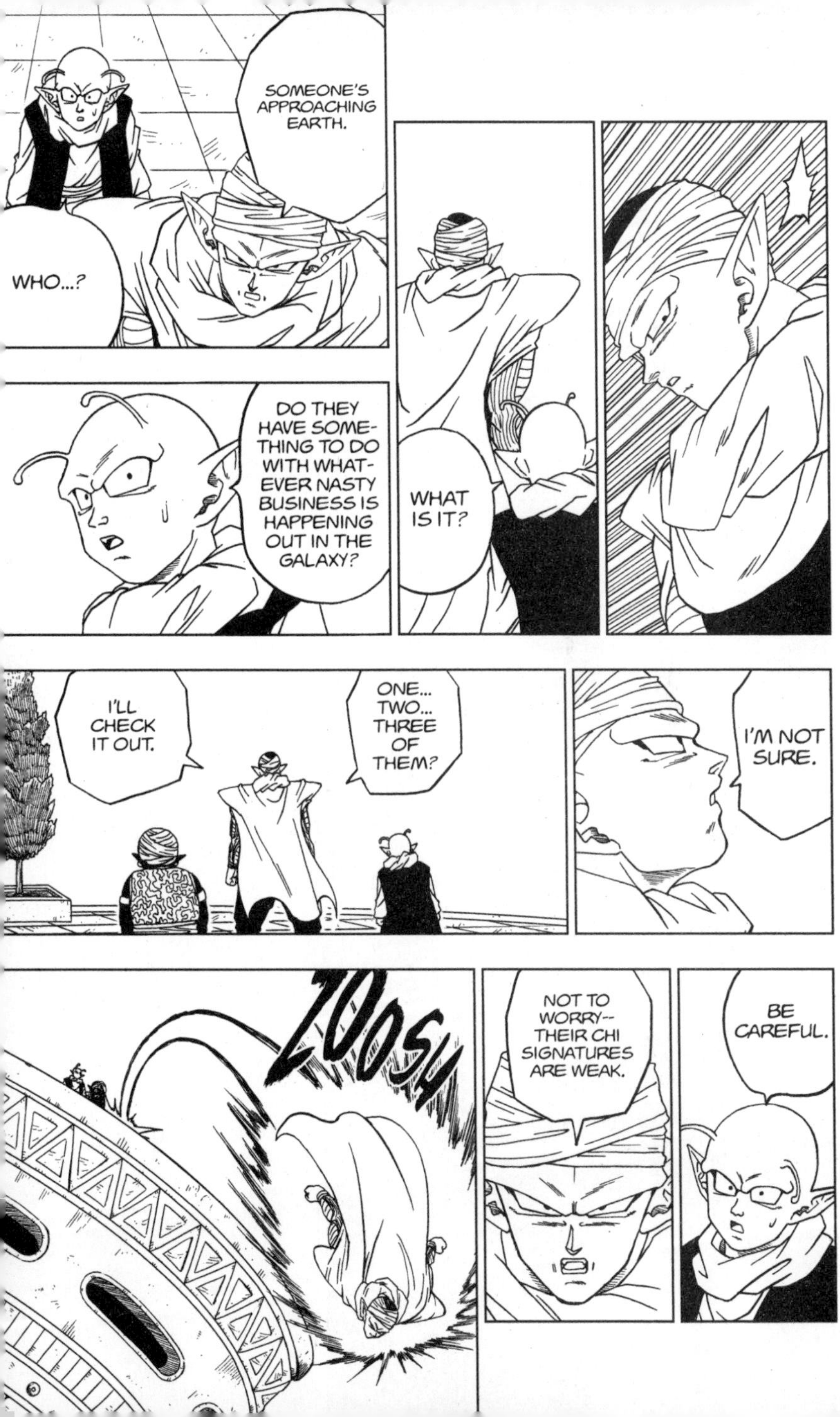
WHAT IS IT?
SOMEONE'S APPROACHING EARTH.
WHO...?
DO THEY HAVE SOMETHING TO DO WITH WHATEVER NASTY BUSINESS IS HAPPENING OUT IN THE GALAXY?
I'M NOT SURE.
ONE... TWO... THREE OF THEM?
I'LL CHECK IT OUT.
BE CAREFUL.
NOT TO WORRY-- THEIR CHI SIGNATURES ARE WEAK.
ZOOSH

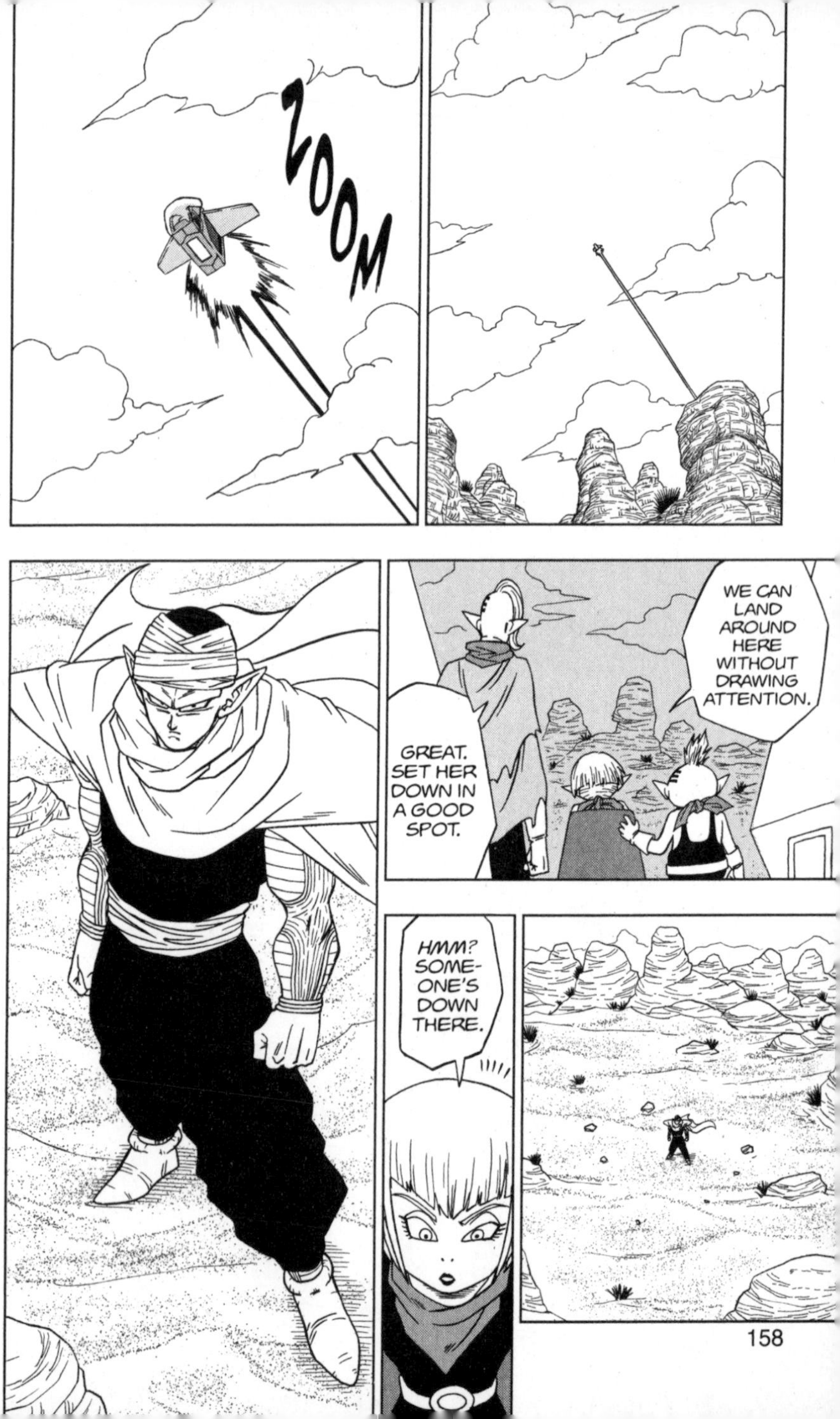
ZOOM
WE CAN LAND AROUND HERE WITHOUT DRAWING ATTENTION.
GREAT. SET HER DOWN IN A GOOD SPOT.
HMM? SOME-ONE'S DOWN THERE.

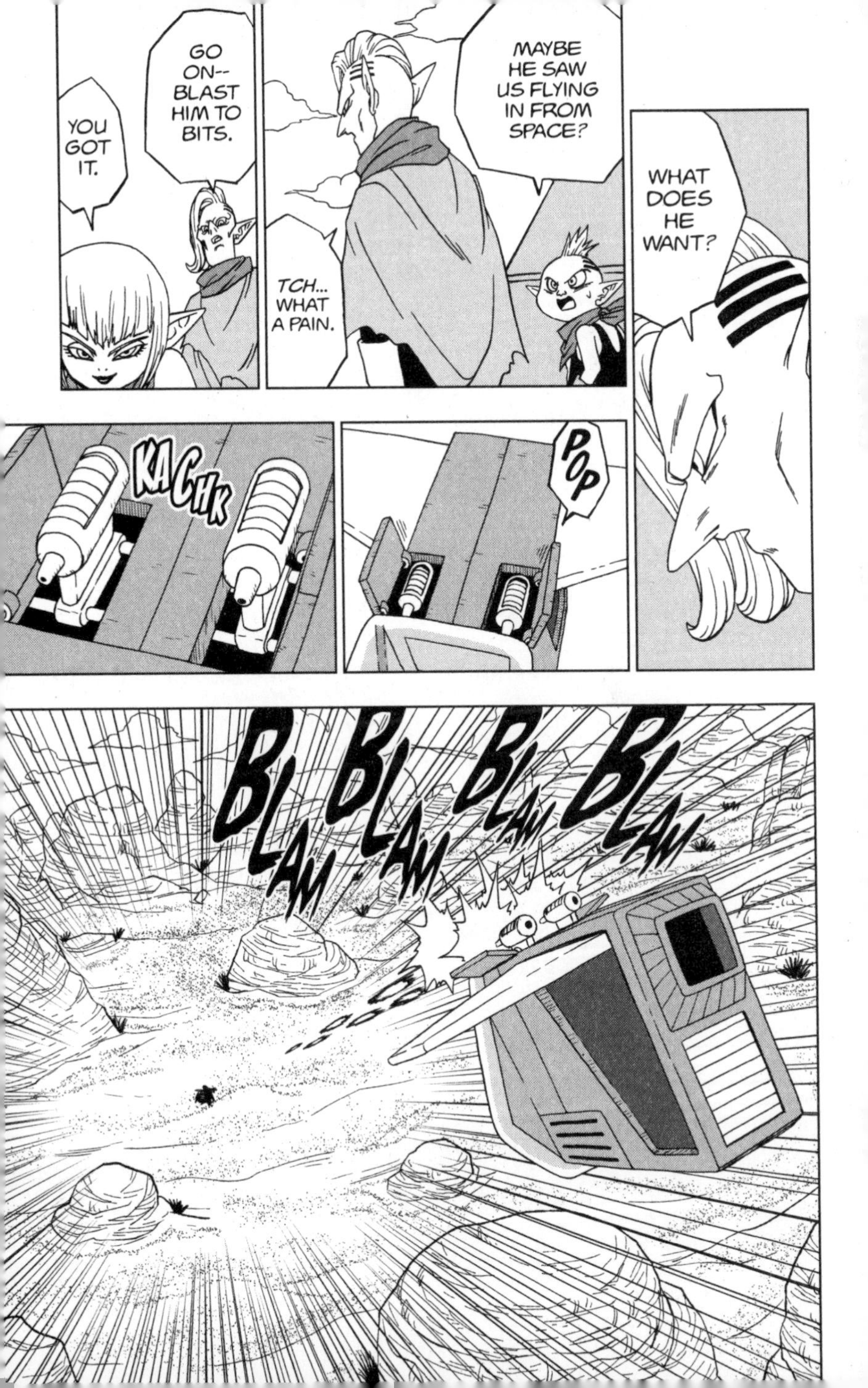
WHAT DOES HE WANT?
MAYBE HE SAW US FLYING IN FROM SPACE?
TCH... WHAT A PAIN.
GO ON-- BLAST HIM TO BITS.
YOU GOT IT.
POP
KACHK
BLAM BLAM BLAM BLAM

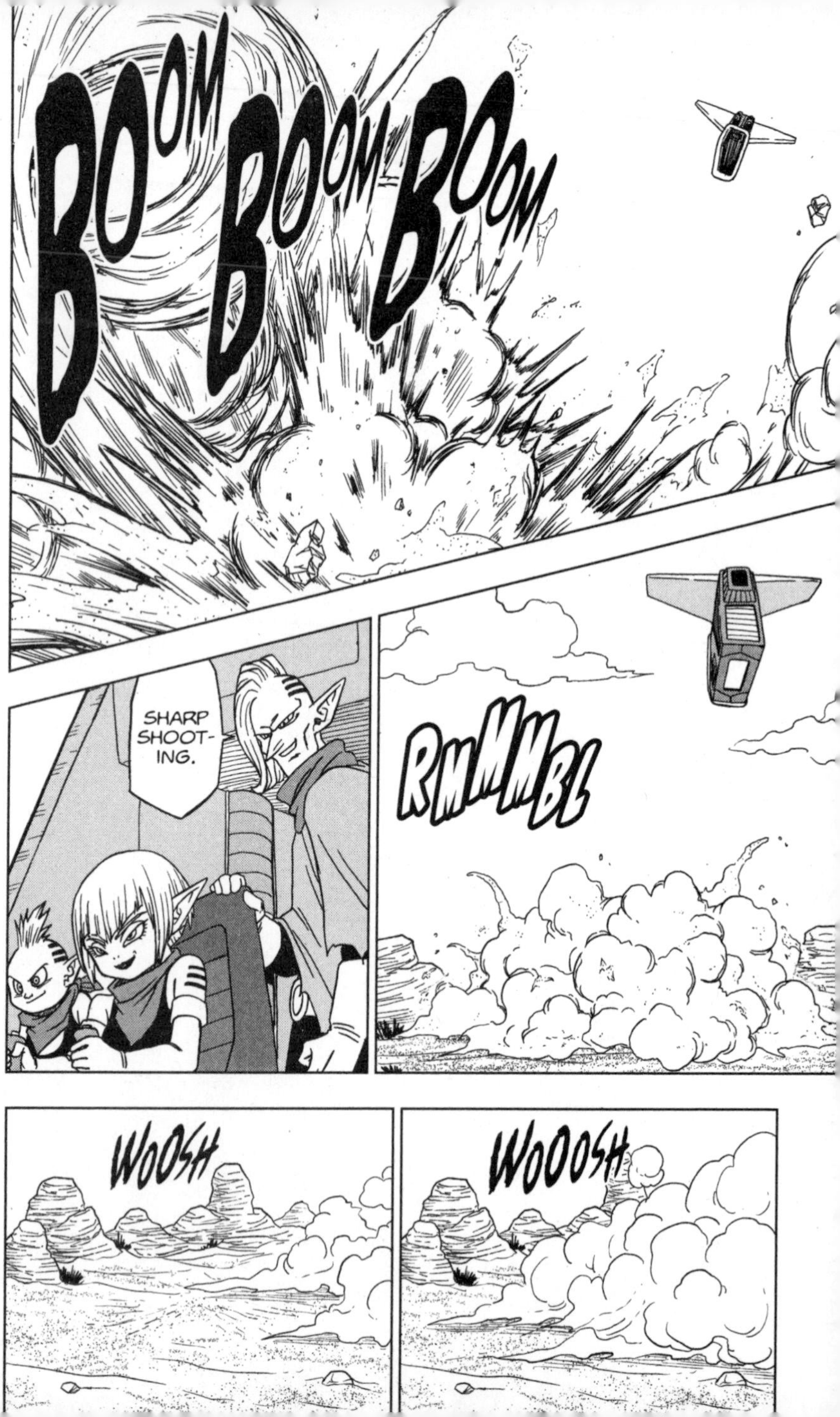
BOOM
BOOM
BOOM
RMMMBL
SHARP SHOOT-ING.
WOOOSH
WOOSH

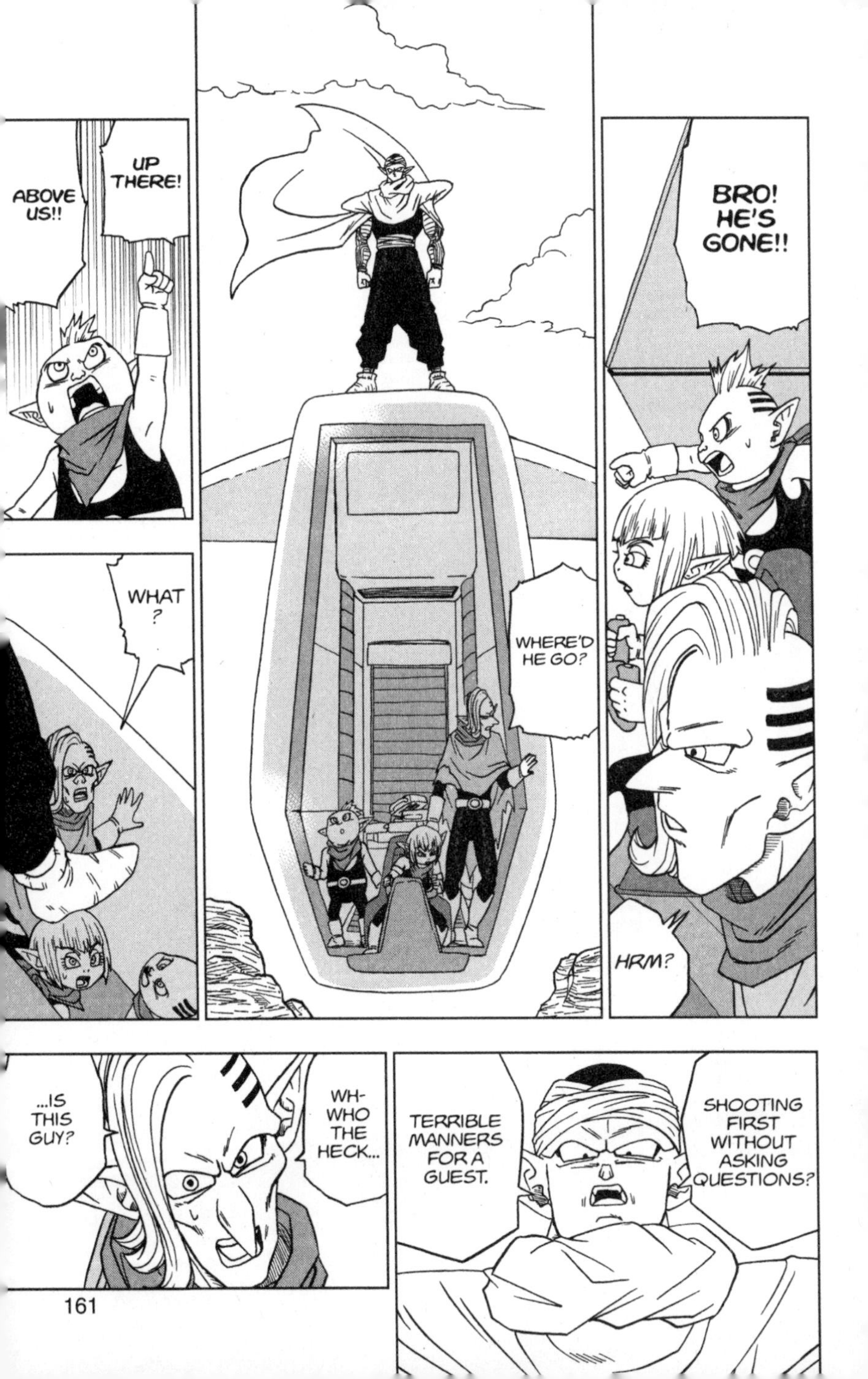
BRO! HE'S GONE!!
HRM?
WHERE'D HE GO?
UP THERE!
ABOVE US!!
WHAT ?
SHOOTING FIRST WITHOUT ASKING QUESTIONS?
TERRIBLE MANNERS FOR A GUEST.
WH- WHO THE HECK...
...IS THIS GUY?

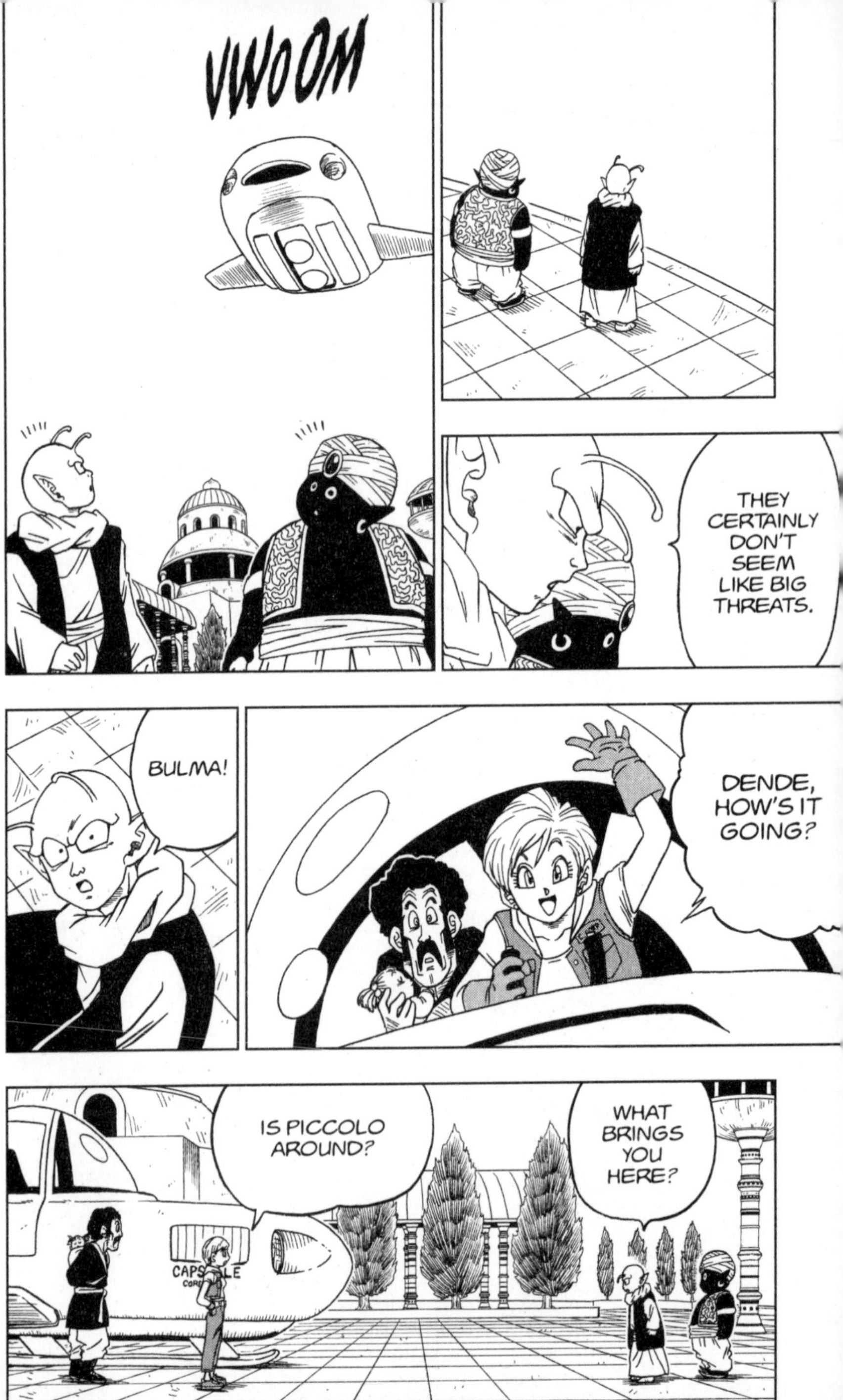
VWOOM
THEY CERTAINLY DON'T SEEM LIKE BIG THREATS.
DENDE, HOW'S IT GOING?
BULMA!
WHAT BRINGS YOU HERE?
IS PICCOLO AROUND?

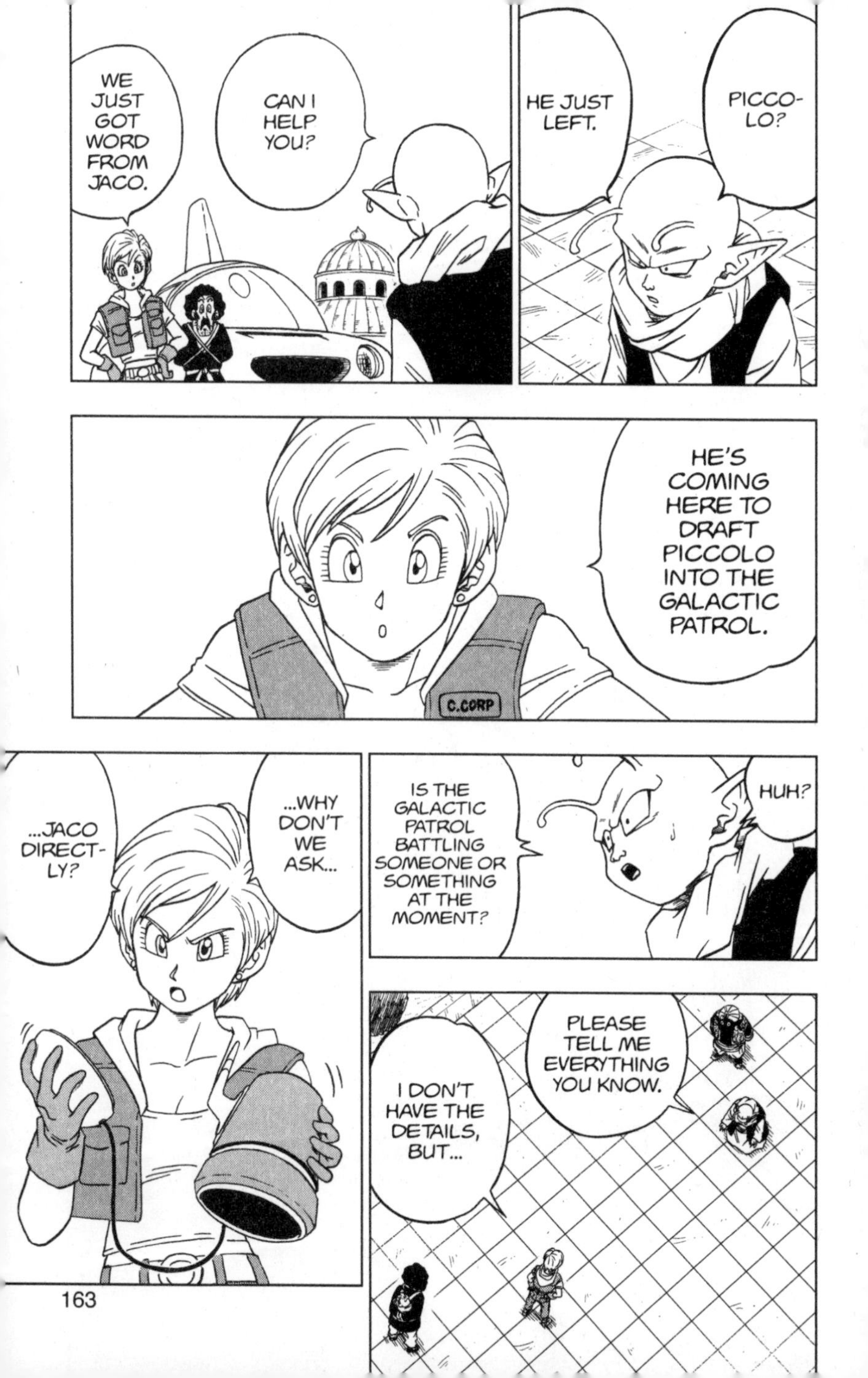
PICCO-LO?
HE JUST LEFT.
CAN I HELP YOU?
WE JUST GOT WORD FROM JACO.
HE'S COMING HERE TO DRAFT PICCOLO INTO THE GALACTIC PATROL.
C.CORP
HUH?
IS THE GALACTIC PATROL BATTLING SOMEONE OR SOMETHING AT THE MOMENT?
PLEASE TELL ME EVERYTHING YOU KNOW.
I DON'T HAVE THE DETAILS, BUT...
...WHY DON'T WE ASK...
...JACO DIRECT-LY?

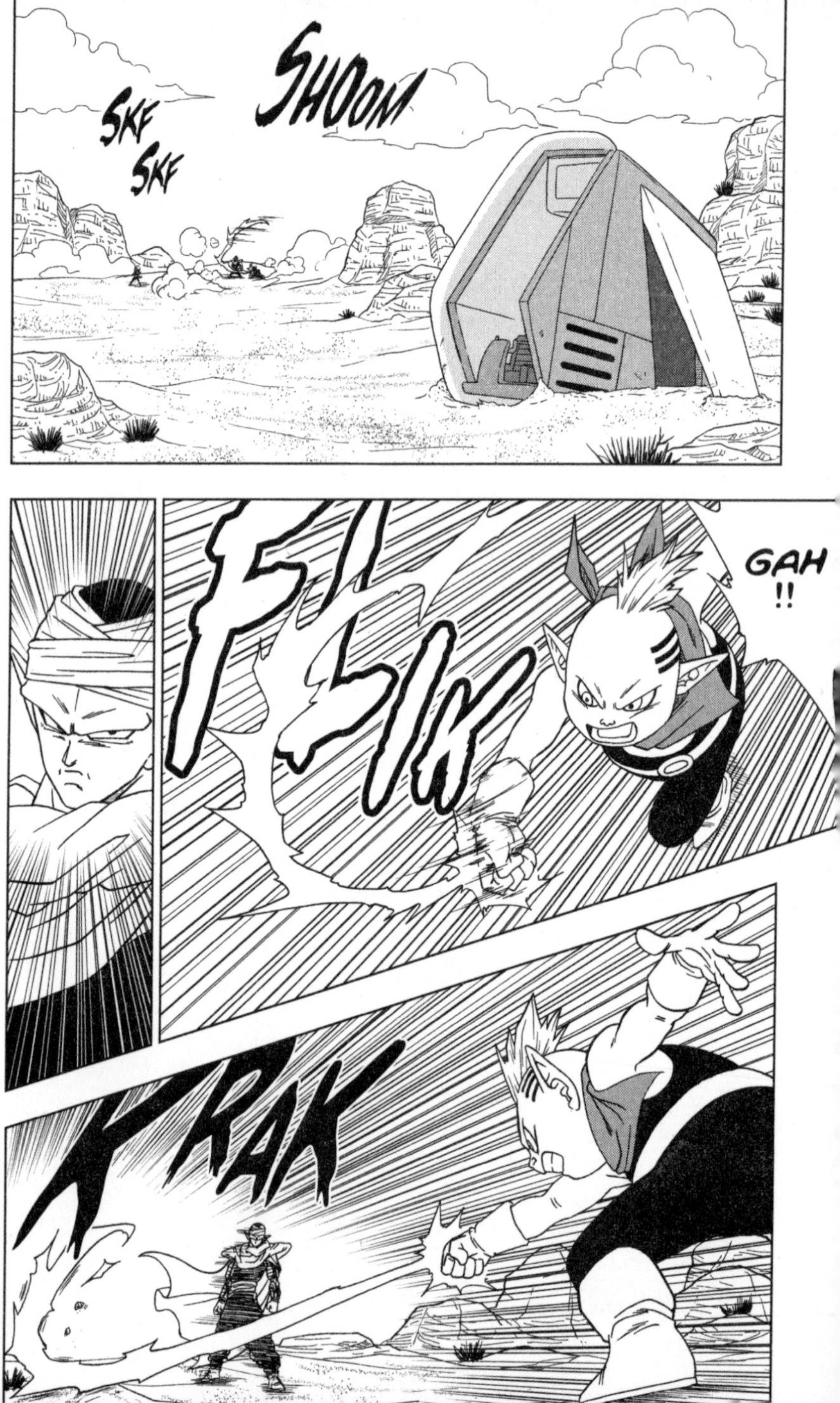
SHOOM
SKF
SKF
GAH !!
KRAK

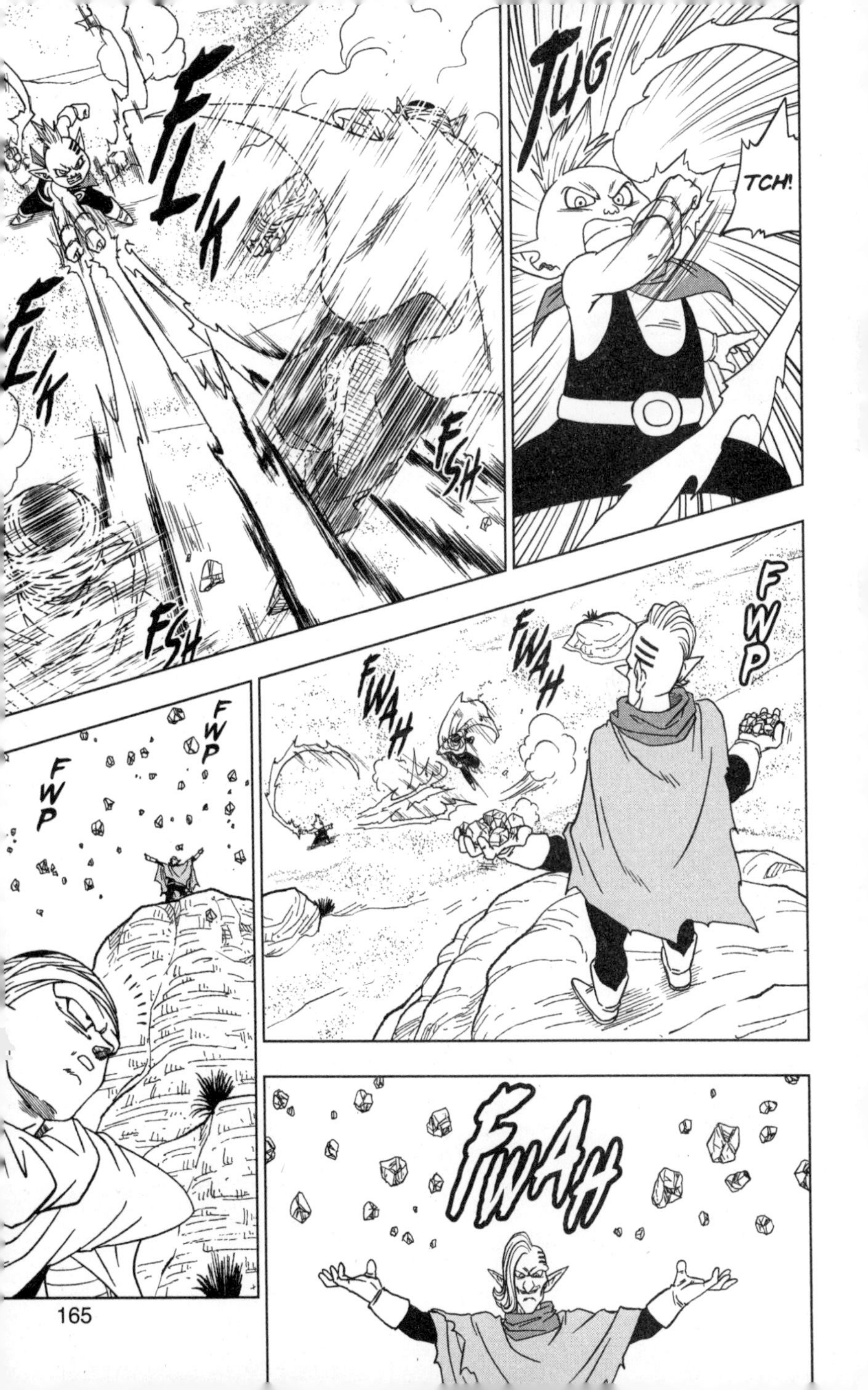
TUG
TCH!
FLIK
FLIK
FSH
FSH
FWP
FWAH
FWAH
FWAH
FWP
FWP

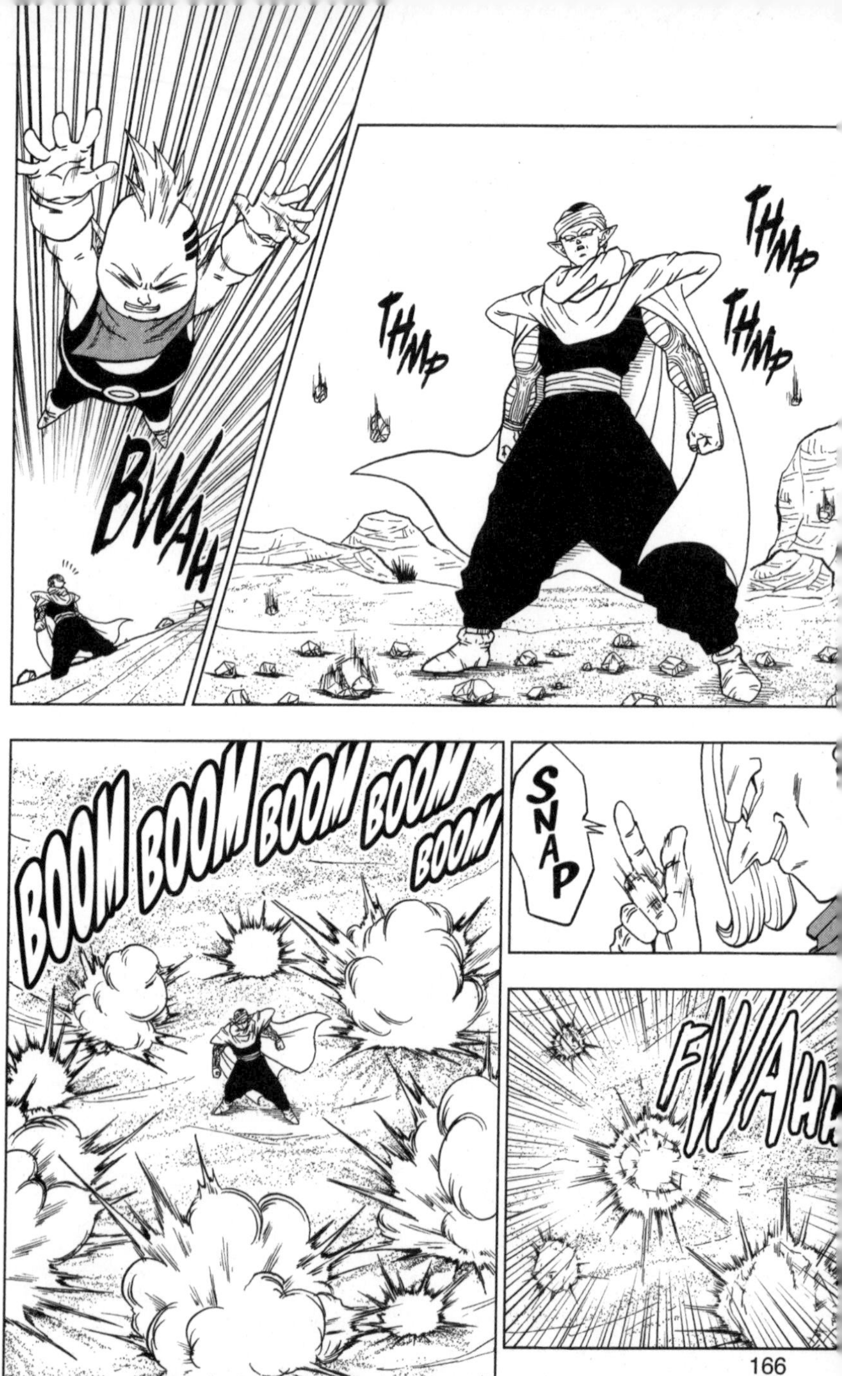
THMP
THMP
THMP
BWAH
SNAP
FWAH
BOOM BOOM BOOM BOOM BOOM

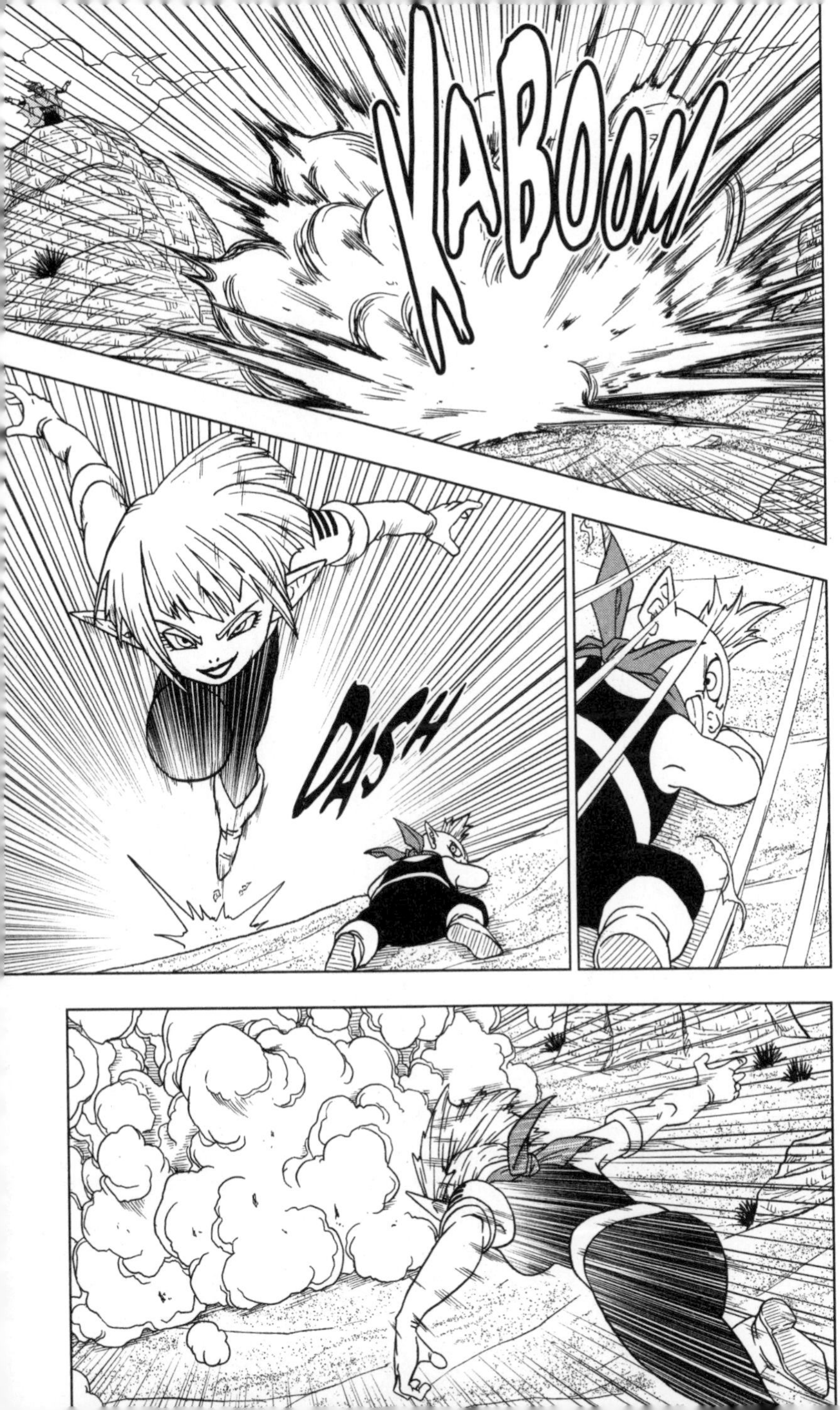
KABOOM
DASH

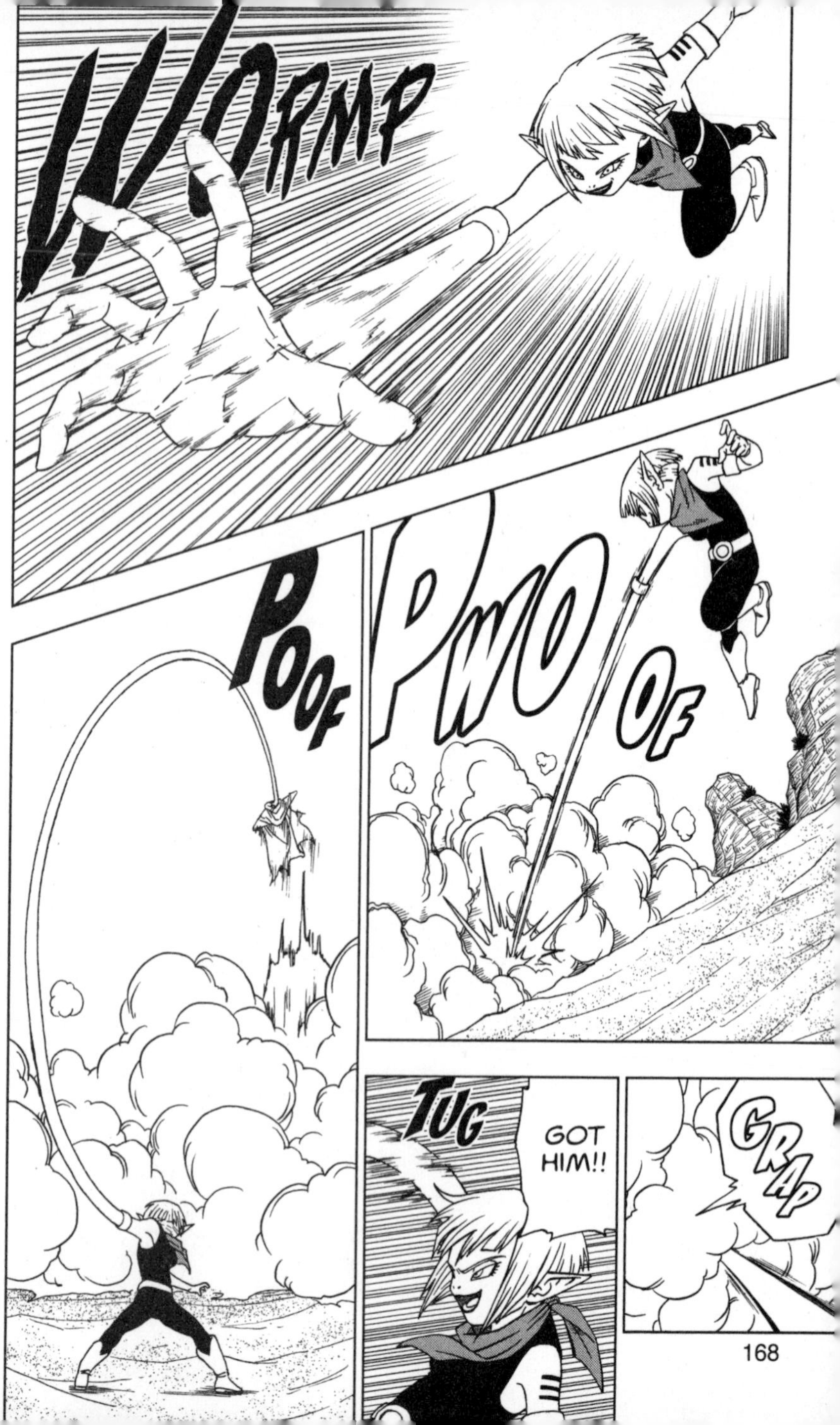
WORMP
PWOOF
POOF
GRAP
GOT HIM!!
TUG

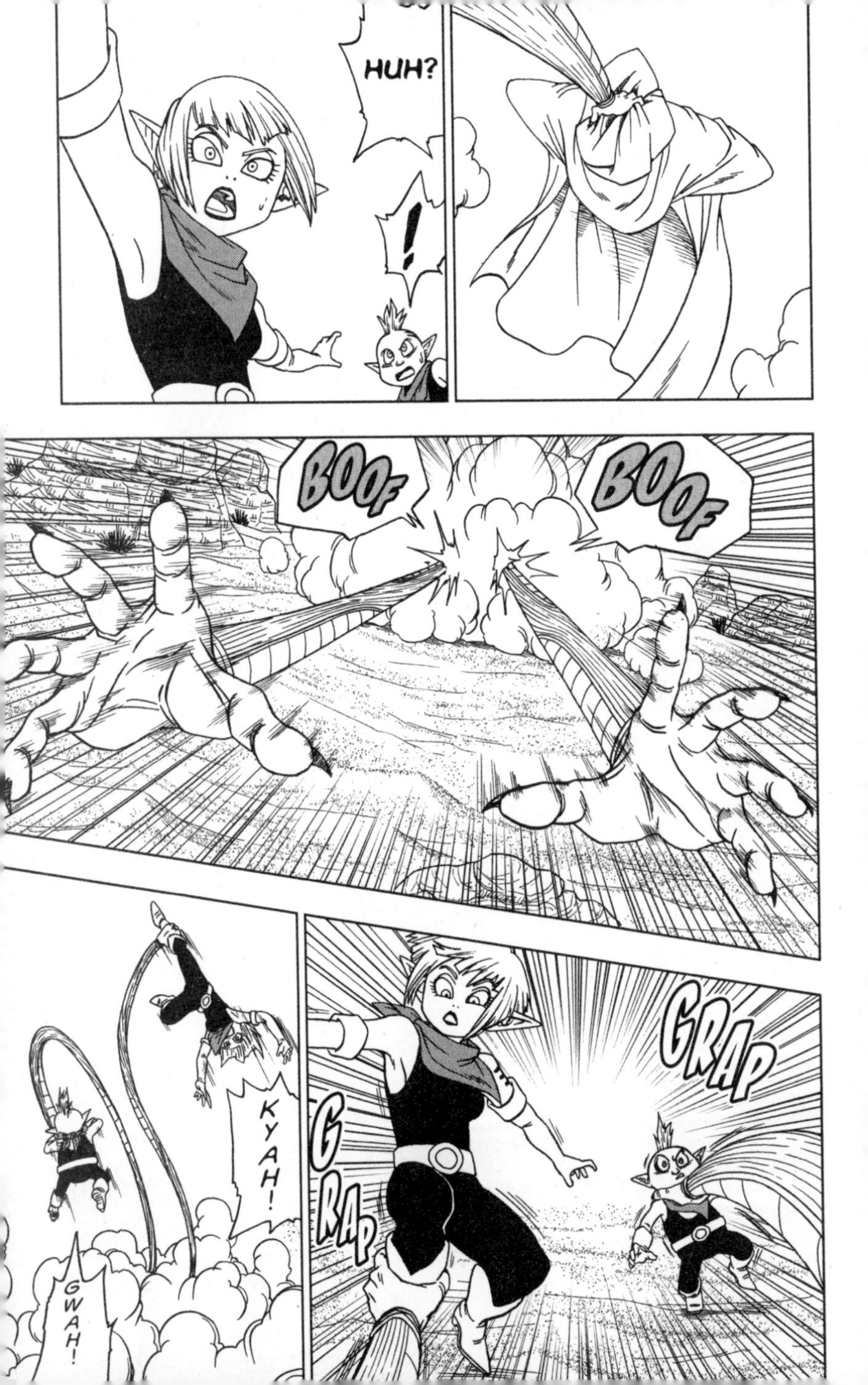
HUH?
!
BOOF
BOOF
GRAP
GRAP
KYAH!
GWAH!

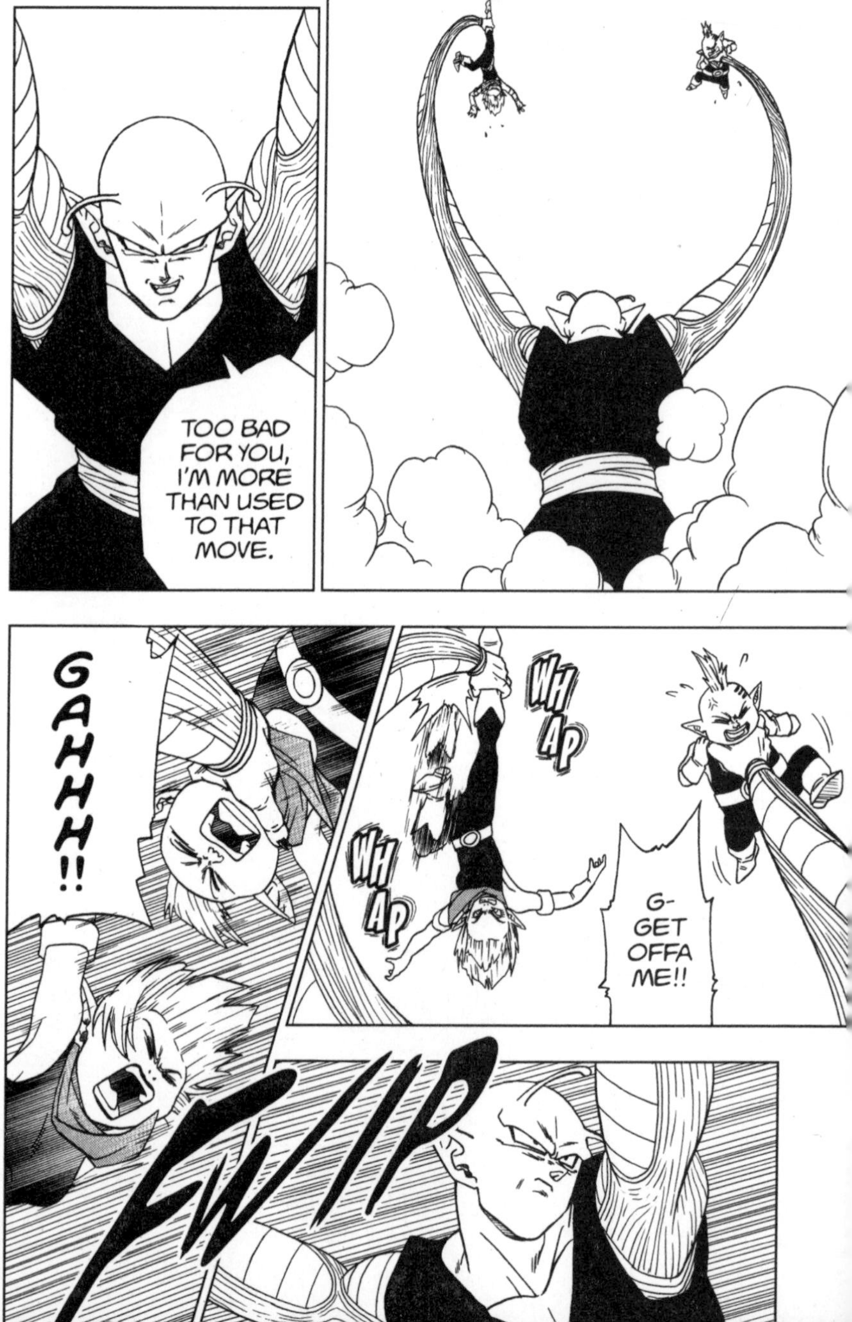
TOO BAD FOR YOU, I'M MORE THAN USED TO THAT MOVE.
WHAP
WHAP
G-GET OFFA ME!!
FWIP
GAHHHH!!

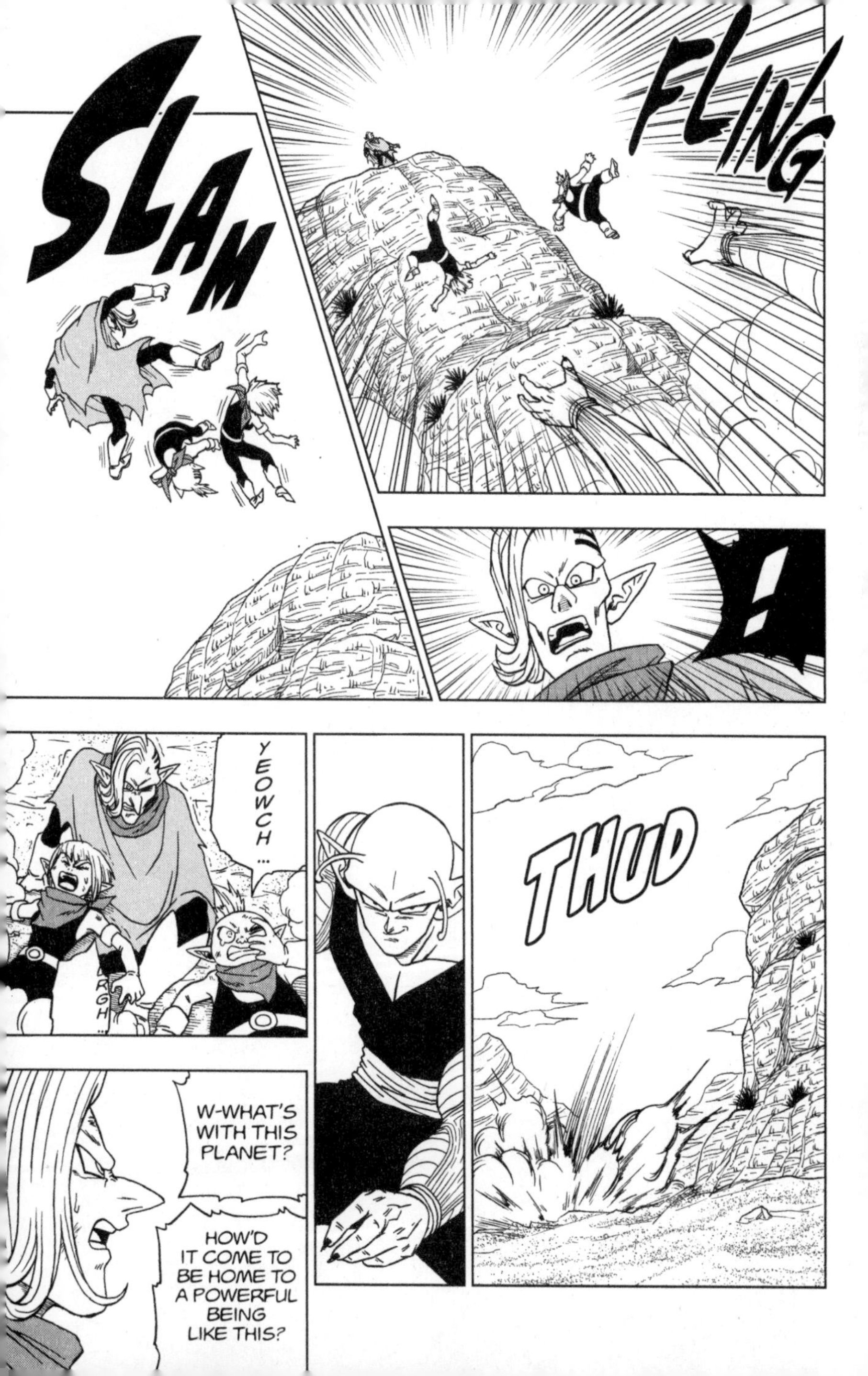
FLING
SLAM
!
THUD
YEOWCH...
W-WHAT'S WITH THIS PLANET?
HOW'D IT COME TO BE HOME TO A POWERFUL BEING LIKE THIS?

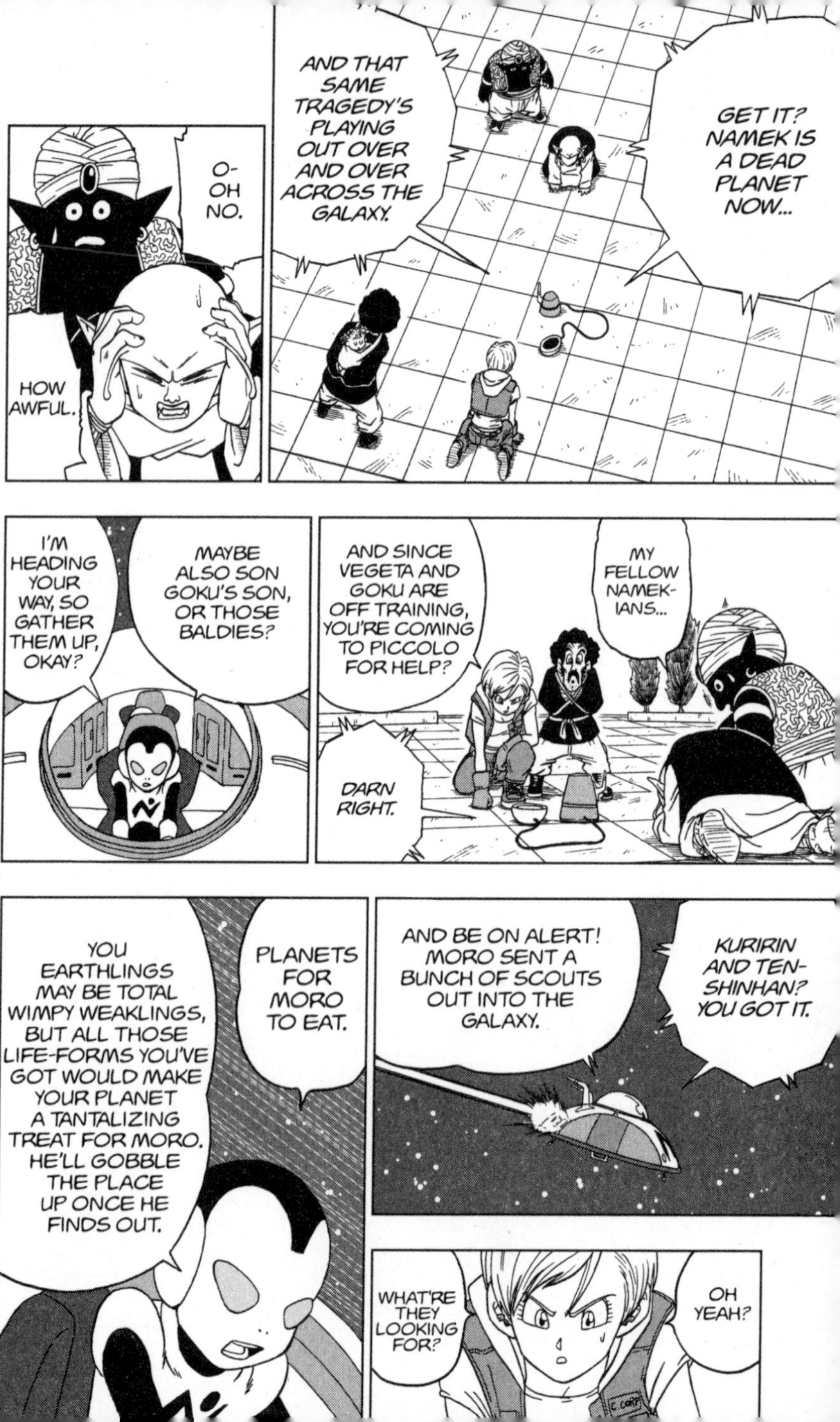
GET IT? NAMEK IS A DEAD PLANET NOW...
AND THAT SAME TRAGEDY'S PLAYING OUT OVER AND OVER ACROSS THE GALAXY.
O- OH NO.
HOW AWFUL.
MY FELLOW NAMEK-IANS...
AND SINCE VEGETA AND GOKU ARE OFF TRAINING, YOU'RE COMING TO PICCOLO FOR HELP?
DARN RIGHT.
MAYBE ALSO SON GOKU'S SON, OR THOSE BALDIES?
I'M HEADING YOUR WAY, SO GATHER THEM UP, OKAY?
KURIRIN AND TEN-SHINHAN? YOU GOT IT.
AND BE ON ALERT! MORO SENT A BUNCH OF SCOUTS OUT INTO THE GALAXY.
OH YEAH?
WHAT'RE THEY LOOKING FOR?
PLANETS FOR MORO TO EAT.
YOU EARTHLINGS MAY BE TOTAL WIMPY WEAKLINGS, BUT ALL THOSE LIFE-FORMS YOU'VE GOT WOULD MAKE YOUR PLANET A TANTALIZING TREAT FOR MORO. HE'LL GOBBLE THE PLACE UP ONCE HE FINDS OUT.

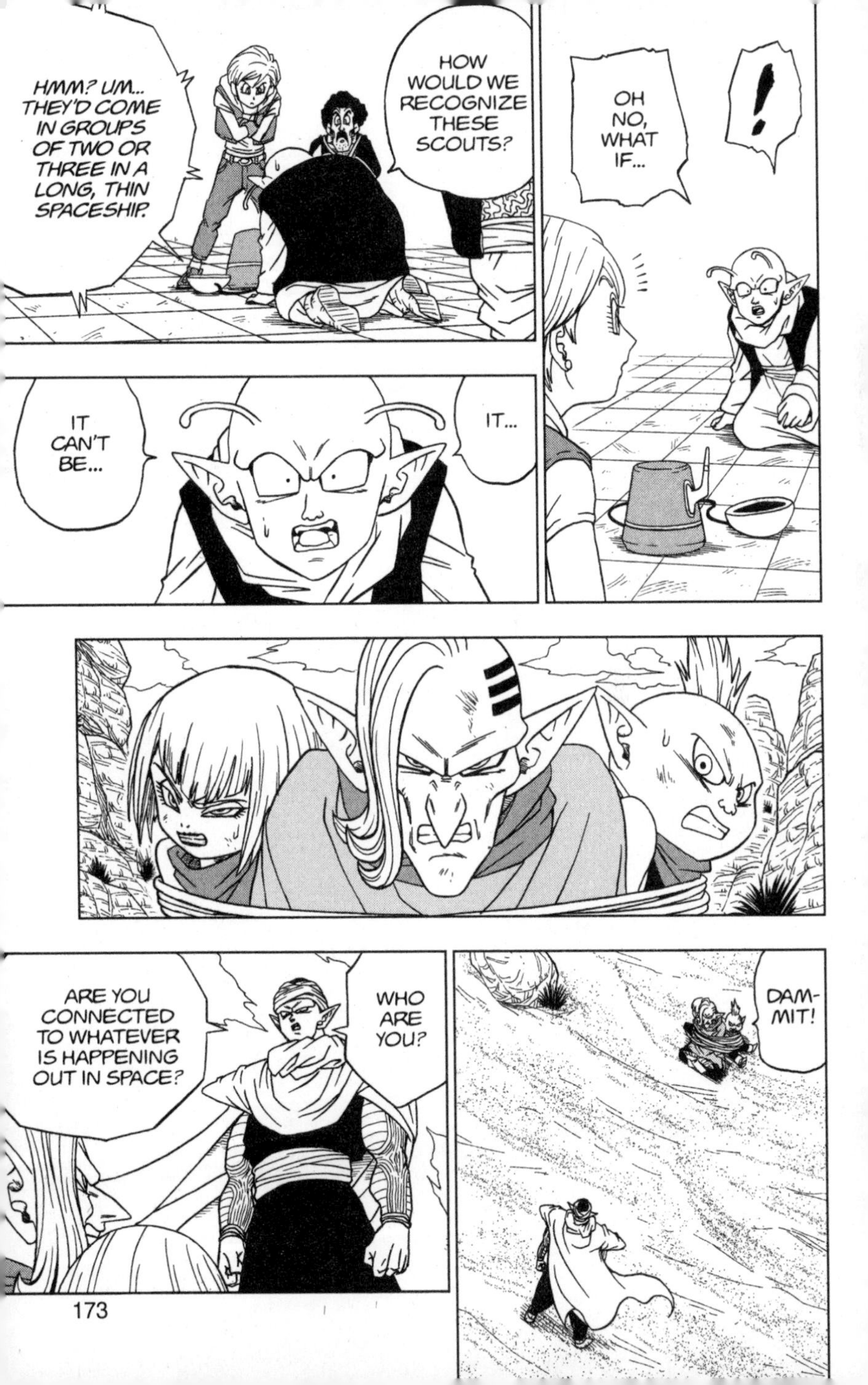
HOW WOULD WE RECOGNIZE THESE SCOUTS?
HMM? UM... THEY'D COME IN GROUPS OF TWO OR THREE IN A LONG, THIN SPACESHIP.
!
OH NO, WHAT IF...
IT...
IT CAN'T BE...
DAM-MIT!
WHO ARE YOU?
ARE YOU CONNECTED TO WHATEVER IS HAPPENING OUT IN SPACE?

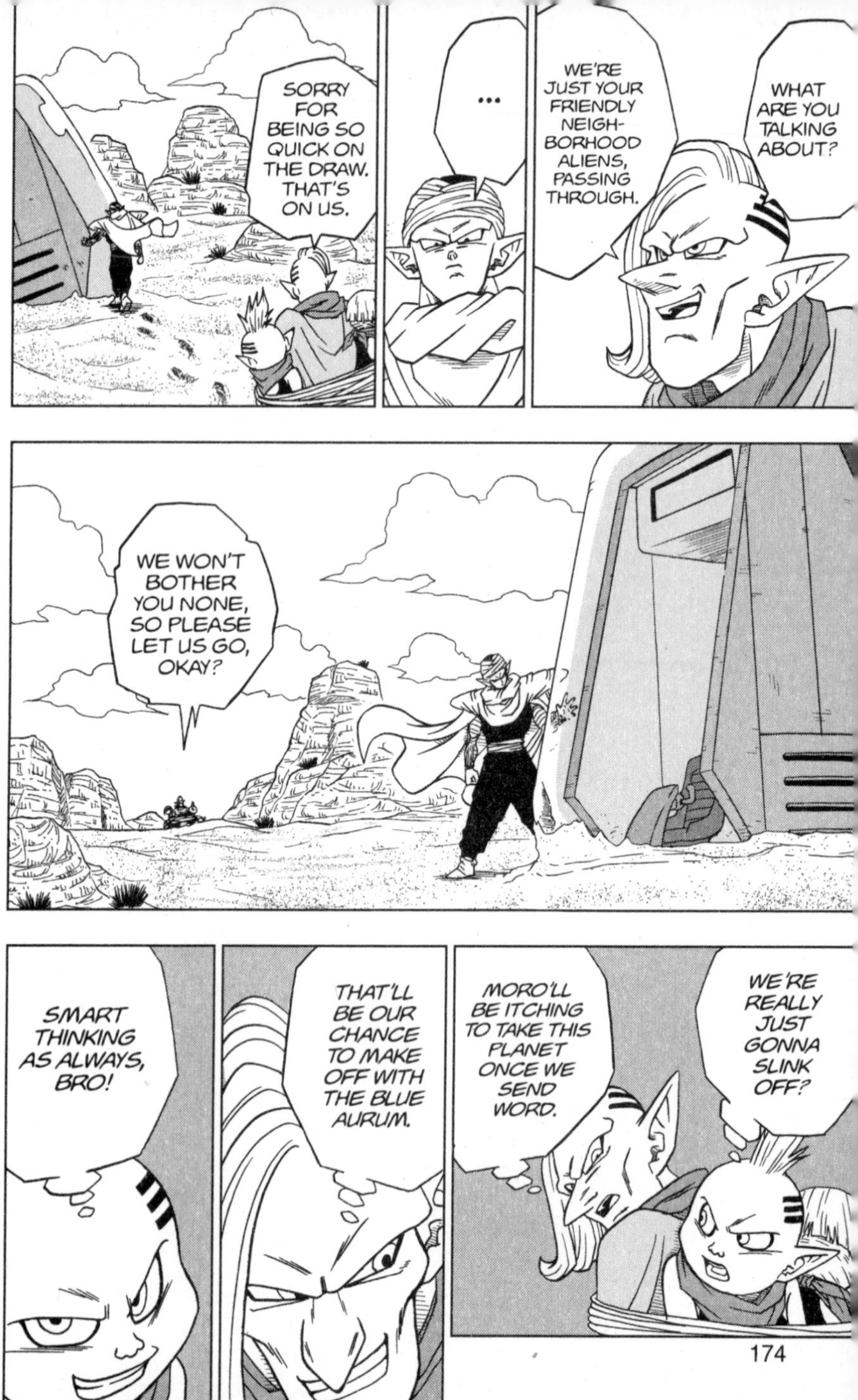
WHAT ARE YOU TALKING ABOUT?
WE'RE JUST YOUR FRIENDLY NEIGH-BORHOOD ALIENS, PASSING THROUGH.
...
SORRY FOR BEING SO QUICK ON THE DRAW. THAT'S ON US.
WE WON'T BOTHER YOU NONE, SO PLEASE LET US GO, OKAY?
WE'RE REALLY JUST GONNA SLINK OFF?
MORO'LL BE ITCHING TO TAKE THIS PLANET ONCE WE SEND WORD.
THAT'LL BE OUR CHANCE TO MAKE OFF WITH THE BLUE AURUM.
SMART THINKING AS ALWAYS, BRO!

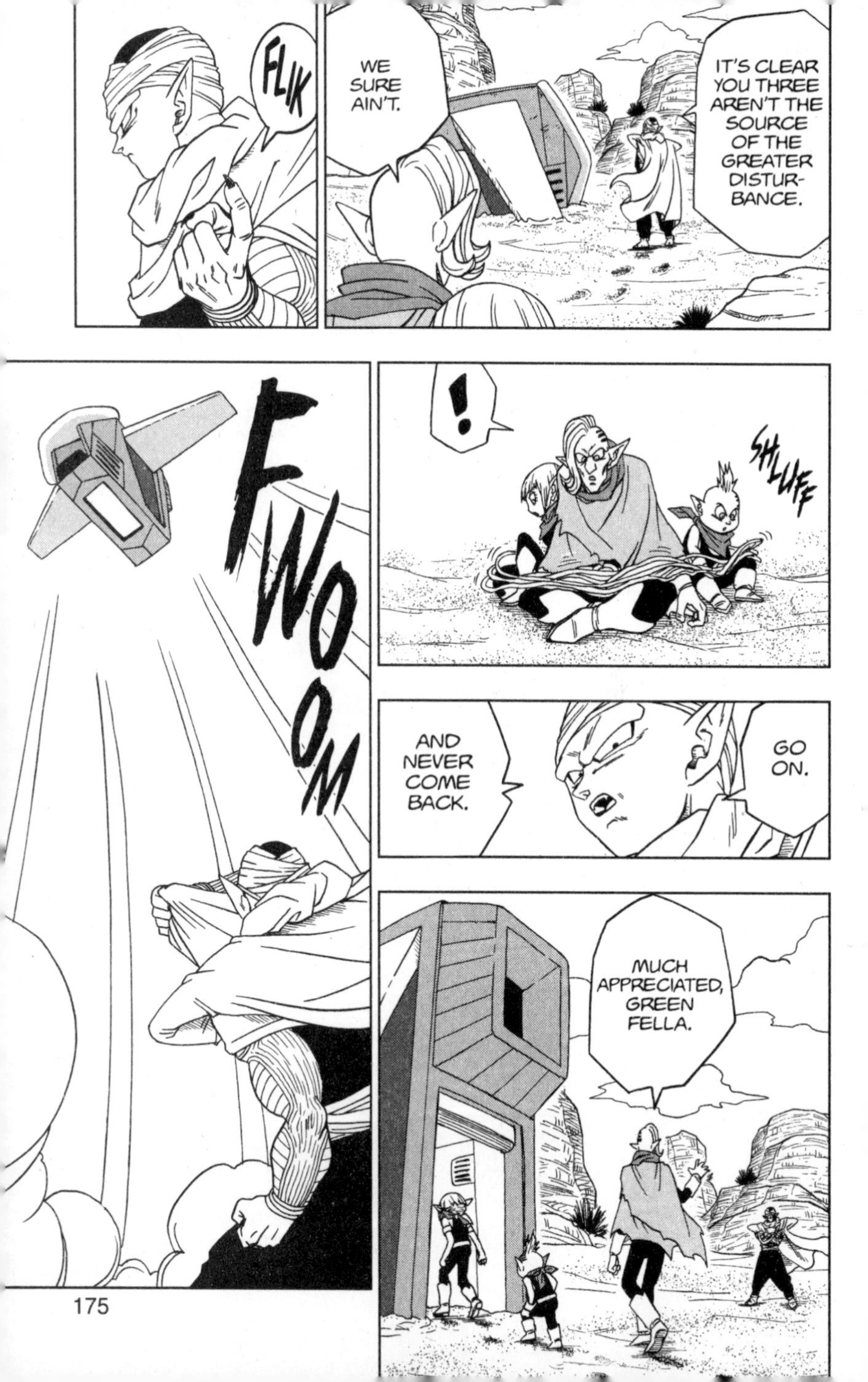
IT'S CLEAR YOU THREE AREN'T THE SOURCE OF THE GREATER DISTUR-BANCE.
WE SURE AIN'T.
FLIK
!
SHLUFF
GO ON.
AND NEVER COME BACK.
MUCH APPRECIATED, GREEN FELLA.
FWOOOM

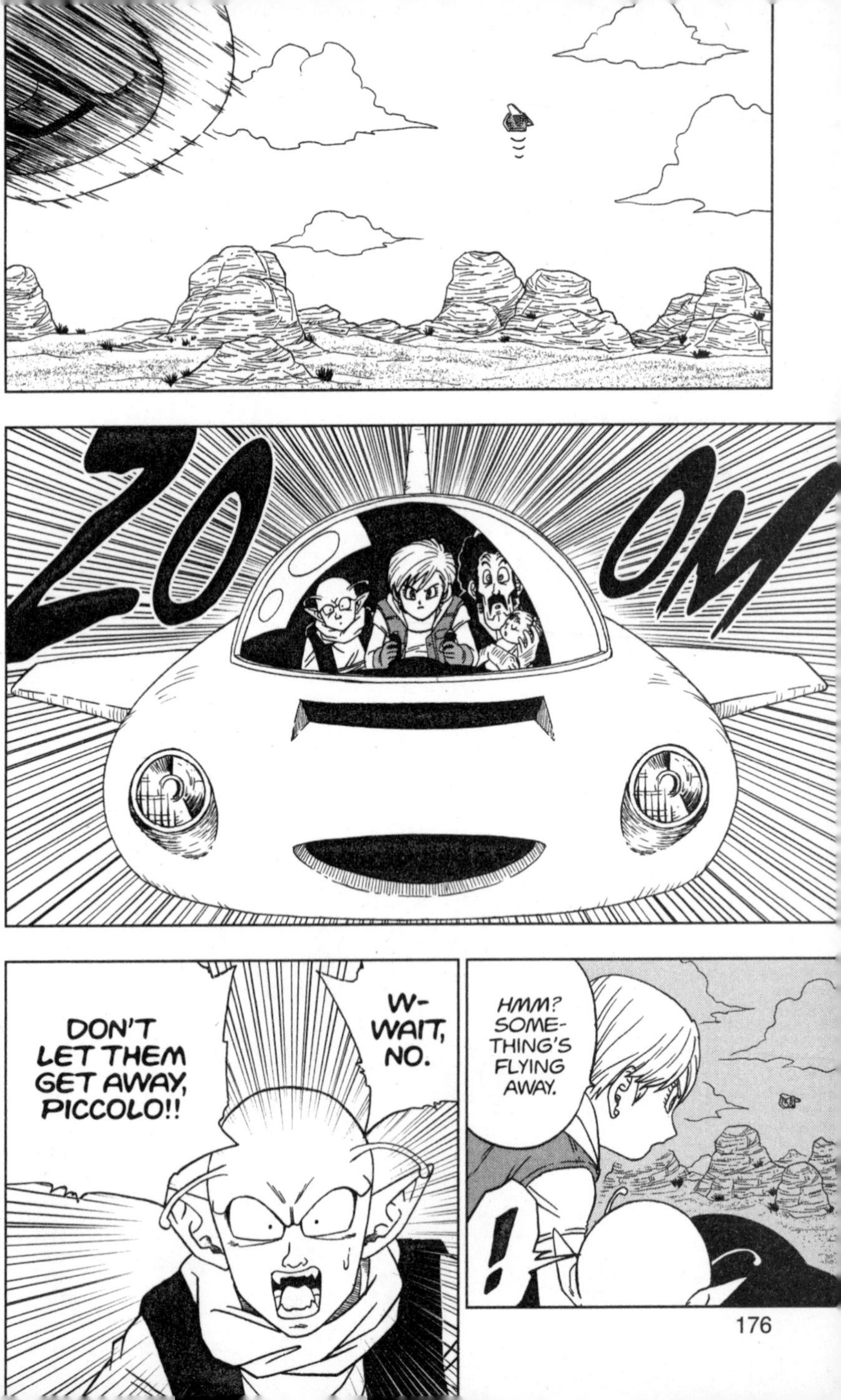
ZOOM
HMM? SOMETHING'S FLYING AWAY.
!
W-WAIT, NO.
DON'T LET THEM GET AWAY, PICCOLO!!

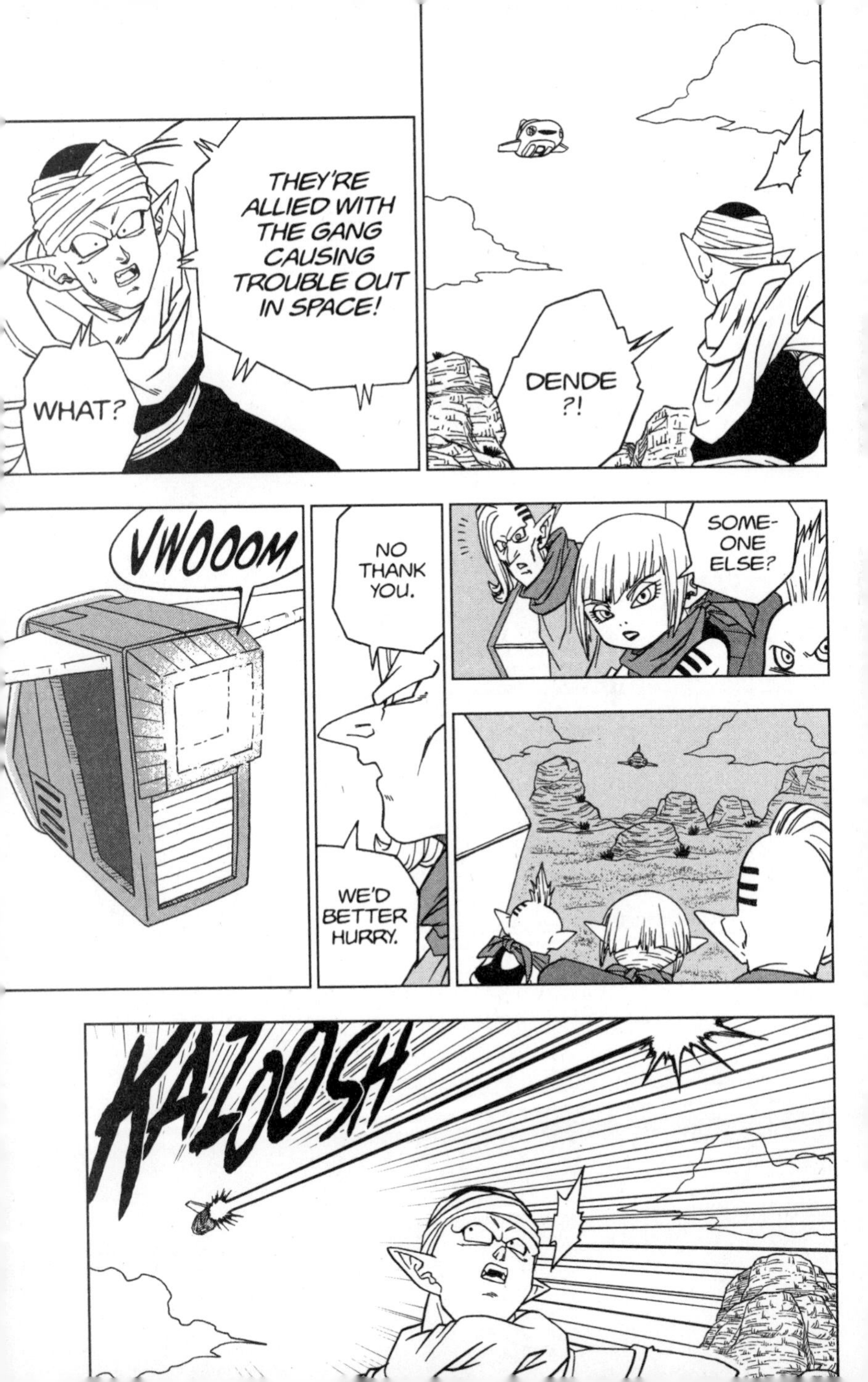
DENDE ?!
THEY'RE ALLIED WITH THE GANG CAUSING TROUBLE OUT IN SPACE!
WHAT?
SOME-ONE ELSE?
NO THANK YOU.
WE'D BETTER HURRY.
VWOOOM
KALOOSH

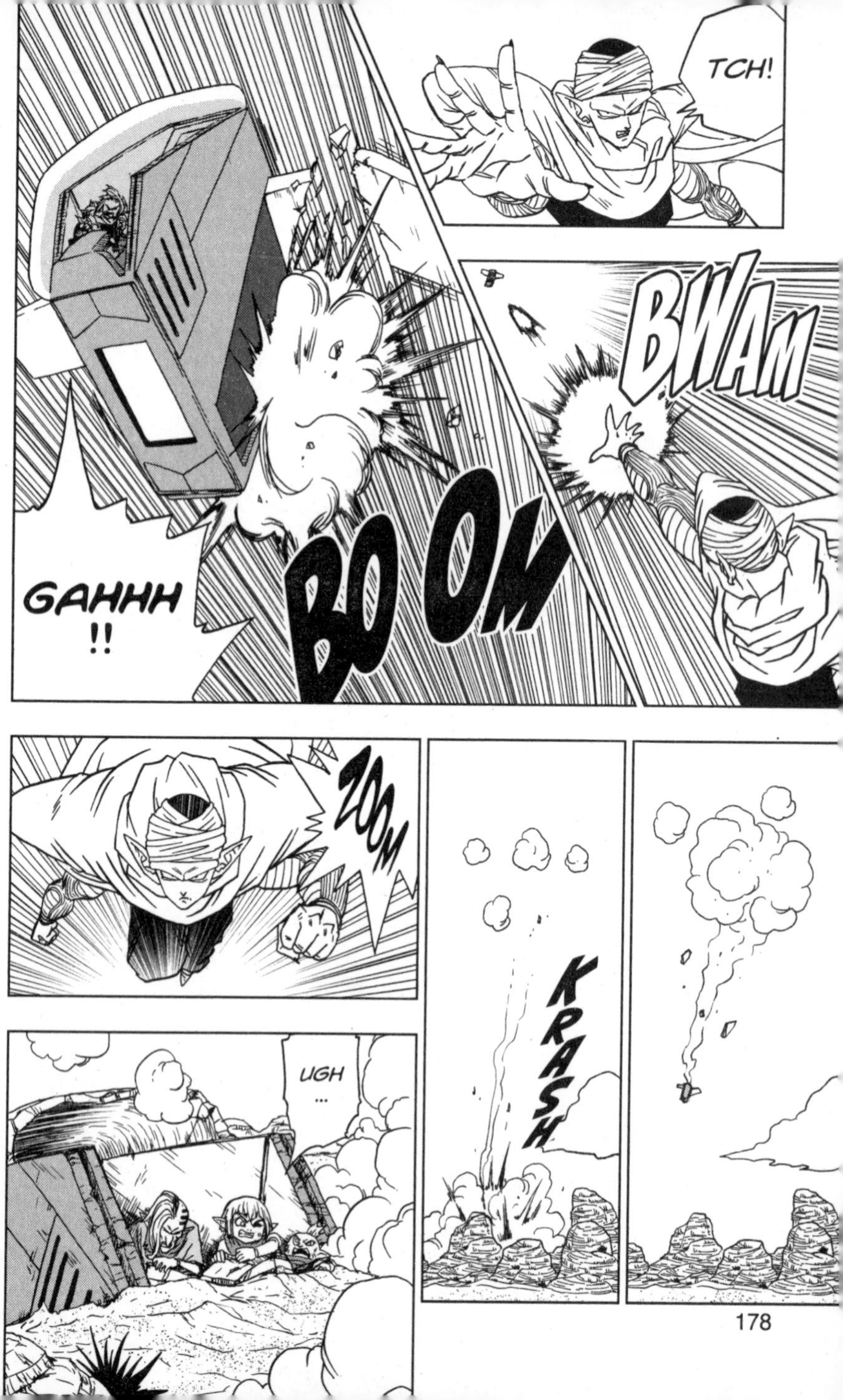
TCH!
BWAM
BOOM
GAHHH !!
KRASH
ZOOM
UGH ...

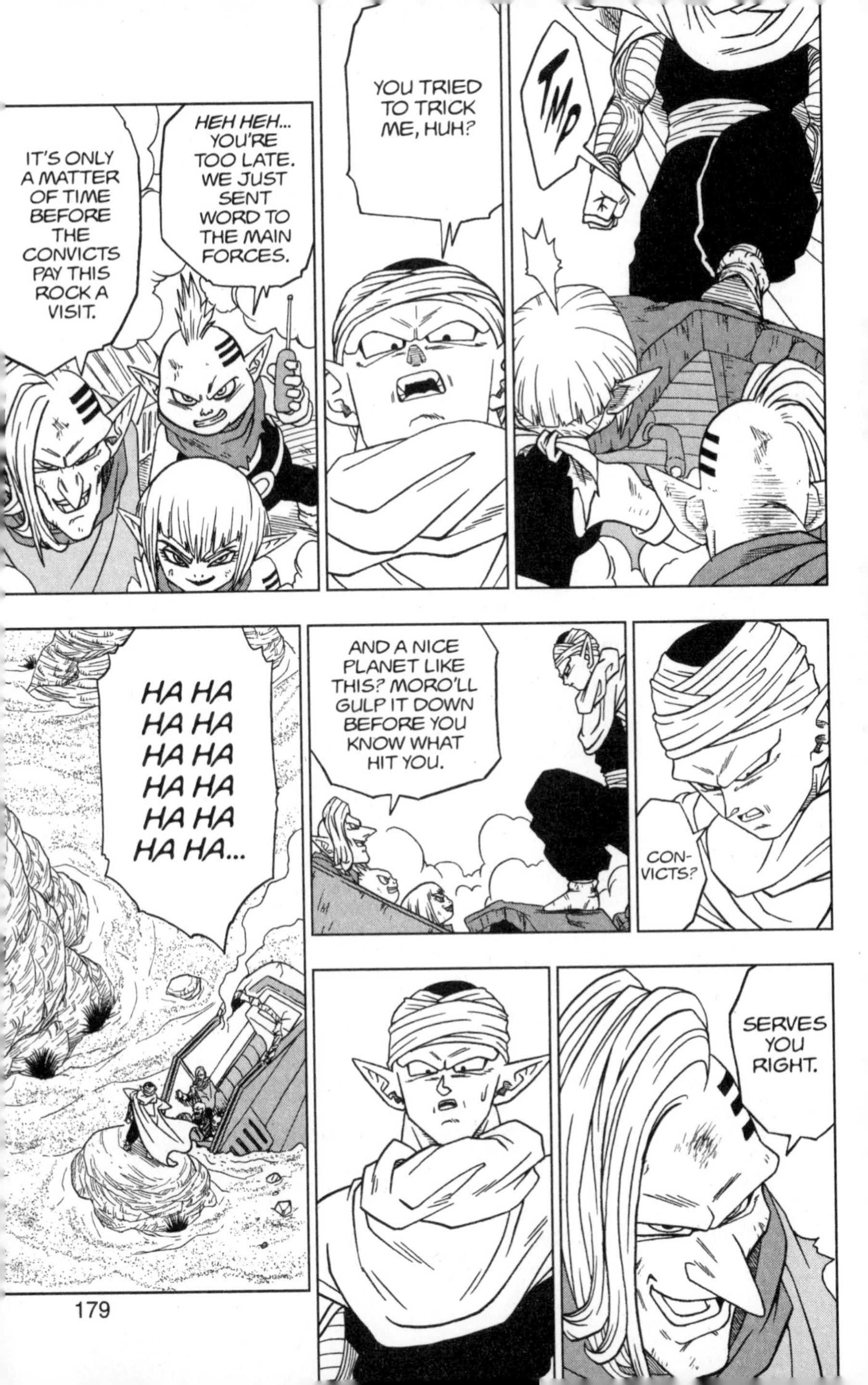
TMP
YOU TRIED TO TRICK ME, HUH?
HEH HEH... YOU'RE TOO LATE. WE JUST SENT WORD TO THE MAIN FORCES.
IT'S ONLY A MATTER OF TIME BEFORE THE CONVICTS PAY THIS ROCK A VISIT.
CON-VICTS?
AND A NICE PLANET LIKE THIS? MORO'LL GULP IT DOWN BEFORE YOU KNOW WHAT HIT YOU.
SERVES YOU RIGHT.
HA HA HA HA HA HA HA HA HA HA HA HA...

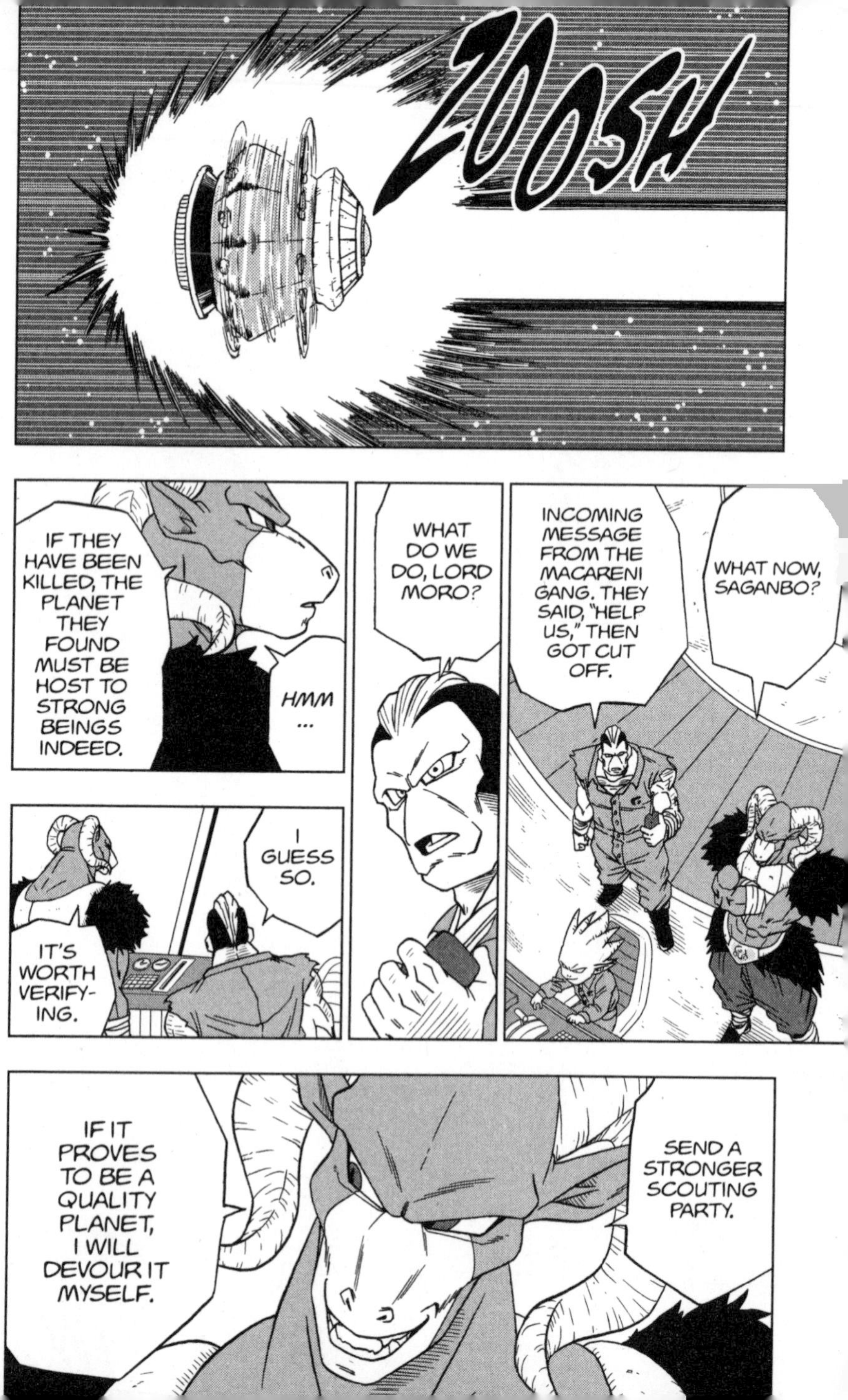
ZOOSH
WHAT NOW, SAGANBO?
INCOMING MESSAGE FROM THE MACARENI GANG. THEY SAID, "HELP US," THEN GOT CUT OFF.
WHAT DO WE DO, LORD MORO?
HMM ...
IF THEY HAVE BEEN KILLED, THE PLANET THEY FOUND MUST BE HOST TO STRONG BEINGS INDEED.
I GUESS SO.
IT'S WORTH VERIFY-ING.
SEND A STRONGER SCOUTING PARTY.
IF IT PROVES TO BE A QUALITY PLANET, I WILL DEVOUR IT MYSELF.

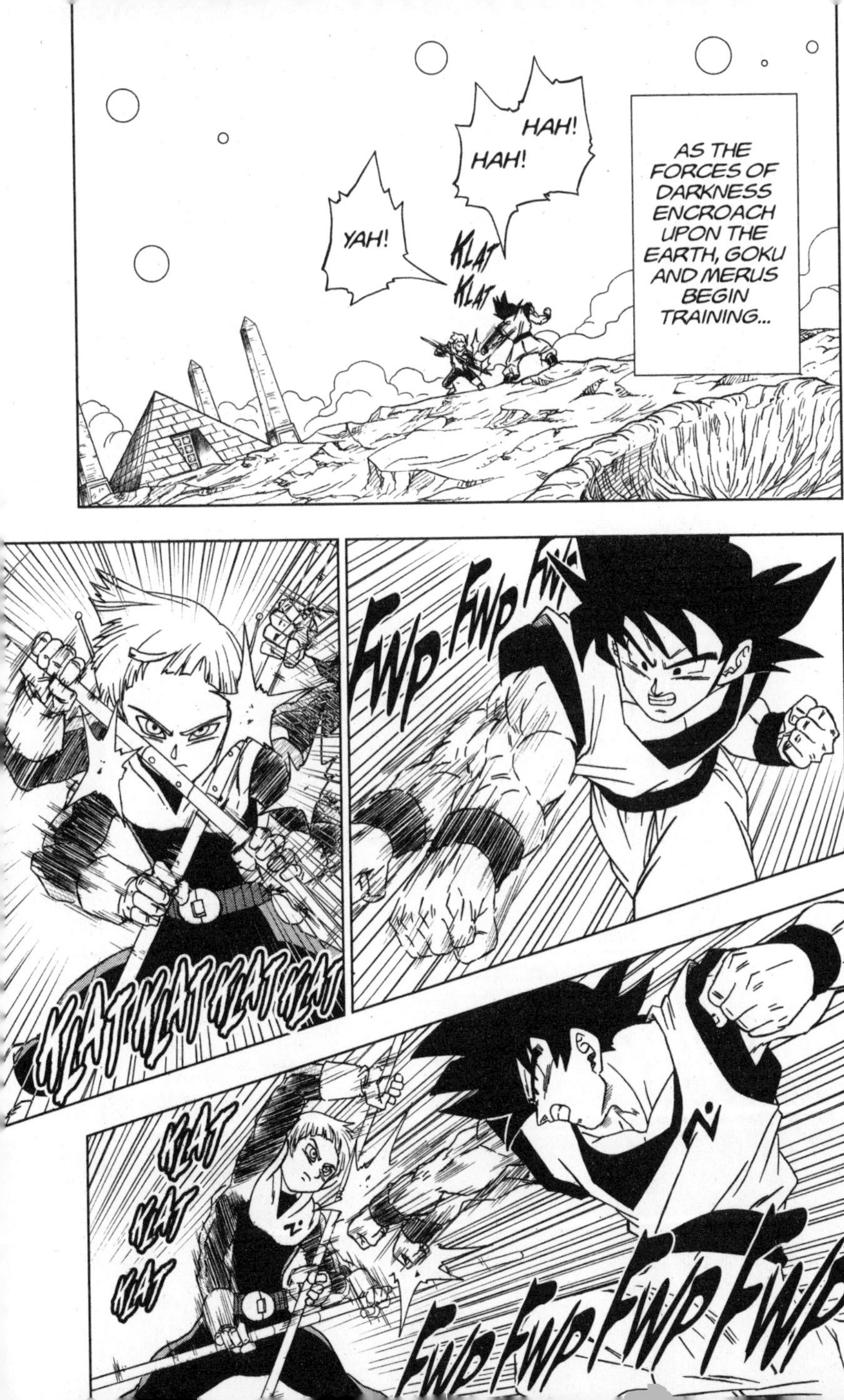
AS THE FORCES OF DARKNESS ENCROACH UPON THE EARTH, GOKU AND MERUS BEGIN TRAINING...
HAH! HAH!
YAH!
KLAT KLAT
FWP FWP FWP
KLAT KLAT KLAT KLAT
FWP FWP FWP FWP
KLAT KLAT KLAT

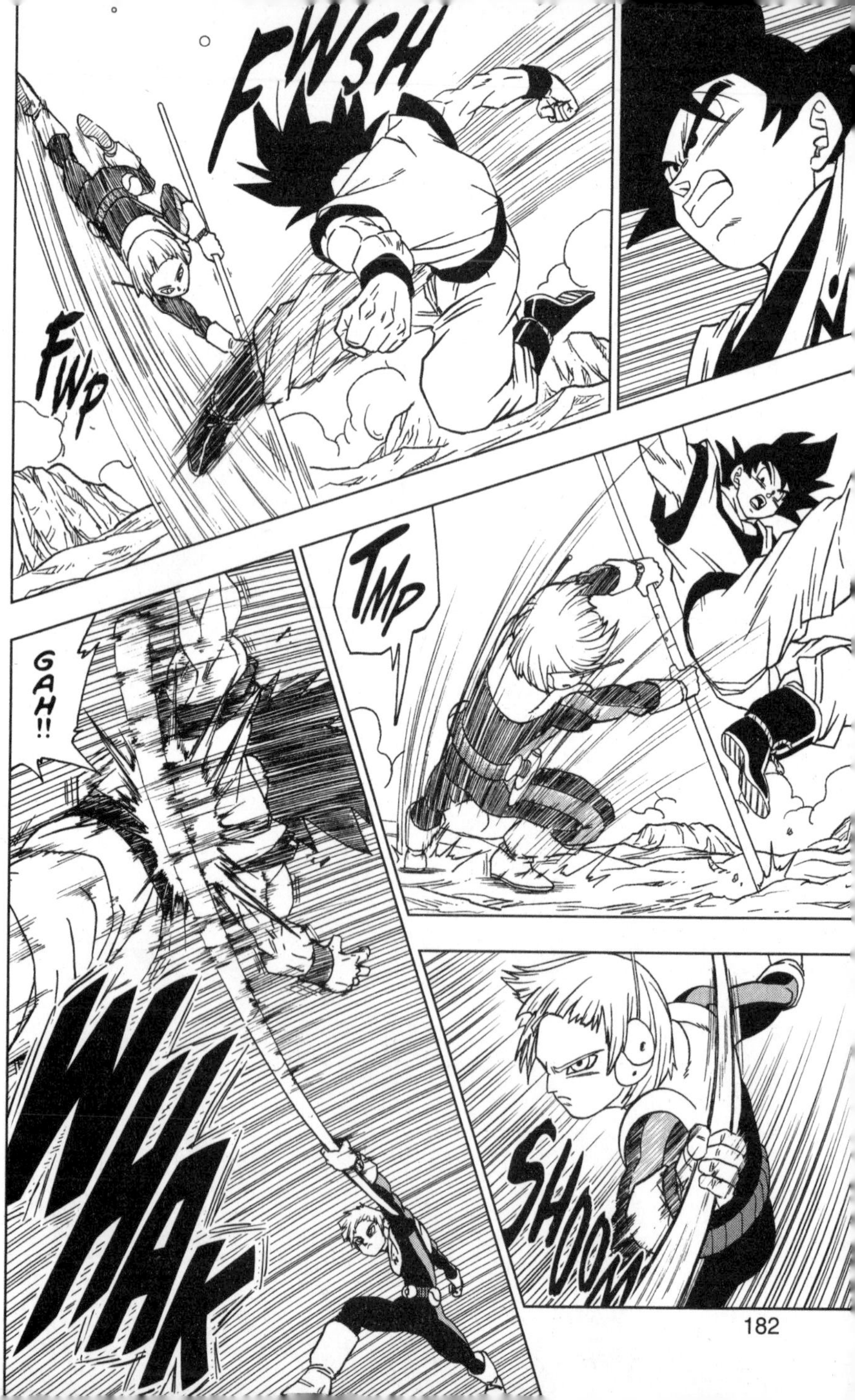
FWSH
FWP
TMP
SHOOM
GAH!!
WHAK

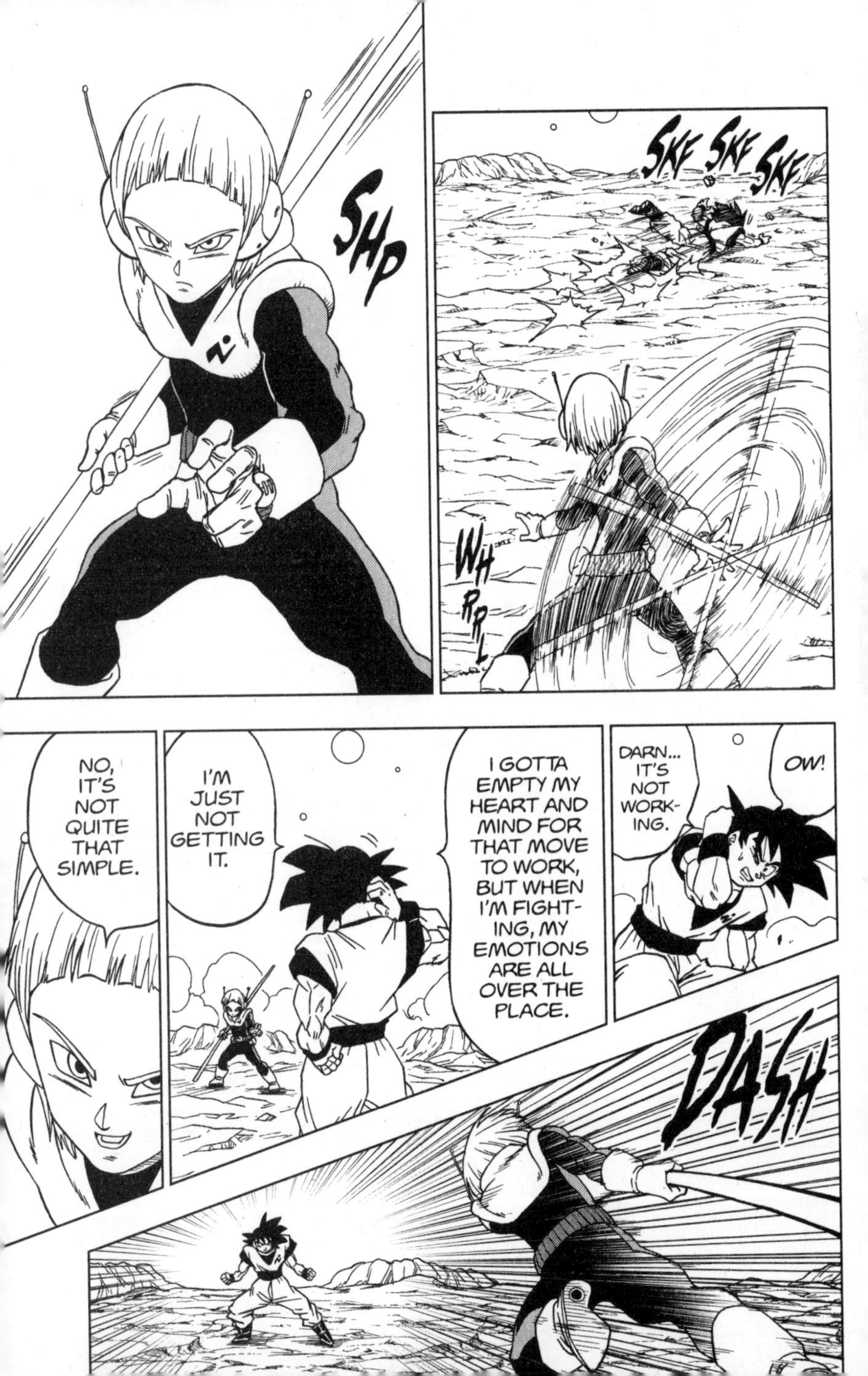
SKF SKF SKF
WHRRRL
SHP
OW!
DARN... IT'S NOT WORKING.
I GOTTA EMPTY MY HEART AND MIND FOR THAT MOVE TO WORK, BUT WHEN I'M FIGHTING, MY EMOTIONS ARE ALL OVER THE PLACE.
I'M JUST NOT GETTING IT.
NO, IT'S NOT QUITE THAT SIMPLE.
DASH

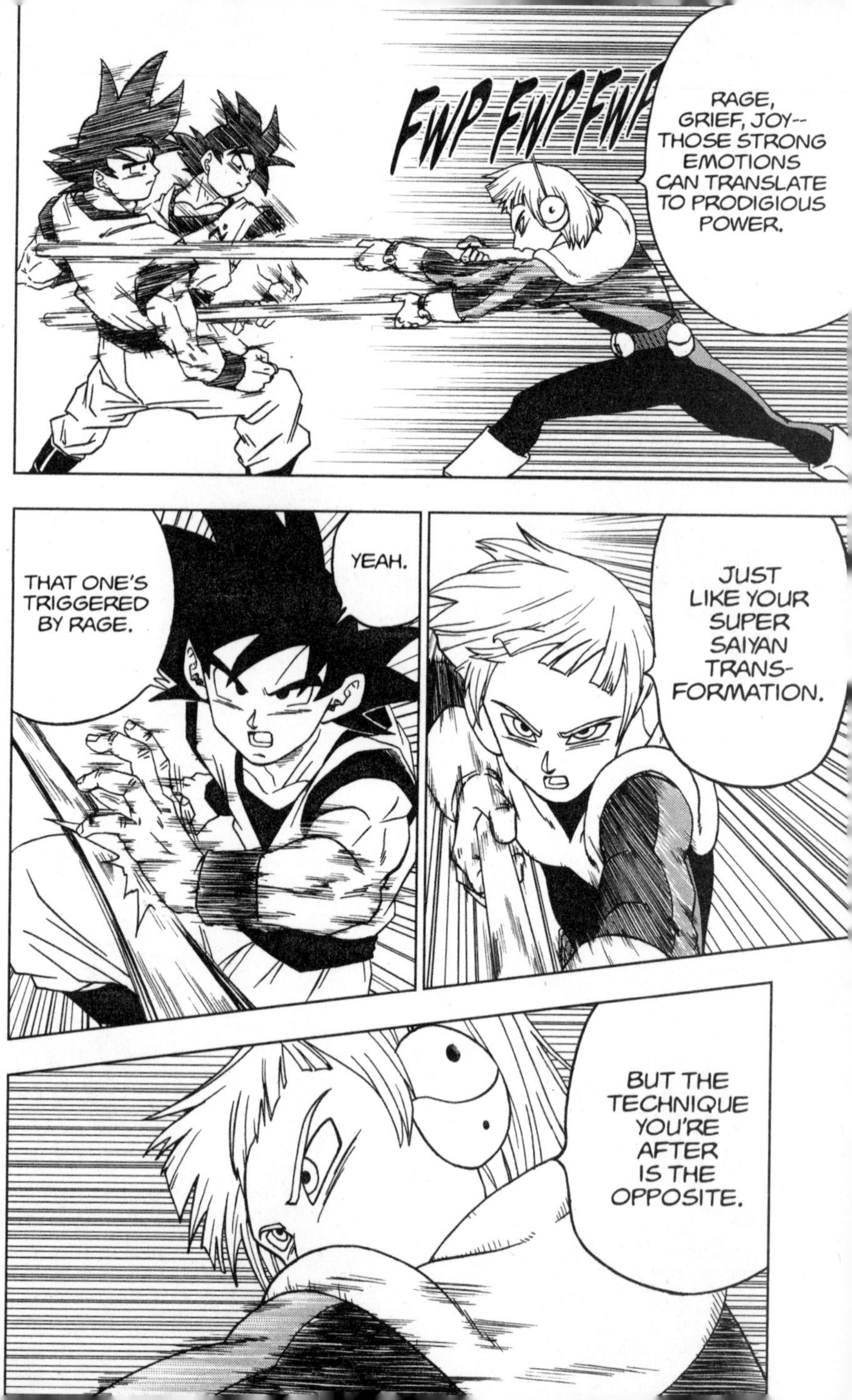
RAGE, GRIEF, JOY-- THOSE STRONG EMOTIONS CAN TRANSLATE TO PRODIGIOUS POWER.
FWP FWP FWP
JUST LIKE YOUR SUPER SAIYAN TRANS-FORMATION.
YEAH.
THAT ONE'S TRIGGERED BY RAGE.
BUT THE TECHNIQUE YOU'RE AFTER IS THE OPPOSITE.

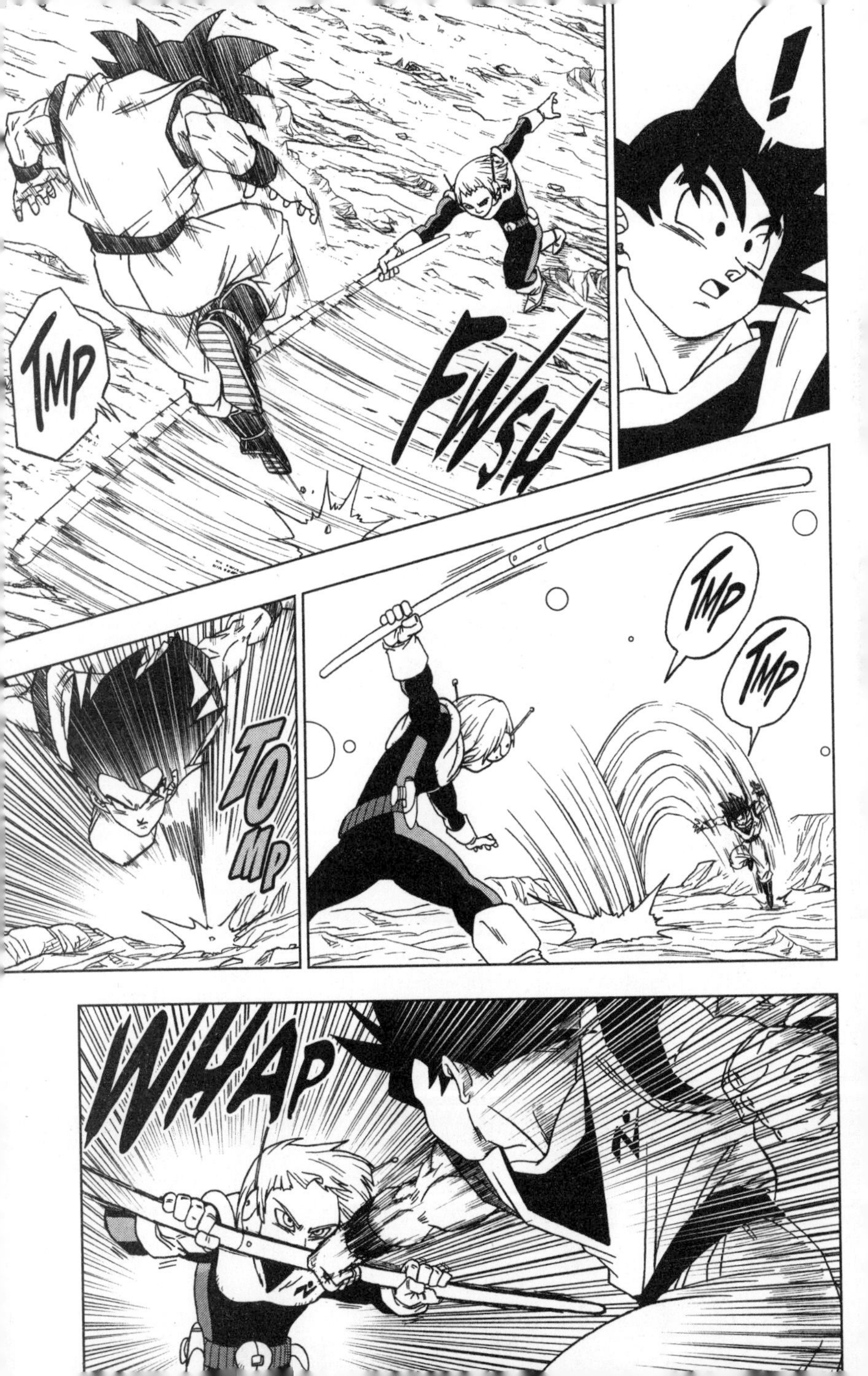
!
FWSH
TMP
TMP
TMP
TOMP
WHAP

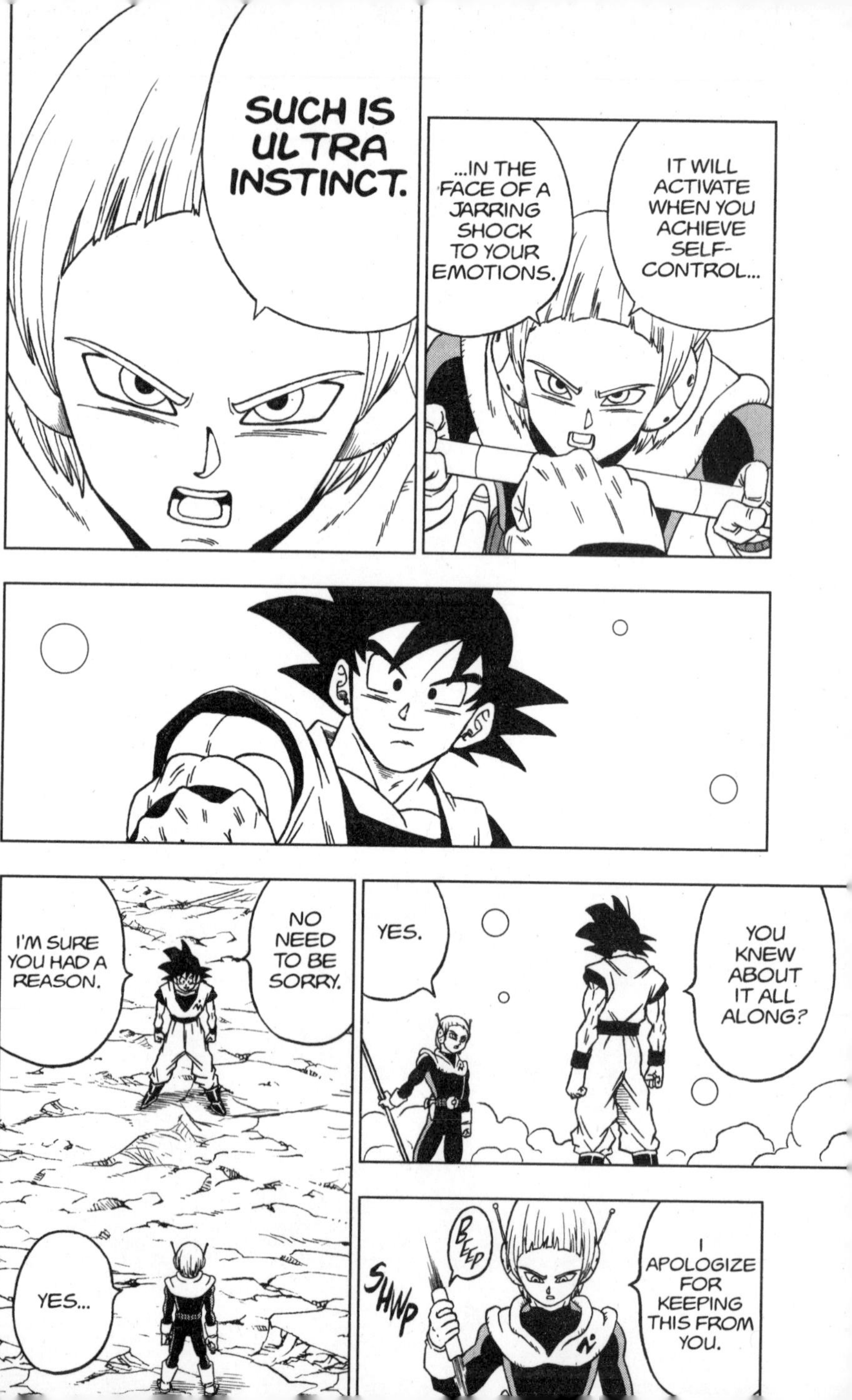
IT WILL ACTIVATE WHEN YOU ACHIEVE SELF-CONTROL...
...IN THE FACE OF A JARRING SHOCK TO YOUR EMOTIONS.
SUCH IS ULTRA INSTINCT.
YOU KNEW ABOUT IT ALL ALONG?
YES.
I APOLOGIZE FOR KEEPING THIS FROM YOU.
BEEP
SHWP
NO NEED TO BE SORRY.
I'M SURE YOU HAD A REASON.
YES...

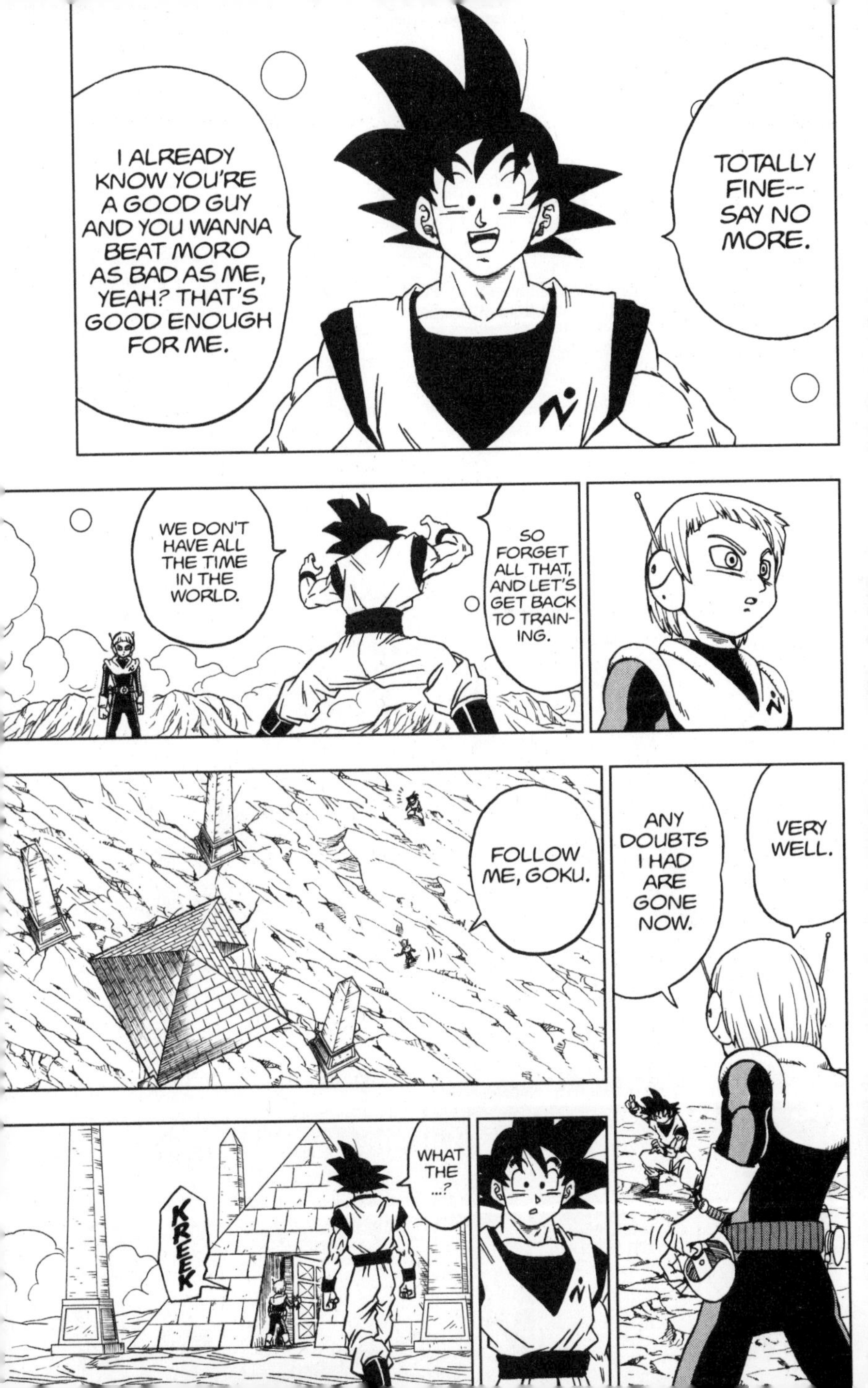
TOTALLY FINE-- SAY NO MORE.
I ALREADY KNOW YOU'RE A GOOD GUY AND YOU WANNA BEAT MORO AS BAD AS ME, YEAH? THAT'S GOOD ENOUGH FOR ME.
SO FORGET ALL THAT, AND LET'S GET BACK TO TRAIN-ING.
WE DON'T HAVE ALL THE TIME IN THE WORLD.
VERY WELL.
ANY DOUBTS I HAD ARE GONE NOW.
FOLLOW ME, GOKU.
WHAT THE ...?
KREEK

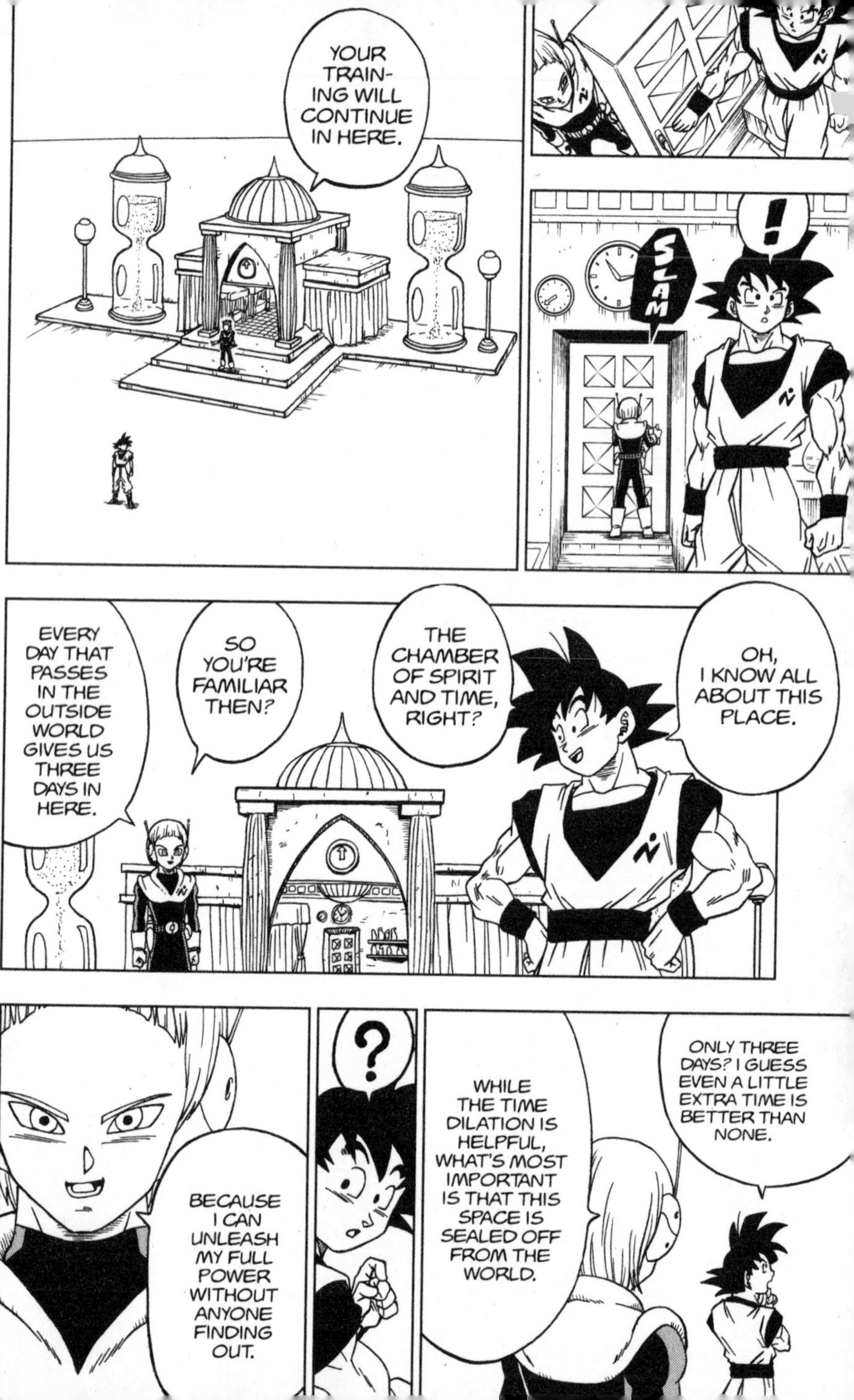
SLAM
!
YOUR TRAIN-ING WILL CONTINUE IN HERE.
OH, I KNOW ALL ABOUT THIS PLACE.
THE CHAMBER OF SPIRIT AND TIME, RIGHT?
SO YOU'RE FAMILIAR THEN?
EVERY DAY THAT PASSES IN THE OUTSIDE WORLD GIVES US THREE DAYS IN HERE.
ONLY THREE DAYS? I GUESS EVEN A LITTLE EXTRA TIME IS BETTER THAN NONE.
WHILE THE TIME DILATION IS HELPFUL, WHAT'S MOST IMPORTANT IS THAT THIS SPACE IS SEALED OFF FROM THE WORLD.
?
BECAUSE I CAN UNLEASH MY FULL POWER WITHOUT ANYONE FINDING OUT.

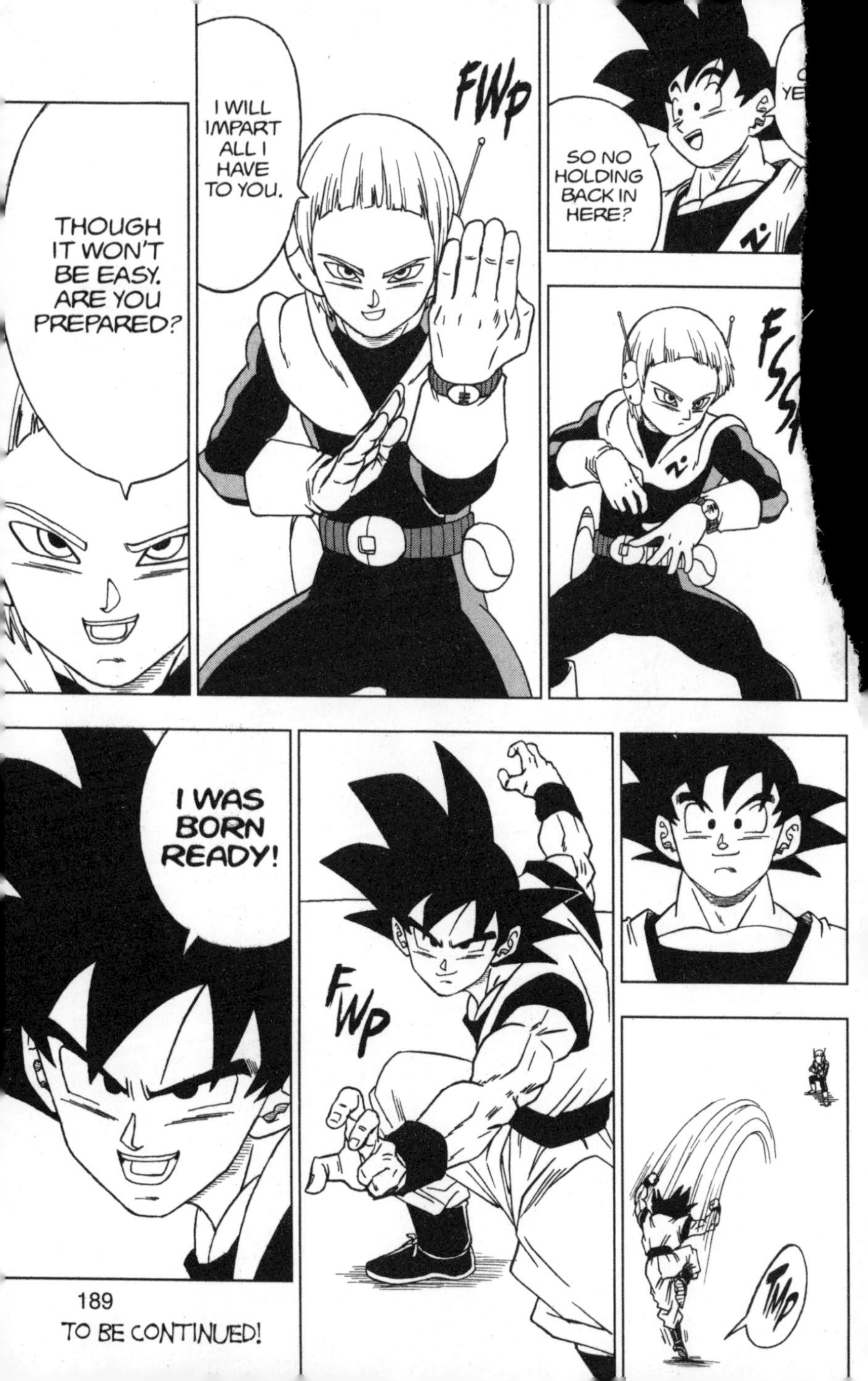
SO NO HOLDING BACK IN HERE?
FSSS
FWP
I WILL IMPART ALL I HAVE TO YOU.
THOUGH IT WON'T BE EASY. ARE YOU PREPARED?
TMP
FWP
I WAS BORN READY!

TO BE CONTINUED!

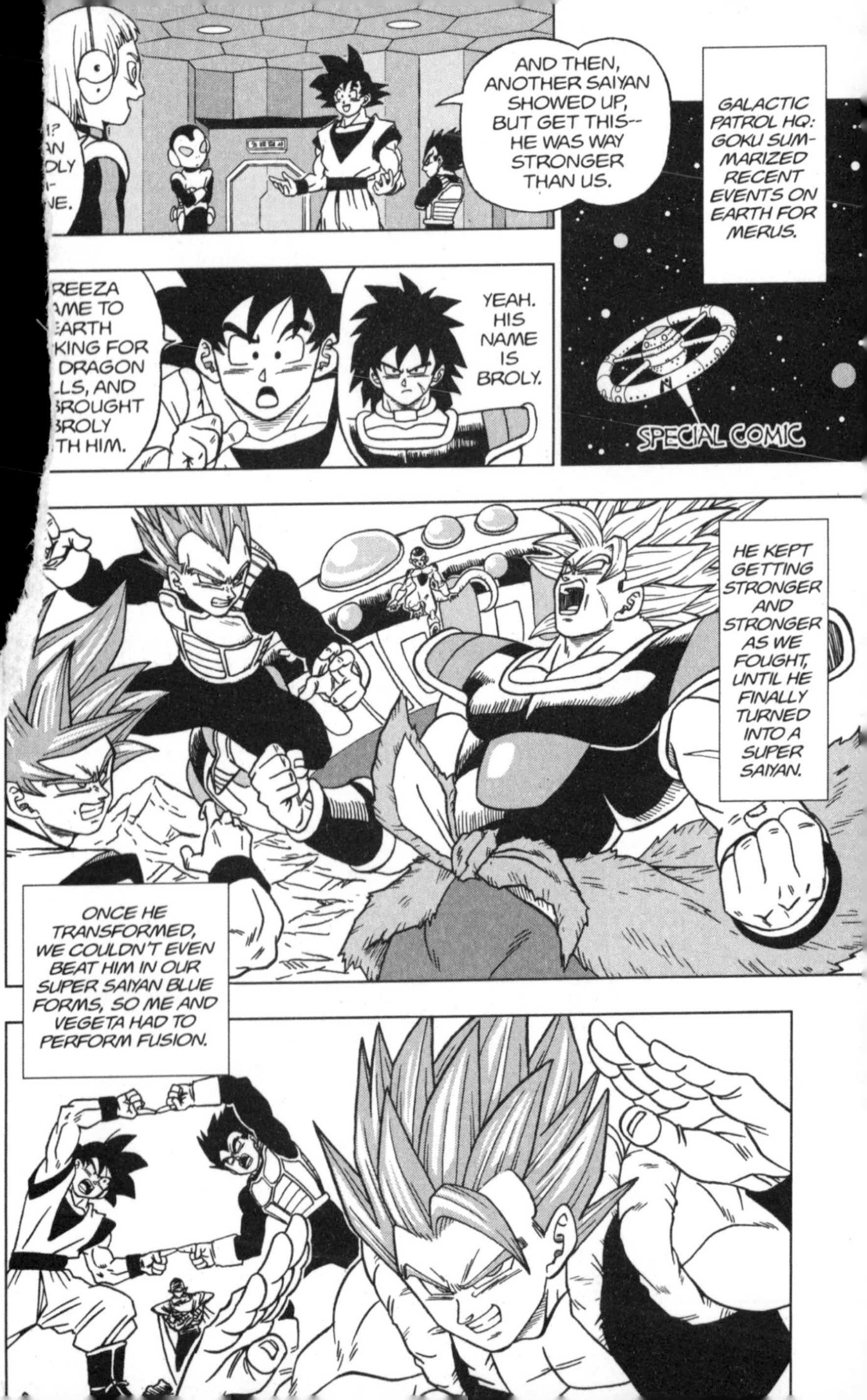
GALACTIC PATROL HQ: GOKU SUMMARIZED RECENT EVENTS ON EARTH FOR MERUS.
SPECIAL COMIC
AND THEN, ANOTHER SAIYAN SHOWED UP, BUT GET THIS-- HE WAS WAY STRONGER THAN US.
YEAH. HIS NAME IS BROLY.
REEZA AME TO EARTH KING FOR DRAGON LLS, AND BROUGHT BROLY TH HIM.
HE KEPT GETTING STRONGER AND STRONGER AS WE FOUGHT, UNTIL HE FINALLY TURNED INTO A SUPER SAIYAN.
ONCE HE TRANSFORMED, WE COULDN'T EVEN BEAT HIM IN OUR SUPER SAIYAN BLUE FORMS, SO ME AND VEGETA HAD TO PERFORM FUSION.

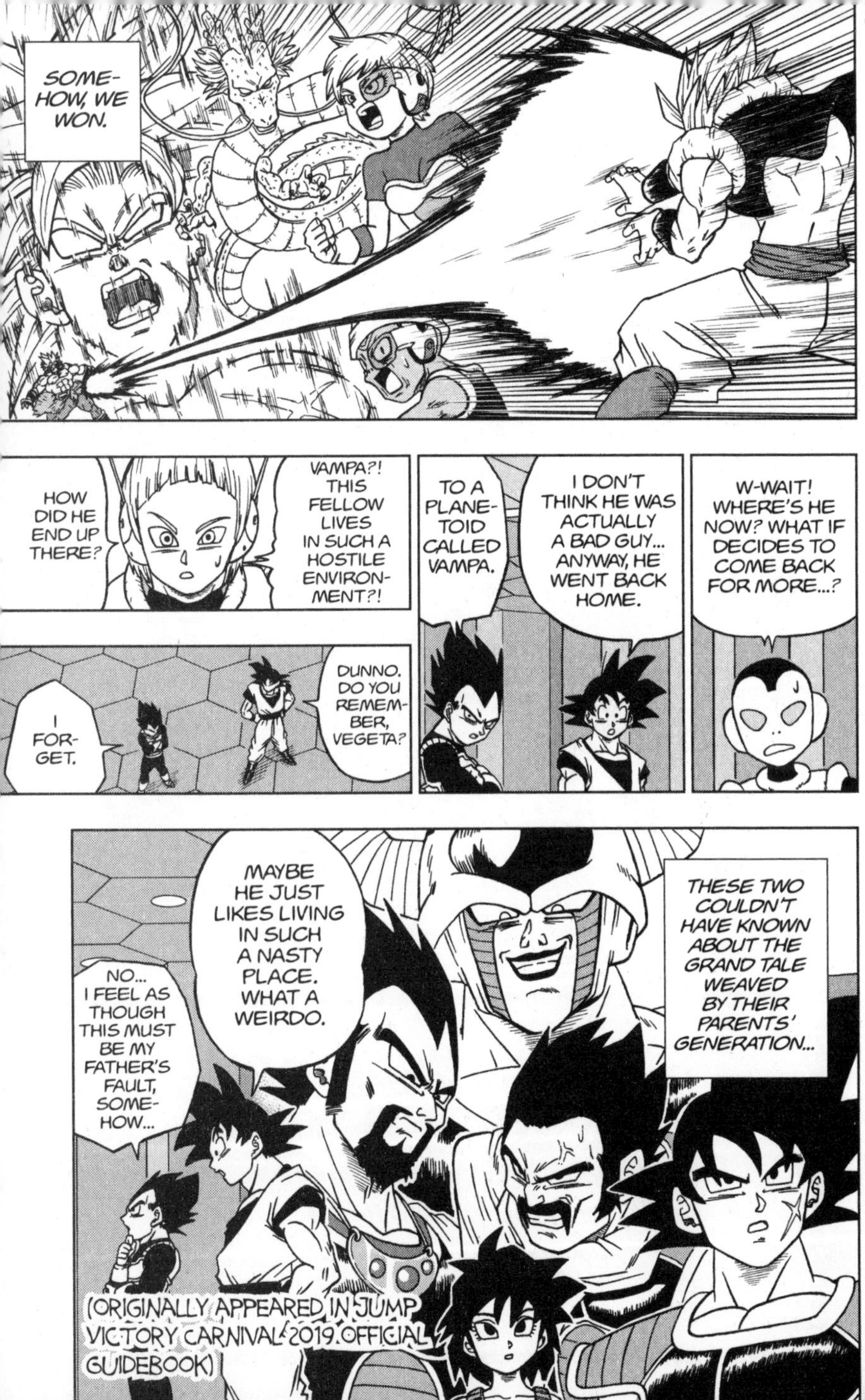
SOME-HOW, WE WON.
W-WAIT! WHERE'S HE NOW? WHAT IF DECIDES TO COME BACK FOR MORE...?
I DON'T THINK HE WAS ACTUALLY A BAD GUY... ANYWAY, HE WENT BACK HOME.
TO A PLANE-TOID CALLED VAMPA.
VAMPA?! THIS FELLOW LIVES IN SUCH A HOSTILE ENVIRON-MENT?!
HOW DID HE END UP THERE?
DUNNO. DO YOU REMEM-BER, VEGETA?
I FOR-GET.
THESE TWO COULDN'T HAVE KNOWN ABOUT THE GRAND TALE WEAVED BY THEIR PARENTS' GENERATION...
MAYBE HE JUST LIKES LIVING IN SUCH A NASTY PLACE. WHAT A WEIRDO.
NO... I FEEL AS THOUGH THIS MUST BE MY FATHER'S FAULT, SOME-HOW...
(ORIGINALLY APPEARED IN JUMP VICTORY CARNIVAL 2019 OFFICIAL GUIDEBOOK)

YOU'RE READING
THE WRONG WAY!

Dragon Ball Super reads from right to left, starting in the
upper-right corner. Japanese is read from right to left,
meaning that action, sound effects, and word-balloon
order are completely reversed from English order.